ANOTHER INDIA

PRATINAV ANIL

Another India

The Making of the World's Largest
Muslim Minority, 1947–77

HURST & COMPANY, LONDON

First published in the United Kingdom in 2023 by
C. Hurst & Co. (Publishers) Ltd.,
New Wing, Somerset House, Strand, London, WC2R 1LA

A Cataloguing-in-Publication data record for this book
is available from the British Library.

ISBN: 9781787388086

www.hurstpublishers.com

Printed in Great Britain by Bell and Bain Ltd, Glasgow

For Polly and Christophe

CONTENTS

CONTENTS

ABBREVIATIONS

AICC	All-India Congress Committee
AIMIM	All-India Majlis Ittihad-ul-Muslimin
AIML	All-India Muslim League
AIMPLB	All-India Muslim Personal Law Board
AISC	All-India Shia Conference
AMU	Aligarh Muslim University
ASI	Archaeological Survey of India
BAMCEF	Backward and Minority Communities Employees Federation
BHU	Banaras Hindu University
BJD	Bangla Jatiya Dal
BJP	Bharatiya Janata Party
BKD	Bharatiya Kranti Dal
BSP	Bahujan Samaj Party
CAD	*Constituent Assembly Debates*
CBI	Central Bureau of Investigation
CD	compact disc
CIA	Central Intelligence Agency
CPI	Communist Party of India
CPM	Communist Party of India (Marxist)

CrPC	Code of Criminal Procedure
CSDS	Centre for the Study of Developing Societies
CWC	Congress Working Committee
CWMG	*Collected Works of Mahatma Gandhi*
DCC	District Congress Committee
DDA	Delhi Development Authority
DMK	Dravida Munnetra Kazhagam
DMMA	Dissolution of Muslim Marriages Act
DS4	Dalit Shoshit Samaj Sangharsh Samiti
ECI	Election Commission of India
EPW	*Economic and Political Weekly*
FAQ	frequently asked questions
HMC	Hyderabad Municipal Corporation
HMSO	Her Majesty's Stationery Office
ICS	Indian Civil Service
IMF	International Monetary Fund
INC	Indian National Congress
ISIS	Islamic State of Iraq and Syria
IUML	Indian Union Muslim League
J&K	Jammu and Kashmir
JI	Jama'at-i-Islami
JMI	Jamia Millia Islamia
JUH	Jamiat-ul-Ulema-i-Hind
JUI	Jamiat-ul-Ulema-i-Islam
KMPP	Kisan Mazdoor Praja Party
KPP	Krishak Praja Party
LD	Lok Dal
LG	lieutenant-governor
MAOC	Muhammadan Anglo-Oriental College
MC	Muslim Convention

MCD	Municipal Corporation of Delhi
MCSI	Muslim Convention of South India
MEA	Ministry of External Affairs
MHA	Ministry of Home Affairs
MHAP	Ministry of Home Affairs Papers
MJ	Muslim Jamaat
MLA	Member of Legislative Assembly
MLC	Member of Legislative Council
MP	Member of Parliament
NAI	National Archives of India
NAP	National Agricultural Party
NAWADCO	National Waqf Development Corporation
NC	National Conference
NISRC	National Integration and Spiritual Rearmament Congress
NMML	Nehru Memorial Museum and Library
NWFP	North-West Frontier Province
NWP	North-Western Provinces
NYT	*New York Times*
OBC	Other Backward Class
PCC	Pradesh Congress Committee
PDF	People's Democratic Front
PSP	Praja Socialist Party
PwC	PricewaterhouseCoopers
RPI	Republican Party of India
RRP	Ram Rajya Parishad
RSS	Rashtriya Swayamsevak Sangh
SAD	Shiromani Akali Dal
SC	Scheduled Caste
SIMI	Students' Islamic Movement of India

SMU	Shillong Muslim Union
ST	Scheduled Tribe
SVD	Samyukta Vidhayak Dal
SWJN	*Selected Works of Jawaharlal Nehru*
TOI	*Times of India*
TOP	*Constitutional Relations Between Britain and India: The Transfer of Power, 1942–47*
UGC	University Grants Commission
UN	United Nations
UP	Uttar Pradesh
UPSA	Uttar Pradesh State Archives
UPSC	Uttar Pradesh Shia Conference
VC	vice-chancellor
VIP	very important person
WDC	Wakf Development Corporation

GLOSSARY

adivasi	tribesman
ahmadiyya	a controversial Muslim sect
ajlaf	low-caste Muslims
akhand	Hindu irredentist
amir	chief
amir-e-hind	ruler of India
anjuman	chapter
arzal	former Untouchable Muslims
ashraf (sing. *sharif*)	high-caste Muslims
ayurveda	Hindu healing tradition
azadi	freedom
bakra	sheep
bazaar	market
begum	Muslim woman of high rank
bhadralok	respectable people
bhai-bhai	brothers in arms
bhangi	sweeper
bidi	cigarette
bigha	3.6 acres
biradari	caste

biradari anjuman	caste association
bismillah	ritual involving the reading of the opening lines of the Quran
chai	tea
dacoity	brigandage
Dalit	former Untouchable Hindu
dar al-Islam	house of Islam
dar al-kufr	house of unbelief
darbari	royal
dars-e-nizamiya	the Firangi Mahal's curriculum, focusing on Arabic and jurisprudence
dawa	God's call
deeni talim-o-tarbiat	religious education
devanagari	alphabet used for Sanskrit and Hindi
dewan	prime minister
dharmayuddha	religious battle
dhoti	loose garment worn by male Hindus
doab	interfluve
durgah	shrine
eidgah	structure for the commemoration of Eid
fatwa	ruling on a point of Islamic law
fez	flat-topped conical red hat
fiqh	jurisprudence
gaddi	seat of power
gaekwar	ruler
ghaleb-e-islam	Islamic rule
ghaleb-e-muslimeen	rule by Muslims
ghazal	lyric poem set to music
goonda	gangster
gurudwara	Sikh temple
hadith	anecdotes culled from the life of the Prophet

hajj	Muslim pilgrimage to Mecca
hajjis	pilgrims to Mecca
hakim	doctor
halal	religiously acceptable
halwa	cheap confection
haram	religiously forbidden
hidiyah	circumcision
hijrat	holy migration
hookah	oriental tobacco pipe
hukumat	government
idara	institution
ijtihad	creative interpretation
ilhad	atheism
imam	person who leads prayers in a mosque
imambara	building where the Shia commemorate the killing of Husain
janab	an Urdu honorific
jawahar	diamond
jhatka	meat from an animal killed instantaneously
jihad	holy war
kaffir (pl. *kuffar*)	infidel
karsevak	Hindu stormtrooper
khair-e-ummat	chosen community
khanqah	spiritual retreat
khatib	sermoniser
Kulturkampf	culture war
kurta	loose collarless shirt
lakh	hundred thousand
madrasa (pl. *madari*)	Islamic school
mahant	priest
maharaja	king

mahfil	musical extravaganza
majlis-e-numaindagan	Council of Representatives
majlis-i-shura	governing committee
makhdoom	teacher
malish	outcaste
maulana	pious Muslim man revered for his religious learning
maulvi	Muslim scholar
mazhab	sect
millat	community
mofussil	the countryside
mohalla	neighbourhood
moi muqaddas	strand of the Prophet Mohammad's beard
morcha	protest
mughlai	Indo-Persian cuisine
muhajir	Muslim migrants from India in Pakistan
mullah	Muslim scholar schooled in law and theology
munazarah	debate
munshi	secretary
murshid	religious teacher
mushaira	poetry competition
mussalman	Muslim
mutawalli	custodian
nastaliq	alphabet used for Urdu
nawab	ruler
nechari	naturalist
nehru	man of the river
nizam-i zindagi	complete system of life
paan	betel leaves used as a stimulant
pandit	Hindu scholar

peshimam	prayer leader
pir	saint
piri-muridi	a master-disciple relationship that verged on enthralment
praja mandals	associations in the Princely States
pugree	lump sum paid to secure a permanent lease
purdah	the practice of screening women from men
qanun-i-markaz	legal centres
qasba	gentrified Muslim township
qaum	Indian Muslim community
qaumi tabligh	proselytisation
qazi	judge
quaid-e-millat	leader of the community
Rechtsstaat	rule of law
sadhu	ascetic
sahib	polite form of address for a man
sangathan	mobilisation
sarsanghchalak	RSS chief
satyagraha	civil disobedience
savarna	upper caste
sayyid	descendant of the Prophet
shakha	branch
sharafat	respectability
sharia	Islamic law
sher	lion
sherwani	knee-length coat worn by men
shuddhi	purification
shudra	lower caste
shura	consultative body
siyasa	politics
sunnah	practices of the Prophet

swaraj / swarajya	self-rule within the aegis of the Crown; independence
tabligh	proselytisation
taluqdar	landlord
tanzim	mobilisation
taraqqi-pasand	a modernist literary movement
tazia	Muslim passion play
tehzeeb	Persianate class markers
tibbia	Muslim healing tradition
ulama (sing. *alim*)	clerics
umma	global Muslim community
urs	saints' days
ustad	expert
waqf (pl. *auqaf*)	Muslim endowment
waqf-alal-aulad	private endowment
waqif	owner
wasiqa	pension for Awadh's royals and their retainers
wasiqadar	pensioners
yagna	sacrifice
yom-e-jung	day of war
zakat	charity
zenana	women's quarters

ACKNOWLEDGEMENTS

In research projects such as this one, debts pile up like artefacts at the Pitt Rivers. Like Blanche, then, one in great measure 'depends on the kindness of strangers'. Happily, many have since become good friends, a testament to the warmth of the South Asianist community.

My biggest debt, as always, is to Sara Perlangeli, helpmeet and editrix, acerbic critic and amateur psychoanalyst. Research can be a lonesome enterprise. Thanks to her, though, it was a veritable *folie à deux*.

Academia is a tribe, and like all tribes, unfathomable from the outside. Fortunately, I have had two rather percipient confidants to help me make sense of this world. Christophe Jaffrelot has been so much more than a mentor—an analytical mind with few equals, as well as a reminder that Protestant productivity and Franciscan generosity can, on rare occasions, complement one another. One cannot exercise better judgement than to defer to Polly O'Hanlon's astuteness. This book is infinitely the richer—more precise, less prolix—for her advice. Equally, one would do well to heed her dictum, of which I have now heard many iterations, that the purpose of writing is not to display erudition, but to elucidate. To them this book is dedicated.

A few more citations are in order. This project would have never got off the ground were it not for the guiding hand of Taylor Sherman, quite possibly the most formidable historian working on postcolonial India today. Sunil Khilnani, Yasmin Khan, and Faridah Zaman were, by turns, sympathetic and incisive, offering precisely the kind of constructive criticism that any young academic wishes for. Maria Misra came to my rescue a dozen times. It was in marathon conversations and friendly jousting with Faisal Devji that many of the ideas contained in these pages developed. David Priestland has been an indirect but substantial influence, getting me to rethink Britain and much else. And it was the sybaritic company of Chiara Ardoino and Lucian George, constants in a revolving cast of friends floating in and out of Oxford and London in life's *chassé-croisé*, that made the last leg of writing such a joy.

For commissions and advice on the craft, dinners and drinks, I thank Rhys Griffiths, Kai Friese, Raphael Susewind, Sidharth Bhatia, Raisa Wickrematunge, Maya Palit, Charlotte de Blois, Gus Carter, Tom Zoellner, and Bryce Becker. Thanks are also due to Surajkumar Thube, Benjamin Graham, Vanita Leah Falcao, Vignesh Rajahmani, and Tobias Scholz for organising conferences where a few chapters of this book were presented. Tanweer Alam and Moin Nizami helped me hit the ground running in Delhi and Aligarh, respectively. I now have Urdu thanks to Imre Bangha. At Hurst, Michael Dwyer, Michael Clark, Alice Clarke, and Daisy Leitch turned an unwieldy manuscript into a concise book.

I must also thank the librarians and staff at the National Archives of India, Nehru Memorial Museum and Library, Uttar Pradesh State Archives, Bihar State Archives, Khuda Bakhsh Oriental Library, Sapru House, *Radiance*, Majlis-i-Mushāwarat, Aligarh's Sir Syed House and Sir Syed Section, Central Secretariat Library, Bodleian Library, Weston Library, Library and Study Centre at St John's College, Nizami Ganjavi Library, British Library of Political and Economic Science, and British Library. Pecuniary matters cannot be ignored, and it must be acknowledged that this book was only made possible by the Clarendon Fund, which covered fees and living expenses, Hilla Ginwala Scholarship, Covid-19 Scholarships Extensions Fund, and my college's eminently sensible four-figure book grant.

Begrudgingly, then, I must accept that the mistakes and misinterpretations in the following pages are mine alone.

Pratinav Anil
Oxford-London
September 2022

INTRODUCTION
A COMMUNITY APART

India's deliverance from empire was not an entirely optimistic affair. The birth of a new homeland for South Asian Muslims in 1947 broached novel anxieties among citizens of the old one. Plurality voting, the exodus of millions of their *confrères* to the northeastern and northwestern tracts of the Subcontinent, and their distinct markers of religious difference—sartorial, linguistic, exequial—at a stroke made India's Muslims a visible minority: politically, socially, and culturally. So how, then, did the world's largest religious minority carve out a space for itself in the Republic?

On the dominant historiography, they did not need to. For, we are told, India's early postcolonial years were characterised by the largely peaceable relationship between the Republic's rulers and its largest confessional minority. The accent here is on the 'liberalism' and 'secularism' of the country's constitution and its underwriters, the Indian National Congress, the party whose long years of uninterrupted rule put it at the centre of efforts to shape Indian political life.

The most fervid apologist of this position, surely, was Mushirul Hasan, the Stakhanovite historian whose oeuvre—over sixty authored, edited, and translated works—traversed the Muslim landscapes of late and postcolonial India. In particular, it was the urgent threat of Hindu nationalism to Indian secularism that animated his writings. So with one eye on the present and the other on the

1

past, Hasan sought, as it were, to mobilise the archive to oppose the insurgent saffron brigades that had flattened the Babri Masjid in 1992, captured power first briefly in 1996 and then for a full term in 1999, engineered the Gujarat riots in 2002, and more generally, embarked on eviscerating the country's largest minority by pogrom, conversion, and emigration.

So it was that Hasan endeavoured to recover in the early postcolonial years a golden age for secularism. Under the premiership of the Congress' Jawaharlal Nehru—the 'generous and magnanimous torch-bearer of secularism' who spent his seventeen years in office to 1964 'consistently championing minority rights and justice'—the 'fears of the beleaguered' community were allayed by his 'healing touch'.[1]

Such 'men with an enlightened world-view'—Nehru and his Muslim allies—moreover, were the legatees of mediaeval syncretism, their 'composite nationalism' defined in contradistinction to the 'communal' nationalism of the Muslim League that had been the moving spirit of the Pakistan demand and the Hindu nationalist Rashtriya Swayamsevak Sangh, its less fortunate counterpart.[2]

And finally, Hasan worked to demolish the 'myth of Muslim unity', that there existed something like an Indian Muslim, sharing in a common ideology, set of practices, and above all, a sense of loyalty to the Muslim *umma* and not the Indian nation-state. Indeed, Muslims could hardly be the bogeymen of the Hindu Right if there was no 'Indian Muslim' to begin with. For Shia and Sunni time and again lock horns in Lucknow, even in peacetime rarely seeing eye to eye on most matters. Sunni Islam itself is a house divided: the Deobandis take inspiration from the Hanafi law books whereas the Barelwis look to Sufi practices that affirm the intercessionary power of saints. Bihari and Tamil Muslims speak mutually unintelligible languages. The high-caste *ashraf*, low-caste *ajlaf*, and ex-Untouchable *arzal* scarcely ever cross paths. *A fortiori*, the ability of Islam to adapt to local milieux renders the festivals, music, cuisine, and culture of Muslims in, say, the Deccan, Bengal, and Gangetic plains incomprehensible to one another, but nevertheless accessible to other cohabiting communities. Ultimately, on his account, region counts for more than religion.[3]

2

But Hasan is not alone in making the case that the Congress best represented Muslim interests from the fifties on; that Muslims, as a fractured community incapable of collective action, after Partition found themselves vilified as a homogenous collective in thrall to atavistic practices and adventitious authorities; that the Congress, upholding precolonial syncretism, was an isle of hope in an Islamophobic ocean; and that under its charismatic postcolonial leadership, it pushed forward a secularising process to which every self-respecting Muslim hitched his wagon, receiving in return state protection and social approval.

Indeed, a number of academics, journalists, and political commentators have concurred with his assessment, giving it the weight of consensus. For the Hyderabadi historian Omar Khalidi, the Congress was 'the natural instrument for the participation of Muslims in the new political process'.[4] M. J. Akbar, author of a life of Nehru and editor of the Calcutta *Telegraph*, too, understood, albeit less charitably, Congress-Muslim relations as a refurbished version of the social contract: 'Tucked in the pocket of the Congress, the [Muslim] vote [was] the protection money Muslims paid in return for the promise of security'.[5] The *Statesman* reporter Saeed Naqvi reached the same conclusion in his autobiography, a volume in equal measure a sociological inquiry into the Muslim condition: 'We saw [Nehru] as one of us, as an embodiment of Awadh's composite culture'.[6]

All of these, it must be said, are essentially riffs on an emic perspective of the fifties. Take, for instance, the Congress' very first election manifesto, which promised, 'as protection of the rights of minorities', to 'make every effort to ensure proper representation for them'.[7] For his part, Maulana Syed Asad Madani, general secretary of the Jamiat-ul-Ulema Hind that represented the clerical interest and was an arm of the Congress, praised 'the glorious example set by Mr Nehru in giving equitable and just treatment to minorities'.[8] 'Protection', 'treatment', 'magnanimous', 'healing touch'. Feudal or mafioso, supercilious or paternalistic, as such an arrangement might appear to contemporary sensibilities, these were precisely the terms in which the Congress-Muslim pact was generally understood.

For another set of writers, Muslim diversity is the point of departure. As Moin Shakir has it, only a small section of the community took to 'communalism'. 'Sectarian differences', meanwhile, precluded religious solidarity, the little of it that existed in any case owing more to the push of Hindu nationalism than the pull of Islam.[9] In a similar vein, Gopal Krishna sees in the Muslim identification with the Congress an 'integrative process at work'. The community, we are told, concluded that 'communal solidarity' was false consciousness.[10]

At first blush, there is more truth here than is apparent from Hasan's boosterism or the more restrained, if still inadequately rationalised, prose of allied opinion. For the weight of evidence suggests that the Congress was indeed the central vehicle for the community. In 1952 and 1957, Congressmen accounted for 78 and 90 per cent of Muslim lawmakers elected at the centre, and 80 and 81 per cent in the states of the Union.[11]

The overall thrust of Nehru's correspondence confirms the received view. The same impression comes through in his entreaties to his party to discontinue education policies delegitimising Urdu as a language of instruction, commitment to increasing Muslim representation in the bureaucracy, and general vigilance, manifest in the absence of major instances of religious violence until the 1959 and 1961 riots, respectively, in Uttar and Madhya Pradesh. Legislative measures corroborate this picture. For instance, in 1956, the Congress pushed through the repeal of the Evacuee Property Act, which had for the most part impounded property owned by Muslims as enemy assets. On the international front, Nehru settled on a mindful foreign policy: 'because of Muslim sentiment within India, a neutrality slanted towards the Arabs' on the Palestinian question.[12] What is more, his party's unbroken reign of three decades was bookended by secular declamations. In November 1947, the All-India Congress Committee, in one of its first postcolonial pronouncements, resolved to 'protect the Muslim minority'. And in December 1976, three months before the Janata coalition ejected it out of power, the party steamrollered the Forty-second Amendment, adding the modifier 'secular' to describe the Republic in the Constitution's preamble.

For yet another cluster of academics, it was the system in general rather than the Congress in particular that offered Muslims avenues of representation. Here, the emphasis is on the polity, not the party. On one such account, India is not so much a nation-state as a 'state-nation', a society of 'robustly multinational dimensions' fashioned through the Herculean efforts of the 'founders of Indian democracy', who 'crafted an inclusionary set of political institutions'. The 'form of secularism India pioneered in the democratic world [*sic*] ... gave equal support and equal respect to *all* of India's religions'.[13]

A variant of this position is to be found in Arend Lijphart's 'consociational interpretation' of Indian democracy. Like the political systems of Colombia, Belgium, Switzerland, Lebanon, Malaysia, and his native Netherlands, early postcolonial India exhibited all the 'crucial elements' of 'consociationalism'—essentially power-sharing. As a result, Indian democracy ably withstood the kind of destabilising centrifugal forces that did in many of its African and Asian counterparts. Muslims were won over by power-sharing at the high table in the form of representative 'grand coalitions', their ranks sworn in as ministers and lawmakers; a 'minority veto' that guaranteed—partial—juridical and educational autonomy, preempting state attempts to muscle in on the *sharia* in the private realm; and, counterpointing the distorting effects of plurality voting, the informal system of 'proportionality' maintained in electoral slates.[14]

These ideas also find currency, if not explicit mention, in historical writing. Granville Austin, for one, argues that despite achieving hegemony, the Congress went through the motions of securing adequate Muslim representation in Parliament.[15] The 'principle of accommodation' was in full view in the constitutional settlement, which granted minorities the right to proselytise and establish educational institutions. Over the next half-century, the fidelity of citizens and rulers alike to the Constitution, coupled with the 'curative character' of the document itself, saw to the protection of minority rights, hence of the minorities themselves.[16] Such enthusiasm for constitutional safeguards is to be found in some of the earliest writings on Muslim politics as well as many of the latest.[17]

Ultimately, in the Whig histories of postcolonial India that dominate popular and academic writing, Nehru ('the father of Indian democracy' to Ashutosh Varshney) and his partisans (for

Pratap Bhanu Mehta, 'symbols of a new awakening India') serve but as characters in a morality play, rallying to the defence of minorities (as the Nobel laureate Amartya Sen sees it, by laying 'emphasis on the toleration of heterodoxy and pluralism in Indian history') and magnanimously writing the laws of the land in concert with Hindu nationalists and Muslim clerics ('Nehru and his colleagues wisely put aside these differences', Ramachandra Guha helpfully notes).[18] It is, it will be argued in these pages, an obliviousness to the power dynamics that shaped interfaith relations in postcolonial India that enables public intellectuals to reproduce uncritically such ideas, and to wax lyrical about India's 'improbable', 'robust', and 'surprising' democracy.[19] Like all consensuses, this one cloaks a concealed bias. It is to disinterring it that we now turn.

A number of uncomfortable facts are conveniently ignored in such narratives of Nehruvian munificence. The few occasions when a divergence between intent and implementation is acknowledged, it is in a declinist context contrasting the rule of the 'tall men' of the fifties, who deftly managed the minority question, and their successors, ever so carelessly playing with confessional fire.[20] It bears more reflection, then, as to why fewer Muslims made it to Nehruvian legislatures than to any other Parliament before 2014, the first time an explicitly Hindu nationalist party secured a clear majority.

Cognisant of this, a number of historians in recent years have been less inhibited in taking the Congress to task. The liberation from orthodox historiography stems from both a shift in focus and method. By fixing on political actors themselves—often in surveys of discrete states and organisations—these works place a premium on state practice rather than ideology. Even when theoretical ambitions are explicit, as in Paul Brass' corpus for instance, a thoroughgoing empiricism precedes the construction of a metanarrative rather than the other way around, the norm in the writings seen above.

A rather different view of the Congress, then, emerges from these accounts. *Pace* Hasan, it appears, independence did not mark the end of history. The dispatch of the League did not make Muslim politics *passé*. Indeed, the community had its fair share of political battles to fight in postcolonial India. For in practice, constitutional guarantees and Congress hegemony were scarce prophylactics against the malaise of majoritarianism.

In North India, for instance, the fifties witnessed a sharp decline in the number of Muslims in government. Short work was made of Urdu, the language used by Muslims as much for quotidian communication as for political mobilisation.[21] Hindi was made the sole official state language in Uttar Pradesh and Bihar. Muslims were counselled 'to refrain from being cantankerous' by the UP Language Committee. The national education policy, dubbed the 'three language formula', was interpreted to mean that students were to be taught Hindi, English, and a third tongue reflecting the 'majority wish of students'—inevitably Sanskrit, the choice of the Hindus.[22]

South of the Vindhyas, in the span of a few months following the wresting of Hyderabad from the Nizam by the Indian armed forces, a pogrom left—in a 'very conservative estimate'—'between 27,000 and 40,000' Muslims dead. Delhi's proxies—first the military governor, J. N. Chaudhuri, and then the appointed chief minister, M. K. Vellodi—turned a blind eye to the violence, imprisoning 13,000 Muslim civilians, firing Muslim administrators wholesale in order to bring in Hindu replacements, squeezing access to Gulf capital to immiserate Muslim institutions of higher learning, and denying Muslims citizenship and rehabilitation.[23]

In Gujarat, in the west, what began as a sin of omission turned into one of commission. Throughout the sixties, job cuts and deindustrialisation delivered thousands of Ahmedabad's textile workers into the arms of Hindu nationalists. The smouldering resentment finally erupted in September 1969 in one of postcolonial India's bloodiest riots. The Congress state government, it appears, was 'partially harnessed to Hindu organisations'.[24] In a town that was one-seventh Muslim, the community accounted for two-thirds of the 660 dead. Muslim assets made up over three quarters of the Rs 42 million lost in damaged property. The upshot was the beginning of an ongoing process of ghettoisation, Muslims seeking safety in numbers by moving *en masse* to 'safe' neighbourhoods.[25]

The Congress' comportment was no better in the east. In consolidating power in West Bengal, it adopted an 'assimilate or leave' policy that killed off the Muslim League, as intended. But it also unleashed a wave of anti-Muslim violence across urban Bengal, forcing Calcutta Muslims to migrate to the countryside. It was, moreover, on the Congress' watch that the most violent Hindu-Muslim conflagration of postcolonial India transpired. These were the riots of 1964 that followed the theft of a relic from the Hazratbal Shrine in which several thousand souls perished. In its wake, more than 800,000 Muslims—one in fifty Indian Muslims—emigrated to Pakistan.[26]

By the end of the Congress' three decades in power, Muslims, accounting for 11.4 per cent of the country's population, made up only 4.5 per cent of its judges, 4.4 and 6 per cent of the Union's and states' civil servants. The community was underrepresented in banking and the constabulary, overrepresented in the carceral population and as riot victims.[27]

So much for the Congress. What of the Constitution? Here, too, the picture is more complex than it appears. In the spring of 1949, the Constituent Assembly set about discarding all the political safeguards that Muslims had secured with the devolution acts of 1909, 1919, and 1935. Not long after, separate electorates vanished. Whereas Hindu ex-Untouchables and tribal peoples were reserved parliamentary seats, Muslims were left out of the process. Plurality voting was adopted over the heads of Muslim objections, making a mockery of minority representation and the popular will.

What of Indian secularism? As Paul Brass has shown, its unwritten rules made it easier for, say, Tamil and Punjabi speakers to have the government's ear than it did Urdu natives. For the former put forward 'regional' demands, the latter 'communal' ones. Likewise, it was easier for Dalits (Hindu ex-Untouchables) to press for quotas than for the *arzal* (Muslim ex-Untouchables), for 'caste' trumped 'communal' demands as well.[28] In postcolonial India, then, the secularism of Muslims had to appear 'more Catholic than the Pope'. Any defence of Muslim communitarian interest, even in the face of gross injustice and discrimination, held the possibility of being denounced as anti-secular, 'anti-national' even.[29] By contrast, Hindu impulses—such as when the ban on cow slaughter was snuck into the Constitution as a 'directive principle' for the states of the Union to aspire to—were exempt from secularist censure.[30]

The informal norms of 'consociational' governance, too, failed to deliver. 'The Congress Working Committee recommendations on minority proportionality were [flouted] at every level of government'. No Muslim made it to the great offices of state in Nehruvian India. Seen as a 'security risk', the Muslim home minister of Uttar Pradesh was forced to resign in 1947.[31] As the fifties wore on, a number of locally influential Muslim Congressmen such as Mehdi Nawaz Jung and Jehangir Kabir were turfed out in the rough and tumble of factional politics, essentially Hindu intercaste struggles that left Muslims sitting uncomfortably at the margins of political life.[32]

In essence, neither the 'Congress system' nor the 'consociational' polity of the 'state-nation' lived up to their conceptual promises. On the contrary, what passed for secularism either put Muslim politics *in extremis* or prompted Muslims to forswear politics proper.

Purging politics from the study of postcolonial India, then, will not do. The dominant historiography would have us believe that Muslims simply did not require a politics of their own, so immensely satisfied they were with constitutional and Congress protection, party and political architecture mutually reinforcing each other.

All that was left for historians, on Mushirul Hasan's account, was to recover and 'enlarge our appreciation of the role played' by great Muslim men in the making of modern India.[33] In other words, it was pointless for historians to carp about divisive figures and unwholesome movements when the more pressing task of building a nationalist pantheon awaited them. But politics is indeed divisive and unwholesome, concerned as it is with, to use Harold Lasswell's pithy definition of it, the business of who gets what, when, and how.

Muslims in India, of course, had much to fight over. They had grouses galore. There is, in fact, a sizeable body of work written in opposition to the nationalist tradition. The story told here is not a happy one. The words that leap out of these pages are not 'protection' and 'representation', but 'victimisation' and 'discrimination'. The titles alone should suffice for our purposes here: *Plight of Indian Muslims*,[34] *Plight of Muslims in India*,[35] *Denial and Deprivation*.[36] A protected community or a marginalised minority: how are we to square the circle?

The question, admittedly a rather uninspiring one, prompts another, a more interesting line of inquiry: what of Muslim agency? Or, as an exasperated reviewer put it in an appraisal of one of his colleague's latest tomes, yet another 'dismal catalogue of Muslim grievances and defects': is there no more to the Muslim experience than their 'depending on the police and existing [as some kind of] protected monuments?'[37] The present study is premised on a kindred dissatisfaction with the literature on Muslim India, by turns fixing on 'protection' and 'plight' while ignoring Muslim agency *tout court*.

Building on the work of the few historians and political scientists who treat India's Muslims as subjects, not merely objects, of history, I set out in these pages to recover the agency of a range of Muslim social actors, elite and subaltern, secular and clerical, activist and apolitical. Early forays include Paul Brass' and Theodore P. Wright, Jr's studies reconstructing, in the Gangetic plain and Malabar, Coromandel, and Deccan respectively, the quintessential dilemma of Muslim politics: 'communal' appeals asked for trouble whereas 'secular' mobilisation cut no ice.[38]

More recently, Joya Chatterji has explored the many ways in which the community contended with Islamophobia in West Bengal: the damascene conversion of Muslim Leaguers to the Congress at Partition; until as late as the mid-sixties, subaltern migration to East Pakistan; depoliticisation and ghettoisation.[39] In her study of Muslim belonging in Hyderabad, Taylor Sherman discerns similar processes at work: an acceptance, if only on sufferance, on the part of a large section of the Muslim elite that the Congress was the only game in town; the cautious and ultimately futile struggle for the recognition of Urdu.[40] Likewise, Roland E. Miller's survey of the lifeworld of Kerala's Mappila Muslims bears testimony to their agency: they threw in their lot with the Muslim League during its slow road to recovery in the late fifties, even as they kept at arm's length from the state, seeking greener pastures in trade and on the Gulf labour market.[41]

Yet others have taken stock of Muslim attempts to secure juridical autonomy and greater representation in government; stave off state interference in the *waqf*—Muslim endowment—regime; and negotiate, even oppose, Islamophobic citizenship and preventive detention laws.[42] A collection of essays edited by the Osellas has reconstructed the trials and tribulations of living as a Muslim as viewed from the perspective of the Muslims themselves.[43] In producing a synchronic snapshot of Muslim women in India, Zoya Hasan and Ritu Menon have used original data to produce an impressive study covering a broad range of themes, *inter alia*, workforce participation, political activism, education, marriage, domestic violence.[44] Taking cues from the works of Vazira Fazila-Yacoobali Zamindar, Yasmin Khan, and Sanjib Baruah, a considerable literature has developed on the bureaucratic battles between Indian Muslims and the unbending functionaries set on disenfranchising them.[45]

All the same, an historical imbalance remains. For both quantitatively—shelves and column inches filled—and in the thought-world of postcolonial India—that is, the scholarly as well as popular consensus, gauged by the near-hegemony enjoyed by secularists in the Indian world of letters—chronicles of protection and plight crowd out accounts of Muslim agency. Besides making a contribution to offset this disparity, the purpose of the present volume is threefold.

First, it sets out to bring the unity of the Muslim experience of postcolonial India under a single focus. In the course of this work, the reader will encounter the *ulama* and lay politicians, Congressmen and Leaguers, Shia and Sunni, *waqifs* and *wasiqadars*, university and *madrasa* students, academics and activists, tycoons and trade unionists, lobbyists and landlords, princes and publicists, workers and women. Even as the accent lies, as it must, on the regions where the bulk of India's Muslims live—the Hindi belt and the Deccan—the peripheries of the Republic, where, in fact, the largest concentrations of the *qaum* as a proportion of the population are to be found—Assam, Kashmir, parts of Kerala and West Bengal—are given generous treatment, too. The picture here, moreover, is not merely synchronic but also diachronic, tracking changes in élan and strategy over time—in the case of the Congress Muslims, for instance, over half a century to the seventies.

True, no single volume can do justice to the bewildering variety of sects and sectional interests that make up Indian Muslim society.

Even so, it is hoped that a clear picture emerges in the pages that follow. We must be careful to avoid the pitfalls of reading too deeply into superficial differences—cultural, linguistic, and regional. Indeed, if there is a single takeaway here, it is the simple observation that it was first and foremost class, and not confession, that counted in postcolonial India. Muslim princes in the Punjab and Uttar Pradesh had more in common with the Hindu royals of Rajasthan and Madhya Pradesh than with, say, the Muslim craftsmen of the same states, employed without contracts and social protection in sunset industries. Likewise, the Muslim rentiers who managed *auqaf* were a world removed from the Muslim working class. The Muslims of Aligarh town and gown, too, were chalk and cheese. Indian Muslims were a community apart.

Second, *Another India* attempts to bridge the material and the ideational—realms artificially separated by the disciplinary ravine that divides intellectual from political and social history—to show that Muslim politics was shaped as much by political ideas as by political realities. For ideas, of course, are not formed in a vacuum. Nor are political strategies independent of regnant *Weltanschauungen*. This, then, is not *histoire événementielle,* moving briskly from one event—or, for that matter, one riot, election—to the next. Rather the focus here is on the strategic responses of Muslims to the challenges of Islamophobia and Hindu nationalism, mass democracy and the nature of the postcolonial settlement.

Third, written in opposition to the discursive turn in historiography, this study uncovers Muslim voices by looking at Muslim actors themselves. For the discourse of Muslim politics is well-trodden ground. We know all too well now that Hindu nationalist ideologues such as Savarkar and Golwalkar were not particularly fond of Muslims, views that were shared and amplified by mandarins, civil society organisations, and, as the Indian term of art goes, the 'scurrilous' press. All the same, we know very little about what the Indian Muslims themselves thought about their predicament and what they did to change it. Put differently, the primary aim of *Another India* is to recover Muslim agency from the back pages of history.

Much ink has been spilled in trying to suss out, theoretically at any rate, the limits of political agency. Are we the product of our actions or our circumstances, or perhaps, in the language of sociology, 'the mutual constitution' of agency and structure? The balance for Giddens has always lain in favour of the former, for Parsons the latter.[46]

More recent writing, however, has tended to look beyond the interpenetration of agency and structure even while acknowledging its irrefutability. Mustafa Emirbayer and Ann Mische, for instance, follow George Herbert Mead in making the case for, as it were, a temporal understanding of agency. For even as 'reality exists in a present', 'the immediacy of present situations is extended by our ability to imaginatively construct a sense of past and future'. Agency, in other words, is conditioned by past habits, present contingencies, and future intentions. On their account, social action oriented towards the past typically is the least agentic, towards the future the most.[47]

Muslims in postcolonial India called on, by turns, all three elements in this 'chordal triad of agency', negotiating the spectres of the past (the shadow of Partition and the blame for it that was routinely laid at their feet), the changing circumstances of the present (subaltern awakening, the growing incidence of riots), and Islamic desiderata for the future (a tolerant society, *sharia* rule for Muslims, commensurate representation in public life and private enterprise).

To some extent, so, too, did Muslim academics. For quite a few of them were writing what, in the first instance, were not works of history, but rather historical manifestoes. Even if never explicitly stated, these were political interventions. Divulging political *raisons d'être*, even party affiliations, was for them par for the course. Indeed, some of them quite evidently put their money where their mouths were. For instance, Rafiq Zakaria, columnist and author of a life of Jinnah, went on to serve as deputy leader of the Congress Parliamentary Party. Less overt party-political affiliations were more common. All the same, there are ample clues in the corpora of, say, Mushirul Hasan, Omar Khalidi, and Moin Shakir to put two and two together. For all of them, identification with the Congress was, in itself, an act of agency. Their works, then, are better seen as an act of delegation of the role of protecting the *qaum* to the Congress rather than a mere historical description of such an arrangement. Therein lies the agency. Much the same process is at work in histories of 'Muslim plight'. For painting a narrative of misfortune serves to build a case for amelioration. 'Things are bad. It is time Muslims got their act together'. An agentic call to arms, after all.

As with historians, so with political actors. The Congress Muslims' was the first kind of agency, oriented to the past. Indeed, as we will see in Part I, theirs was a politics of guilt and circumspection, overdetermined by Partition and cast in a renunciatory mould. Here was a subtle and peaceable agency, yearning for a return to the syncretism of old. The long and short of it was to appeal to the better nature of Delhi's Hindu rulers.

What of the second kind of agency, aligned to the present? Emblematic of it were Muslim modernisers, as it were, figures such as the education minister Mohammedali Currim Chagla and the atheistical polemicist Hamid Dalwai, both of whom we will meet in Part II. Theirs was a decidedly pragmatist politics, the kind that gets described as sensible, premised on a concern with 'backwardness'—understood in terms of literacy and participation rates, a deficient patriotism—and apparently in possession of the ministrations required to extricate the community from it. What was needed was more of the same: more toleration, more secularism, more state intervention, more schooling, and more *Kulturkampf*.

Finally, the third kind of agency, disposed towards the future. India's Islamists and clerics fit this bill. Here, one witnesses a curious temporal pincer movement. For even as they nostalgically journeyed through the past—revisiting the Rashidun Caliphate when disposed to history, otherwise a chimerical world inherited from the Holy Book and the *hadith*—the aim was never to 'return' to it. Instead, it was to envision a rather different future, one in which Muslim India was governed, in the private realm at any rate, exclusively by Muslim laws, an *imperium in imperio* fashioned in Azad's millenarian fantasy by an *amir-e-hind*—ruler of Muslim India.

If the form of agency limited political possibilities, so, too, did systemic constraints. It must be remembered that in the three decades to 1977, India was effectively a one-party state. When it came to Muslim politics, then, inadvertency often counted for more than determinacy. As we will see at greater length in Chapters 4 and 5, the major achievement of the clutch of Muslim parties that lined up against the Congress lay not in their electoral record but in their ability to alter the balance of opinion in Delhi. Much like the Red Scare that occasioned welfarism in the West, the Green Scare sparked off a serious conversation about India's Muslim question. What is more, with it came pork-barrel funds, patronage, representation in Parliament. The bugbear of a largely imaginary communalism produced a veritable affirmative action programme.

It is not hard, then, to see why the Olympics of who best represented Muslim India is a rather profitless discussion. In the event, there will be little methodological reflection in this study on what constitutes, or is representative of, 'Muslim' politics, or indeed who is a 'Muslim'. This seeming indifference, however, should not be mistaken for incuriosity. For it appears fair to me to accept claims of Muslimhood at face value. To do otherwise would entail policing boundaries—who is a 'real' and representative Muslim?—a futile exercise that has been the preserve of secularists and Islamists whose semantic sleights of hand allow them to exclude one another as *bona fide* representatives of the community. There are no true Scotsmen. Also, the more the tesserae, the more nuanced and complex the mosaic of Muslim India. Far better, then, to be ecumenical than cast about for 'real' representatives.

Such a methodology is also in keeping with the expansive turn in our understanding of representation as a concept, one that has prompted a reappraisal of the link between representative and represented.[48] On the newer, more accommodating account, democratic representation is so much more than electoral consent. Here, the break with Hanna Fenichel Pitkin, whose presence has towered over the literature for well over half a century, has been especially liberating. True, she contends that her analysis holds good not just for electoral democracy, but for political life in its entirety. The general thrust of her analysis, though, suggests the reverse. A German *émigré* who fled Berlin at the time of the Enabling Act, and then Prague the year of the Sudeten Crisis for the United States, it was not by accident that Pitkin concerned herself primarily with the business of voting and liberal democratic systems, which in her opinion were, unlike Nazism and Bolshevism, truly representative.[49]

The recent literature on representation, by contrast, points to a more ecumenical direction. We find, for instance, in Nadia Urbinati's discussion of Rousseau a much more capacious conception than an electoral contract.[50] Indeed, the conceptual leaps made of late are plain to see if one compares Pitkin's *locus classicus* of 1967 with a more contemporary account, say Mónica Brito Vieira and David Runciman's, written in 2008.[51] Both take their cue from Hobbes, albeit with a crucial difference in standpoint. For Pitkin, authorisation and representation are one and the same thing. Once the people authorise a sovereign, they effectively surrender their right to reject their ruler. In Vieira and Runciman's reading, on the other hand, the two are distinct. Sovereigns only represent the Commonwealth, that is the sum of individuals, and not the individuals themselves, enabling the latter to reject the former. In other words, if Pitkin's version of Hobbes found himself in the age of Trump, Brexit, and Modi, he would profess a rather poor opinion of the Resistance, People's Vote, and *azadi*. The people, for they voted in their leaders, had forfeited the right to oppose them until the next election. But if Vieira and Runciman's Hobbes had a contemporary avatar, he would support the defenestration of a sovereign so long as the masses had lost faith in him.

This shift, tilting the balance in favour of the represented over the representative, makes it harder to sustain the minimalist claims of Mushirul Hasan, who deems the Islamist Jama'at-i-Islami beyond the pale, or indeed the JI itself, which discounts liberals as Muslims. No Muslim in these pages will be considered less Muslim than the other.

If superseded in sophistication by her heirs, Pitkin nevertheless presents what is a striking variety of representations on offer in modern societies. Her typology is not without its uses. So, in the course of this study, we will encounter *descriptive* representatives of Muslim India, that is representatives that resembled the represented in that they were both 'Muslim' and 'leaders'—luminaries from Azad to Zaheer. We will also meet *substantive* representatives, who acted on the behalf of Muslims in Parliament and in society, though, as we will see in the conclusion, very few figures in fact lay at the intersection in the Venn diagram of the two. This we will call an 'ashraf betrayal', on which we will discuss more later. All the figures we will come across were, after a fashion, *symbolic* representatives of Muslim India, in that they, through their position in power and public life, embodied the represented, as a poster child does a cohort. Finally, we will come upon *formalistic* representatives, who stood for the community by being authorised by its members. Of these there were not many. Suffice to say that few Muslim leaders were in point of fact put to the task by their community. Instead, they drew their influence from other sources—for example, from juridical circles in Chagla's case, clerical in Nadwi's, the trade union movement in Asaf Ali's.[52]

I originally set out to write a narrative history of Muslim high politics during the first three decades of postcolonial rule, 1947 to 1977, years of uninterrupted Congress rule, widely understood, as we have seen, to be a golden age of liberalism and religious tolerance. My book, then, was to be a chronological account tracing the rise of Muslim consciousness from its mid-century nadir to its Mushāwarat apogee. The virtual absence of records on this period, however, meant that it was not long before I was disabused of my linear historical arc.

Indeed, there was only so much material to be had in the Indian archives. One came up against incomplete series of papers, private collections that were but meagre stacks of newspaper clippings, to say nothing of the state of records at the Bihar State Archives and the Aligarh Muslim University, uncatalogued in both instances. In Patna, I was informed that the entire archive—hundreds of thousands of documents—was being digitised, and so would be inaccessible for some years to come. Every day, I was shown ten files in no particular order, and with no relation to my research, on a CD, the scans scarcely readable. The original files, I was told, had been destroyed.

By contrast, the collection at the Sir Syed House in Aligarh was indexed, though not a single corresponding file could actually be found. As for the Sir Syed Section—an eponymous but altogether different enterprise at the Azad Library, a stone's throw away—there was, as in Patna, no catalogue. To my dismay, records on the handful of shelves that made up the institutional papers dried up after *circa* 1920. Equally, a visit to the headquarters of the Majlis-i-Mushāwarat in Okhla proved unprofitable. No documentation had survived the five relocations in as many decades. Likewise, I drew a blank at the Central Secretariat Library, where I found only a handful of the reports boasted by its online catalogue. On inquiry, I was informed that the rest had gone missing.

The historical reconstruction of events was possible only in Swiss cheese fashion. It made more sense, then, to swap chronology for compressed surveys of myriad Muslim sectional interests. I had better luck with the National Archives of India and Nehru Memorial Museum and Library, both in Delhi, and Lucknow's Uttar Pradesh State Archives—all, by comparison, eminently professional affairs. Here I found a plenitude of material on Congress Muslims, many of whom gave unvarnished interviews in the seventies and eighties as part of the NMML's oral history project. The correspondence of Chagla, Mahmud, Kabir, and Saadulla at the NMML, along with their published memoirs, proved an unrivalled source on political possibilities in the age of Nehru. The reconstruction of *mutawallis*, *wasiqadars*, and the Aligarh Muslim University are based on home ministry files at the NAI and UPSA.

Archival impediments—par for the course in the Subcontinental setting—and plague apart, the other obstacle lay in finding sources where Muslims could be quoted in their own words, so central to the business of recovering agency. Here, newspapers and journals came to the rescue. In particular, four stood out. *Radiance*, the weekly of the Islamist Jama'at-i-Islami, whose numbers I found mildewed and moth-eaten at the paper's headquarters in Okhla, is by far the best source we have on Muslim India of the sixties and seventies. Its suspect provenance, in fact, is quite misleading. For in it we find a record not only of the Jama'at's activities, but the community's at large. Nor are heterodox opinions found wanting in its pages. Another indispensable source is *Link*, a contemporary weekly attached to the Communist Party of India whose editors and writers—many of them Muslim—expressed a thorough interest in Muslim affairs, preserved on grainy microfilm at the NMML. Then there is the *Times of India*, the newspaper of record, available online, and Syed Shahabuddin's *Muslim India*, in equal measure a monthly digest of Muslim high politics in the closing decades of the twentieth century and a compendium of the lives and works of nineteenth- and twentieth-century luminaries, stored at Sapru House.

The limitations of this book, then, should be clear. I have had to rely on a rather narrow base of sources to build my arguments on. *Faute de mieux*, I have had to depend on a fragmentary archive, piecing together material from newspapers and reports to see if details from memoirs check out.

Colonial sources, of course, I have read against the grain. The *Transfer of Power* documents have bias written all over them. They contain, primarily, the correspondence of the men on the spot, none of whom were particularly sympathetic to Congress Muslims, a small sectional interest that they took to be a nuisance. All the same, their missives are of value to us. For one thing, the Raj was able to intercept large amounts of mail. In a sense, then, Delhi had a more complete picture of the situation on the ground than any single Indian actor. For another, prejudice notwithstanding, their letters tell us what contemporaries thought of these figures at the time. Memoirs written after the event lack the immediacy of these documents.

Oral history, too, can be misleading. Both Raza Khan and Syed Mahmud, for instance, were at pains to display their impeccable nationalist credentials in their interviews. Newspapers and private papers strike a different note—by turns more agentic and reflective, questioning decisions made by party leaderships and critically weighing up the pros and cons of their actions.

Perhaps the most important limitation imposed by my sources is the near-absence of subaltern voices. One hears a lot about the Muslim working classes, *petite bourgeoisie*, and lumpenproletariat, though it is rare to hear *from* them—from the horse's mouth, so to speak. I hoped to survey Aligarh's locksmiths, Firozabad's bangle-makers, and Banaras' weavers, perusing at length papers such as *Working Class*, the organ of the Marxist trade union CITU, its Congress equivalent *Indian Worker*, the Bombay *Blitz* and *Link*. To little avail. No sustained account of the subaltern Muslim predicament could be gleaned from these pages.

I could, of course, have interviewed Muslim old-timers in these towns myself, learning a thing or two about 'Muslim trades'. That was the plan before the pandemic struck. In the event, I don't regret the absence of interviews, not least on account of my desultory experience with them on a previous book. I have come to distrust the vagaries of human memory, so much more fallible than the written word. To paraphrase Barnes' dictum, oral history is 'that certainty produced at the point where the imperfections of memory meet the inadequacies of documentation'.[53]

In any case, my aim here is to outline the Indian Muslim Ideology, as it were, placing it in its context, tracing its lineage and ramifications. Ideologies, by definition, are high-political creations, the work of a thinking elite: politicians, clerics, the lettered classes. Unsurprisingly, these are the kind of figures who populate these pages. A more complete study encompassing the thought-world of Muslim subalterns could quite possibly take up another volume, not to mention turn into the work of a lifetime.

What follows, then, is very much a first cut at writing a postcolonial history of Muslim India. Mushirul Hasan, as we have seen, made a stab at just such a volume, only to produce an inventory of elite political manoueverings in which Muslims are little more than spectators.[54] Much the same can be said of Omar Khalidi's smaller and staider tome.[55] Yoginder Sikand's study, *Muslims in India since 1947*, despite its ambitious title, profiles only a handful of marginal Muslim journals and organisations. Likewise, the definite article in the subtitle of Saeed Naqvi's largely autobiographical essay, *Being the Other: The Muslim in India*, seems largely misplaced. And there is little information about the general élan of Muslim politics in Hilal Ahmed's *Siyasi Muslims*.

A fuller statement will have to await the opening of more archives, not to mention a writer fluent in half a dozen regional tongues and with unparalleled access to the Who's Who of Muslim India—an endeavour rather beyond my ken.

That said, every effort has been made to range widely in this study. The Hindi belt, where the better part of India's Muslims live, commands centre stage. But even so, the peripheries play strong supporting roles. Indeed, these are not mere cameos. Substantive sections of Chapters 3 and 4 concern Assam and Madras, respectively. Chapters 4 and 5 cruise Bombay and Bengal, Kerala and Kashmir, Chapter 7 the Punjab and Hyderabad. Equally, care has been taken to place developments in their proper comparative perspective, contrasting changes in Hindu to Muslim personal law, the political safeguards bequeathed by the founding fathers to Muslims to those to the Scheduled Castes, the fate of Urdu to that of other minority tongues, the Aligarh Muslim University to the Banaras Hindu University.

Part I documents the ascendancy, meridian, and decline of the 'nationalist Muslim' from the beginning of the Khilafat movement to the end of the Emergency. The theme here is the diminution of the Indian Muslim elite. Chapter 1 considers the birth of the nationalist Muslim, a new style of politician forged in the maelstrom of devolution, clerical modernisation, and incipient nationalism. The next two chapters look, in turn, at how the nationalist Muslims fared in the Constituent Assembly and in government. Part II, titled 'Communalists' to send up the exnominated Manicheanism of the fifties that divided the community into the latter (read: bad) and nationalists (read: good), follows Muslim parties in Chapter 4, an important Muslim pressure group in Chapter 5, and India's Islamists in Chapter 6. The picture is much of a muchness. The 'communalists' had a lot in common with the 'nationalists'. The more important cleavage, in fact, was class. Indeed, some of these sectional interests never had it better than they did in postcolonial India, otherwise synonymous with anti-Muslim prejudice. Part III considers precisely these figures, the custodians of Muslim endowments, aristocrats and princely pensioners, and the patrician landed interest in charge of the AMU's board of trustees.

The community's *ashraf*—upper class and upper caste—elite mobilised in the name of the entire community, but ultimately attended to the select few. This was the *ashraf* betrayal. Mass mobilisation by Muslims was conspicuous by its absence. Indeed, this was the upshot of the political élan—essentially anti-political and juridical—adopted by 'nationalists' and 'communalists' alike. 'Muslim politics' in postcolonial India, I conclude, has been a politics *manqué*.

21

An accent on Muslim agency can at first blush appear unsettling. What is more, to talk of an *ashraf* betrayal can even seem exculpatory—why blame Nehru and Modi when Nadwi and Mahmud are at hand? Still, such an historical verdict, I hope, has its own value. For at a time of left-liberal despondency and Hindu nationalist preponderance, no greater historical service to the Muslim community can be performed than to recover its agency, foregrounding not only displays of it, but also its limits.

PART I

'NATIONALISTS'

1

IDENTITY POLITICS

The 'nationalist Muslim' was, incontrovertibly, the most powerful Muslim force in modern Indian history. For it was the policies, and more importantly, political élan, of this rather small section of the *qaum*'s elite that shaped the lives of multiple generations of Indian Muslims.

But who were they? Golwalkar, chief Hindu nationalist ideologue of the fifties, derisorily refers to them in his *Bunch of Thoughts*, singling out that 'greatest nationalist Muslim' Maulana Azad for foolishly spurning Jinnah when he could well have followed him to the new homeland and 'had a decisive voice in the affairs of Pakistan'.[1] Chagla, Nehru's Muslim education minister—who, as a votary of 'real secularism', consciously distanced himself from the nationalist Muslims—too, railed against them for their insincerity: they 'were really communal at heart'.[2] Nehru, for his part, heaped praises on them and mourned the 'pitiful story' of their 'collapse and elimination'; at the time he wrote this, in the thirties, their postcolonial renascence was not a foregone conclusion.[3] The editors of the Congressman Syed Mahmud's letters simply title their volume *A Nationalist Muslim and Indian Politics*.[4]

But the nationalist Muslim is as much an actor's category as it is an historian's category. Barbara Metcalf, for one, uses it, albeit warily, to refer to figures whose anticolonial politics stemmed from their religious identities.[5] Meanwhile, in his life of Ansari, *A Nationalist Conscience*, Mushirul Hasan registers his discomfort with the worldview of his subject, who contrasted the 'nationalist Muslims' with those for 'whom the freedom of the country came merely a bad second to communal privilege'. For Hasan the appellation was entirely without purchase, as various Muslim champions of *swaraj* shared little else in common. Instead, there existed only 'Congress Muslims' (a term of approbation) and partisans of 'Muslim communalism' and 'Muslim separatism' (both terms of opprobrium).[6] So who, then, were the nationalist Muslims?

Despite its ubiquity, few have interrogated this curious nomenclature, let alone probed into the thought-world of this circle. Its uses as an empty signifier in nationalist historiography are plain enough: these were, as it were, the good Muslims, the nemeses of 'communalists'. Beyond that, their beliefs and actions have attracted little comment. But before we proceed, three short observations are in order. First, to use the language of linguists, the 'nationalist Muslim' was a marked category; there was, of course, no 'nationalist Hindu'. Second, that the description, in a sense, is a *faux ami*. For these figures are not to be confused with 'Muslim nationalists', Muslim Leaguers campaigning for greater representation and eventually a separate homeland. And third, the nationalist Muslim was a high-political creation. For the ideology of the men who described themselves, and were described in the press, as such only mattered because these were important men who held positions of power and commanded the ear of the—mostly Hindu—Congress leadership. As mediators between the largest party and largest minority, they were the movers and shakers of Muslim India.

What follows is an interpretative essay in which I attempt to break new ground by looking at a wide range of nationalist Muslims over half a century to argue that beneath all the complexity and variation in their thinking, there lay a common set of assumptions, a common worldview that shaped their politics. No matter what the period under consideration, or which nationalist Muslim in question, on balance their purchase holds true. Like the dependable presence of the Kaaba through the ages—built, rebuilt, and renovated *ad nauseam*, from

Rashidun times to ours—this vision remained a permanent fixture in the nationalist Muslim political landscape. One could survey the nationalist Muslims of the twenties, forties, or sixties: every *coup d'œil* would reveal the same picture.

In a word, nationalist Muslims were Muslim Congressmen. Early figures included Mukhtar Ahmad Ansari (1880–1936), Abul Kalam Azad (1888–1958), Syed Mahmud (1889–1971), Rafi Ahmed Kidwai (1894–1954), and Humayun Kabir (1906–1969), all of whom were roughly coevals; enjoyed a personal rapport with the Congress' Hindu leadership; passed through clerical institutions or were favourably disposed to religious authority at any rate; and, more generally, were influential in shaping party, and even state, policy towards Muslims. They were, to all intents and purposes, seen by fellow Congressmen, Raj apparatchiks, and the press as *the* representatives of Muslim India, even if their competitors, the separatist Muslim elite, occasionally vied—and, as time wore on, often with greater success—for that title. Ideologically, they shared three assumptions that set them apart from their co-religionists.

First, a conflation of nation and the party to which they belonged. In essence, to these men, the fortunes of the Republic were a function of the ease with which the Congress could conduct its affairs, and for this reason, their co-adherents from other political persuasions were seen by them variously as 'communal' or 'anti-national'.

Second, on the question of strategy, a firm belief that it was the forceful and refractory style of politics—the kind that the League represented—that had forced the Congress' hands and brought on Partition. Better then to appear biddable to the party high command and circumscribe political demands, they felt. Their hot-headed brothers had let them down once, and with disastrous consequences. As a result, henceforth they would only tiptoe around the party leadership, always wary of Hindu sensibilities. This was both atonement and course correction. Theirs was a politics of guilt.

And third, an unflinching belief—perhaps a reflection of their clerical character, for many of them were trained as priests—in the autonomy of Muslim personal law, the profundity of the *sharia*. This

27

was a colonial inheritance, borne out by happenstance but quickly accepted as a shibboleth by Hindu and Muslim alike.

What follows in the rest of Part I is a rudimentary sketch of the ascendancy, meridian, and decline of the nationalist Muslim from the Khilafat movement that began in the aftermath of the First World War to the close of the Nehruvian period. The focus here will be on the United Provinces—the cynosure of nationalist Muslim politics—but sections will also explore territories further afield, Assam and Bengal included. The next part on 'communalists', by contrast, will centre on the West and the South, where Muslim political formations had greater salience.

In this chapter, synthesising a mass of secondary material and using autobiographies, letters, reports, and the *Transfer of Power* documents drawn from viceregal and the India Office records, I argue that in the interwar period, the ecumenicism of Muslim high politics during the first two decades of the century gave way, in the span of a few years, to a new dynamic: leaders of the community were increasingly drawn to either one of two poles, the Congress and the League. A distinct nationalist Muslim ideology, centred on the three assumptions seen above, emerged in this period, and a separatist challenge, building on the work of turn-of-the-century revivalists and modernists, consolidated in opposition to it. The quarter of a century to independence, then, is best characterised as a dialectic between the 'nationalist' and 'separatist' Muslim, which, as we will see, for various reasons culminated in a victory for the latter. But defeat for the nationalist Muslims was not without its silver lining. For with Partition and the attendant migration of the League elite to Pakistan along with the decimation of the party's remnants across India barring in the South, the upshot was that nationalist Muslims came to achieve complete hegemony as representatives of Muslim India. The show was still on the road.

This state of affairs lasted well into the Nehruvian period, the subject of Chapters 2 and 3, coming to a close only a few months after the passing of India's first ruler in 1964, when the Majlis-i-Mushāwarat (on which more will be discussed in Chapter 5) came into existence. In two snapshots—one from the Constituent Assembly, the other the executive—I show how depoliticisation became the order of the day. Everywhere, nationalist Muslims beat a retreat. In the assembly, they led the effort to rescind separate electorates and reservations for Muslims and retain simple plurality voting, whose distorting effects, to the detriment of minorities, were well known to lawmakers. And in government, they received a raw deal—obtaining 'difficult' ministries, being edged out in factional struggles on account of their faith, and the like—which they accepted sanguinely, occasionally petitioning the premier, but to little avail. In the world of law, however, they found greater success. Indeed, what they achieved through their spirited defence of the *sharia* was unique in world-historical perspective. At a time when Islamic laws were being torn up, or radically rewritten at the very least, across the Muslim world—Pakistan, Tunisia, the United Arab Republic—in India, Muslim personal law remained untouched.

The origins of the nationalist Muslim, I argue below, lay in the peculiar elite Muslim response to a concatenation of developments spurred by late nineteenth and early twentieth century devolution that forced Muslim notables to become more articulate in their political positions, either as loyalists or nationalists; the rise of Indian nationalism and the embrace of identitarianism by the Congress; and the modernisation of the *ulama*, who were gradually won over to the cause of party political associationalism.

So it was that a trinity of actors—Muslim notables, the Congress, and the *ulama*—thus became aligned. While theirs, it appeared in the twenties, was an unstoppable juggernaut, it must be remembered that there was nothing inevitable about it. Instead, it was the result of a number of historical contingencies. For each of these sectional interests was responding to a discrete problem—for Muslim notables, the devolution of power to Indians that threatened their position as a privileged minority; for Congressmen, the glacial pace of reform; and for the *ulama*, the erosion of clerical authority in a secular age—whose solution lay in their pooling of resources. Solidarities were forged only on sufferance.

Ideally, Muslim notables would have wanted no truck with popular politics; Congressmen, with Muslim clerics; the *ulama*, with secular political formations. Yet when push came to shove, each party grew more accepting of the other two. In what follows, we will look at the factors leading to this reconciliation, and by extension, to the birth of the nationalist Muslim. First, we will consider Muslim notables, before proceeding to Congressmen and the clergy.

'Sit Down and Be Off to Madras'

Muslim notables, in the main the gentry, had been unlikely political actors to begin with. All the same, the late nineteenth century had witnessed them mobilise in ever-increasing numbers in response to the assaults on their hegemonic position by a cluster of *parvenu* Hindu commercial groups.[7] What was demanded was not a commensurate share of power for the Muslims—the *ashraf* elite had much more than that—but a return to an era of untrammelled Muslim preponderance.

Indeed, as Francis Robinson has it, while the *cri de coeur* of the Muslim political elite of the North-Western Provinces was 'backwardness', the Muslim condition itself pointed to a rather different malaise.[8] For while the community continued to account for between a third and a half of government employees well into the 1880s even as its ranks made up only a seventh of the provincial population, it was the relative decline *vis-à-vis* Hindus—on account of communal quotas and education requirements—that stung its leadership. In a word, then, Muslims were not so much the have-nots as have-not-much-more-than-enoughs.

Luckily for them, when Raj administrators such as Hunter and Mayo based on their experience of dealing with the immiserated Muslims of Bengal, the bridgehead for British rule, wrote of the Muslim condition as if India was that province writ large, the 'backwardness' fictive took on a life of its own. This, moreover, came at a time when heartland elites were exchanging class for confessional identities.

Through most of the late mediaeval and early modern period, the ruling elite and the bureaucracy and clerisy that depended on it— in the main *ashraf*, but also Bania, Brahmin, Rajput, and Kayasth— had shared in a 'Persianate ideology' that cut across sectarian and confessional lines even as violence on such axes was not absent.[9] Capital, culture, cuisine, and corps had circulated taking scarce cognisance of confession. Not even the switch from Persian to Urdu, abetted by Raj policy, in 1837 had succeeded in curbing the cosmopolitanism of the *crème de la crème*.

By the end of the nineteenth century, however, both Persianate cosmopolitanism and *ashraf* hegemony had come under stress. Mobilisation around a Hindu identity had rendered odious the Islamic practices—sartorial, linguistic, culinary, cultural—that once served as class markers of the Subcontinental rich in a manner not dissimilar to the French affectations of the Russian nobility. As a result, wearing the *sherwani*, speaking Urdu, eating *mughlai* food, and luxuriating at *mushairas* and nautch parties became decoupled with class, their association shifting by transference to faith.[10] These became, as it were, 'Muslim' practices. On the face of it, nothing about, say, Urdu was distinctly Muslim. It was the work of nineteenth century revivalists that drove a wedge between the Muslim and Hindu registers of what essentially was 'Hindustani'. 'Muslim' Urdu came to be characterised by Persian inflections and the *nastaliq* script, 'Hindu' Hindi by Sanskritised argot and *devanagari* letters.

Spurred by the work of Hindi propagandists such as Babu Shiva Prasad and Bharatendu Harischandra in the 1860s and 1870s and Madan Mohan Malaviya in the generation that followed, Hindu revivalists successfully persuaded the administrators of the Central Provinces in 1873 and of Bihar in 1881 to substitute Hindi for Urdu as the language of government. In 1899, the North-Western Provinces followed suit, giving parity to both tongues as languages of administrative communication, effectively benefiting Hindus, who were more likely to have a better command of both than Muslims. Hindus, who generally attached no real importance to clerical learning, also found it easier to embrace Western education, which had become the *entrée* into the administrative services. In the NWP, Muslims fell from 64 to 35 per cent of the clerks in the government's employ between 1857 and 1913, while Hindus grew from 24 to 60 per cent. The production of Urdu books outpaced Hindi ones by 57 per cent in the 1880s; by the 1910s, it was works in Hindi that were pouring out of the printing presses 43 per cent faster than titles in Urdu.[11] With devolution proceeding apace, Muslim notables had other reasons to be worried, too.

For democratisation, inevitably, played into the hands of the majority. In a bid to offload prohibitive welfare responsibilities, education, healthcare, and public works were handed to natives in the North-Western Provinces in 1882. At first, because of the limited franchise, the elective principle was coolly accepted by Muslims, who were in the main wealthier than the Hindus. But with the ascendancy of the Hindu bourgeoisie, elections quickly became a major stumbling block for the *qaum*, whose members fell from 34 to 30 per cent of the province's municipal councillors between 1884 and 1907.[12]

It was no surprise then, that in the associative avalanche of the last third of the nineteenth century, it was well-heeled Muslims of the North-Western Provinces who were in the lead. This period witnessed the establishment of the Muhammadan Anglo-Oriental College (1875), Muhammadan Educational Conference (1886), United Indian Patriotic Association (1888), Muhammadan Anglo-Oriental Defence Association of Upper India (1893), Urdu Defence Association (1900), Muslim League (1906),[13] and the seminaries of Darul Uloom in Deoband (1866) and Nadwatul Ulama in Lucknow (1894).

The *qaum*'s strides served it well. For after initially blaming Muslims for the Revolt of 1857, the Raj, deciding against reforming Indian society—now seen as a hopelessly utopian Macaulayesque venture—opted to restore the *ancien régime* to its pride of place.[14] *Taluqdars* were returned their lands and also given partial juridical powers to aid in their management.[15] The Muslim elite, once again seen as the Subcontinent's natural rulers, were mollycoddled with all kinds of patronage. The MAOC was for all intents and purposes funded by the state, which also rescued it every time it tumbled into some financial crisis or the other. Sops from the Raj, especially under Mayo, Ripon, and Dufferin—viceroys between 1869–72, 1880–4, and 1884–8, respectively—too, stood the Muslim elite in good stead, paternalism to the rich being perfectly compatible with the High Tory ideology of the Raj at its apogee.[16]

Paradoxically, it also helped that the government laid the blame for the Revolt squarely on the shoulders of Muslims. For it was the mortal fear of Muslim extremism that prompted the Raj to cave in to the Muslim demand for separate electorates in 1909, and not—as in the writings of nationalist historians such as Gyanendra Pandey and Venkat Dhulipala—a premeditated intention to 'divide and rule'.[17] Better to mollify the Muslim than risk the wrath of every extremist Islamic current—what with Wahhabism, pan-Islamism, and the possibility of an elite revanchism—it was thought. *Ashraf* politics was off to a good start.

Identities hardened. The suggestion, common in *ashraf* circles, that Muslims ought to have it better inevitably meant casting Hindus as villains, and *vice versa*. 'If you accept that the country should groan under the yoke of Bengali [*sc.* Hindu] rule and its people lick the Bengali shoes, then, in the name of God, jump into the train, sit down, and be off to Madras [*sic*]', Sir Syed Ahmad Khan, founder of the MAOC, asseverated in 1887.[18] Hindu revivalists described Muslims in equally intemperate terms.

The same went for language. Here, too, a class element cannot be divorced from the *ashraf* mobilisation around Urdu. It was, after all, the language of the courtly and scribal elite—or, in the words of the pamphleteers of *A Defence of the Urdu Language and Character* of 1900, 'the language of refinement and upper and civilised classes of people ... Are these two classes [Hindus and Muslims] then merely to be judged by their quantity and not quality, by their size and not their importance?'[19]

Building religious solidarity wasn't a tough ask. For one thing, the Muslim elite, in the main heirs of the bureaucratic and military administrators of the Mughal era, were already a very closely knit group, bound by ties of kinship, a common ancestry—or the belief of one—and endogamy.

All the same, the *ashraf* élan, which served them well in the nineteenth century, was ill-suited for the twentieth. Indeed, with devolution and the extension of the franchise, it was a millstone around their necks—doubly so. For as Muslims, they were now more plainly a minority, and as the Muslim elite rallying around a small set of upper-class grievances, incontrovertibly a minority within a minority.

They were, in short, caught in the horns of a dilemma. Campaigning to reverse devolution was not an option. It had a logic of its own. Ending religious rivalry, too, was easier said than done, now that the Pandora's Box of religious hatred had been opened. Both communities had come to use local office as a site to play out confessional antagonisms. In preponderantly Muslim Moradabad in the 1880s, for example, at the instigation of the town's new Hindu administrators, Muslim butchers were prevented from tanning hides within the confines of the city. Chandpur banned cow slaughter. Muslims in Bijnor were beaten for selling beef. When Muslims gained control over Najibabad, they set about decimating the local bovine population simply to rile up Hindus.[20]

What's more, among Muslims a generational cleavage had opened up. This was ineluctable. For devolution was at its outset designed to bolster colonial rule. Its winners, by design, were primarily the landowning classes, magnates, and other men of standing—all figures if not advanced in age, representative of the old order nevertheless. Still, the young guard, men from the professions, succeeded in capturing a modest number of elective positions in towns, where, in contrast to the *mofussil*, the Raj's filtration mechanism proved weaker. These were men who had passed through the MAOC, which by the turn of the century was churning out a quarter of India's Muslim graduates every year. Better educated than their predecessors but still *déclassé*, theirs was a politics of resentment. Convinced that the subservience of the previous generation had worsened their predicament, their comportment was the veritable antithesis of the old guard's: vigorous and confrontational.

The early nationalist Muslims emerged from the ranks of this impatient cohort. The crystallisation of the nationalist Muslim élan, however, was still some time away. For in the early years of the twentieth century, the young guard was still animated by what can be called representational-separatist concerns—quotas for the *qaum*; its incompatibility with the Raj's Hindu subjects—that were soon to become the preserve of the League, as opposed to national-cultural ones—a *sharia*-minded patriotism; a belief in, as the tired apothegm goes, 'unity in diversity'—that were to become the pillars of the nationalist Muslim. But the direction of the thinking of the young publicists was unmistakably clear. Ghulam-us-Saqlain, one of them, was among the early figures who was ready to countenance tactical alliances with the Congress' professionals, who, as he saw it, were members of the same class and had similar priorities—lower taxes and more jobs.

Greater ideological clarity came with the creation of the League in 1906. At its founding, a high entry fee, capped membership, and income thresholds saw to it that the old had edged out the young. Indeed, this was a coup for the old guard, who in receiving the sympathies of Minto, the viceroy, for their cause—separate electorates and Muslim quotas for those elected on them—ended up appropriating representational-separatist politics for the League. The young insurgents, now on the side-lines, felt compelled to adopt more nationalist positions to challenge the loyalist League, which had fallen into the hands of Muslim *taluqdars* such as the Rajas of Mahmudabad and Salempur. At the same time, these striplings were also increasingly drawn to the *Kulturkampf* playing out at Aligarh. For one thing, students and staff alike were taken up by pan-Islamic solidarity, a cause championed and led by the *ulama*. For another, the 'Muslim University movement' for autonomy and state recognition was gaining momentum.[21]

By the time of the First World War, then, the *ashraf* faced a brave new world. No longer could Muslim notables afford to be reviled by the *ulama* as Sir Syed Ahmad Khan once was; to clerics, his ideas—which in equal measure drew on Shah Waliullah, a proponent of *ijtihad*, or interpretation, and Bishop J. W. Colenso's Biblical exegesis, reconciling 'Genesis and geology'—had reeked of apostasy.[22] Nor could they ignore mass politics, the full force of which was registered at first in Aligarh in 1913, when a cluster of Muslim publicists, Ansari and the Ali brothers included, returned to the university town amidst national fanfare after having arranged the Red Crescent medical mission to the Ottoman Empire, and then when Gandhi's organisation of the peasant and millworker strikes in Champaran, Ahmedabad, and Kheda created a stir in 1917–8. Muhammad Ali, for instance, remembers in his memoirs that *circa* 1913, all at once educated, well-heeled Muslims like him found that 'their mental and spiritual horizon ha[d] suddenly expanded and they ha[d] been brought into the closest touch, on the one side, with old world conservatism and orthodoxy, and on the other, with the masses whose troubles they now began to share as comrades in arms'.[23]

The reversal of the partition of Bengal in 1911 was similarly instructive. With the disappearance of the Muslim-majority province in Eastern Bengal and Assam also vanished Muslim clout. The next year, the British refused to grant university status to Aligarh. Agitating Hindus had had their way, petitioning Muslims had not. The lesson was learned. It was time to mobilise. An early indication of the uses of public outrage was the Kanpur Mosque incident of 1913. The ham-fisted demolition of a part of it was followed by a march of 15,000, a few of whom died in clashes with the police. Criticism of the heavy-handed response poured in from even staid and normally loyalist quarters: Mahmudabad, Sir Ali Imam, Mian Muhammad Shafi of the Punjab. As it was, the viceroy was forced to row back on the demolition.[24]

Unsurprisingly, it was the early converts to mass politics—Gandhi, Ansari, the Ali brothers—who were best placed to turn populism to good account. These were initially peripheral figures who were to play a key role in yoking their communities to the cause of nationalism.

A brief prosopography could begin with Mukhtar Ahmad Ansari, surgeon turned politician, whose was among the earliest modern South Asian forays into pan-Islamism. Hailing from a family of *hakims*, doctors, whose clients had once included Mughal emperors and now did Hyderabad's Nizams, Ansari, on account of his upbringing and associates, was able to straddle two seemingly irreconcilable worlds. As it happened, one of his brothers was a disciple of Gangohi's, chief of the Deoband *madrasa*. As for Ansari himself, the product of both a traditional Yusufpur *madrasa* and an Edinburgh medical degree, he was an intimate of the Ali brothers—all three cut their teeth with the Red Crescent—who in turn were Gandhi's comrades.

It is easy enough to register the shifts in his worldview in his correspondence. Before the Great War, Ansari's circle seemed unduly concerned with British opinion: 'if our mission fails, we will be made a laughing stock of all the English clubgoers in India', a colleague wrote to him in 1912.[25] After it, there was a greater emphasis on 'the people', 'Muslim society', 'the will of the people'.[26] With new ideas came new contacts. 'Captivated by the charisma, prestige and personal authority of Gandhi', Ansari soon found his *métier*.[27] Settling into his iconic 10,000 square yard estate on 1, Daryaganj in Delhi, Ansari made his house a hub of Congress politics in the twenties. Like most nationalist Muslims a religious man, he was a regular at the local mosque, counting Maulanas Mahmud Hasan and Husain Ahmad Madani, both of whom were arrested for their nationalist activities and exiled in Malta, among his friends. He went on to serve as Congress president in 1927.[28]

But his role was not confined to Congress affairs. On the eve of the Montagu-Chelmsford reforms of 1919, it was at his instigation that an insurgency of *imams* arrived to take over the reins of the League. Having one foot in both party doors allowed him to use his position as chairman of the League's reception committee at its December 1918 session—not long after the publication of the Montagu-Chelmsford report, which, in falling short of League expectations, strengthened the hands of the young guard—to see that the Firangi Mahal *madrasa*'s Maulana Abdul Bari's entryist putsch succeeded.[29] Still, because his preoccupations were elsewhere, his control over the League, but little of use of it, atrophied the party. The upshot was that the League was rendered impotent, a shadow of its former self, lacking a constituency, an agenda even. It could well be said that it was the Khilafat movement that did in the League.

Ansari, of course, was just one of many figures in this constellation. Of equal note were the Ali brothers, Muhammad and Shaukat, scions of Rampur administrators. While both began their careers in the services, Shaukat as a sub-deputy opium agent and Muhammad a Baroda functionary, both developed an interest in Aligarh politics. Working at cross-purposes with the League's old guard, they made a name for themselves by taking up two issues, one anticolonial and the other religious.[30]

The first found the brothers and the British on opposite sides of the fence: the duo were after university accreditation for Aligarh, whereas the government wanted to keep the college on a tight leash. When a loyalist committee made up of Leaguers and Raj staffers worked a compromise in April 1917 on the lines of the deal struck with the Hindu university at Banaras—little autonomy, but government oversight aplenty—the Alis led the charge against it. But to no avail. Parliament passed the Muslim University Bill in September 1920, leaving the Alis and their allies to set up shop next-door. The Jamia Millia Islamia, the 'nationalist' alternative to the AMU, was established in a local mosque with the blessings of Deoband administrators. Greater success came their way with the second issue. In 1913, along with Ansari, the Alis—who had by then exchanged their Savile Row wardrobe for 'traditional' Islamic robes—raised relief funds for the Turks, organising a Red Crescent medical mission to the Porte during the Balkan Wars.

Such concerns were amplified in their organs, the English *Comrade* and Urdu *Hamdard*, and chorused by literary vehicles such as the Calcutta *Al-Hilal*, edited by the cleric Abul Kalam Azad, the Lahore gentry journal *Zamindar*, and Hasrat Mohani's *Urdu-e-Mu'alla*. But the burst of literary energy was cut short by the Great War. The Porte entered the conflict on Germany's side. With the Ottomans battling the British in various theatres, *Comrade* was shuttered and the Alis, Mohani, and Azad interned, their release becoming the *cause célèbre* of nationalists across the Subcontinent.[31]

The picture that emerges from such profiles is clear. Once indifferent to confessional and national attachments, many young Muslim notables were coming around to ascriptive categories. Even figures who wanted to have no truck with religious politics, some of whom would go on to become the League's leading lights, were drawn to the Congress. Indeed, in the 1910s, Jinnah, famously impatient with all matters religious, was still a Gokhale understudy, and Khaliquzzaman, who opposed the entryism of the *ulama* into the League in 1918, a rising star of the Congress' Lucknow branch. A reputed Bombay barrister, Jinnah had unsuccessfully tried to tether the League to Congress nationalism at Allahabad in January 1910. But by the end of the year, he had convinced his colleagues. Under the secretaryship of Wazir Hasan, a friend of Muhammad Ali's, the League continued its drift towards the Congress. And in March 1913, the troika—Jinnah, Ali, Hasan—lobbied Leaguers into resolving in favour of a 'suitable' form of self-government, making it more palatable for Congressmen to join the Muslim party.[32]

In the event, while radical clerics such as Azad and Shibli continued to dismiss the League as a bastion of loyalism, it was nevertheless inching towards the Lucknow Pact of 1916, when the Congress accepted separate electorates for Muslims in the provinces— reversing its position since 1909—and proportional representation in the councils in exchange for the League's acquiescence to the elective principle in central and provincial legislatures and greater Indian representation on the viceroy's and governors' executives.[33] A year later, won over to popular politics after the arrest of his colleague Annie Besant, Jinnah took up the presidency of the Bombay Home Rule League.[34] By autumn secretary of state Montagu, responding to the unity shown in Lucknow, had declared in favour of more devolution.

Mass politics appeared to be working. True, all that the Montagu-Chelmsford report had promised so far was 'dyarchy', greater provincial autonomy but even greater central power—a kind of federalism Indians would readily adopt when free but found unacceptable in the interwar period. Still, old guard figures ill-disposed to mass politics such as the party secretary Wazir Hasan, and even their sympathisers like the party president Mahmudabad, young radical turned loyalist critic of Lucknow, were losing ground. Both were forced to resign in February 1919. The passage of the Rowlatt Act, extending wartime legislation including preventive detention, in March despite Indian opposition in Parliament came as a further blow to League loyalists.[35]

By the time the Ali brothers were released, ahead of the League and Congress sessions in Amritsar in December, they found themselves in an altogether different political landscape. The League was riven by factional struggles. Meanwhile the same year had witnessed the birth of two powerful nationalist Muslim outfits, the short-lived All-India Khilafat Committee and the Jamiat-ul-Ulema-i-Hind, the largest and best organised confederacy of clerics that the Subcontinent has ever witnessed, which survives to this day as an important auxiliary of the Congress. Nationalist Muslims were moving from strength to strength.

Its thunder stolen by a nationalist publicist-priest combine, the League fell out with the zeitgeist, all but disappearing from the political scene in the interwar years. But this triumph of the nationalist Muslim was no independent achievement. Indeed, it would have scarcely been possible were it not for the support of Hindu politicians.

'A Question of Love at First Sight'

Clerical entryism into the League was mirrored by a coup in the Congress. Here the insurgents were Gandhi and his set, better disposed to both interfaith alliances and mass politics. As in the League, disillusionment with constitutionalism had set in, especially after Rowlatt. The lure of *satyagraha*, civil disobedience, a political élan piloted by Gandhi during the score of years he spent in South Africa, was stronger than ever.

Moreover, just as the League had struggled with devolution, its nemesis, too, strained to develop a wider following—and, likewise, with mixed results. For on the one hand, its younger leadership from Tilak through Gandhi had ably transformed the Congress from a sodality of lawyers and functionaries into a popular movement. Yet on the other, its repeated stabs at attracting Muslims and Untouchables had thus far failed to win them over.

To be sure, already in the late nineteenth century, a battery of elite Muslims had joined the Congress. But these, even collectively, were still a small minority. What's more, thanks to censuses, devolution, and print-capitalism, minorities were increasingly becoming aware of the crippling disadvantages that minority status conferred upon them. The Congress was, as it were, too Hindu for most of them.

The undying enthusiasms of some of its leaders to 'reconvert' Muslims to Hinduism and outlaw the slaughter of cows were of little help in this regard. But these Hindu revivalist elements the Congress very much needed, for it was only through such mobilisation that it could expand from the maritime provinces and its lawyerly networks, both undeniable curbs on its growth since its founding in 1885. The traditional demands of the party's coastal elite—first and foremost, the holding of Indian Civil Service examinations not only in England, but in India, too—had failed to cut any ice in the heartland. It was opposition to high inflation and taxation and calls for greater devolution that won it a greater following.

Taking politics to the byres achieved the same ends. As the Arya Samaj and the circle around Malaviya gained ascendancy in the party in the NWP, so, too, did the emphasis on cow slaughter and *devanagari*. But even as the Congress expanded its base and reach, its ranks remained overwhelmingly upper-caste: Chitpavan Brahmins in the west, the Bengali *bhadralok* in the east, Tamil Brahmins in the south, Punjabi *savarnas* in the north. Unsurprisingly, Muslim notables were never attracted to it. And they were not alone. A testament to the Congress' minority problem was the emergence of a string of parties that railed against it: the Muslim League (1906), the Akali Dal of the Sikhs (1920), and Depressed Classes Federation of the Untouchables (1930). Not for nothing did Syed Ahmed Khan spend his dying days cursing it. His League heirs built a constituency opposing the trifecta of devolution, competitive examination, and Hindu revivalism—all Congress platforms.

For Congressmen, the way out of the confessional impasse was at once to appear more inclusive and exoticise the Muslim, who apparently was impervious to a universal political lexicon and required understanding on his own terms.[36] This required intermediaries. While the bulk of the Muslim leadership had thrown in their lot with the League, a few figures were nevertheless up to the task. Intellectually speaking, therein lay the birth of the nationalist Muslim.

The guiding logic was not solidarity, but *quid pro quo*. Here was identity politics in one of its clearest manifestations. Gandhi, fresh on the heels of successful campaigns in Natal and Champaran, pledged the backing of the immense Congress party machinery to the Khilafat cause—an end to British interference in the Porte and the restoration of the Caliph's powers—that had become the obsession of Muslim politicians and the *ulama* alike in exchange for Maulana Abdul Bari's efforts to enlist the support of Muslims to the Congress *satyagraha* against the Rowlatt Act and a 'voluntary' relinquishing of 'cow slaughter'—an issue that resonated all the more with the Hindu leadership since the riots of Shahabad in September 1917, occasioned by Hindus objecting to the sacrifice of cows on Baqr Id.[37]

What explains the heteroclite alliance? The choice of striking a deal with Bari was either a disingenuous call or a masterstroke, depending on one's predisposition to the Mahatma. For when riots had broken out in Calcutta in 1918, the violence in part had been spurred by Bari, who mobilised angry Muslim crowds against Hindus after, so he claimed, the Prophet had been slandered in an English daily. Whatever his intentions may have been, Gandhi's role was instructive. In countenancing his talk of Ram Rajya, pan-Islamists in effect paved the way for their nationalist Muslim heirs to accommodate Hindu revivalism as well. Indeed, after Khilafat ran its course, its protagonists—Shraddhanand, Bari—took up the cudgels for religious revivalism themselves. Hindu *shuddhi* and *sangathan* on the one hand, and Muslim *tabligh* and *tanzim* on the other, proceeded in tandem.[38]

Leaders, for Gandhi and Bari, represented the communities they hailed from, rather than a de-confessional amalgam of them. 'I can wield no influence over the Mussalmans except through a Mussalman', Gandhi had reflected at the height of the non-cooperation movement in November 1921.[39] Similarly, while he presented his 1919 anti-Rowlatt *satyagraha* to Hindus as a protest idiom rooted in the Hindu tradition of non-violence, to Muslims he sang a different tune:

> I have discussed the Mahomedan question [*sc.* the Caliphate] with [Bari, Ansari,] and many other Mahomedans throughout India and I feel that this question is the greatest of all, greater even than that of the repeal of the Rowlatt legislation; for it affects the religious susceptibilities of millions of Mahomedans ... Bari-*sahib* assured me that there was warrant enough for *satyagraha* in the Holy Koran.[40]

Bari's worldview was of a piece with his. Hindus and Muslims had different interests. Solidarity, then, was not without a transactional element. 'The Hindus will judge our faith, and rightly, by our conduct towards them. That is why I say: if we take from you, we must give to you', he said to Gandhi.[41] Here, 'we' referred to Muslims, and 'you' to Hindus. National consciousness, as such, was nowhere in sight. Missing, in Benedict Anderson's formulation, was the 'ironical intimacy', the 'deep, horizontal comradeship' so integral to the national *imaginaire*—'us Indians' as it were.[42] This bias was to become a mainstay in the decades to come. As we will see, nationalist Muslims would see themselves, and be seen by parties and the press alike, foremost as representatives of Muslim India. This marked identity—as *Muslim* Congressmen—while an asset, would also see to it that they stayed a community apart. Even as political insiders, then, nationalist Muslims would remain perennial outsiders.

In essence, the Mahatma and the *maulana* were building a bridge between the two faiths by throwing a plank between two cliffs. They were not, to stretch this metaphor, shifting the tectonic plates underneath to disappear the ravine altogether. But the Gandhi-Bari pact must not be seen as an instance of some kind of Foucauldian discontinuity; it was, instead, merely a clearer manifestation of a not uncommon worldview. For many others shared in this vision, both at that time and before. For instance, in 1912, in conjuring a utopian 'political entity' in *Comrade*, Muhammad Ali had revealingly noted that 'it would have to be a federation of faiths'.[43] Small wonder, then, that when Gandhi later recounted his first encounter with the Ali brothers—the one a Gitaphile, the other two Koranheads—he did so effusively: 'It was a question of love at first sight between us'.[44]

So it was that during the Khilafat movement, Hindu revivalists such as the Arya Samaj's Swami Shraddhanand could be found sharing stages with *ulama*, calling for Hindu-Muslim unity. Hindus, for the first time, were allowed to frequent Azad's Nakhuda Mosque in Calcutta. Deal-making trumped nation-building. This was to have profound consequences on interfaith relations—both before and after independence.

For something of a 'pact' sensibility continued to define Congress-Muslim relations. Even at the onset of Khilafat, were one to draw a Venn diagram of Hindu Congress and clerical Muslim interests, one would be hard pressed to find overlapping ground. Bari was in search of a mass following to pressure the government to free the interned Ali brothers. Gandhi, meanwhile, hoped to consolidate power within the Congress; the task, he felt, would be infinitely easier if he could bring Hindus and Muslims together to press for *swarajya*, self-rule under the Crown. And Gandhi was candid about this: 'by helping the

Muhammadans of India at a critical moment in their history, I want to buy their friendship'.[45] But buy it to what end? To Muhammad Ali: 'my interest in your release is quite selfish ... [For] in the proper solution of the Mahomedan question lies the realisation of *swarajya*'.[46] And to Chelmsford, the viceroy, Gandhi pledged to turn Muslims into loyalists if he released the Alis. In practice, of course, he could do no such thing.

At first, Gandhi's bluster failed to pay off. On his advice, the brothers wrote to the viceroy, but the plan backfired. Laced with innuendo and threat, the missive only wound up converting their internment into incarceration. Still, Gandhi had secured his longer-term objective. By April 1919, Bari was convinced about the merits of *satyagraha*.[47] So much so that when push came to shove, it was Bari and the Muslims who were calling for non-cooperation, while a reticent Gandhi, who had by then developed cold feet, advised caution. Bari's brand of non-cooperation, the Mahatma thought, was too violent to be efficacious. When Khilafatists rampaged about the Punjab that month, his reaction was withering: 'I find utter lawlessness bordering almost on Bolshevism', Gandhi wrote to the viceroy's secretary. 'Englishmen and women have found it necessary to leave their bungalows and to confine themselves to a few well-guarded houses. It is a matter of the deepest humiliation and regret for me'. All the same, there was only so much the Mahatma could do: 'The ferment among the Mahomedans is too great to be checked for ever', he conceded. 'I have not hesitated to tell the Mahomedans, whom I meet, that rather than harbour discontent, ill-will and finally hatred, and depend upon methods of violence, it behoves them to depend on the peaceful and royal way of *satyagraha*'.[48]

Indeed, evidence suggests that Bari embraced Gandhi's non-violence claptrap with some cynicism. After all, he was his own man. As he argued in a 1920 pamphlet, *Unanimous Fatwa of the Indian Ulama*, making common cause with 'infidels'—*sc.* Gandhi—was *halal*, accepting their leadership *haram*.[49]

For the *ulama*, non-cooperation was little more than a power-grabbing opportunity. They wanted to assume judicial and fiscal authority for themselves, running *sharia* courts and collecting taxes in the form of *zakat*, usually understood to be charity, a voluntary contribution for the poor. Azad, in particular, was feverishly animated by a vision of Islamic juridical sovereignty, running from district *sharia* courts headed by *amirs* all the way up to provincial *amirs* and a national *amir-e-hind*. He spent the summer of 1921 piloting his programme in Bihar and pushing unsuccessfully for his own coronation as *amir-e-hind*; outside his native province, though, his plans went nowhere.[50] Whereas Gandhi and other Hindu leaders only reluctantly, and very gradually, came around to a clean and complete break with empire, the *ulama*, led by Maulanas Abdul Bari (Firangi Mahal), Mahmud Hasan (Deoband), and Abul Kalam Azad (JUH), had long been at the forefront of Indian nationalism.

'A Muslim First and an Indian Afterwards'

In world-historical perspective, it was rather atypical for the Muslim clergy to be at the vanguard of nationalism. Indeed, India's *ulama* were quite unlike most of their Asian and African counterparts who, if not always loyalists, were most certainly hostile to bourgeois nationalism.[51] The Indian anomaly can be explained by a historical peculiarity: the considerable synergies between clerical activism and Indian nationalism.

Here, anticolonial pan-Islamism drew on an older repertoire. Well over half a century before Khilafat, the peripatetic preacher Jamal al-din al-Afghani's pointed barbs against the Raj and, as he saw it, heretical Muslim modernists such as Syed Ahmed Khan had found a substantial following, as did his paeans to pan-Islamic cosmopolitanism.[52] Many clerics cheered on the Turks in their war with Russia in 1877–8. Khan and other modernists, however, turned the other way, reassuring the Raj's apparatchiks that the community was still 'loyal'.

Crucially for the Khilafatists, their anticolonialism was not ground in an economic critique of imperialism, as was the case with a number of other nationalists from Naoroji to Nehru. Its leaders, who could scarcely conceal their contempt for mundane political matters, spoke in a language of Islamic millenarianism that had little time for common people. 'True Home Rule for Muslims', Bari declared, meant 'the enforcement of the *sharia*'.[53] Unsurprisingly, a popular response was found wanting. Indeed, outside Sind, where *piri-muridi*—a master-disciple relationship that verged on enthralment—held sway, and perhaps Bengal, the movement failed to find a mass following.[54]

This was a harbinger of things to come. Indeed, their want of popularity was to prove one of the biggest stumbling blocks of nationalist Muslims in the postcolonial period, when they readily accepted to mute their demands in exchange for religious guarantees, such as the autonomy of personal law. As we will see below, the high-political and legal worldview of the clerics in Nehru's government—Azad, Kidwai, and others—inhibited the development of any mass base that could unite the community behind nationalist Muslims, leaving even these very same leaders carping bitterly about the Congress' betrayal of the *qaum* towards the end of their lives. Still, they could ill afford to leave the party, so dependent were they on it. Azad, for instance, in at least four instances in his autobiography describes Congress policies as 'great blunders'; on other occasions, what he has to say about the party's leadership is, if not more damning, of a piece with such appraisals. All the same, the interminable frictions notwithstanding, it appears that not once did the *maulana* consider quitting his party.[55]

What mattered most to this set were questions of faith, issues a world removed from the bread-and-butter concerns of their co-believers. Hence the cathexis on the Caliph, who to Sunni Muslims was the spiritual and temporal leader of the world. A dying institution in 1919, the cause of the Caliphate was taken up by India's *ulama* who called for a return to the *status quo ante bellum* in Turkey. For the clerics, moreover, this meant restoring not only the spiritual authority of the Caliph, but his temporal power as well, a clear enough indication that they were out of step with their times. Already a nominal authority since its late nineteenth-century revival after the Tanzimat, the Caliphate was all but moribund after the deposition of the pan-Islamist Sultan Abdülhamid II in 1909.[56] But the politics of the Porte was one thing, of the Indian *ulama* another.

Indian Muslims had previously raised money for the Ottomans during their war with the Russians in 1877, the Greeks in 1897, and the Balkan League in 1912. Given this habit of mind, it was hardly surprising that the Khilafatists could scarcely believe their eyes when they were confronted with press reports of rising Arab nationalism and anti-Ottoman sentiment. To Shaukat Ali, it was fake news, plain and simple.[57] Khilafatists were unable to countenance any political identification outside religion. Nor was this the last time they were stung by betrayal. The final blow to the Khilafat cause was struck not by the British but by Kemal, who, in his bid to consolidate his presidency, did in the Caliphate in 1924.

To Gail Minault, the movement's foremost historian, even as its spokesmen swore by extraterritorial loyalties, its referent was always the Subcontinent: its 'distinctively national character' trumped, if never fully, its pan-Islamism.[58] It appears to me, however, that the adjective was always secondary to the noun in 'nationalist Muslim'. This was thrown into sharp relief in a droll exchange between Muhammad Ali and H. A. L. Fisher, the number two at the India Office, in March 1920. Ali had made the voyage to London ahead of the Treaty of Sèvres to make the case against Western interference with the affairs of the Caliph; to which Fisher wondered how he could nonchalantly accept British rule in the Subcontinent while vehemently opposing Middle Eastern mandates. 'Hastily dodging the implications of this', all that the befuddled Ali could do was mumble that 'the two cases were entirely different'.[59] In April 1924, Ali put his views more pithily in the *Times of India*: he was 'a Muslim first and an Indian afterwards'.[60] If Ali, a religious man but no cleric, held such views, so did the *ulama*—all the more fervently. 'It is not a question of Khilafat or *swarajya*', Bari said to the press that year, 'but of danger to the land of the Hejaz and its desecration'.[61] The Holy Places came first, self-rule and even the Caliphate—by then abolished—second. Indeed, the movement was exemplary of the Muslim political style that was to become common currency for the rest of the century, where an Islamic cultural logic prevailed over political impulses. Part of this was down to the very nature of the Khilafat movement, constructed around an entirely new breed of politician: 'part journalist, part orator, part holy man'.[62]

Who were these men? In the main, they were up-and-coming clerics trained at some of the Subcontinent's most powerful and rapidly modernising *madrasas*. All of them, it appears, were

47

institutionally modern and pedagogically traditional, an admixture that made those who passed through them accomplished orators, hence great politicians, but also deeply conservative ones with a predilection for Islamic jurisprudence and a disdain for the hoi-polloi. This sense of superiority often stemmed from an exaggerated concern with lineage. To Bari, for one, his self-worth ultimately derived from the fact that he hailed from a very long line of illustrious *ulama,* the Firangi Mahallis: 'there is no theologian who is my peer', he announced in 1920, 'we have been theologians for a hundred generations, but others cannot put forward this claim. They are raw youths'.[63] If he thought nothing of his coevals, he suffered Muslim laymen, let alone Hindus, even less. Azad, for another, not to be outdone, was given to genealogical *amour propre* as well. In *Tazkirah,* an early work, he extolled his ancestors, tracing his own precocious achievements to them.[64] One of them, apparently, had been described by a contemporary as the kind of figure who 'would have nothing to do with worldly people'. 'This was a source of great delight to me', Azad wrote, 'the idea that our family had always distinguished itself with the pursuit of learning and the zeal to serve the cause of *hadith* and *sunnah* [teachings and practices of the Prophet], that was from the very beginning our claim to distinction, gladdened my heart and made my mind drunk with happiness'.[65] Azad, then, had little time for those of lesser stock. 'Towards Westernized Muslim leaders, Azad's attitude was one of aloofness, if not hostility', Minault writes. For less Quranically minded publicists, 'Azad had nothing but disdain': Shaukat Ali was 'inferior intellectually', his brother a mere '*munshi*'—sc. secretary, a term of abuse in Azad's book.[66]

Consequently, for the nationalist Muslim clerics, authority trumped popularity, and hubris tolerance. Still, it was acknowledged that Muslims could be brought under Islamic rule only if the British were thrown out of the Subcontinent. This required coming around to the trappings of political modernity: associations, alliances, mass mobilisation. Gradually, then, it dawned upon them that they would have to embrace the Congress.

Azad realised that the religious utopia he had in mind could hardly exist alongside the colonial state. Regime change was needed. In a 1920 pamphlet on *The Question of the Caliphate,* he argued that the Holy

Law and government were inseparable. Social orders turn on *qanun-i-markaz*, 'legal centres', without which they fall apart. For Muslims, their legal centre was none other than the *sharia*. 'True government and conformity with the will of God is that which the *sharia* has brought into being', he noted.[67] Summing up the worldview of Azad and the JUH, Peter Hardy notes that they 'visualised a free India in which Muslims would live in a juristic ghetto', governed by the *sharia* and virtually independent of the state, which in any case was to be a largely emasculated enterprise shorn of its vital functions.[68]

Many of the earliest nationalist Muslim clerics were alums of Deoband, the more muted successor of Waliullah's eighteenth-century Delhi *madrasa* that exchanged violent *jihad* for Islamic rectitude. Founded in 1867, Deoband was decidedly modern, drawing funds from alumni networks and offering consistent syllabi. In other aspects, though, it embodied tradition, one of its faculties, the Department of Juristic Rulings, even responsible for issuing *fatwas* to help the faithful negotiate the moral dilemmas of modern life. In the four decades to 1951, Deoband issued no less than 147,851 *fatwas*—a veritable empire of law, which included decrees on the acceptability of learning English, wearing caps, usurious lending. As Sufis of the Qadiri and Naqshbandi orders—where a totalising *piri-muridi* relationship was the norm—Deobandi clerics commanded the attachment of their pupils in no uncertain terms.[69] This hybrid quality was to play a vital role in forging links between the *ulama* and Muslim notables.

The Deobandis' peregrinations spread their alma mater's philosophy far and wide. The Jamiat al-Ansar, an old boys' network, was inaugurated in Deoband in 1910 and placed in the hands of an impassioned Sikh convert to Islam, Ubaidullah Sindhi, who, with the help of Ansari and fellow Deobandi Mahmud Hasan, set up the Nazarat al-Ma'arif al-Quraniya, a Quranic school that doubled as a forum for the local elite. It was at this institution that Muhammad Ali, Ansari, Azad, and Sindhi discovered their overlapping views, their divergent professional paths notwithstanding.

Lucknow's Firangi Mahal, too, boasted a clutch of nationalist clerics. A fixture since the time of Aurangzeb, the Mahal was best known for its curriculum, the *dars-e-nizamiya*, with its focus on

Arabic and jurisprudence, which had become something of a gold standard in the centuries since. Its hereditary chief at the turn of the twentieth century was none other than Maulana Abdul Bari, who, as it happened, was also *pir* to Ansari, Hasrat Mohani, and the Ali brothers—all future leading lights of Khilafat. Bari, too, belonged to a Sufi order—two of them, in fact: Qadiri and Chishti—which gave him a vice-like grip over his disciples.[70]

As with Deoband, the lure of modernism proved too infectious to resist. In 1905, he set up the Madrasa-e-Nizamiya, an enclave within the Mahal that broke from its familial pattern of education. In its place came a slicker affair. The *dars-e-nizamiya* was retained, though given modern pedagogic touches to attract Anglophone students. Finally, a trip to Turkey and work with the Red Crescent led Bari to cast in his lot with the nationalists.

As it was, there was little apart from the affairs of the Porte that tied this salmagundi of sectional interests together. There was, on the one hand, Seth Chotani, a Bombay lumber merchant who had usuriously profited from the Great War and had little patience for non-cooperation. Likewise, Zulfiqar Ali Khan, a *zamindar* in the Punjab, and Sayyid Raza Ali, a Shia lawyer of the United Provinces, had plenty to lose from blanket boycotts of British goods. Meanwhile the clerics, Maulanas Bari, Mohani, and Salamatullah included, feverishly supported such measures.

Once the Caliphate had ceased to exist, the nationalist Muslim alliance quickly came undone. Seen from the mid-twenties, their only lasting contribution was to have facilitated Gandhi's consolidation of power. Only in May 1920, he had failed to win the Congress over to non-cooperation in Banaras. But in September, an insurgency of *ulama* stormed the Calcutta Congress, allowing Gandhi to coast to victory—his programme was carried 1,885 to 883—taking the party with him on non-cooperation. Crucially, of the 5,500 delegates present, more than 2,000 were Muslim. 'Never had so many Muslims attended a Congress', Francis Robinson observes—and never would so many ever again.[71] Indeed, in less than two decades, the Congress was to transform into a very different beast, with its 2.2 per cent Muslim membership and its inability to field even a single candidate in nine out of ten Muslim constituencies.[72]

'Their Pet Theme of a Joint Electorate'

If at the time of Khilafat, nationalist Muslims held the upper hand, the years that followed saw an inversion of roles: it was the Hindu leadership in the driving seat with the nationalist Muslims firmly ensconced behind. In March 1920, it was because the *ulama* threatened to abandon him that Gandhi had flip-flopped on non-cooperation. After defending the 1919 reforms and declaring boycotts a 'form of violence', he finally came around to *satyagraha*. It would take him another two years to unshackle himself from the clerics. But before he did, they would score one final victory over him, pushing the Congress to move from non-cooperation, the first stage of the protests, to civil disobedience, the next entailing mass resignation. After initially resisting this, Gandhi capitulated in November 1921. The radical clerical support was crucial because he risked being outflanked by Malaviya, Jinnah, and the other moderates who had opened talks with the viceroy. Nor could the Mahatma alienate his base. So, he promised to pilot civil disobedience in February in Bardoli, where he would observe its efficacy, as if under lab conditions.[73]

In the event, the trial did not last long. The movement was called off just days into it, with the storming of a police station in Chauri Chaura in the United Provinces, a *deus ex machina* providing Gandhi the cover to declare that civil disobedience had 'failed'. While he drew criticism from Muslim clerics, the upshot was clear.[74] A new hierarchy had been established. Gandhi—and subsequently, other Hindu leaders—would be in command and the nationalist Muslims in tow.

The quarter-century that followed witnessed the secular decline of the nationalist Muslims, and the rise of the Muslim League at their expense. A financial scandal in the summer of 1922 implicated nearly every Khilafatist, the Ali brothers included, cutting short many careers. Death and disillusionment did for the rest. Death: Bari passed away in 1926, Ajmal Khan in 1927, Ansari in 1936.

Disillusionment: both the Ali brothers turned against the Congress when it produced the Nehru Report of 1928, recommending joint electorates and reservations in Muslim minority provinces. It was too little, too late. Jinnah's response, his Fourteen Points, became the rallying cry of a more impatient generation of publicists: the retention of separate electorates; reservations for both the minority and majority provinces on a population basis; a third of the central legislature for Muslims.[75]

Chaudhry Khaliquzzaman, who was to take over as Congress president from Ansari when he went to jail, was another nationalist Muslim heavyweight who switched sides. Before he could fill in his mentor's shoes, differences over reservations emerged between him and the Nehrus, *père* and *fils*, who blocked his ascent. In the end, Khaliquzzaman plumped for a career with the League, consolidating power on the back of Oudh *taluqdars*. Particularly formative was the contretemps surrounding the Nehru Report. Initially, in 1927, Jinnah had been ready to drop separate electorates for reservations. One in three seats in the central legislature was the asking price. At the time the Congress had seemed amenable. But with the volte-face of the Nehru Report, reducing the figure to a quarter, it became clear the spirit of compromise was not reciprocated. The complacency of its author, Motilal Nehru, was equally telling: all that remained 'to settle the Hindu-Muslim question', he had written Annie Besant reassuringly a few weeks later, was to be achieved 'by throwing [the League] a few crumbs here and there'.[76] More important to him was winning over the Hindu revivalists who threatened his hold over the party: Lajpat Rai, Moonje, Jayakar, Malaviya.

Crumbs for the *qaum*, the whole cake for the communalists. Khaliquzzaman understandably felt betrayed. Later in his memoirs, he wrote scathingly: 'the Hindu leadership lost the chance of securing their pet theme of a joint electorate, to which even the Muslim League under Mr Jinnah's guidance had committed itself ... Let the Hindu youth of India ponder over these bunglings of their leadership before they blame Muslims for Partition'.[77]

Likewise, in the Punjab, disillusioned nationalist Muslims on the Congress Left decided to strike out on their own. In 1929, they joined Chaudhuri Afzal Haq's Ahrar movement, attacking the *ahmadiyyas*, whom they saw as apostates, and demanding a ban on usury, education for all, lower taxes for smallholders, and *sharia* rule.[78] In Bengal and the United Provinces, nationalist Muslim lawmakers were deselected ahead of the 1926 elections; by the end of the decade, most of them were unsurprisingly in Jinnah's camp.[79] What was left of the nationalist Muslim was only the party *pur et dur*, figures like Azad and Kidwai.

By the thirties, it was clear that they had been dealt a losing hand. Forces outside their control were conspiring against them. As Paul Brass argues in what is, perhaps, the most persuasive theorisation of Partition, a separatist minority nationalism is bound to succeed when its 'rate of social mobilisation' outpaces the 'rate of assimilation' into the majority community. All of this can, of course, in keeping with ethos of much political science, be 'mathematically' proven. Were, for instance, some 100,000 Urdu-speaking Muslim students emigrating from the countryside to receive instruction in cities where there was a capacity to enrol only, say, 20,000 in Hindi-medium institutions, the rest—80,000 students—would, perforce, create Urdu ones. With the right amount of 'symbol manipulation', in outstripping Hindi 'assimilation' by a factor of four, 'social mobilisation' around Urdu could further entrench a constituency for Muslim separatism.[80] With this schema at hand, Brass culls a wide array of statistics— on urbanisation, literacy, employment—to suggest that this was, indeed, what came to pass in late colonial India. Once a community, Muslim India became a nation.

On Brass' account, the Muslims of the United Provinces were urbanising much faster than Hindus in the half-century to 1931, providing a constituency to the rapidly mobilising Muslim League, which was able to corner half the urban Muslim vote in 1937 and 71 per cent in 1946. The same went for that small, but decisive for the purposes of separatism, minority of Anglophone literates—some 0.36 per cent of the population in 1901—in the province: Muslims accounted for 17.6 per cent of them at the turn of the century; 22.3 per cent in 1931. These developments were mirrored in the vernacular world: while Urdu students grew fourfold in 1860–74, Hindi students did by less than a third. The picture, then, was clear. Muslims were mobilising faster than Hindus were assimilating them.

Put differently, nationalist Muslims were very rapidly being put out of business by separatist Muslims.

Brass has come under fire from Francis Robinson, in whose view objective differences between Muslim and Hindu counted for more, a sentiment shared by Farzana Shaikh.[81] To be sure, the Muslimness of Muslim separatism is an undeniable fact. But the two interpretations need not be read in opposition to one another. For religious essences and political agency were mutually reinforcing. If music before mosques was *haram* according to the tenets of Islam, it took political entrepreneurs to help set a riot into motion. Likewise, if the *sharia* was the final word on Muslim law, it took a not inevitable *ashraf* agency to will it into constitutional reality.

The separatists shared in the nationalists' firm belief that only Muslims could speak for the *qaum*. Crucially, they preached this message with more fervour. Famously for Jinnah, writing in March 1940, it was a 'dream that the Hindus and Muslims can ever evolve a common nationality ... They are not religions in the strict sense of the word, but are in fact *different and distinct social orders* ... They neither intermarry, nor interdine together and, indeed they belong to two different civilisations'.[82]

Such an unforgiving worldview was compounded by deft political acumen. While the nationalist Muslims were busy discrediting themselves with their extremism (from the Afghanistan *hijrat* to Malabar),[83] infighting (financial and factional), and lost causes (the Caliphate, *amir-e-hind*), League separatists set about to win over the Muslim majority provinces in the northeastern and northwestern strips of the Subcontinent. These became the core constituencies for the demand for Pakistan: in the main Bengal and the Punjab, but also Sind and the NWFP. The decade to 1937, especially, was a crucial one. By reopening the debate on reservations with an eye to the Punjab and Bengal, and currying favour with the gentry, Jinnah built a convincing case for separatism.

When the results of the 1937 elections—the first to feature a statistically significant franchise, some 5.5 million voters—came in, the true balance of power between the nationalist Muslims and the separatists became apparent. True, the League's middle-of-the-road showing—it won only 109 of the 482 Muslim seats, mostly from Bengal and the United Provinces—disappointed its leadership. But it nevertheless put the Congress to shame. The party won a mere 26 Muslim seats. Assam, Bengal, Orissa, the Central Provinces, Bombay, Sind, and the Punjab returned not a single nationalist Muslim.

As was to become clear with Nehru and K. M. Ashraf's 'Muslim mass contact campaign' after the electoral *bouleversement*, there was no love lost between Muslims and the Congress. An avalanche of complaints revealed the communal prejudice that lay under the carapace of Congress secularism. Muslims were prevented from joining the party and contesting PCC and DCC seats. Leading Congressmen held simultaneous membership in Hindu revivalist organisations. Essentially the party of nationalist Hindus, the Congress cornered three in five general seats, coming in at pole position in nine of British India's eleven provinces. The figures spoke for themselves. It could win handsomely without Muslim support. It might be surmised that the question many Congressmen were asking themselves in 1937 was: why bother with the *qaum* at all?

Talks between the League and the Congress broke down that spring. Before the polls, the two parties had come to an understanding in the United Provinces. A common programme was not absurd. Jinnah's ideas, after all, broadly concurred with the Congress Left's. They were agreed on the efficacy of protectionism for domestic manufacturers, writing off rural debt, promoting cottage industries, greater devolution, and free primary education. The Congress was to stand down in all but one Muslim seat—so that the League could battle the NAP without triangular contests—the one being Rafi Ahmed Kidwai's, where the League withdrew. The *modus vivendi* also implied a coalition after the election. The JUH, a branch of the Congress in all but name, went so far as to campaign for the League. Khaliquzzaman and Ismail Khan, both League luminaries, were promised cabinet positions by the Congress.[84] But this was not to be. The League won 27 seats, the Congress 134. With enough numbers and a firm belief that its two nationalist Muslims—in addition to Kidwai, the Congress had acquired a second one in Hafiz Mohammad Ibrahim who defected from the League; both were inducted into its ministry—were evidence enough of cross-confessional support, the

Congress reneged on the alliance, forming a government on its own. What's more, it called for the League to disband.

The Congress' bluster only strengthened League resolve. In the autumn of 1937, Jinnah went on the offensive, striking a deal with the Unionists in the Punjab, and in Bengal sealing a pact with Fazlul Haq, once a Congress general secretary and now chief of the KPP, polling third. Initially, Haq was to align with the Congress. Azad, then the foremost nationalist Muslim of the day, and Humayun Kabir, KPP notable and rising trade unionist, had been leading the coalition talks. In the event, Nehru and Sarat Bose, president of the Bengal PCC, declared themselves opposed. The parleys broke down.[85] A KPP-League coalition was sworn into office shortly after. Already a weak agency, the nationalist Muslims had proven themselves to be singularly incapable of standing up to the Hindu leadership.

The League, meanwhile, continued to press home the advantages of being in opposition. Many of the damning findings of its Pirpur and Shareef reports of 1938 and 1939 were in fact corroborated by the Congress' very own Muslim Mass Contacts Office. The Congress governments had made full use of their newly acquired muscle power to enforce bans on cow slaughter and impose Hindi. Muslim functionaries found fewer roles. Muslim manufacturers found themselves discriminated against, as religious prejudice intruded into industrial policy. On one occasion, staff and students at an Urdu school in Chandwar were instructed to worship a portrait of Gandhi's—*shirk,* idolatry, of course being an unforgivable crime in Islam.[86]

The confessional make-up of the Congress reflected its comportment. Even after 'mass contact', when the number of Muslim heads more than tripled to 100,000, the *qaum* made up a mere 3.2 per cent of its total membership—at the time, of course, one in four Indians was Muslim.[87] Still, a year into it, the party high command 'deliberately abandoned the struggle of mass contact', in the words of Ashraf, who complained that he had been thrown to the wolves.[88]

Gandhi's Wardha Scheme, an education programme for national rejuvenation that effectively turned primary schools into centres of Hindu traditional learning, too, gave the League ammunition to denounce the Congress. That it was placed in the hands of a nationalist Muslim, Zakir Husain, and implemented in Bihar by the province's education minister Syed Mahmud, another member of this genus, only made it easier for the League to portray Congress Muslims as Uncle Toms. As the League's Pirpur Report pointed out, history courses were saturated with the life and works of 'Hindu divinities and Hindu heroes and saints'—all patriotic *laudatio* with scarce critical comment—while Muslim history was given short shrift.[89]

The League, then, scarcely needed to lift a finger for Muslims to come flocking to it, abandoned sheep in search of a shepherd. The Congress was doing its work for it. As Gurharpal Singh and Ian Talbot have it, 'Jinnah's main asset was to sit tight and let his opponents make mistakes'.[90]

Historical contingencies worked to the League's benefit. For, with the Second World War raging and the Congress waging its Quit India Movement, the British came to increasingly rely on it, along with the princes and Unionists, for local support. The League obliged. Throughout the war, the Raj placated Jinnah's demands in return. The trajectories of the League and the nationalist Muslims, then, were a study in contrasts. Jinnah drove a hard bargain, achieving more or less what he wanted from the Raj. Nationalist Muslims, on the other hand, suppressed their demands, closing ranks and receiving next to nothing from the Hindu leadership.

'A Politically Reactionary Minority'

The question arises how far nationalist Muslims could have gone had they adopted a more assertive élan. A provisional answer is to be found in Syed Mahmud's contretemps with Nehru. As the 'top leader of the province', in Azad's estimation, Mahmud in 1937 was set to be sworn in as prime minister of Bihar.[91] As it happened, however, he was pushed out of the competition by Rajendra Prasad, who was orchestrating intra-party—in effect, intra-caste—rivalries from on high. The premiership instead fell to Shri Krishna Sinha, a Bhumihar, and Anugraha Narayan Sinha, a Rajput, was made his deputy. Mahmud had been thrown under the bus. That was not all.

In the years that followed, he found himself cowed into submission by Nehru, who had been a junior of his at Cambridge. When Mahmud, in an effort at conciliation, wrote to Gandhi in the run-up to the war suggesting that the Congress hold out an olive branch and bring the League into the Bihar government to ensure a minority veto, Nehru became apoplectic:

> the whole background of [your proposal] seems to me utterly wrong ... In some ways it shows entire ignorance of the present position ... The proposal is so astonishing in its futility and dangerous consequences that I am surprised that you should have permitted any one to make it in your name ... As a matter of fact the whole conception of the memorandum is politically so reactionary that it is difficult even to criticise it seriously ... It seems to me that somebody has imposed this very extraordinary and very childish note on you and that you have not considered it at all with care.[92]

The gaslighting worked. Still, Mahmud was not ready to beat a full retreat, even if the nationalist Muslim tendency to circumscribe political agency was in full display in his response:

> It is just possible that the language may have played me false and created the unfortunate impression on your mind that the background of my note has anything to do with reactionary outlook. You know that your influence on my life has been so great that it is impossible for me to have any reactionary outlook ... Let me tell you in general terms again that the Congress has failed to properly and efficiently govern, particularly in this province [Bihar] where it has definitely misgoverned. The Congress is full of provincialism, caste prejudices and rivalism [sic] ... The Congress in power has further failed to win the confidence of the minorities, not only Moslems but Christians and others.[93]

The advice to be more mindful of minorities was not heeded, and he received another tongue-lashing:

> It is absurd for a politically advanced majority to give up its advanced views to please a politically reactionary minority ... I wish you had spoken to me about this matter and shown me

your note before you gave it to Gandhiji. You have upset him completely and he is very unhappy about it. As a matter of fact you should try to forget all that is happening and look after your health. A person who is not well enough to take part in public activities fully is not competent to judge.[94]

Mahmud fell in line. There was no more correspondence on the issue. But even in defeat, he was vindicated—twice over. Linlithgow, the viceroy, had already hinted at a minority veto to Jinnah a month earlier. Amery, secretary of state, more formally did the same in August the next year. Moreover, on 22 December, two weeks after Nehru had brushed off Mahmud's warnings, Muslims celebrated— alongside Ambedkar and the Dalits—a 'day of deliverance' from the Congress regimes, which resigned protesting Indian involvement in the war. In Bihar, Congressmen were treated like lepers, as Mahmud discovered on his return to Chapra in the spring of 1940. He came to bury his mother-in-law, but found that few were ready to partake in his grief. 'Muslim League people', apparently, had instructed the townsmen to keep away from the burial. Ostracising the grieving was particularly noteworthy in this context, for, as Mahmud noted, 'amongst the Mussalmans this is the greatest form of insult conceivable'.[95]

As it was, it took another episode to fully bully Mahmud into submission. This one, however, was of his own making. Always a sceptic of civil disobedience—his biographers attribute this to his 'Anglophilia' and tendency to reminisce 'his days in England with great affection', which, we are hastily told, did not detract from his 'firm nationalism'—Mahmud found himself pushed by the rising tide of nationalism into supporting the Quit India Movement, his role in which wound him up in prison in Ahmednagar Fort with Nehru and Azad. Weary, ailing—a violent reaction to a cholera inoculation (an epidemic was raging nearby) was making him 'bleed from his gums'—and with time on his hands, he took to penning a history of Hindu-Muslim relations, an aborted effort that he abandoned shortly after his release. Only he wasn't. At first, Congressmen could not fathom why Mahmud alone was freed from prison. But then the truth came to light. As Azad later wrote, recalling his eureka moment,

Mahmud had been 'in correspondence with the government ... It is true that he had consulted some of us about certain English phrases and idioms. Jawaharlal and I thought he was engaged in writing a book and wanted to be sure about the correct usage of some phrases. It never entered our heads that he was composing a letter of apology to the viceroy'.[96]

Weeks after his release, when the letter was leaked, it emerged that Mahmud had pleaded loyalty, reminding the viceroy that he had voted against civil disobedience at an AICC meeting in July 1940. While Wavell, the new viceroy, felt that Mahmud's claim was 'probably untrue', he had nevertheless seen fit to release him, for 'he is a weak simple man who could now do very little harm'.[97] Congressmen, Nehru included, were stunned by the duplicity. Mahmud, for his part, tried to explain away his letter as the tragic upshot of divine afflatus. It appears that 'he consulted the Quran three times by opening the pages at random. On each occasion, his eyes lighted on a passage which said that he should act according to his wishes. Dr Mahmud said that he regarded this to be an indication from Providence and accordingly sent the letter to the viceroy'.[98] His colleagues naturally found this unconvincing, and came to be view him 'as a Muslim League fifth-column'.[99] Thereafter, whatever little independence Mahmud had shown gave way to a political style we are now familiar with: muted in its demands and subordinated to party interests.

While nationalist Muslims were being discredited in the eyes of Hindu Congressmen, so, too, were they falling in the Raj's esteem. Linlithgow's contemptuous dismissal of the Convention of the Nationalist Muslims—which sought to impress upon Cripps' mission that they, indeed, were representative of the *qaum*—bore sad testimony to their marginalisation: theirs was a heteroclite coalition of 'Ahrars, Jamiat-ul-Ulema, extremist Shias, a section of Momins, Ittihad-i-Millat, and Red Shirts. None of these bodies is important, and their combination would be artificial'.[100]

A further indication of their relegation came in June 1945, when Wavell brokered the Simla Conference to get the Congress and the League behind his plan for a new executive council—this time fully Indian barring the viceroy and commander-in-chief—to run an interim government. Insisting that the League have a monopoly on Muslim members on it, Jinnah scuttled the talks. Crucially, this he did not so much to hit at the nationalist Muslims—they had already been consigned to irrelevance—but to get back at Tiwana, the leader of the Unionist Party in the Punjab who had refused to turn his party into a League appendage at Jinnah's instigation in 1942.[101] That Jinnah could single-handedly do in a policy convinced many Unionists to defect to the League, now seen as the real locus of Muslim power. Not even second place, then, for the nationalist Muslim.

Azad cut a lonely figure at Simla, ignored by Jinnah, who refused even to meet him, and similarly disregarded by the British in attendance. Wavell, by all accounts a friend of Azad's—the *maulana* would write glowingly of the viscount in his memoirs[102]—had this to say of his role at the summit: 'Azad is an old-fashioned scholar with pleasant manners, but I doubt if he contributes very much to Congress policy. His main object is to get even with Jinnah and the League Muslims who despise him as a paid servant of the Congress'.[103] To this end, the *maulana* had mustered a motley crew of nationalist Muslims at Simla to demonstrate Muslim support for the Congress. His intended audience, Leaguers and the British, was unconvinced.[104] It didn't help his cause that despite understanding English 'quite well', he chose not to speak it, relying instead on G. B. Pant, his interpreter—and UP premier—who was never fully up to the task.[105]

But the Simla débâcle was no isolated incident. Indeed, throughout his lengthy presidency—seven years to 1946—Azad never escaped its lame-duck quality. His correspondence with the British was vetted, at times even ghost written, by Nehru, and Raj officials were well aware of this.[106] To the government, then, he was small fry. When he was in prison in 1944, Alfred Porter, secretary to the governor of Bengal, noted that his bosses were eager to see the back of him. 'It was generally agreed that Azad's release would make no difference to the political situation at all'.[107] The same was true for Kidwai and Ibrahim.[108]

Away from the high tables, the nationalist Muslims fared no better. In the NWFP, the Congress-friendly Khan Abdul Jabbar Khan's premiership was followed by four years of governor's rule, which ended with the province falling to the League's Aurangzeb Khan in 1943. In Sind, Allah Bakhsh Soomro, the premier favourably disposed to Quit India, was dismissed in 1942 and replaced by Ghulam Hussain Hidayatullah, who soon joined the League. Electorally, too, Jinnah's party did exceedingly well. In the five years to 1943, of the 73 Muslims elected to legislatures, 40 were Leaguers, 12 Unionists, and a mere six Congressmen.[109]

The nationalist Muslims were also alienating the *ulama*, who had generally been hostile to Jinnah. Understandably. The League conjured—however fuzzily—secular state power. To begin with, it had little time for extraparliamentary action, let alone a meddlesome clergy bent on juridical sovereignty. At the time, it was the League that was the secular alternative to the Congress—and not the other way around—whose gentry and professionals preferred to couch their class interests in confessional terms. The rhetoric of nationalist Muslims, especially, was inflected by a strong religious tenor—and this was true not merely of clerics. Indeed, in the thirties, it was hard to tell apart a 'socialist' Congress Muslim from a *maulana*. Mir Mushtaq Ahmed of the Congress Socialist Party was a case in point: his was a world of '*kaffirs*' and 'divines', 'un-Islamic' reactionaries and 'great Muslim thinkers'.[110]

Clerics and Leaguers, moreover, worked towards rather different objectives. In 1937, the *ulama* lobbied lawmakers into passing the Shariat Act, giving the *sharia* precedence over local custom in courts. Watering down its redistributive potential to keep the gentry on board—making the piece of legislation less Islamic, as it were, on questions of inheritance and land—the League, for its part, aroused the ire of the *ulama*.[111]

Likewise, the clerical campaign to restrict the competence to enforce the Dissolution of Muslim Marriages Act in 1939—a progressive law allowing Muslim women to sue for divorce cynically endorsed by the *ulama*, alarmed at the spike in divorces secured through conversion—only to Muslim judges was frustrated in Parliament by secular lawyers, Jinnah included.[112] Throwing the divide between the League and the clergy into dramatic relief, the act was the last time the judiciary involved itself in the religious affairs of Indian Muslims until the 1980s. That Hindu law was subject to controversy nearly every decade in the intervening period, while Muslim law remained cast in stone, was testament to the leverage of the *ulama* over the Congress. It was also the last time Leaguers joined hands with Congressmen to defeat the clergy. Thereafter, they went to great lengths to paint themselves as pious Muslims.[113] Throughout the forties, Jinnah talked of 'Islamic democracy', an oxymoronic turn of phrase whose constructive ambiguity he exploited in full measure.[114]

That the League was forced to don a confessional armour—in effect trade in corporatist for confessional politics—was, after a fashion, a resounding victory for the nationalist Muslim position; though this, of course, came at the expense of the nationalist Muslims themselves. In ideological victory lay political defeat.

Luckily for the League, in purely class terms the clergy counted for little to begin with. In the United Provinces in 1921, for example, to some 10,650 clerics there were nearly 80,000 in the other professions.[115] What's more, the *ulama* made for poor communicators, preferring harangues to the hustings. But issuing *fatwas* was one thing, persuading people across the spectrum another. Good enough for the early twenties, by the mid-thirties— Congressmen and Leaguers by then both veterans of popular politics—they were quickly becoming an anachronism. The League stole a march on, and devolution did for, them.

True, the Deobandi chief of the JUH, Husain Ahmad Madani, organised the Azad Muslim Conference in 1940 to denounce the League's Lahore resolution. But he was inconsequential. The League, meanwhile, was attracting clerics in droves. In October 1945, it established the Jamiat-ul-Ulema-i-Islam, an obvious reference to the organisation it was hoping to undercut. The JUI quickly outshone the JUH. For while the League *ulama* had a formidable party machinery and a chiliastic vision of the future to sell to the masses, the nationalist Muslim clerics—Azad and others now reduced to sycophants—had neither.

The view from London confirmed the new balance of power. 'The large majority of educated Muslims now follow the League', read a dispatch doing the rounds at the India Office in January 1946. 'The Congress are now left with no Muslims of national importance except Maulana Kalam Azad. The Congress claim to represent more than the Hindus of India now rests on very slight foundations'.[116]

The League also received a fillip from the polls that month, ably hoovering up Muslim candidates from across the spectrum: the gentry, independents, defectors from the NAP and Unionist Party. Its biggest asset was its schizophrenic ideology. It spoke to the millenarianism of Muslim youth, the conservatism of the *ulama*, the progressivism of socialists, the aspirationalism of the bourgeoisie. *Pirs* and *makhdooms* campaigned for it in Sind and the Punjab. The *ashraf* elite of the United Provinces convinced themselves that jobs awaited them in the new homeland. Southerners dreamt of Moplastan. Price ceilings won over consumers, the promise of land reform producers.[117]

While the Leaguer and the nationalist Muslim stood for more or less the same things—juridical autonomy; jobs in the services; a just order based on religious parity—it was patently clear to voters that it was Jinnah's party, and not Azad's, that was ready to back up this vision with the full weight of state power. The League's quest for political sovereignty was a means to that end. By then, Jinnah was pushing for two constituent assemblies, inching closer to a fully sovereign Pakistan. To many Muslims, then, the separatist's was the more convincing argument. In urban Muslim constituencies of the United Provinces, the Congress polled a mere 0.75 per cent. Across the Subcontinent, the League carried 86 per cent of the Muslim seats, improving its vote share over 1937 from 4 to 75 per cent.

The Congress' Hindu leadership remained in denial. Like a whingeing child, Nehru sought refuge in comforting fictions in order to deflect attention from his own actions, infantilising the *qaum* and crying foul, pinning the blame for the results on Muslim susceptibility and vote-rigging:

> The voters' registers were prepared and manipulated in such a way as to favour the League and large numbers of bogus names were intrdouced [*sic*]. In Banaras we have the remarkable instance of more names on the Muslim register than there are Muslim inhabitants in the city … As a whole Muslims are politically backward, with no sufficiently developed middle class and

hardly any notable leaders, with the exception of Jinnah. They can be more easily moved by a religious cry than the Hindus ... Pakistan as such is hardly understood or appreciated by most members of the League; it is a sentimental slogan which they have got used to.[118]

In the sixteen months from the time the new premiers assumed office in April 1946 to independence and Partition in August the following year, a cataract of cataclysms—some willed; others blundered; yet others entirely contingent—provoked a chain of events that led to the creation of Pakistan. Complete distrust between Hindu and Muslim at the levels of both high and low politics—words were exchanged at the high tables; on the streets, blows were—made any kind of reconciliation impossible. The Raj wearily came to accept this sad reality. London's final attempt to rescue a single, albeit decentralised, Union ultimately came to nought.

As it happened, the final disagreement between the League and the Congress turned on the legitimacy of the nationalist Muslim. For the interim government, Jinnah had in mind a cabinet of twelve Indians, five each from the League (all Muslim) and Congress (all Hindu)— parity—and two others. Nehru, on the other hand, was bent on having fourteen members, six Congressmen (including a Muslim and a Dalit), five Leaguers, and three others. Wavell felt this was a fair deal. Jinnah did not.[119] The inclusion of Azad proved to be a thorn in his flesh. But the *maulana*, who had been keen to join the executive council at Simla, was now ready to stand down.[120] Gandhi would have none of it.[121] If Azad wouldn't rise to the challenge, another nationalist Muslim would have to be sought. For how could the Congress insist on its right to include a nationalist Muslim if it did not have one who was up to the task in the first place? In the event, a replacement was found in Zakir Husain, later president of India.[122] But the League once again put its foot down. The impasse, then, remained.

'The Cheap Butter of Insincere Compliments'

After briefly temporising, the Congress joined the interim government in September, as did the League a month later. In the scramble for ministries that followed, the Congress sought to deprive Jinnah of the one he coveted for himself, defence. Moreover, it did not budge on its right to nominate a nationalist Muslim; three of them had been inducted in the League's absence. This, of course, was not a reflection of the strength of the nationalist Muslims, but the Congress' desperate need for them. But not for long. That they were expendable quickly became clear. Indeed, among the five Congress cabinet ministers made to step down to make way for Leaguers on 26 October, two—Shafat Ahmed Khan and Syed Ali Zaheer—were nationalist Muslims. Only one nationalist Muslim, then, was left standing in the reconstituted cabinet: Asaf Ali. Ultimately, what mattered to the Congress was not the representation of Muslims per se, but its right to represent them, and be seen—by the Raj, the electorate, the wider public—representing them.

No one, however, was fooled. Here's Wavell's appraisal of the nationalist Muslim troika: Zaheer had been put up to the job because he was 'a friend of Nehru's ... [As for] Asaf Ali and Shafat Ahmed Khan [they were] very poor specimens indeed. They have neither capacity nor character'.[123] Khan, in fact, only joined the Congress a few days before he became minister. A former high commissioner to South Africa, he was 'stabbed seven times in the head, neck, and chest' days after he resigned from the League.[124] Zaheer, president of the All-India Shia Conference and sometime Lucknow lawyer, was not even the heavyweight of his household. The governor of the United Provinces put him below both his father, ci-devant chief judge of the Oudh Court, and brother, commissioner at Gorakhpur, in the familial pecking order. 'Zaheer himself' was 'of little or no account'.[125] Ali was Azad's locum. Not long before entering the interim government, he had in a CWC meeting—along with the maulana—voted against nationalist Muslim representation on it.[126] During his brief tenure, it was widely understood that he was keeping the seat warm for Azad, who was vacillating.[127] And sure enough, when the cleric was inducted as education and arts member in January 1947, Ali was sent off to the US as an ambassador.

A month into their terms, Wavell took stock of the trio again in a memo to George VI. The viceroy's opinions, of course, serve as a useful barometer of their political weight and reputation. Khan: 'seems to me almost a half-wit (five-eighths as a maximum). At his first interview with me, he let off a few platitudes about his portfolios, and interlarded them with the most servile flattery of myself ... a lightweight, if not indeed a featherweight ... as high commissioner he was unstable, tactless, and tiresome ... exudes the cheap butter of insincere compliments'. Zaheer: 'seems fairly sensible and wide awake, but I have seen little of him yet'. Ali: 'a man of no weight, looks scared, and has always been rather a worm'.[128]

Lest it seem that Wavell's judgment was prejudiced, it should be noted that his remarks can be corroborated by a brief survey of their performance in government. Indeed, they were inexperienced, inept, and put in positions above their pay grade primarily because, one suspects, they happened to tick the right box. Khan at health, ironically, had to worry about his more than the nation's. Reeling from his stab wounds, he spent the early weeks of his tenure in convalescence.[129] In health ministers' conferences and statements to the press, it appears, it was not him but Nehru, vice-president of the interim government, who set the agenda on health policy: a premium on the *mofussil* over cities, on prevention over cure, on autarkic production over imports.[130] Khan, evidently, was not his own master.

Zaheer, responsible for posts and air, could not quite dispense with his capacity for wonder. He saw himself as less a member than observer of the elite. In other words, he remained a bit of a *parvenu*: 'I shall have the privilege of working with the cream of Indian leadership', he exclaimed beamingly to the press on his appointment.[131] In the event, his vision did not extend beyond a few facile soundbites relating to the need for more deregulation and less red tape. Out of step with the rest of his administration, he reassured the industry majors that there were no plans for nationalisation and heaped praise on the efficiency of the private sector. But his press statements of the time suggest not so much an interest in his portfolio as in the more pressing concern of weaning the *qaum* off the League—perhaps why he had been brought into the executive in the first place—and in using his platform to lobby for a Shia quota in the Constituent Assembly.[132]

Ali, by contrast, threw himself into his ministerial responsibilities. Unlike the others, he was a man of experience. A veteran of the Congress Assembly Party, he had acquired a formidable reputation for grilling British ministers in Parliament.[133] As member for transport and railways, he was receptive to worker interests, often pinning the blame for strikes on management, even if he did not hesitate to put pressure on unions when they crossed him.[134] He took policy initiatives—thereby demonstrating that he was more than just a Muslim face—recruiting armed forces personnel to protect freight and staff from *dacoity*, and taking steps to abolish the practice of 'communal' vending, wherein hawkers advertised their faiths along with their wares—*chai mussalman!*—to attract co-religionist customers, but not without ratcheting religious tension.[135] Still, he proved incapable of liaising with other ministries and securing funds from Delhi. He felt compelled to jack up fares to cover the ever-widening deficit. Nor was he able to fend off charges of 'indifference' and 'neglect'.[136] All in all, none of them left much of a mark on their ministries. Moreover, all were gone—two replaced by Leaguers, the third by Azad—by mid-January.

In the months that followed, the Congress Right suffered sleepless nights on account of the League Left. Liaquat Ali Khan's socialist budget of February 1947 sent markets crashing; plantation owners and industrialists complained of higher taxes and duties, and Congressmen decried what they—incorrectly—saw as 'anti-Hindu' discrimination. Even Nehru admitted as much: truth be told, it was 'the poor man's budget'.[137]

Jinnah, lawyer no more, decided to meet the Congress' intransigence not in the corridors of power, but on the streets. He declared 16 August 1946 'direct action day'. Violence broke out in Calcutta as the League tried to enforce a lockdown. Some 4,000 were slaughtered, another 15,000 injured. From what came to be known as the Great Calcutta Killing to Gandhi's killing in January 1948, ceaseless waves of violence swept across the Subcontinent.

It was against this backdrop—executive obstruction; boundless rioting—that both Congressmen and Leaguers resigned themselves to Partition. Nationalist Muslims signed up to it as well, if only very late in the day. Around the same time, the British set themselves to the task of decolonisation. On 2 June 1947, when it was decided to transfer power to two successor dominions of the Commonwealth, the plan was accepted across the board—reluctantly by Jinnah, nonchalantly by Gandhi, and with both hands by Nehru.

With the troika on board, the only dissident of some standing to the Mountbatten Plan, then, was Azad. Averring that Partition would 'spell disaster for the Mussalmans', and that 'blame in the first place must be laid on Congress', he made one final stab at rescuing the Cabinet Mission Plan—for a decentralised, three-tiered but single Union—in the summer of 1947. But both his party colleagues and the British, let alone the League, wanted nothing to do with it.[138] By July, the *maulana* had become a liability. His very public criticism of Gandhi, who had 'betrayed' the nationalist cause—so Azad felt—by acquiescing to Partition left the Mahatma foaming at the mouth. Infuriated, Gandhi sought to deprive Azad of a place in government. More manipulable Muslims would have to be sought to replace him, he recommended in a letter to Nehru:

> I did not say anything yesterday about the *maulana saheb*. But my objection stands. His retiring from the cabinet should not affect our connection with him. There are many positions which he can occupy in public life without any harm to any cause … It should not be difficult to name another Muslim for the cabinet. I have destroyed the two copies you sent me yesterday.
>
> Blessings from Bapu.[139]

Gandhi then sent Azad a hectoring letter. 'Make way for a younger man' was the message.[140] Flanked on all sides by mounting criticism, Azad reconciled himself to Partition. 'Now there is no alternative', he said painfully to the AICC on 14 July. Let bygones be bygones. He set himself to the task of seeing through a soft partition, as it were, advocating a single army for both Unions instead of a communal carve-up, and convincing Muslims to stay on in the Indian bureaucracy.[141] All to no avail.

After the Mountbatten Plan, there was no looking back. So it was that the British left India 'to anarchy', just as Gandhi willed it, after having only reluctantly acceded to Partition in order to avoid escalating casualties on their hands.[142] In the event, the rushed transfer of power at a time of collapsed state capacity and heightened identitarianism, pushed through by the Congress, eager to lay its hands on as large a centralised state as possible, and accepted by the League, determined to have a nation-state before Nehru consolidated his position, left over twelve million displaced, perhaps half a million dead.

But Partition need not be seen, as in Paul Brass' words, as a 'massive Pyrrhic victory' for the heartland League elite.[143] Instead, it must be recognised as its success. For the *muhajirs* were able to control the commanding heights of the economy in the new homeland, an improbable prospect had they entered into a power-sharing arrangement with Hindus. But more importantly for our purposes, it was a victory for the nationalist Muslims, too, who at a stroke became the sole spokespeople of the *qaum*. It is here, by contrast, that Brass' verdict appears apposite. For Muslim politics in postcolonial India was incontrovertibly scarred by, and continues to reel from, the effects of Partition, and the conundrums—political, economic, legal, moral—it threw up.

All the same, the transformative effects of this rupture must not detract from the core beliefs of nationalist Muslims, a set of concerns which were commonly expressed on either side of Partition, temporally speaking. Indeed, there was the common political grammar based on the three assumptions that we encountered at the beginning of this chapter: a conflation of party and nation; an eschewal of refractory for biddable politics; and an espousal of legal and cultural autonomy.

First, the nationalist Muslim belief that the Congress was the only game in town. From Ansari's enchanted encounter with Gandhi— the former 'captivated' by the latter's 'charisma'—to Mahmud's mesmerised correspondence with Nehru—'your influence on my life has been so great'—it is clear that the nationalist Muslims had all fallen under the Congress spell. Such language suggests that theirs was not the kind of admiration that one has for one's peers. Unmistakably, there was a self-abasing quality to it, an element of uncritical slavishness. By contrast, Leaguers were the enemy. To be sure, at crucial moments in 1937 and 1946, figures like Azad did strike a conciliatory tone. But here, again, this stand stemmed from patriotic and pragmatic commitments. A Manichaean worldview was never in doubt. Accommodating the League was only the means to an altogether different end: winning the *qaum* over to the Congress cause, and later, preventing Partition.

Second, the meekness of the nationalist Muslim. Admittedly, early nationalist Muslims were anything but meek. Bari, as we have seen, was the prime mover of non-cooperation, Gandhi nervously tiptoeing around his ambitions. But after Khilafat, everything changed. Death took away leaders who could hold their own (Ansari, Bari). Disillusionment drove others into the arms of the League (Khaliquzzaman, Mohani). What was left was a much smaller set, figures who in the following years would consent to their own emasculation (Azad, Ashraf, Husain, Kidwai, Kabir, Mahmud). They learned to live with Hindu revivalists, who dominated the provinces, PCCs, and DCCs, finding comfort in the fact that at least in the realm of discourse and high politics, the Congress represented some kind of secular ideal. They put up with the party's spurning of the League in 1937. They tolerated widespread discrimination. They swallowed insults from the Hindu leadership (Nehru on Mahmud: 'ignorant', 'dangerous', 'reactionary', 'childish', 'incompetent'). And they accepted their fate as marginal men in a momentous movement. Azad, occasionally bitter but generally stoical, came to terms with political isolation.

Third, the nationalist Muslim idealisation of Islamic law and authority. An early harbinger was the obsession—surplus of nationalist uses—with the Caliphate. Religious to a man, and clerics disproportionate among them, they organised the JUH. Time and again, Quranic sanction was needed to justify political decisions: *satyagrahas*, alliances with infidels. Indeed, an idea of agency was alien to the nationalist Muslim. Bari saw independence primarily as an opportunity to impose *sharia* rule on Muslims. Azad concurred. To him, Muslim India was to be an *imperium in imperio*, with separate (*sharia*) courts, tax authorities (notional *zakat*), and rulers (*amir-e-hind*). Suspicion towards secular authority stemmed from a contempt for lay politicians, lesser clerics too: 'raw youths' to Bari, mere '*munshis*' to Azad. The nationalist Muslim was, after all, forged in the crucible of *madrasa* politics. Deobandi and Firangi Mahali clerics played an important role. In Peter Hardy's evocative words, their dream was a 'juristic ghetto'. No wonder they detested the League. For they were working towards entirely dissimilar objectives: the League aspired to economic and political, nationalist Muslims to cultural and legal, sovereignty.

As we will see in Chapter 2, each of the three trends were to deepen after independence. Nationalist Muslims became ever more committed (to both the Congress and the cause of nationalism), cautious (circumscribing demands even more so than before), and conservative (closed to any ideas that did not emanate from the Quran or the Constitution).

2

CULTURE WARS

No single life encapsulates the depoliticisation of the nationalist Muslim that followed independence better than Azad's. In his case, a habit of forbearance was followed through on pain of historical erasure. Once a pan-Islamist revolutionary, a mellowed Azad in his late years was keen to banish the memory of his radical past when he set about writing his autobiography—more accurately, dictating it in Urdu to Humayun Kabir, fellow cabinet minister and nationalist Muslim—a volume he, tellingly, dedicated to 'Jawaharlal Nehru, friend and comrade'. Here, but for a few banalities about the 'Khilafat problem', the *maulana* registers little else of this formative phase of his career.[1] Azad's, then, is one of those rare instances where, as Faridah Zaman writes, 'the colonial archive generates a life more revolutionary than the one that is penned in the first person'. Indeed, government reports put him at the centre of the Silk Letters Conspiracy. The cleric, it appears, honed his political skills as a pan-Islamist, liaising with revolutionaries in Lahore, Afghanistan, and the Porte, 'preaching *jihad*', recruiting 'fanatical schoolboys', and 'building secret societies'.[2]

That he did all these things should not be surprising. They are of a piece with his background. Born in Mecca, Azad grew up in Calcutta studying the *dars-e-nizamiya*, before rebelling against his father, a Sufi martinet, by reading Syed Ahmad Khan's Quranic commentaries—frowned upon by the *ulama* for their greater emphasis on reason than revelation—as well the reformist writings of Abduh, chief mufti of Egypt. At the same time, he drew on the works of Shibli, al-Afghani, and Rida—a wellspring of Islamic conservatism. Such a hybrid intellectual formation lent itself to both nationalist iconoclasm and pan-Islamism. Azad's rage against *ilhad* (atheism) and *kuffar* (infidels), lexical favourites of his, makes this patently clear. At the heart of his politics was an ambition that was both a means and an end: a return to Islam's roots by fixing on the Quran. In the fifties, however, as Indian nationalism increasingly became synonymous with Hindu traditionalism—Muslim separatism, by then a bogeyman with no real referent, serving as a useful foil—it made greater sense to downplay his pan-Islamist past, and play up his links with other transnational revolutionary circles, such as the Hindu-dominated Jugantar.

Almost as if to bolster the case for postcolonial depoliticisation, there exists a second layer of circumscription in Azad's tale: the censoring of his autobiography by his Man Friday and stenographer, Kabir. In his dying days, disillusioned with the Congress and overtaken by delirium, Azad approached his memoirs as a tell-all, spilling the beans on its inner workings. His narrative was on good authority. For the *maulana* had been, since his resignation from the League's Parliamentary Board in May 1937, at the nerve centre of the Congress, serving as party president from 1939 to 1946. At the time of Partition, he readily laid the blame for the violence at Patel's doorstep, shielding the rest of his party from criticism. In his autobiography, however, he threw caution to the wind. All the same, it would take another three decades before his jeremiad saw the light of day.

For after Azad's death, when the task of editing the manuscript—and, as it were, the mantle of the *ne plus ultra* of the nationalist Muslim—fell on him, Kabir assumed the very self-censoring élan of Muslim Congressmen of old that Azad had desperately been trying to cast away on his death bed. Feeling 'a little uncertain' about the contents of twenty-four pages that reflected badly on Nehru and the Congress, he 'marked them in red pencil' and sent them to the premier.[3] Unfortunately for our purposes, there are no more letters among Kabir's papers on the matter. Nehru's role, then, is not entirely clear. What we do know is that the posthumous volume that was published in 1958 was an expurgated version. The unabridged memoirs were placed under lock and key at the National Archives for thirty years. (In this, it could be parenthetically added, the Congress had form: Syed Mahmud's tell-all, too, was censored before publication; the Mahatma, Nehru, and Azad had taken umbrage at Mahmud's 'less-than-just' chapters on the Congress government in Bihar).[4]

When the manuscript resurfaced in 1988, and legal battles to secure its publication were gotten out of the way, it emerged that Azad had lain the blame on himself for his 'Himalayan mistake' of acceding to Nehru's promotion as Congress president after him. For the man who went on to become India's first premier was also the man most amenable to Partition. 'India was not divided by the Muslim League but by the Congress', Azad had written plainly. The rest of the unredacted material, thirty pages of it, was much of a muchness. Khurshed Framji Nariman, on this account, was denied the Bombay premiership in 1937 because 'Patel and his colleagues could not reconcile themselves' to the elevation of a Parsi; in the event, B. G. Kher was sworn in as prime minister, and Nariman, who cried foul, found himself silenced by Nehru at the CWC meeting that was meant to be his coronation, where India's premier-to-be 'treated him harshly and tried to shout him down'. In Bihar, it was a Muslim who met the same fate: Mahmud was cheated out of the premiership, which fell to S. K. Sinha. 'Merit', in Azad's estimation, gave way to majoritarian concern.[5]

'A Muslim Show-Boy Congress President'

The unabridged edition now affords a fuller picture of this nationalist Muslim life, warts and all. It is now amply clear that Azad was a mere figurehead president, unable to prevent—in his opinion—the untimely Quit India resolution, what with the Japanese Imperial Army inching towards Imphal. Likewise, he failed to scuttle the Gandhi-Jinnah talks of 1944, which he felt would only increase the latter's prestige. He also proved utterly incapable of swaying his party against the war when Gandhi flip-flopped his opposition to it—by which time, ironically, Allied victory was assured—proclaiming that a free India would share in the war effort. Jinnah's rebuke—'cannot you realise you are made a Muslim show-boy Congress President?'—may have been a bit of an exaggeration, but it was not too far off the mark.[6]

It was only towards the end of his tenure that Azad tried to reverse the fortunes of his straitjacketed presidency, prevailing over Nehru on two occasions. First, against the wishes of the premier-to-be who was against any kind of power sharing arrangement, Azad stitched together the Unionist-Congress-Akali coalition, bringing his party to power in the Punjab for the first time. Second, also in the summer of 1946, the *maulana* defeated the *pandit*'s bid to trim his powers. By defending his right, as Congress president, to remain, as convention dictated, the sole representative of the party in future parleys with the British—the Cabinet Mission was in the capital—Azad thwarted Nehru's machinations to make the party president a creature of the CWC.[7]

Nehru regained the upper hand, however, calling for a strong central government. Azad, groping for a federalist *via media* to forestall Partition, increasingly became side-lined in the endgame of empire. As an intercept of a letter to Gandhi reveals, he had been tirelessly pushing, albeit to no avail and 'in his personal capacity and not (repeat not) as Congress president', his win-win scheme since at least August 1945: Partition was 'defeatist', federalism the only option. Muslims would sign up for a united India if Muslim units were given the 'right to secession', parity with Hindus in Parliament and the executive in the short run, a system of alternation of Hindu and Muslim premierships. The takeaway was clear. 'Unless Hindu Congress leaders take a new line, nationalist Muslims will desert them'.[8] Gandhi's reply—also intercepted—was revealing of how protective he was of Hindu interests, and by extension, scornful of Muslim ones:

> I do not infer from your letter that you are writing about *my Hindus*. Whatever you have in your heart has not appeared in your writing ... Whatever you want to say about the communal

problems should not be said without consulting the Working Committee ... My opinion differs from your [*sic*] ... Your letter I think should not be published.[9]

Gaslighting, again. It would take some time before Azad felt confident enough to air his views in public. A fuller statement would have to wait until 15 April the next year, when he argued both dispassionately—in his own judgement—and presciently that 'the situation in India is such that all attempts to establish a centralised and unitary government are bound to fail'. The only way out of the impasse, then, was to 'meet the fear of the Muslim majority areas' without giving in to the demand for Pakistan. Anything short of that would mean sleepwalking into a two-state settlement wherein Indian Muslims—'backward industrially, educationally, and economically'—would be 'left to the mercies of what would become an unadulterated Hindu raj'. Crucially for Azad, a weak federation did not amount to a capitulation to the League. It was only ever a temporary concession.

> I am one of those who considers the present chapter of communal bitterness and differences as a transient phase in Indian life ... When India attains her destiny ... opposition among political parties will continue, but it will be based not on religion but on economic and political issues. Class, and not community, will be the basis of future alignments.[10]

But this was not to be. For scarcely ten weeks passed before Nehru publicly pooh-poohed the federal alternative, setting the Subcontinent on an unalterable course to Partition and realising Azad's worst nightmare.

If in the decade to 1947 Azad could still hold higher office, however tenuously, then the decade that followed saw through the completion of his marginalisation. He resigned himself to his fate, a venerated has-been, a man without agency. To the journalist Abdurrazzaq Malihabadi, a friend of his from one of his spells in the Raj's jails, describing his Constituent Assembly days, he confided: 'My new prison is this Government House'.[11] As education minister, he was equally morose: 'too aloof to concern himself with persons, too proud to think in terms of alliance, affiliation, or opposition ... he was so engrossed in principles that he could not become an efficient administrator. He had to be taken for what he was, with no credentials other than his personality', a mostly sympathetic observer wrote in a brief sketch.[12]

Throughout the fifties, 'the *maulana* seldom participated in debates in Parliament', one of his obituarists remembered.[13] Fellow lawmakers regularly inveighed against his prolonged truancy. Whenever his presence was needed, Azad would send in a stand-in. In 1955, the *Times* reported that he had absented himself from Parliament for 'a year now'. What's more, he 'never answered questions', democratic accountability being infra dig for this cleric.[14] Perhaps it was not arrogance, but his dipsomania that was to blame. 'A sadly misunderstood man', his biographer writes, Azad spent most of his 'later years drinking alone'.[15]

Politics proper, then, mattered little. Azad retreated into cultural activities, leading prayers in Delhi,[16] promoting cultural dialogue between India and Pakistan (on his view, a 'political' partition did not have to entail a 'cultural' one as well), and corresponding with Muslim youths about the Quran. His letters and speeches of the time suggest a growing appreciation for Vedanta and the Bible, and contempt for the orthodox Muslims who had come to resent him—a world removed from the pan-Islamism of his prime. 'Despairing of any following among the *ulama*, it appears that he was determined to range far and wide, finding a mental resting place wherever he found hospitality to the idea of a common humanity', his biographer speculates. But his immersion into the world of bromides— variously, 'world citizenship', 'unity in diversity', 'international peace'—was also a reflection of how distant quotidian politics had become for him.[17]

His counsel to the *qaum* was of a piece with this vision: 'live as loyal citizens'.[18] Loyalty, of course, is not a sign of agency, nor so much a programme, but a demonstration of submission. Similarly, in the wake of the 'police action' in Hyderabad, Azad tried to explain away the killing of 40,000 Muslims on Delhi's watch before a Muslim audience: it 'was an inevitable consequence of the minority community's misdeeds and excesses. The laws of nature were immutable and every action had its reaction'. Better than 'crying over spilt milk', he recommended Muslims to steer clear of government and work towards the 'rehabilitation and uplift of their fallen brothers and sisters' themselves. For 'in a large measure' this burden 'rested with the community' itself, not with the state.[19] If depoliticisation suited him, then he hoped that it would suit other minorities, too. In 1956, for instance, he advised the Akalis to 'totally give up politics'.[20] The choice of words, it hardly needs telling, hinted at reduced agency. To fight against injustices against the Sikhs, he went on, as if to remove any lingering doubts, the Akali Dal could well 'raise its voice' as a 'religious and cultural organisation ... It is not necessary for an organisation to be political'.[21]

To Azad, then, there existed a neat separation between the political and cultural. The former needed to be relinquished, the latter defended. For nation-building depended on unity, and while there could be unity in cultural diversity, political differences could be fatally divisive. This was the lesson of Partition. Better then to take up the cudgels for the Congress, circumscribe demands, and concentrate energies on cultural concerns—as we have seen, the holy trinity of nationalist Muslim thinking.

Early postcolonial Muslim politics was immeasurably shaped by this worldview. As we will see below, its upshots were most forcefully felt in the Constituent Assembly, where nationalist Muslims exchanged political for cultural safeguards.

'We Were Only Asked To Dress the Baby'

India's founding document has attracted endless reams of comment. The contretemps in the halls of the Constituent Assembly, the lives and works of the founding fathers, individual amendments even— none have been spared analysis and scrutiny. In what follows, however, I set out not so much to rehearse, theorise, or summarise this material—not least because there already exist two very fine, 'definitive' even, to use an old-fashioned word, accounts[22]—but instead to bring attention to a rather specific, and, for our purposes, rather significant, aspect of the assembly debates: namely, the singularly nationalist Muslim aversion to agency, and the long shadow it cast on Muslim politics in postcolonial India. Remarkable was the allergy to politics proper on the part of these career politicians.

Remarkable, too, is the fact that, as far as I know, their distinctly anti-political vision has gone unnoticed. One can only conjecture the reason for this elision. It appears that academic focus has been on constitutional outcomes, not their ideological origins, and for good reason. It makes for a telling contrast: Muslims in the assembly saw moderate success with cultural safeguards even as they were confronted with complete failure when it came to political ones.[23]

However, the cause of this divergence has been insufficiently understood. All too often, it has been suggested that, in the wake of Partition and Gandhi's murder, Delhi's rulers became uncomfortable with political safeguards of any kind. Outside the realm of culture, religion came to be seen as poison. So it was that the minority rights regime evolved mirroring this thinking.[24] An allied narrative has it that this settlement was the product not of the leadership's wishes per se, but national ideology at large. That cultural trumped religious safeguards was of a piece with the *pensée unique*.[25]

What is lost in this picture is Muslim agency. Indeed, it was neither the Hindu leadership in particular nor the prevailing dispensation that produced this singular outcome. Rather it was the nationalist Muslims. For they enjoyed what amounted to a minoritarian veto, and made full use of it. To be sure, there were undeniable pushes and pulls, carrots and sticks—the seductions of public office, the fears of admonishment—at work in the assembly. But on balance, agency weighed over structure here. In the event, it was a reflection of their efforts that Muslim personal law found a foothold in India, even as the stab at guaranteeing Muslim representation in government went nowhere.

If cultural safeguards became the bailiwick of the nationalist Muslims, political safeguards fell to the southern Leaguers. As before, there was a clear tension between the juridical and political in the nationalist Muslim imagination: in the assembly, Azad and his *confrères* defended the autonomy of the *sharia* even as they relinquished claims to greater representation in legislatures. Separate electorates, reservations, and a more egalitarian electoral system were sacrificed on the altars of national and party unity. For southern Leaguers, obverse priorities obtained. The fundamental cleavage between the League and the Congress had stayed the same.

The relative balance of power between the two parties sealed the fate of the safeguards regime. Tainted by Partition, decimated by migration, and confronted by a strident opposition, the League proved spectacularly unsuccessful at swaying the assembly behind its schemes. Hence the failure of political safeguards. The nationalist Muslims, on the other hand, were to all intents and purposes *the* representatives of the *qaum*. While they boasted fewer faces in the assembly, their party affiliation saw to it that their desiderata found a receptive audience. Consequently the success of cultural safeguards—the only kind that they put up a fight for.

This important chain of causality has been lost—perhaps buried amidst the welter of other insights—on account of the tendency to take rhetorical positions at face value and present the founding fathers as stand-ins for various ideological persuasions. Rochana Bajpai's account, for example, which argues for the subordination of function to form, and for the need to 'bracket off' the 'social origins' of ideologies, illustrates this well.[26] But despite her emphasis on the autonomy of the ideational, her narrative cannot avoid the role of objective factors. Muslims, for instance, Bajpai acknowledges, are sometimes 'pressured' to adopt certain positions.[27] She also concedes that 'rhetoric' at times 'served to blur political conflict of interests'.[28] Besides internal inconsistencies, what is more, such a view not only detracts from politics proper, but obscures the complex motivations—personal, sectional, communal—that prompt political actors to behave the way they do. Politics, after all, was a vocation for most of those in the assembly. It is only by bringing Muslim agency into sharper relief—bringing politics back in, as it were—and pushing back against this political-scientific impulse to read politics only through overarching categories and stilted taxonomic exercises that we can uncover the real reasons why cultural trumped political safeguards.

In fixing on assembly members themselves, their actions and motivations, it becomes clear that the *coupure* of Partition has been overdetermined. Being more mindful of Muslim thought goes some way in providing a corrective. Indeed, the nationalist Muslims behaved with almost admirable consistency. This is not to suggest that Partition had no effect on them. It did. And time and again, they alluded to it and regretted it.[29] But, when the balance sheet is drawn, the continuities counted for more than the discontinuities. Azad in the assembly, in short, sounded a lot like Azad the Congress president. And why would he not? He was, after all, still the same man. While Partition had shaken his beliefs somewhat, it had not drastically altered them. If the *dramatis personae* were the same and so was their élan, there is no reason to believe that it was Partition that impelled Muslims to do for political safeguards.

Muslims did have an important say in India's constitutional settlement—on the question of minority safeguards, a veto even. Even so, if they were not passive victims, they were not entirely free agents either. Written against a backdrop of upheaval—Partition in August 1947; the appearance of Pakistani irregulars in Kashmir in October; Gandhi's killing in January 1948; India's invasion of Hyderabad in September; high inflation, rationing, floods, and famine throughout—India's Constitution was a product of its time. There is no denying that its authors wanted a safer and more secure republic.

In concrete terms, this translated into sanction for a kind of regime that could be described as a national security state, one that places a considerable premium on the use of paramilitary power, censorship, and incarceration to vanquish enemies of all stripes, be they democratic dissidents or unreconstructed revolutionaries. Consequently, liberal precepts, the *Rechtsstaat* included, were not foremost on the founding fathers' minds. 'Integration' and 'unity' are the watchwords that leap from the pages of the twelve-volume *Constituent Assembly Debates* at regular intervals. Significantly, this was the lexicon of not only the Hindu traditionalist Congress Right and its sympathisers without. Ambedkar, the leader of the Dalits and *de facto* architect of the Constitution, made use of it, too, as did the Left. As Christophe Jaffrelot has persuasively argued, the constitutional settlement was forged by the improbable entente between Jacobinism and Hindu traditionalism.[30]

No dissent could be brooked from this consensus. Muslims were in for an uphill struggle. This was compounded by a second impediment. Crushed under the unforgiving wheels of Congress hegemony, never before so acutely felt, they were, in some measure, both unrepresentative and unfree. Unrepresentative because they did not, electorally speaking, represent Muslim India. For the only Leaguers who took their seats in the assembly in July 1947 were the dissidents who had decided against emigration. This meant that the party that had won 86 per cent of the Muslim seats in 1946 was scarcely represented on the benches.

Granville Austin, the founding document's finest biographer, then, was hardly exaggerating when he noted that in the assembly 'the representatives of nearly 100 million Indian Muslims were absent'.[31] The League had won 73 of the 80 seats reserved for Muslims, the Congress a paltry four. After Partition, most of the former found themselves in, or found their way to, Pakistan. By October 1947, a mere twenty-seven Muslims were left in the assembly.

To be sure, the Congress had, in its kaleidoscopic fashion, gone through the motions to represent minorities on the assembly. Parsis, Christians, Anglo-Indians, and women had wound up on it through the 'general' category. Non-Hindus, Dalits, and tribesmen made up some 37.5 per cent of the assembly, in keeping with their demographic weight.[32]

The Muslims were not only unrepresentative, but also to some extent unfree. Now, as it happens, the assembly debates themselves, paradoxically, tell us very little about the actual drafting of the Constitution, its attendant contretemps and the pressure brought to bear on lawmakers. Many of its details were hammered out *in camera* by the Congress Assembly Party and its committees. Only then were matters taken up in the assembly, which, the occasional verbal sparring aside, served primarily to authenticate laws placed before it. This was resented by many, including Syed Mohammad Saadulla, a Leaguer on the assembly's Drafting Committee who was soon to jump ship and join the Congress, becoming, as it were, a belated nationalist Muslim. As he noted in a rare, embittered remark that made it to the *Debates*:

> The Drafting Committee was not a free agency. They were handicapped by various methods and circumstances from the very start. We were only asked to dress the baby and the baby

was nothing but the Objectives Resolution [that was virtually entirely the work of Nehru] which this Constituent Assembly passed [in December 1946].[33]

The 'debates', then, if not entirely notional, certainly fell short of the argumentative premise of the word. Procedural concerns were the subject of much discussion, substantive matters less so.

These constraints apart—unrepresentativeness, relative unfreedom—it would be remiss to suggest that the nationalist Muslims had no agency whatsoever. Indeed, it is possible to recognise the obstruction they faced without detracting from the role they played in shaping the Constitution, the minority safeguards regime and electoral system in particular.

'Forget the Past'

Political safeguards—separate electorates; reservations; proportional representation—were systematically dismantled over five set pieces in the two years to May 1949. In each of these, nationalist Muslims— both newly minted, for many Leaguers joined the Congress, and of old—played an important part, even if only through their silence. Azad, in fact, was part of what Austin calls 'the Oligarchy', the quartet—Nehru, Patel, Prasad, and the *maulana*—whose writ ran virtually unchallenged. Speeches by other nationalist Muslims at crucial moments swung the assembly in favour of scrapping safeguards. It could be said, then, that they were the protagonists of their own political marginalisation. This they consented to, speaking in the language of pragmatism and conciliation, for an admixture of communal and personal reasons. The interests of party and nation, along with vocational imperatives, were placed above those of the *qaum*.

But before we move on to the first set piece, a few remarks on the lay of the land—ideologically speaking—are in order. At the outset, the minority rights subcommittee operated with the assumption that separate electorates would survive the transfer of power. After all, they had been a mainstay of Indian political life since 1909. In fact, all those who sat in the assembly had wound up there on the back of separate electorates—Muslim, Sikh, and General. The subcommittee also hoped to reserve seats in Parliament, ministries, and the services. At the time, Muslim opinion was agreed on this. Not that it counted for much—quite literally so. Only one Muslim was represented on the subcommittee of twenty-six: Azad. Interestingly, there were more Parsis—Mody and Sidhwa—on it. The latter accounted for 0.03 per cent of the national population, the former 10 per cent. It was only after Mountbatten announced his partition plan, and a score and a half recusant Leaguers decided to stay on in India, that three of them were inducted into the subcommittee at Patel's instance: Saadulla (who was to join the Congress), Chundrigar and Khaliquzzaman (both of whom were to leave for Pakistan soon after).[34]

How did this quartet fare? On 25 July 1947, eight weeks after the partition plan, Leaguers led by Khaliquzzaman and Dalits by Ambedkar together fought tooth and nail to prevent the scrapping of the principle of weightage, guaranteeing minorities supernumerary representation in legislatures. Azad, true to character, sat out the debate. Weightage was rejected by a vote of nine to four.[35]

But there were limits to such solidarities. Two days later, it was decided twenty-eight to three to do away with separate electorates, the League troika very likely making up the dissenting trio.[36] Azad and the Dalits were against them. Still, he joined the Leaguers in demanding the retention of reservations for Muslims in the services, a proposition accepted nine to seven. While there's no record of who voted how in the subcommittee report, we can make fairly educated guesses based on remarks made in the advisory committee the next day, 28 July.

Moreover, we know that when members of the subcommittee resolved to water down affirmative action by voting eight to seven against reservations for Muslims, Sikhs, and tribesmen for public positions requiring examinations, Muslims across the board declared themselves opposed; Khaliquzzaman and Chundrigar abstained in protest.[37] We also know that Zaheer proposed a system of minority consultation for public appointments, which was carried in the advisory committee on 31 July.[38]

Despairing, Khaliquzzaman then suggested that perhaps it would be better for a few Muslims to 'authoritatively' liaise with the Congress high command than go through the motions in the minorities subcommittee, where, paradoxically, minority voices did not count for very much. He had a point. Eight of its twenty-nine members were caste Hindus. Four were Christians (2.3 per cent of India's population), and three were Anglo-Indians (0.1). In other words, the largest minorities of the Republic—the Muslims (10) and the Scheduled Castes (14) and Tribes (6)—were in a minority in the minorities subcommittee, with a total of nine members between them.[39] Khaliquzzaman's counsel was roundly rejected. So was his proposal to have proportional reservations for all minorities in public employment.[40] Two months later, he left for Pakistan.

In the event, by the time the advisory committee took up the matter up, all was done and dusted. It was decided to dispense with separate electorates and reservations in the ministries. Fifty-five voted against separate electorates for Muslims, and three in favour, possibly the same trinity that defended it in the subcommittee: Saadulla, Chundrigar, Khaliquzzaman.[41] No nationalist Muslims, then. The battle for reservations was left for another day.

Crucially, Patel, chairman of the advisory committee, used the meeting to declare open season on the nationalist Muslims, who, while complaisant (they rejected separate electorates, after all), were evidently not complaisant enough (they still insisted on reservations). A fine insider's account of his machinations is to be found in the Munshi Papers. According to K. M. Munshi, who was witness to these parleys, Patel recruited two northern League rebels, Tajamul Hussain, Shia landlord from Bihar, and Begum Aizaz Rasul, League chief in the UP legislative council and the only Muslim woman in the assembly, to scuttle the work of his party colleagues Azad and Hifzur Rahman, both in favour of reservations.[42]

When Patel tried to reopen the minority question in the committee, Ambedkar interjected, noting that the matter had already been settled. But Patel prevailed. With the Sardar behind him, Hussain, 'in a vehement speech, criticised the nationalist Muslims for seeking reservation', Munshi tells us. 'Indirectly attacking Maulana Azad, [he] urged Muslim representatives to forget the past and help in creating a secular state'. The Shia landlord, in turn, 'emboldened Begum Aizaz Rasul to put her point of view': 'now that

Pakistan had been formed, in the interest of Muslims who are left in the country, it would be better not to isolate [our]selves from the general community by asking for reservations'.[43] How the tables had turned. The nationalist Muslim was now painted as a communalist, the separatist until yesterday now his nationalist traducer.

Patel, for his part, 'sat in stolid silence, interrupting the discussions only by some humorous remark'. His work was done here. Having sown the seeds of doubt, he made out that it was too soon to declare in favour of parliamentary quotas. Why was he so determined to stamp out safeguards for Muslims? Part of it was down to sectional interest. Patel was minister for states, and from 1948, home minister as well. The concern with 'unity' came with the territory. His predisposition militated to the same end. By all accounts an intemperate man, he also had strong feelings on this subject. As he saw it, 'a minority that could force the partition of the country is not a minority at all'.[44] When Syama Prasad Mookerjee wrote to him questioning Muslim 'loyalty' to the Union, playing into a pet peeve of Patel's—'we very often forget the part by some smooth and shallow talks [sic] in which some Muslims now in India indulge, declaring their outward loyalty to India. I feel we are not taking sufficiently strong action to watch their activities and guard against any open or secret revolt organised by them'—the Sardar's reply was unequivocal: 'I entirely agree with you'.[45]

Still, Patel's ambush notwithstanding, the advisory committee report recommended reservations for Muslims in legislatures and the services in August.[46] This was a second volte-face, a 360-degree turn, as it were. First, the subcommittee had called for reserving posts for Muslims in the services; then, when Khaliquzzaman raised the matter, rejected the proposition in the advisory committee; and now, in the report, accepted it again—all in ten days. The pirouetting served the nationalist Muslims well. In the judgement of Ralph Retzlaff, one of the assembly's earliest chroniclers, the August report represented nothing less than 'the high watermark' of the Congress' accommodation to Muslim India. Critically, this came a good two months after the partition plan, by which time the Congress no longer needed to placate minorities with overgenerous schemes.[47] A counterfactual then arises: what might have happened had lawmakers finished their business on schedule and delivered the Constitution that autumn as planned—instead of taking another two years at it? Muslims would probably have had reservations.

'A Very Dangerous Innovation'

As it was, reservations were as far as Azad and his kind were ready to go. When more expansive demands were made twenty days later, stoking the tempers of Hindu Congressmen, nationalist Muslims sat out the controversy. They wanted nothing to do with the bolder electoral reforms that Leaguers were proposing.

In the second set piece in our quintet, the nationalist Muslim is conspicuous by his absence. Azad and his *confrères* did what was expected of them, appearing biddable, nationalistic, and decidedly not sectional. What greater demonstration of unconditional acceptance than silence? Politically speaking, the mantle of representing the *qaum*, then, had fallen on southern Leaguers. Their northern counterparts, since Patel got to them, had become, as it were, nationalist Muslims by osmosis. Hereafter, the most imaginative electoral reforms proposed came from the southern League duo of B. Pocker, the leader of the Malabar Muslims, and Madras' K. T. M. Ahmed Ibrahim, general secretary and brother of the party president Mohammed Ismail. Their *bête noire* was plurality representation, whose distorting effects they endeavoured to dampen.

To this end, on 28 August, Ibrahim recommended that candidates in reserved seats require at least three out of ten votes from the reserved community. For, as K. S. Karimuddin, his colleague from the Central Provinces and Berar, put it, under first-past-the-post, 'even a man of straw, or even a false convert, will be able to defeat a genuine or real member of a community'.[48] The Bengal Leaguer Naziruddin Ahmad appealed to the better instincts of the Hindus: 'no danger or harm can follow if the elder brother [the Hindus] listens to the grievances of the younger brother [the Muslims]', to which Patel replied, riffing on the fraternal metaphor, 'I regret to say that if I lose the affection of the younger brother, I am prepared to lose it because the method he wants to adopt would bring about his death'.[49] To others, too, Ibrahim's scheme, which in the end was defeated, came off as a bit desperate: 'it is nothing but unadulterated separate electorates', a suspicious Shrimati Dakshayani Velayudan, Congresswoman and the assembly's sole Dalit woman, noted of a similar scheme.[50]

But the proposal needs to be placed in context. It did not appear from nowhere, as Ibrahim himself pointed out. It had its antecedents in the recommendations proposed at the Third Unity Conference of 1932.[51] It was also in keeping with the zeitgeist. In both of the Congress' most sustained efforts to craft a constitutional architecture for postcolonial India, there had been safeguards in spades. The Nehru Report of 1928 had promised proportional representation, apparently 'the only rational and just way of meeting the fears and claims of various communities'.[52] The Sapru Report of 1945, similarly, had recommended reservations and a 'parity of representation between Muslims and [caste] Hindus'.[53] The Raj had done its bit, too: since 1925, a quarter of civil service positions were reserved for Muslims; and from 1943 onward, a twelfth—and from 1946, an eighth—for the Scheduled Castes.[54]

In the assembly, however, history could be hastily buried thanks to the Congress' comfortable majority. Not unlike after the French Revolution, this was a chance to start over at Year One. Not just Leaguers but also Dalits proposing a similar scheme were painted as reactionaries. Leading the charge was the Sardar. Patel's philippic deserves to be reproduced *in extenso*:

> Those who want that kind of thing have a place in Pakistan, not here (*Applause*). Here, we are laying the foundations of One Nation ... You have got what you wanted. You have got a separate state and remember, you are the people who were responsible for it ... To the Scheduled Caste friends, I also appeal: Let us forget what Dr Ambedkar or his group have done. You have very nearly escaped partition of the country again on your lines. You have seen the result of separate electorates in Bombay, that when the greatest benefactor of your community [Gandhi apparently] came to Bombay to stay in *bhangi* quarters it was your people who tried to stone his quarters. What was it? It was again the result of this poison.[55]

Patel won out, and both the Muslim and Scheduled Caste schemes were put down, the former in a vote and the latter when its author withdrew it. The 'Anglophone provincialism' of Congressmen, in the words of Perry Anderson, also came to Patel's rescue.[56] Its leaders did not so much as even entertain the possibility of rival electoral systems. For first-past-the-post was familiar, fathomable even to India's illiterate masses, and functional, if one went by the first-world experience of it. Here's Patel: 'this country better adopt the parliamentary system of constitution, the British type of constitution, with which we are familiar'.[57]

The League, then, failed to wean Congressmen off their status quoist Anglophone parochialism. The United Provinces' Aziz Ahmad Khan made the case for the Swiss system, where the federal council—the executive—is elected by the federal assembly. Along these lines, he argued, Indian lawmakers could elect representatives of their faiths to cabinets. Khan enjoyed the support of his entire party—not only hardliners like Ibrahim but also, remarkably, figures like Rasul, who was soon to become Patel's poodle. Karimuddin went further, demanding mandatory coalitions of all parties. The scheme was, in a sense, of a piece with the anti-political worldview of the nationalist Muslims. Needless to say, it was shot down.[58]

Ten days later, two Dalits, Jagjivan Ram and H. J. Khandekar, made another stab at pushing for reservations for minorities in cabinets. This was rejected by a thin majority of eight to seven, indicating that—contrary to what might be inferred from the few but forcefully expressed views in the assembly—there was still considerable support for safeguards. The subcommittee felt it necessary to insert a word of advice into a constitutional schedule: all governments—it recommended in counsel following the Instrument of Instructions of 1935—should attend to minority interests while forming cabinets.[59]

When the matter came up before the assembly on New Year's Eve the next year, opinions ranged from Ambedkar's, who wanted the Instrument to be merely prescriptive, to Naziruddin Ahmad's, who instead wished for it to be justiciable.[60] Importantly, there was no serious questioning of the Instrument itself. Ambedkar's position carried the day. But six weeks before the Constitution was adopted, the Instrument was thrown out of the Schedule. Political norms prevailed over constitutional safeguards. As it was, postcolonial norms were considerably weaker than colonial safeguards. Governors, for instance, had followed the two interwar acts to the letter in providing for 'inclusive' administrations. Jinnah had discovered this the hard way when the League, anything but a cross-section of Indian society, was passed over by the Punjab governor in 1946. Despite having fewer seats Tiwana's Unionist-Congress-Akali coalition, a veritable confessional potpourri, was invited to form a government.[61] No such discretionary powers obtained in postcolonial India, and perhaps understandably so. For no modern democracy built on the legitimacy of electoral validation could justify a system of nomination that rested on the probably more equitable, but certainly more arbitrary, notion of representative fairness.

Another ambitious minoritarian scheme to check executive powers, too, went down in defeat. Here, a belated nationalist Muslim was a bit player. Over the summer of 1948, Ambedkar, Saadulla, and N. Madhava Rau—a Dalit, former Leaguer, and princely state mandarin, respectively; all, in other words, a poor fit with Delhi's new rulers, and, for this reason, more wary than most of unchecked Congress hegemony—tried to drum up support for their innovative, but in the end doomed, scheme to rebalance power between the branches of government. They proposed an advisory board of fifteen lawmakers from both houses, elected by proportional representation, which would act as a break on the executive. Parliament was to step in if differences arose between the cabinet and the board. The amendment, of course, failed to make the cut.[62]

'Slaves of the Congress'

Once more, on 4 January 1949, when the final showdown on first-past-the-post took place, the nationalist Muslims kept at arm's length from the proceedings. Here, again, their silence served but to validate the 'correct' Congress position.

That day, not one of them rose to Hasrat Mohani's bait in the assembly. Addressing the Hindu Congressmen in attendance, the Leaguer insinuated that the 'question of reservation of seats has been raised by the nationalist Muslims who had [*sic*] always been your slaves and slaves of the Congress'. The way he saw it, reservations were a mere ploy to allow Congressmen to burnish their secular credentials by returning unelectable and unrepresentative Muslims to legislatures.[63] Curiously enough, the subjects of his broadside, quiet as mice to a man, issued not even a perfunctory remark to refute him.

Sixteen months had elapsed since our second set piece. Desperation had driven the League to adopt a change of tack. It proposed to substitute proportional representation for first-past-the-post. Two of its more articulate members, Karimuddin and Baig, took the lead. They appeared to have the sympathies of the Akali Dal, the party of the Sikhs. This time around, importantly, the demand was made in universalist spirit, a far cry from the world of confessional crutches, concessions, and compromises. No one could accuse it of being sectional, even if few Congressmen nevertheless did—unconvincingly.[64] To Karimuddin, first-past-the-post was the 'tyranny of the majority'. Proportional representation, on the other hand, 'is not based on religious grounds and it applies to all minorities: political, religious, or communal'.[65] In fact, he was even ready to see the back of the quotas that were so dear to the nationalist Muslims. For him, proportional representation was the only bulwark against the barbarians at the gates: namely, the communists. Here, he betrayed a not atypical mid-century impulse, one common to his class at any rate. An AMU alum for whom lawyering was both a *métier* and an heirloom, Karimuddin was a scion of the Muslim *haute bourgeoisie*. It was either us or the reds, he argued:

> Communism is knocking at our door. We are about to transfer the Government of this country from the middle classes to the wage-earning class ... The Congressmen are of opinion that they are bound to sweep the polls ... They are wrong ... No organization in the world has reconciled the conflicting claims of labour and capital, tenant and landlord ... Look around us, communism is spreading with alarming speed and once it catches the imagination of the working classes, its potentiality is very grave. Suppose the working classes take a fancy for socialist dogmas or communist dogmas, they, being in majority, are bound to capture power ... I want the Congress to live longer

because they have given peace, tranquillity, and a secular state to all the communities in India, but this cannot be guaranteed unless the system of proportional representation is introduced.[66]

Its paradoxical quality aside—improbable League paeans to Congress longevity—his speech was couched in the language of liberalism, not separatism in any sense of the word.

If the Sikhs were on the League's side and nationalist Muslims nowhere to be found, the other minority of some consequence, the Scheduled Castes, by contrast, came hard on the heels of the Congress in their support for first-past-the-post. Here, the Dalit-League minoritarian combine crumbled under the strain of conflicting objectives. Ambedkar was of the opinion that strong and 'stable governments', perforce, demand artificial electoral majorities. He went on to paint a picture of anarchy under proportional representation: governments 'would fall to pieces'.[67] The assembly agreed.

The goodwill earned by the nationalist Muslims in the summer of 1947 by consenting to the scrapping of separate electorates, then, had by early 1949 become a wasting asset.

'They Are More Arabs Than Indians'

Four months later, on 11 May, Patel's insurgents mounted an attack on the *qaum*'s sole remaining safeguard: reservations.

Azad had defended parliamentary quotas in July 1947. Now, in the constitutional endgame, the *maulana* made a stunning volte-face. Whether this was elicited under duress we will never know. But what we do know from the Munshi Papers is that when the question cropped up in the committee, 'the representatives of the nationalist Muslims sat silent'. Azad, apparently, 'had instructed them not to press for reservation'.[68] Here, again, silence was submission by proxy. That silence in this instance, not unlike the Church's on everything from mediaeval slavery to modern clerical paedophilia, was pregnant with meaning is evident. It meant consent to whatever the Hindu party high command saw fit.

At first blush, Azad's silence is surprising in view of his position in four of the eight major assembly committees, not to mention his distinction as the party's longest-serving president. All the same, figures like the *maulana* may have been important men, but they also tended to be self-effacing, and, appropriately enough, they were often effaced. Therein lies the rub for the historian: to write about the nationalist Muslim is to be repeatedly confronted with the silence of one's subject, the uncovering of their agency a journey through so many *cul-de-sacs*. Still, historical fragments leave some room for interpretation.

Two weeks later, when Saadulla insisted that the committee's views were not a reflection of Muslim thinking on reservations, Patel rather tellingly replied:

> Azad is not a cipher: he has a conscience. If he felt that it was against the interests of his community he would have immediately said so and protested. But he did not do so, because he knew and felt that what was being done was right. Therefore, if Mr Saadulla interprets his silence as neutrality, he is much mistaken.[69]

That this needed saying, especially when Saadulla had insinuated no such thing, only hints at the obverse. Recall Nixon's post-Watergate plea, 'I am not a crook', or Indira Gandhi's comment after the Emergency: 'I am not guilty'. Patel's 'Azad is not a cipher' was just another such laboured denial that rang hollow.

It appears, if we are to infer from one of Tajamul Hussain's interventions, that the only Muslim to defend reservations in the committee was his 'honourable friend' Syed Jafar Imam, a Leaguer from Bihar.[70] The two clerics, Azad and Rahman, had maintained a studied silence. The fourth Muslim present was Rasul—more on her below. It seems other nationalist Muslims, both within the assembly and without, were on board.[71] Colonel Bashir Hussain Zaidi, the Shia representative for Rampur who was soon to join the Congress, in a bizarre analogy likened the community to the kind of 'patient who has lost the use of his legs and is given crutches [but] will stick to them even when some good surgeon has given him back the use of his legs ... [Reservations] would make [Muslims] cripples for the rest of their lives'.[72]

All the same, the consensus was not as wide as it appeared. Congressmen needed to find more consenting Leaguers to fend off charges of majoritarianism. But few were prepared to give up both separate electorates and reservations. In the event, Patel had his way, but not without some arm-twisting. This was necessary because Hussain, his usual Muslim confidant, was on a delegation abroad. Once more, then, Rasul was trotted out. She played her part, but the manner in which she did belied consent. On Munshi's testimony, she was inveigled into being the poster-girl of the 'secular' Muslim:

> Begum Aizaz Rasul, afraid of being severely attacked by the nationalist Muslims, could not summon up courage to speak ... Sardar looked at me significantly. I, in my turn, whispered to Begum Rasul, who was sitting next to me, that Sardar expected her to speak. Ultimately, somehow, she summoned up courage and walked up to the lectern. She pleaded in a very hesitant manner for abolition of reservations, [adding that Muslims] should play their part in the general electorate ... No sooner had she resumed her seat than Sardar ... said: "I am very glad that the Muslims are unanimously in favour of joint electorates without reservations. We will now adjourn".[73]

Meaningful glances, hushed tones, hesitant pleas. Only the smoke-filled rooms are missing in this le Carresque landscape. None of this sits well with Patel's comment about unanimity. If anything, it points to the lengths that Congressmen were ready to go to create a semblance of consensus when none existed.

When the advisory committee reconvened, the abolition of reservations was passed fifty-eight to three. Crucially, no Muslim, nationalist or otherwise, was part of the dissenting trio: Saadulla and Hussain were absent; Chundrigar and Khaliquzzaman had left for Pakistan; Imam was in attendance but not a voting member; Azad and Rahman sat out the vote; Rasul was now behind Patel. In fact, all three were Dalits—and they objected not to the abolition *tout court*, but merely to the scrapping of reservations for their ilk. One of them, Muniswami Pillai, put forward an amendment to exempt Dalits, which was accepted. It was then agreed to abolish reservations for all minorities other than the Scheduled Castes.[74]

Pillai's success could have prompted the Muslim elite to follow in his footsteps. But it didn't. Consequently, Dalits would—and still—have seats reserved for them in legislatures, while Muslims did—and still do—not. It must be said that ultimately there was not much, conceptually speaking, that distinguished the Muslim from the Dalit. Both were, in the language of political science, 'ethnic' groups. Both mobilised around these signifiers, forming parties— the Scheduled Castes Federation, the Muslim League—that even as wildly successful enterprises, nevertheless had little purchase outside the party-political setting, where internal differences and caste hierarchies got in the way. That Dalits emerged out of the constitutional settlement relatively unscathed while Muslims did so battered and bruised owed in no small measure to agency.

To be sure, language mattered. As Rochana Bajpai has pointed out, where the Scheduled Castes and Tribes shifted their register to 'backward' classes, demanding reservations to better 'integrate' into national life, Muslims proved singularly incapable of such transhumance between 'secular' and sectional categories.[75] The select few demands they made were presented in terms of difference, disadvantage, and discrimination, all of which, of course, were some distance removed from integration, incorporation, and assimilation—the kind of words India's Hindu leadership would have liked to hear. In other words, the one embraced agency and mobilised around economic backwardness, the other shied away from it and espoused an anti-political worldview.

Still, the contrasts need not be overdrawn. While they fared better than Muslims, Dalits nevertheless lost on separate electorates, quotas in cabinets, the principle of weightage, and the Instrument of Instructions. Subaltern solidarity was rare, and rather easily overcome. Dalits disassociated themselves from 'racial minorities'. As the Congress Dalit S. Nagappa put it: 'well, Sir, I do not claim that we are a religious minority or a racial minority. I claim that we are a political minority'. Muslims, on the other hand, were both religious and racial aliens:

> Really speaking, they do not deserve to be here because they are not Indians. They are more Arabs than Indians; they are more Persians than Indians; they are more Turks than Indians ... We have a right to ask the Mohammedan, the invader, to go out of this country.[76]

As for the Muslim representatives, most of them *ashraf*, they mobilised around cultural difference over economic marginalisation. Here, Pocker's remarks are instructive:

> I say that even if a non-Muslim does his best to do what he can for the Muslim community, to represent their views, he will find it impossible to do so because he is not in a position to realise, understand, and appreciate the actual needs of the members of that particular community, so long as he does not belong to that community ... How would the Hindus feel if the Muslims were to represent their grievances in the legislature and provide effective remedies as regards, say, temple entry, marriage customs, *et cetera*?[77]

Such a Manichaean mindset had allergy to solidarity written all over it. There was no love lost between Muslims and the Scheduled Castes. In his autobiography, Khaliquzzaman notes how the two communities worked at cross-purposes in the advisory committee:

> Both my demands, for separate electorates and reservation in the services, were rejected ... The Scheduled Castes representatives again abstained from voting with us. When lastly the Scheduled Caste matter came up, Dr Ambedkar claimed reservation of seats in the legislature and the services. I was in a temper and opposed both of them on the ground that Scheduled Castes were part and parcel of Hindu society and did not require any separate rights to safeguard their interests. If the Muslims could not claim them, then surely the Scheduled Cases were not entitled to any special safeguards.[78]

In a word, the antipathy was mutual. What, then, of the other important minority community, the Scheduled Tribes? Here's Ambedkar in the *Annihilation of Caste*:

> The Hindu has not realised that these aborigines are a source of potential danger. If these savages remain savages, they may not do any harm to the Hindus. But if they are reclaimed by non-Hindus and converted to their faiths, they will swell the ranks of the enemies of the Hindus ... Apart from the question of whether their exclusion from the new Constitution is proper

or improper, the fact still remains that these aborigines have remained in their primitive uncivilised state ... Not only are they not civilised, but some of them follow pursuits which have led to their being classified as criminals.[79]

Worse, they worship:

demons of all denominations and dead ancestors of all antiquity. Witchcraft, sorcery, animal and human sacrifice make up their religion. Without education, with no idea of Science or of the knowledge of the working of nature, steeped in ignorance and superstition, these Primitive Tribes have been living on the outskirts and in close conformity with civilization in a savage stage which has been their lot for ages.[80]

Torn by mutual prejudice and unconcern, no Muslim-Dalit-Tribe combine emerged to mount an opposition to the caste Hindus. The upshot, inevitably, was an electoral system rigged in favour of the Congress. In the fifties and sixties, with vote shares in the mid-forties, it would control more than two-thirds of Parliament. In the Hindi belt, it would take until 1977, the first time voters returned a non-Congress government, for caste Hindus to be reduced to a minority-majority in Parliament. In short, minorities paid a heavy price for their lack of solidarity in the assembly.

'Muslims are Realists'

Two weeks later on 25 May, it was time for the *coup de grâce*. Ironically for the Leaguers, it was delivered by one of their own—a former Leaguer, more precisely.

The gamut of proposals tabled by the League that day ranged from the unattainable to the realistic. Ismail called for both separate electorates and reserved seats. Very much a last-ditch effort, it was palpable that he was clutching at straws. On the other end was Z. H. Lari's demand for cumulative voting in multi-member constituencies, which, in a bid to mollify the majority, came with an explicit rejection of separate electorates.[81] Saadulla then took to the floor, imploring his Hindu colleagues to accept either of the two schemes, lest risk witnessing very soon the 'sad day' when 'democracy will dwindle into oligarchy'.[82] Perhaps this had been the strategy all along. As if some kind of good cop/bad cop routine, Ismail's scheme was probably meant to provoke indignation, and Lari's to then appear reasonable, the knock-on effect of which, it was hoped, would be the acceptance of safeguards in some form or other.

Whatever was the case, the Congress was not having any of it. Ismail's suggestion was brusquely rejected as impracticable and Lari's shot down after Congressmen ruled it too 'complex' for Indians, illiterates accounting for 88 per cent of them.[83] But Rasul's remark, dredging up the dreaded bugbears of the time, probably hit closer to the real reason why Congressmen were so eager to see the back of Ismail's scheme (and by extension Lari's, too): 'it keeps up [sic] the spirit of separatism and communalism alive'. The basic thrust of her argument was simple enough: constitutional safeguards were, in effect, a form of ghettoisation. They gave 'no chance to the minorities to win the good-will of the majority'.[84] Better, then, to assimilate into the 'mainstream'. 'The majority', it seems, was a polyvalent construct: at once the Republic's Hindu majority and the Congress' parliamentary majority, the will of the people as well as its representatives. Minority safeguards were of no account. Azad, of course, had nothing to say.

Materially, what was in it for Rasul? Certainly, career advancement cannot be discounted. She had ahead of her a long line of sinecures as a Congress politician: a Rajya Sabha seat in 1952, a state cabinet portfolio in 1969, a Padma Bhushan in 2000. To be sure, life came full circle. At death's door—a terminal illness killed her a year after her award—during the Hindu nationalists' first full term in power, she expressed the need for Muslim reservations anew. But this final regret should not detract from a career spent assiduously cultivating Congressmen and appearing 'reasonable' when Islamophobia in party and society was rife. A lifetime consumed and baubles collected, she only lowered her guard on her death bed. Reservations, she hinted at the *fin-de-siècle*, held the possibility of 'improving the educational and socio-economic conditions of Muslims'.[85] In her prime, however, she had struck a different note. 'Muslims are realists', she had said in the assembly: 'They are not a static people and they have no static ideas. They have always advanced with the times'.[86] New realities demanded new thinking, and she was happy to oblige. Note the use of the third person to describe her community, the impersonal pronoun possibly a deliberate contrivance to deflect the charge of communalism.

Nor can her conversion in the assembly be removed from a more personal kind of political agency—a quest not for higher office, but self-realisation. She had had it with the *ulama* and 'conservative old men, steeped in old ideas and so much against women's lib', she wrote in her memoirs, *From Purdah to Parliament*, where she recounted her titular transformation—why bargain with patriarchy when one can reject it?—jettisoning the veil and joining the legislative council in 1937. A *taluqdar*'s wife descended from a family of princely mandarins on one side and Punjabi royalty on the other, she championed the abolition of *zamindari* and the redistribution of land to the 'tenants who toil and sweat'.[87] She was not a prisoner of ascription. Class and faith allegiances were of little account. A contrarian by instinct, her intellectual formation has to be understood as a struggle against her milieu. Doing for separate electorates, then, was just another act of individual emancipation.

What's more, the very existence of the League had become something of a liability. She recalls having felt 'very embarrassed and ashamed' by Khaliquzzaman's departure. 'It was not a gentleman's act', she writes with characteristic restraint. 'We all felt humiliated'.[88] She had the option of joining him. Liaquat, in fact, had written Rasul a warm letter, inviting her to follow in the footsteps of her family, many of whose members had migrated to Lahore. She politely declined the offer.

It was soon decided that the League had 'no utility'—more accurately, that it had outlived its usefulness.[89] By May 1948, its provincial branches across the North had disbanded. Rasul and others, then, were forced to adapt to new realities even as they were in a position to shape them in the assembly. Carping about the Congress could only achieve so much. By contrast, playing a constructive role inside it, even from the margins, could lead to meaningful change. Rasul leveraged her new position as a Congress-friendly Leaguer to get Shastri, the United Provinces' home minister, to tide over the lock-makers of Aligarh, who, in dire straits with the emigration of the middlemen in the lock trade, were set to follow them to Pakistan.

For all that, it is important to register that that she harboured no illusions about tolerance in the new Republic. Far from it. Writing some fifty years after Partition, she tried to disabuse the post-millennial Muslim reader of the notion that life under Vajpayee was worse than it was under Nehru:

> It is not possible for the Muslims of today to realise the conditions of those days ... Even a broken knife found in a Muslim house could send the family to jail ... What difference would a few seats more or less in the legislatures have made for the Muslims if reservation had been retained? It was the goodwill of the majority that was essential.[90]

Rasul was convinced that she was acting in the interest of the greater good. Nehruvian India was no utopia, but if the *qaum* did not bend over backwards to appear eirenic, it could become a considerably worse place for it. At a personal level, the strategy paid off. In the run-up to the first election, Rasul and her husband formally joined the Congress. Both were handed tickets. Nehru even joined Mr Rasul on the hustings once. Both won handsomely. She was elected to the Rajya Sabha. He made it to the UP assembly.[91]

Rasul was not alone. Karimuddin followed her into the Congress, becoming a Rajya Sabha MP in 1954 and spawning a dynasty of nationalist Muslims. A brother would go on to become a Congress MLA in the fifties, two sons-in-law bit players in Andhra Pradesh and Maharashtra, a grandson—in his own words—a 'popular Congress leader from Adilabad'.[92] Tajamul Hussain, too, got on the gravy train. A decade after independence, he was to be found on the benches of the Rajya Sabha as well, this time reincarnated as a Congress die-hard, cheering on Delhi's latest round of preventive detention laws even while decrying that they were, in fact, 'very lenient': 'those detained for traitorous acts should be shot dead. Unless you rule the country with an iron, you can never manage the affairs of the country'.[93] For a leader of the community he once claimed to represent, it was not a very judicious remark. For, as we will see, ordinary Muslims rather effortlessly found themselves accused of treason under the provisions of the Preventive Detention Act. Hussain went on to serve two full terms.

In the final analysis, it was, ironically, an indirectly elected body whose members were selected as representatives of their communities by a tiny electorate—which, in turn, had no mandate from the people to form a constituent assembly—that sealed the fate of political safeguards. Too few, too inconsequential, and too averse to politics proper, the nationalist Muslims were completely out of their depth. Theirs was a worldview where cultural took precedence over political concerns, national trumped sectional interest, meekness was preferred to assertiveness.

The upshot was that they squandered the minoritarian veto bestowed upon them by the Hindu leadership, seeing off political safeguards in their bid to appear loyal, better their career prospects, and focus attention elsewhere. Indeed, if Islam had failed to find a footing at the level of state policy, it could still eke out an existence in Muslim homes. Consequently, they concentrated their energies on the private realm. If the political war had been lost, the culture war could still be won.

'A Juristic Ghetto'

That the *Kulturkampf*, and not political representation, was foremost on the minds of nationalist Muslims should hardly come as a surprise to the reader. Many among their ranks were clerics, and, as such, were steeped in *sharia*-minded juridical thinking. They were also remarkably well organised. Indeed, they had in the Jamiat-ul-Ulema-i-Hind—whose ranks included figures such as Maulanas Azad, Rahman, and Asad Madani—a powerful lobbying outfit that had the ear of government. What's more, in Hindu Congressmen they had strong allies in the assembly. With friends like these, and a well-defined *Weltanschauung* like theirs, it was on foreseeable lines that for all their weaknesses, the nationalist Muslims nevertheless saw through most of their cultural agenda.

First, it was agreed that religions institutions of learning would not be exempt from state aid, allowing *maulvis*, religious teachers, to ply their trade on public payrolls and for Muslim youth to be educated in Urdu in government schools. Second, in deciding on a national language, a compromise was arrived at—to the detriment of the Hindi 'diehards', and by extension to the benefit of the 'moderates'—which gave plenty of room for manoeuvre to minority tongues, Urdu included. And third, it was felt necessary to give the common code a wide birth in consideration of minority sentiments. Consequently, the convergence of the Muslim and civil code proceeded more sluggishly than did the assimilation of secular laws into the Hindu code. By the close of the Nehruvian period, then, the world-historical import of this development was plain to see. Rather improbably, while it received a battering across the Muslim world, in India by contrast, the *sharia* emerged with scarcely a scratch from the upheavals induced by decolonisation, high statism, and secularisation.

Gazing into the future at independence, India's *ulama* had reason to be confident. Certainly, the state was stronger, and its people more Hindu, than ever before. Still, they had history on their side. For while Western Europe had to await early modernity to theorise secularism, South Asia in the early second millennium had already put it into practice.[94] If the Delhi Sultanate and the Mughals had for all practical purposes separated church and state authority, the Raj proved no different. After a few fits and starts in the opposite direction, the colonial state abandoned social reforms soon after the Revolt, formally instituting seven years later a separation of state and personal law, its lineaments sketched out by the clergy.[95] As the decades rolled by, clerical power only grew. The Raj, for the better part a chaotic affair, focussed its legal energies on taming the more consequential property regime, leaving personal law to the *pandits* and *ulama*.[96] At independence, the head-start made for convenient precedent. Lawmakers felt constrained by the regnant legal practices of the time.

Still, at the outset, Hindu opinion militated against state aid to religious institutions of learning. Emblematic was the view of Congressman Damodar Swarup Seth:

> The recognition of minorities based on religion or community is the very negation of secularism. Besides, Sir, if these minorities

are recognised and granted the right to establish and administer educational institutions of their own, it will not only block the way of national unity, so essential for a country of different faiths, as India is, but will also promote communalism, and narrow anti-national outlook as was the case hitherto, with disastrous results.[97]

Generally speaking, Hindu Congressmen treated the rights of linguistic minorities with concern, but those of confessional minorities with contempt. The nationalist Muslims, however, would have none of it. Cultural safeguards had to be defended, even to the exclusion of political safeguards. On 24 July 1947, just four days before Hindu Congressmen made their opening salvo against political safeguards, Rahman and Ansari's minds were elsewhere: 'the Supreme Court should have a Muslim judge to judge the propriety of any cultural right', they wrote in a memo.[98]

As it was, the minority subcommittee declared that 'all minorities' were 'free to establish and administer educational institutions of their choice', and that the government would not, 'while providing state aid, discriminate against schools under the management of minorities based on religion'.[99] Two years later, both provisions found their way into the Constitution as fundamental rights.

Here, it must be said that nationalist Muslims agency remains enshrouded in a thicket of mystery. But we can be certain, all the same, that Azad approved of state aid. A clue lies in one of his rare parliamentary interventions where, as education minister, he set out his policy objectives, one of which was to ensure 'that the mother tongue of the child would be the medium of instruction in primary schools'.[100] Another clue is to be found in a January 1948 speech, in which Azad deployed his characteristically cool sophistry to argue that the remedy for the very Indian malaise of 'religious fanaticism' was not the adoption of a 'purely secular curriculum for government schools'—that would only privatise pious pedagogy—but the embrace of confessionalism. Counterintuitive as this seemed, Azad had a perfectly rational explanation for placing *pandits* and *maulvis* on public payrolls: 'If we want to safeguard the intellectual life of our country against the danger' of religious bigotry, he suggested, 'it becomes all the more necessary for us not to leave the imparting of early religious education to private sources. We should rather take it under our direct care and supervision'.[101]

The provision, admittedly, was a compromise. Lari and the Leaguers would have preferred to go further, but failing Hindu allies—barring a lone Congressman, Kunzru—their efforts to return to an older, more capacious wording were shot down. Initially, it had been agreed that 'minorities in every unit shall be protected in respect of their language, script, and culture, and no laws or regulations may be enacted that may operate oppressively or prejudicially in this respect'. Here's the drafting committee reworking: 'any section of the citizens ... shall have the right to conserve the same'. The burden had shifted from the state to the faithful.[102]

On similar lines, the assembly opted for more universal language on the question of discrimination: the draft constitution changed 'no minority ... shall be discriminated against in regard to admission into state educational institutions' to 'no citizen ...' Many Leaguers felt that this left too little wiggle-room for positive discrimination.[103]

Lari also demanded a right to primary education in one's mother tongue. He noted that his son of six years had returned home from school one afternoon in July 1948 complaining that 'today my master asked me that I should do all the sums in Hindi and Hindi only'. He was 'further told not to bring [his] Urdu book'.[104] But if it was solicitude that Lari was after, he was mistaken. 'You may go to Pakistan', a heckler shouted in response to Hasrat Mohani's defence of his colleague.[105]

It was a revealing comment. It showed that while the Oligarchy could concede state aid, language was an altogether different affair. Here, passions ran high. Since the Congress' decision in 1920 to form provincial committees based on a linguistic criterion—the result of its stubborn refusal to accept the provincial boundaries of the Raj, based as they were on administrative convenience, not on regional identity politics—vernaculars had become veritable weapons. Independence came to mean not only freedom from foreign rule, but from the foreign tongue, too. Congressmen passed resolution after another in praise of Hindi and regional languages—all, curiously, in the language of the metropole.

Taking up the cudgels for local loyalties was always going to be a complicated affair. The dangers of blowback were never far away. To be sure, the Congress tried getting minorities on board. The Karachi resolution of 1931, for instance, promised to protect minority tongues and scripts. During the war, it weighed in favour of mother-tongue instruction. With independence, however, these promises vanished. Protection gave way to self-conservation. Minorities could conserve their languages, unimpeded by state interference. That this was not of the same order as state encouragement and subsidy was not lost on Muslims.

But Urdu was not alone. Telugu speakers in Orissa's borderlands, Bengalis in Bihar's, and Marathi speakers in the Central Provinces', too, struggled to achieve government recognition. But unlike Urdu, they nevertheless found a modicum of state protection in the 'bilingual areas' policy, announced in August 1949. If a fifth of a region's population spoke a minority tongue, it could officially be classed as such. Unfortunately for Urdu speakers, while nationally a force to be reckoned with, the logic of geographic clustering militated against them.

At all events, Leaguers proved utterly incapable of fording these passional marshes. Too outspoken, they came off as too threatening. The nationalist Muslims, by contrast, kept their counsel. It is here, then, that the dividends of complaisance come into full view. It was thanks in no small part to their élan that they scored a victory over intemperate Hindu opinion. Where Lari's bold gambits struck a sour note, they struck a moderate tone, rendering themselves practically invisible and pushing back against Hindi supremacists as part of a large coalition, of which they were only bit players. The final settlement, while not ideal for their pan-Indian elite Muslim *lingua franca*, left considerable elbow room.

It is important to stress how important winning allies across the aisle was to success in the assembly. For instance, Karimuddin convincingly made the case for temperance in concert with Tyagi. Together—the latter arguing in Gandhian terms, the former in the language of the Holy Book, the Quranic being Gandhian *avant la lettre*—they saw through the adoption of prohibition as a 'directive principle': that is to say, it was not made state policy but deemed a worthy ideal for future governments to aspire to.

Likewise, in an opposite scenario, another portent of the juridical and anti-political worldview of the people of the book, nationalist Muslims and Leaguers failed to influence the due process regime. Due process, Saadulla argued, was needed to curb preventive detention, which, since its first use in 1818 in Bengal, had become ubiquitous in the Subcontinent. Since independence, twelve provinces had already passed Public Order and Public Safety Acts to curtail freedoms in the name of the *Rechtsstaat*. Influential opinion—Nehru, Patel—in the assembly was against due process. The Constitution's technocratic draftsman B. N. Rau, under the influence of US Supreme Court justice Felix Frankfurter, was also of the opinion that it was undemocratic. Accountable as they were to the people, the argument went, legislatures were not to be impeded by pesky judges. What's more, were judges to time and again come to the rescue of the people, the juridical regime would breed complacency, and in slackening popular vigilance fatally weaken democracy.

The American experience was instructive. During the Lochner era—the four decades to 1937 that witnessed unprecedented levels of judicial activism by Smithian *laissez-faire* judges—US courts, citing due process, had struck down some 150 pieces of progressive legislation limiting work hours, outlawing child labour, and defending the right to unionise. Liberty of contract trumped worker rights.[106] On Rau's recommendation, then, the drafting committee did away with due process in January 1948.[107] The right kind of alliances, in short, could make even the League's desiderata palatable; the lack thereof, even the nationalist Muslims objectionable.

What of the balance of opinion on the language question? At first, it was agreed that there would be no national language. Instead, Hindi was to serve as the official language—alongside English for fifteen years, after which the foreign tongue was to lose that distinction, unless Parliament decided otherwise—of inter-provincial communication. But what was 'Hindi', as it were? Here, a cleavage developed. To the moderates, to which the nationalist Muslims belonged, Hindi was to be a snapshot of its contemporary usage, a reflection of the cultural and confessional diversity of the Subcontinent—its 'composite culture', as many put it. Because many of them happened to be southerners, they wished the replacement of English to be a long-drawn affair.

The heartlanders—in the main the products of, first, a convent education that they railed against, and, second, Hindu universities at Banaras and Allahabad—by contrast, hoped for an overnight transformation. Further, the Hindi-*wallahs* wanted to rewrite the lexicon with top-down diktat, French-style. Sharing in the conservatism of the Académie Française, they were bent on trading in unedifying loanwords for purer Sanskritisms—incomprehensible to most Hindi speakers. They pushed for making *devanagari* the sole Hindi script. The moderates, meanwhile, struck a more ambivalent note. Like Gandhi, who had resigned from the Hindi Sahitya Sammelan in 1945 to protest its advocacy for *devanagari* over *nastaliq*, they believed in a parity of scripts. 'Hindustani', they believed, could be written in either. Some—Masani, Mehta—even preferred Hindustani in the Latin script.[108]

Given the balance of opinion in the assembly, things looked bleak for the nationalist Muslim initially. After Partition, especially, in the words of K. Santhanam, a Madrasi Congressman, 'the anger against Muslims turned against Urdu'.[109]

If Urdu rankled, so, too, did Hindustani, its very dextrosinistral promise some kind of national humiliation. In mid-July 1947, the moderates were outmanoeuvred in the Congress Assembly Party, which voted sixty-three to thirty-two in favour of Hindi over Hindustani, sixty-three to eighteen in favour of *devanagari*.

But the Hindi-*wallahs'* extremist bluster in the event proved to be their Achilles' heel. Symptomatic of their smugness was Seth Govind Das: 'I want to tell my brethren from Madras that if after twenty-five years of efforts on the part of Mahatma Gandhi they have not been able to understand Hindustani, the blame lies at their door'.[110] Funnily enough, his vituperation, delivered in Hindi, was lost on most southerners, and Ayyar had to put in a request for a translation. Moreover, the Hindi-*wallahs* began haemorrhaging support once the Hindi translation of the constitution got underway. Replete with Sanskrit neologisms and scarcely coherent, it elicited an interesting response when it dropped in Nehru's lap. The first premier, a native speaker, famously 'did not understand a word of it'.[111]

There was another practical impediment: namely that a bilingual constitution was a logistical nightmare. For one thing, the grafting of common law required a sensibility that rested on its framing in English. Hindi had cadences entirely of its own, which came with a worldview utterly unequipped to handle such an operation. For another, a constitution in multiple languages would throw up impossible dilemmas of interpretation and precedence.

If intransigence was their undoing, the Hindi-*wallahs'* defeat was hastened by the handmaiden of political agency, the nationalist Muslim's included. For both Azad and Saadulla found representation on the language committee. Working from within an entente was at once a rewarding and frustrating experience. Rewarding: their presence signalled their usefulness to the Hindu leadership. Frustrating: a seat at the high table did not guarantee that their voices were heard. Ginger group or window-dressing? Which side the scales tilted towards became clear when talks broke down over which numeral system to adopt. The moderates threw their weight behind Arabic numerals, Hindi-*wallahs devanagari* ones. In considering the lexical sources of Hindi, the former wanted to include Hindustani and Urdu alongside Sanskrit. The latter refused to budge.

Disappointed, Azad resigned from the language committee over the impasse. 'I would like to tell you that by accommodating Urdu the heavens will not come down', he tearfully lamented in the assembly. 'Urdu is one of the Indian languages. It was born and bred and brought up in India and it is the mother tongue of millions of Hindus and Muslims'. He went on to proffer a potted history of Hindustani and a genealogy of Arabic numerals that placed 'India's' contribution at the heart of it. 'Vedic physicians' apparently brought 'Indian numerals' to the court of the Abbasid caliph, Al Mansoor, in the eighth century, which, in the event, became 'famous as Arabic numerals'. 'These numerals are India's own'. What of the national lexicon? Here, again, Azad was at his persuasive best. 'Languages are never made, they evolve ... The law of language is beyond your reach. You can legislate for every other thing but not for ordering its natural evolution', he rebuked the Hindi-*wallahs* for their philological artifice.[112]

This was one of Azad's lengthiest interventions. Language, incontrovertibly, was an issue dear to him in a manner that more pointedly political questions—representation, affirmative action— were not. This imbalance—silence on political safeguards, speech after speech on cultural ones—is clear enough indication of the preoccupations of the nationalist Muslims. Mohani, meanwhile, was the mirror image of his fellow-*maulana*. While Azad punctiliously pursued a *via media*, the League cleric pursued a zero-sum game. The obduracy was surely a sign of disinterest. 'Thoroughly disgusted by the policy of appeasement adopted by Azad', Mohani had thrown up his hands in despair: 'I shall simply oppose the whole thing'.[113]

To be sure, there was more to their mutual dislike. There was bad blood. In December 1947, the two clerics had had an especially bitter palaver at the Carlton. Suspicious as ever of anything resembling politics proper, Azad had counselled depoliticisation. 'Terminate all political activity' and 'merge into the Congress'. Mohani was furious. As he wrote in his diary:

> I took a dig at Abul Kalam which was like a cold douche to all his scheming, and which made him extremely annoyed. I said, 'you are doing exactly what Sir Syed did in 1857. In order to allay the suspicions of the British Government, he urged the Muslims to concentrate purely on educational and social matters and to pledge political loyalty to Britain. Exactly in the same way you, in 1947, are preaching to Muslims unconditional loyalty to the Congress and are determined that Islamic organisations shall confine themselves to social matters'.[114]

Eventually, the language question was settled behind closed doors. Whether Azad's resignation was of any import we will never know. At worst, it was entirely ignored, which would once again point to his peripheral position. At best, it fostered some kind of *mea culpa* and then a change of tack. The *maulana* certainly seemed to think that this was the case. 'After my resignation this question was raised in the committee afresh and an effort was made to introduce breadth of vision in solving the problem to a certain extent', he explained to the assembly. 'The amendment of Mr Ayyangar was a product of this effort'.[115] No one contradicted him. There is, perhaps, an element of truth here, which makes Azad's demission one of the first, and most remarkable, instances of nationalist Muslim agency in postcolonial India.

The Munshi-Ayyangar formula—Hindi in *devanagari*, Arabic numerals—left the door ajar for Urdu. What's more, it simultaneously slammed it shut on the ultra-Sanskritised declension of Hindi. Indeed, it was to serve, culturally speaking, as an important bulwark against the worst instincts of Hindu majoritarianism, premised as it was on a trinity of monolithic logics: Hindi, Hindu, Hindustan. Under its terms, Parliament could extend the fifteen-year period in which English held equal status to Hindi. A few concessions were made along the way: lexically, Hindi would draw 'primarily on Sanskrit and secondarily on other languages'.[116] But then again, Hindi was meant to reflect the 'composite culture of India'. On 12 September 1949, the assembly accepted the formula.

In the end, then, there was a surfeit of cultural safeguards in the Constitution: the right to proselytise was recognised (in Article 25), to establish religious institutions and charities (26), preserve scripts and tongues (29), and run religious schools (30). While the nationalist Muslims certainly did not make the running—given the circumstances and their disposition, they could not help but be accompanists rather than soloists—their inputs and desiderata dovetailed with the constitutional settlement.

What of the *sharia*? Here, the nationalist Muslims secured a victory by stealth. Indeed, the cool acceptance of Muslim personal law appeared to come from nowhere. For one thing, the nationalist Muslims were completely absent from the discussion on the civil code. The *Constituent Assembly Debates* record not a single intervention. The only Muslims who weighed in were Karimuddin, Ismail, Baig, Pocker, Imam, and Ahmad—all Leaguers. Nor is there any trace of the nationalist Muslims in B. Shiva Rao's study on *The Framing of India's Constitution*, which, along with its four-volume pendant, *Select Documents*, ever so often ventures behind the scenes. Here is Tahir Mahmood, author of over a dozen studies on constitutional history and Muslim law: while 'it is claimed by

111

some Muslims that Azad and Kidwai did not favour the idea of a uniform civil code, no authentic account of their opinion on the subject is, however, available'.[117]

The late colonial record bespeaks clerical urgency, the postcolonial one nothing at all. It is a puzzle. In the assembly, meanwhile, lawmakers made much of the 'sentiments of the Muslim community', which, apparently, were always in need of reassuring once the trigger words—'uniform civil code'—were uttered.[118] Leaguers had their fears, to be sure. But these, as we have seen, often went ignored on the floor of the assembly. It can be conjectured, then, that all the concern with allaying minority distress hints at points of pressure that have been rendered invisible by the archive. Perhaps the nationalist Muslim penchant for working clandestinely has led to this erasure.

The Parsi Congressman Minoo Masani's stab at incorporating the establishment of a uniform civil code into the directive principles was stealthily nipped in the bud. On 30 March 1947, the fundamental rights subcommittee shot down his proposal five to four. The next day, for good measure, the directive principles were made non-justiciable in the courts; in contrast to fundamental rights, these were now to be merely prescriptive. When Masani and two of his subcommittee allies, Amrit Kaur and Hansa Mehta, brought the matter up in July, insisting that the question be reopened in light of Partition, they were once again frustrated. The common code remained—and remains—a directive principle, a neglected desideratum for the progressive Left and Hindu Right detested by every consequential political current in between.[119]

Leaguers, on the other hand, hoping to convert the *de facto sharia* victory into a *de jure* one, ended up overplaying their hands. Less inhibited about affronting Congressmen, but also for this reason alienating them, Baig and Ismail demanded an unequivocal disavowal of state 'interference' in personal law. Needless to say, the proposal was still-born. All the same, Baig found a somewhat receptive audience, if not when he called for the civil code to be struck off the directive principles, then certainly when he defended separate religious codes to govern the private lives of Indian citizens:

Now, sir, people seem to have very strange ideas about [*sic*] secular state. People seem to think that under a secular state, there must be a common law. That is not the correct way to look at this secular state. In a secular state, citizens belonging to different communities must have the freedom to practice their own religion, observe their own life and their personal laws.[120]

Such was the *mentalité* of the assembly. While few would have cared to admit it, the Leaguer, nationalist Muslim, and Hindu Congressman were one when it came to the autonomy of personal laws. The task that India's postcolonial rulers had set for themselves—sharing in the vision of their colonial predecessors—was not to create a state that had no time for religion, but to cede enough space to confession as to rule unimpeded by fanaticism. 'Communalism' was the problem. Religion was not. Its codes in the private sphere, then, were mostly harmless, even if they did not conform to the egalitarian pretensions of progressives.

Keeping personal laws one step removed from the state helped maintain eirenic church-state relations, so the argument went. By forsaking a *Kulturkampf*, and letting *pandits* and *maulvis* score an easy victory, India's rulers were conserving their energies for what they felt were worthier causes, *inter alia*, the consolidation of borders, quashing of the *zamindars*, constitutional advance. Reform, then, had to come from within communities, not imposed from on high. If the *qaum* wished to preserve the *sharia* for a bit, so be it. It was left to future parliaments to decide.

It helped that personal laws had become immutable by force of habit, closing the roads to radical reform. The Congress had no intention of overturning Anglo-Muhammadan law, a late-eighteenth century contrivance first used by the East India Company to secure local cooperation at a time when it had no state apparatus to speak of. More importantly, its hybrid nature—signalled by the brigading of 'Anglo' and 'Muhammadan'—pointed to a fledgling division of labour that came of age during the second half of the nineteenth century. Public law—matters governing commercial life, taxation, and such like—became decidedly British. Conversely, private law became emphatically native. Muslim personal law was happily outsourced to *qazis*. From 1772 on, the Company was committed to enforcing in the private realm—marriage, inheritance, succession—'the laws of the Koran with respect to the Mohamedans, and those of the Shaster with respect to the Gentoos'.[121]

In the event, barring a brief mid-century utilitarian hiccup, when attempts were made to reform religious practices, the British 'ruled on the cheap', leaving clerics to their own devices.[122] To be sure, the colonial state undermined Muslim clerical authority in all sorts of ways, subordinating *qazis* to English magistrates and substituting English for Persian in 1832. But, on balance, the relinquishment of the private realm to the *qazis* and *ulama* made them stronger.

After the Revolt detonated, nearly every vestige of 'Islamic' law was excised from public law books. But unsurprisingly, the personal code—as systematised and simplified in the late eighteenth century—remained untouched. It was no accident, then, that the new generation of politically conscious Muslim lawyers identified whole-heartedly with the spavined *sharia* of Anglo-Muhammadan law. In a world of flux, no greater certitude existed than the reassuringly 'Muslim' personal code.

Two centuries after the 1772 edict, religious personal laws had become a habit of mind. Indeed, the *khadi*-clad nationalists in power could not quite shake off this most colonial of institutions, a telling instance of the internalisation—or, in Frantz Fanon's famous formulation, *épidermisation*—of the thought-world of the coloniser by the colonised.[123] Unable to unfetter themselves from the logic of Hindu and Muslim codes, they were prisoners of their cognitive constraints. The nationalist Muslims did not need to go out of their way to recruit lawmakers to their cause. That would have meant preaching to the converted. Indeed, the common code never had a fighting chance in the assembly.

* * *

All the same, depoliticisation and juridification were to cast a long shadow. Indeed, the nationalist Muslim's silent acquiescence to first-past-the-post was nothing if not a suicide note on behalf of the community. 'Better not isolate ourselves', Rasul had argued while doing for political safeguards. Ironically enough, plurality voting did precisely that, rendering the community's representatives as veritable Robinson Crusoes.

On the cultural question, by contrast, the postcolonial years were kind to the nationalist Muslims. In the early fifties, Nehru busied his administration with his protracted, and ultimately not particularly successful, stab at reforming Hindu personal law. No commensurate effort was made to bring Muslim personal law in line with the times, which was to become a sore point for Left feminists and Hindu nationalists alike.[124]

During his final years in office when, egged on by the Cambridge-trained progressive jurist A. A. A. Fyzee, Nehru made his eleventh-hour bid to reform the *sharia*, nothing came of it. Fyzee had been pressing the premier to follow the lead of the Muslim world and modernise India's ossified Muslim personal laws. Indeed, across the crescent from Morocco through Libya and Lebanon to Pakistan, Muslim personal laws were being rewritten wholesale. At the close of the Nehruvian period, for instance, only in Saudi Arabia, Iran, Indonesia, and India did polygamy enjoy state sanction. Two issues animated him in particular. First, he found it unjustifiable that Muslim women leaving their faith were denied the right to divorce. Second, he felt triple *talaq*—instant divorce, secured by the husband's invocation of the very word thrice—to be 'unjust to the point of absurdity'. Only Parliament, he believed, could reform Muslim law. The courts, inevitably, would lose themselves in a quagmire of minutiae. Nehru, however, left the business of reviewing the reforms to a judicial commission, the Committee on Muslim Personal Law, convened in 1962. In the event, the vice president Zakir Husain's discomfiture, together with the unease expressed by Aligarh's leading lights, killed off the initiative.[125]

It was not until the eighties that a serious threat emerged to Muslim personal law, which, in the event, was quickly put down when Parliament, pressured by Muslim politicians and clerics, passed the ironically titled Muslim Women (Protection of Rights on Divorce) Act of 1986, reversing the offending Supreme Court judgement that had allowed a Muslim divorcée to claim alimony through a Code of Criminal Procedure provision that worked at cross-purposes with Muslim personal law.[126] Triple *talaq* was criminalised only in 2019.

3

EMINENT NEHRUVIANS

As in the assembly, so in government. Here, too, was the same forbearance. A quietist élan certainly had its uses, it is true. It was also in keeping with the zeitgeist. It dovetailed with contemporary political science orthodoxy, which held that assertive minorities, for they were feared, inevitably generated majoritarian backlash; better, then, to work from within larger parties and institutions.[1]

The Indian setting, of course, was no stranger to this dynamic. Indeed, for the forty million Muslims left behind in India, the early postcolonial period was a time of unprecedented Islamophobia. 'The vast majority of the Muslims in India were not loyal to India. For such people, it was better to go to Pakistan', Patel had counselled Gandhi in September 1947.[2] It was not an uncommon opinion. But nationalist Muslims had to put up with more than disdain. Their Hindu colleagues routinely cast aspersions on their very status as nationalist Muslims. Patel, underscoring what he felt was the category's incongruous character, noted that 'there is only one genuinely nationalist Muslim in India—Jawaharlal'.[3] The rest—actually existing Muslims—by contrast, were not. But the Congress was also the bulwark against a more belligerent Hindu confessionalism, a point highlighted in 1948 by Pant, the chief minister of Uttar Pradesh who purged the state's services of Muslims and oversaw bans on anti-RSS protests:

Muslims 'should try win over the good will of the majority ... if they persisted in their old ways, the establishment of a purely Hindu raj was inevitable'.[4]

How, then, did these eminent Nehruvians navigate these troubled waters? The picture that emerges from the prosopography that follows is a grim one. Influential at the time of Khilafat, not inconsequential in the assembly, later in government their decimation was complete.

Recovering nationalist Muslim agency in this period is a tough ask, for, as it happens, there isn't much agency to speak of in the first place. The three lives presented here form a pendant to Azad's, which opened the previous chapter. All three struggled to have their voices heard. They had to put up with insufferable colleagues, who routinely doubted their loyalty to party and country; intractable ministries, which they were given only because it was a polite way to put them out to pasture; and incorrigible factionalism, in which they could not partake on account of their Muslim character, Hindu caste groups being the building blocks of Congress coalitions.

'Just Like a Dog'

Faute de mieux, the nationalist Muslim had to swallow his pride—and he did, but not without rancour. In 1948, for instance, when a surprised Syed Mahmud had his car stopped and searched by the police for arms, he fired off a missive to a Hindu party colleague of his. 'Half my life I had to suffer humiliation as a Congressman at the hands of the British Government. Now it seems for the remaining period of my life I will have to suffer indignities and insults at the hands of the Congress Government'. Mahmud, moreover, had not been singled out for this treatment. 'Even Muslim ladies of high families have not escaped insult ... even the cars of your lieutenant-governor of police, excise commissioner and other high Muslim officials of the Secretariat have been searched', he wrote. 'This, I think, is the limit'.[5] But it wasn't. Even at the close of the Nehruvian period, Mahmud could be found railing against the future deputy prime minister Morarji Desai for 'hurting nearly the whole Muslim community' and snubbing him at the Democratic Convention: 'even if I were a stranger, I [am] one of the oldest Congressmen alive and, if I am permitted to say, once a leading Congressman. Was it not due me that you should have given me an opportunity to explain to you my conduct? I think you regard me a sinner or a communalist'.[6]

What, then, made men like Mahmud stay on? Evidence from their private papers suggests that their association with the country's Hindu rulers was a mixed bestowal—in other words, not without its advantages. To be sure, Nehru and his party men often turned a deaf ear to their demands. Moreover, in factional struggles, they rarely came out on top. Furthermore, their ability to effect social change was niggardly at best; to shape high-political outcomes, even poorer. Still, as the adage goes, something was better than nothing, and personal rapport did indeed count for something.

Mahmud, for one, got considerable mileage from his friendship with the Nehrus, though by no means could it be said that he owed his career to the first family. His was an archetypal nationalist Muslim background. Hailing from a 'respectable *zamindar* family' in Bihar, Mahmud passed through Aligarh, Cambridge—where he read history and became 'fast friends' with Nehru—and Münster, where he finished a PhD, before rising to prominence as a *protégé* of Mazharul Haq's, whose niece he married, and serving on the Khilafat Committee.[7] Early on in his life, he learnt the importance of securing support on the other side of the communal aisle from his brother-in-law, Mohammad Oomar, a councillor from a 'purely Hindu ward', a lesson that was to prove of great use once he began his swift ascent in the Congress.[8] Mahmud carved a spot for himself as a Muslim man on the Left, forming the Muslim National Congress alongside Ansari in 1929 and calling for the abolition of *zamindari* and the implementation of the Wardha Scheme, encountered above.

In the late forties, he kept a steady correspondence with Nehru, who on many occasions sought his advice—as did the premier's daughter, to whom he was 'Mahmud Chacha'. At the time of riots in Bihar in early 1947, Nehru sent Mahmud, then a minister in the provincial government, Rs 5,000 to 'use for relief work in Bihar according to your discretion', independent of official channels. Impressed with his work, Nehru sent more cash his way from his own account, despite not being 'very flush with money at present'.[9]

If working outside the framework of the state, even as they held positions in government, gave their relationship a distinctly premodern colour, so, too, did the nature of their friendship, marked as it was by a bond of fealty. Mahmud's biographers note that he was 'the older man, but in practice his was the subordinate position in the relationship; an arrangement which he fully accepted and acknowledged from the very beginning'. This they put down to his character: 'Mahmud was an emotional man, lacking in self-confidence, responsive to appeals to his affections rather than to his intellect'.[10] Instead it appears to me that Datta and Cleghorn have stumbled upon a broader phenomenon. For many other nationalist Muslims—from the later Azad through Kabir, Kidwai, Zakir Husain to Fakhruddin Ahmed—seem to have been cut from the same cloth. For this constellation, as with their forebears and successors, there was a tendency to mute their demands and privilege party discipline and loyalty over all else. Mahmud made this clear when he wrote to Nehru on the occasion of his thirty-fifth birthday: 'Now the only present that I can offer is my life-long devotion and fidelity to you and to the Nehrus. I am painfully conscious of the worthlessness of my devotion, but then, my boy, just like a dog I have nothing else or better in my possession to give my master—a thought which sometimes makes me bitter and sad'.[11] Mahmud went on to christen his son Jawaharlal, a patently Hindu name that riled up his Muslim friends and even embarrassed the eponymous friend: 'For heaven's sake, don't call your son Jawaharlal', Nehru wrote Mahmud.[12] The nationalist Muslim had his way.

Personally, Mahmud profited from the premier's patronage. Such declarations of canine loyalty earned him the post of minister of development and transport in the Bihar government in 1946—despite his fall from grace only two years earlier, when, as we have seen, his *faux pas* resulted in his denunciation as a fifth-columnist British collaborator—and union minister of state for external affairs in 1954. Politically, all the same, he failed to have his voice heard in the administration. Indeed, despite being *the* heavyweight Muslim leader of the Congress in Bihar—Azad had no following in his native state and was elected from Rampur, UP—Mahmud found his advice routinely rejected. In 1949, he called for an alliance with Pakistan aimed at containing China, renewing his call for 'joint defence' in Parliament four years later. The plan was welcomed by prime minister Mohammad Ali Bogra, but not his Indian counterpart. Nehru 'was not sympathetic'. During his stint at the MEA, Mahmud was often sent as an emissary to the Middle East, but when he tried being more proactive, he was similarly rebuffed. In 1953, for instance, Nehru shot down his bid to take part in the World Peace Conference in Vienna, where he hoped to open channels with Karachi. The 'so-called' peace conferences were 'bare communist propaganda' came the curt reply—'if you go there ... you will just increase the prestige of the Communist Party here'. In any case, participation in a Soviet summit was pointless: '[Pakistan foreign minister] Zafrulla [Khan] has been anxious to tie up with the United States for a long time'.[13]

If he failed to make his mark in foreign policy, his domestic political clout was a shrinking asset. In 1957, he was dropped from the council of ministers, leaving him to grumble that he had been 'discarded by the Congress'.[14] 'There is a great criticism in new persons not being taken in and the same persons continuing', Nehru explained.[15] This logic, however, did not apply to, *inter alios*, Nityanand Kanungo, Manubhai Shah, Keshav Malaviya or Surendra Dey—Mahmud's contemporaries who rose to higher offices despite their incumbency. The last straw was in 1961, when he failed to place his men on Nehru's National Integration Council. The next year, he failed to get them nominations ahead of the polls.[16]

Mahmud's efforts to represent the *qaum* from outside similarly floundered. Hoping to influence the Muslim predicament through pressure groups, he headlined the Muslim Convention of 1960, calling for proportional representation and trying to bring to the North the kind of assertive politics that had already taken root in the South. Yet it was in the North that the backlash was the strongest. Indeed, Mahmud, along with a Congress colleague of his, A. Q. Ansari, found themselves routinely arraigned as communalists. A sometime Bihar PCC president and leader of the Momins—Muslim weavers—Ansari, too, felt that Muslim interests were best advanced both from without (he led the All-India Momin Conference) and from within; he founded the Congress Muslim Front, a ginger group that sought to 'cure the Muslim League mentality, which still exists among a large body of Muslim masses', a hangover from the forties when 'Muslims alone were injected with the virus of two-nation theory' [*sic*].[17]

As it was, the work of the Front consisted primarily of discrediting the *ashraf* leadership and supplanting it with men who shared Ansari's backward-caste background. For A. M. Noor, another of its conveners, 'aristocratic Muslims' had no place in the Congress. They were 'fifth-columnists'. This was a thinly veiled attack on his rival, Jafar Imam, law minister and a Leaguer of old.[18]

But they were ironically hoist with their own petard. Both Mahmud and Ansari were made targets by K. B. Sahay and M. P. Sinha and their ruling faction of the Bihar Congress, which, as part of a new programme, had decided to take a 'tough' line on communalism. Imam and the *ashraf* hitched themselves to this wagon, the law minister even turning the stick in the opposite direction, insisting that it was the Front that was the 'separatist organisation', not his clique, which worked with Hindu Congressmen and had little time for identity politics.[19]

The author of the piteous letters to the premier we saw above, then, was in the eyes of his party colleagues less the loyalist than the Leaguer of yesterday. This was the conundrum of the nationalist Muslim. For every Mahmud, there was another Imam. This was not merely a party-political problem. Rather it was a reflection of a deeper social malaise. In Rajasthan, for example, against the backdrop of the Indo-Pakistan war of 1965, the cleric Asrarul Haque was to be found calling for the imprisonment of his *confrères*. He wrote to Nehru demanding that all 'suspected Indian Muslims with the [*sic*] anti-national and communal leavings [*sic*] be interned without any delay', before hastening to add that 'Muslims of this country would shed their last drop of blood in the defence of the motherland'.[20]

If Hindu leaders held the *qaum* to a higher standard of nationalism, such declamations suggest that some Muslims hoping to curry favours with the regime did so too. Whether this was on account of a culture of fear, snitching, or opportunism, or perhaps a combination of all three, can be speculated. The upshot, however, was clear. No nationalist Muslim was above suspicion.

Unsurprisingly, Mahmud's postcolonial career was marked by a gradual drift towards the opposition, even if he left the Congress to join the Majlis-e-Mushāwarat only in 1964. Certainly, he was not afraid to break party ranks by lending a hand to the competition. In the fifties, he helped Sheikh Abdullah—the leader of the National Conference incarcerated by Nehru for demanding a plebiscite on Jammu and Kashmir's accession to the Republic, as had been agreed upon in 1947—find a 'suitable counsel' to aid him in his legal battles with the local magistracy.[21] For all that, even during his Mushāwarat years, Mahmud continued to view the Congress in a positive light, attempting, whenever the occasion arose, to influence its Muslim policy from without. And in 1968, three years before his death, he resigned from the pressure group once it entered the electoral fray on its own terms.[22]

'For the Few'

Humayun Kabir's career followed a similar trajectory. Like Mahmud, he, too, hoped to reconcile Congressmen and Leaguers to one another early in his career; enjoyed a good rapport with his party's Hindu leaders; failed in his efforts to lobby the high command for more substantive benefits for the *qaum*; became disillusioned with the Congress; and in the mid-sixties, just a few years before his death, left the party and struck out on his own. While in the final analysis, the Bengali fared marginally better than the Bihari, there was more that was common in their careers than has generally been recognised.

This is perhaps because Kabir was not one of nature's nationalist Muslims. Born to a family of mandarins, he read Modern Greats at Exeter, Oxford, before rising to prominence in the trade union movement, representing railwaymen and dockers. In 1937, he stood on a KPP ticket and lost to Tamizuddin Khan, a Leaguer who went on to become speaker of Pakistan's Constituent Assembly. Luckily an assembly seat in Bengal opened up a few months later, which he comfortably won. It was only during the closing months of the Second World War that he joined the Congress, when Azad, then party president, brought him in as his political adviser. After independence, Kabir reprised this role in the education ministry when the *maulana* came to head it, all the while consolidating power in the 24 Parganas.

Like Mahmud, Kabir initially tried to push the Congress into a more ecumenical direction. As we have seen, his efforts to forge a pact between the Congress and the KPP in 1937 came to nought. A decade later, in November 1947, alongside S. A. Brelvi, editor of the *Bombay Chronicle*, and Dr Z. A. Ahmed, Communist Party of India leader and Congress alum, Kabir embarked on a new mass contact campaign, as it were, calling upon Muslims to join the Congress. This time around, he found his Hindu colleagues more obliging. It helped that, on account of factionalism induced by the flood of east Bengali Hindu politicians into India, Bidhan Chandra Roy's control over the Congress was weaker than before Partition. He was not in a position to be picky.

All the same, disappointment came early. As Kabir was to discover, the League entryists were much more powerful figures than their nationalist brethren. In 1950, Jehangir Kabir, his brother, was deselected despite his loyalty and long record as a Congressman. The assembly ticket instead went to a neophyte, one of the insurgents defecting from the League.[23]

Still, just as Mahmud did, Humayun Kabir ably made use of his good rapport with the party's Hindu bosses to secure government positions for his familiars in the fifties. He was able to lobby Roy to hand out one of the three Rajya Sabha seats on offer in 1952 to a Muslim. Four years later, he demanded at least two of the 'eleven or twelve' seats in the legislative council for the *qaum*, and a third—here Kabir appeared to be building bridges with other minorities—for 'a Christian or a Buddhist'.[24] In 1962, Kabir could be found petitioning Nehru—unsuccessfully as it turned out—to have the Rajya Sabha MP Mustafa Rashid Shervani inducted into the cabinet.[25] Kabir's advocacy for Muslims was not confined to electoral politics. In 1958, for instance, we find him asking Nehru to give M. N. Masud, Azad's private secretary, a 'permanent post in government'. On another occasion, Kabir called on him to have the nonagenarian maestro Ustad Alauddin Khan play at a state banquet. On yet another, he introduced him to the director of the Dairatu'l Ma'arif, the publication arm of Osmania University in Hyderabad, which was 'doing some outstanding work in the field of Arabic and Persian scholarship'.[26]

Such efforts at securing descriptive representation for Muslims was complemented with more substantive concerns. Early in his career, Kabir used his platform at the education ministry to help establish an engineering college at Kollam and a polytechnic for women in Malabar, both created with the intention of opening up technical education opportunities for Muslims.[27] Convinced that 'it is through education that integration has been achieved' in the most successful of multi-ethnic states—the United States and the Soviet Union, in his opinion—Kabir put himself to the task of touring foreign capitals—Kuala Lumpur, Dacca, Canberra, Moscow, Belgrade, Bonn, London, Paris, Cairo, Damascus, Jerusalem, Athens, and Rome—during his tenure as minister for scientific research and cultural affairs to study how his peers were handling the minority question.[28] In each place, a careful study was followed by a detailed report to the prime minister.[29] Not only 'social mixing' in schools, but also positive discrimination 'at all levels, especially in medical, engineering, and technological studies' was the way forward, he concluded.[30] In Parliament, Kabir often called attention to Islamophobia. In 1967, for example, he brought to the house's attention the 'harassment' of 50,000 Muslims who returned from Pakistan to Jammu and Kashmir.[31]

In essence, Kabir's interventions, and those of the nationalist Muslims in general, concerned, in Berlin's famous distinction, the pursuit of negative freedom—here, against discrimination by the state—as opposed to positive freedom—for instance, more state intervention to secure justice and equality through protest and mass organisation.[32]

There was only so far the politics of circumscription could take the nationalist Muslim. Apart from helping out fellow members of the Muslim elite and occasionally decrying discrimination, much of what they did was only of symbolic importance. Symptomatic of the kind of allusive Muslim politics that thrived in Nehru's India was the concern with monuments. Here, the objective was to reassert their use as a communitarian, instead of public, space. Kabir's protest in 1958 at the use of the Red Fort for 'civic receptions' was an early instance of the politicisation of monuments. Places like the Red Fort were in effect 'living monuments', not unlike temples or mosques, and accordingly ought to be treated as such, Kabir wrote to Nehru. 'No dinners, lunches, or parties should be held in such tombs, as they involve an element of gaiety, which is inconsistent with the funerary associations of the monument'. It was, of course, hard for the prime minister to take his plea seriously. Understandably, nothing came of it.[33]

All the same, by the seventies, petitions like Kabir's had become an accepted idiom of Muslim politics. In 1974, Muslim notables wrote to Devaraj Urs, chief minister of Karnataka, demanding that the Sixteen Pillar Mosque at Bidar Fort, under lock and key at the ASI's instance, be opened to worship. Urs forwarded the letter to Indira Gandhi, who noted her reservations. The 'conservation of heritage' benefitted the many, whereas the mosque's use 'as a place of worship served only a few'.[34] But that was precisely the logic of Muslim demand. They were, after all, mobilising as a minority—in the name of the 'few'. To no avail.

In 1981, Mrs Gandhi turned down a similar demand—Delhi Muslims wanted to use the mosque next to the Safdarjung Tomb as a 'site of worship', that is, they wanted it to be free of charge for Muslims not just on Fridays, but every day—opining that the 'use of national heritage for such ends could only be damaging'.[35]

All the same, weaponising monuments was not entirely without valence. As we will see in Chapter 7, the politics of monuments was closely tied to both religious authority and private property, contestations that could descend into riots. Such disputes, in other words, were very much part of the grammar of Muslim politics. Hindu nationalists in the nineties, of course, would prove more adept at this discourse, making the demolition of the Babri Masjid the *cri de coeur* of Hindus across the Republic.

If Kabir's activism points to the limits of nationalist Muslim discourse, it also hints at a peculiarity of its audience: it was not always the *qaum*. Indeed, at times, it was directed not at the Muslim but the Hindu. One of Kabir's many initiatives was to rename the AMU after Syed Ahmed Khan—'many universities in Europe and America are named after their founders'—in order to pre-empt Hindu nationalists. In the spirit of 'secularism', the BHU could be renamed as well—perhaps the Madan Mohan University, Kabir gamely suggested.[36] His counsel was of a piece with a common postcolonial reflex, exemplified by the contemporaneous campaign of the Muslims of Dhulia to end 'unauthorised cow slaughter'.[37] The nationalist Muslim worldview, then, was both a reflection and the most notable illustration of a singular style of Muslim politics.

Humayun Kabir's brother Jehangir, in contrast to him, presented himself as a more assertive kind of Muslim politician. In 1960, along with Kaseem Ali Mirza, the Muslim leader of Murshidabad, he lent his support to the Muslim Convention, a pressure group calling for proportional representation. Admittedly, it is hard to gauge the seriousness of this demand. For Jehangir, it seems from press reports, joining the Convention was some kind of brinkmanship. He was hoping to catch the eye of Atulya Ghosh, the state party boss, and so secure a seat in the state cabinet, a stepping stone to the national one where he would join his brother.

His prospects seemed good, since a 'Muslim' cabinet seat had emptied with the retirement of the animal husbandry and community development minister Dr Rafiuddin Ahmed, who had quit politics 'in disgust' after being made redundant by Roy. However, the gambit failed to pay off. The party satraps were not going to replace Ahmed, who had been an outspoken opponent of Muslim quotas, with someone who had ideas beyond his station. As it turned out, not only did Jehangir not receive a ministership, but he left the Convention, too, grovelling before Ghosh and promising to mend his ways. So it was with Mirza, scion of local *nawabs*, whose cabinet bid was found equally inadmissible. His insubordination only convinced the Bengal PCC that more vigilance was needed to monitor 'separatist' demands in the borderlands.[38]

For all that, as the more successful Kabir's career demonstrates, it would be remiss to see nationalist Muslims merely as 'Muslim' politicians. For they were regional leaders, too. As Humayun's hagiographer has it, 'Kabir was Bengalee to the bone'.[39] In Delhi from the mid-fifties onward, he used his ministerial platform at the centre—first as minister for civil aviation; then scientific research and cultural affairs; education; and petroleum and chemicals—to press for demands for his state. His lasting legacy, so it seems from his life and obituaries, was as an 'educationist', a man of letters, one of Bengal's early institution builders of repute, remembered for his role in founding the Ramakrishna Mission Institute of Culture and securing central grants for the Calcutta and Jadavpur Universities.[40]

Like Mahmud, he grew disillusioned and left the Congress, possibly because, Theodore P. Wright, Jr speculates, he realised that he could never entirely make himself at home in a party whose building blocks were Hindu caste composites. Of little use to Ghosh's dominant faction, he was practically squeezed out of the Congress.[41]

Other Muslim politicians, too, found themselves shut out of the party on account of their inability to gravitate towards the party's caste-centred factions. Take Mehdi Nawaz Jung. A Hyderabadi plutocrat who ran charities and hospitals, not to mention, as the town's municipal commissioner, also gentrified the now fashionable quarter of Banjara Hills, he discovered that he was no longer wanted. In 1960, he was dropped from D. Sanjivayya's cabinet, his 'only fault' that he 'did not belong to any of the cliques in the state Congress'. He was appointed Gujarat governor soon after, a ceremonial but powerless post.[42]

In the summer of 1966, Kabir joined Ajoy Mukherjee's new Bangla Congress, forging an alliance with the Communists in backroom intrigue. In this unlikely coalition, one finds a useful injunction against the temptation of reading too deeply into ideology in the Indian setting. Mukherjee was a notorious immigrant-baiter, having built a constituency railing against east Bengalis swamping the west, whereas the cause of migrants, especially Muslim ones entering Assam and Jammu and Kashmir, was dear to Kabir. The latter was also, famously, a longstanding anti-communist. A formative experience in 1946 had seen him kidnapped by 'Muslim League and Communist firebrands'. He emerged unscathed only because both fell out over what to do with him. His worldview, as summed up by his biographer Dipankar Datta, was a peculiar *laissez-faire* liberalism. State-led rural electrification, he believed, would 'encourage self-reliance', unleashing 'private initiative and enterprise'. Families would turn into 'miniature factories'. Atomised thus, 'such units' would 'eliminate the problem of labour conflict'.[43]

The coalition was to be a masterstroke in triangulation— Mukherjee would sway the *bhadralok*, Kabir the Muslims, the CPI and CPM the working classes and peasants—and for the better part it was. The United Front government they formed was the first time a non-Congress government took power in Bengal.

Kabir, nationalist Muslim no more, could take some credit for the victory. But before it could bring about any substantive change, the Front collapsed. The strikes and expropriation spearheaded by the Communists proved too much for Kabir. His 'Marxist colleagues were functioning in a way that threatened the country's security', he would decry in Parliament.[44] As the heckling response to his speech and his biography make clear, it was Kabir's machinations that led to the fall of the Front. Pulling the rug from under Mukherjee's feet, he helped Prafulla Ghosh, the gentry-friendly former agriculture minister who had vetoed compulsory procurement to lower food prices, replace him as chief minister. But within the year, the Progressive Democratic Front went the way of the United Front.

Now, in 1969, came Kabir's first real test as a popular politician. He formed his own party, the Lok Dal, his brother Jehangir following suit with the Bangla Jatiya Dal. Did they, in fact, represent the Muslims of Bengal? A Gallup poll was sanguine: 'the Kabir brothers might possibly hold 10 per cent of the popular vote'.[45] But the optimism proved to be unfounded. In the event, the vote share of the LD and BJD combined stood at 1.2 per cent. Even the new Progressive Muslim League, a throwback to the League of old, whose very name registered Muslim discontent with the status quo, polled higher—1.5 per cent—quickly establishing a bridgehead in the Muslim-majority regions in the east.[46]

The drubbing in part owed to the general impression that, post-election, the Kabirs would throw in their lot with the Congress. The LD and BJD, then, could never quite shake off the image that they were simply minority appendages of the Congress. Both were disbanded. Jehangir found his efforts to join the second United Front government of 1969 thwarted by the Bangla Congress. Humayun, for his part, joined and left Charan Singh's BKD, a party of the gentry that he thought was too critical of the Congress, not long before he died in 1971, out of luck and out of government.[47] Both brothers, *in fine*, achieved little hopping from one party to another, unable to free themselves from their reputation as nationalist Muslims at a time when being one had become a wasting asset.

'Fired with the Zeal of a New Convert'

A life cut short by an early death, Saadulla's political career could be described as a condensed pastiche of Kabir's: dominance in the world of state politics as an independent Muslim, damascene conversion to the Congress, early disappointment, and then death, all in the span of a decade. The speed of these developments was a reflection of what a poor fit Saadulla was with the nationalist Muslims. In this sense, he was the exception that threw light on the rule. The hasty departure from the Congress betrayed the little patience he had for the politics of circumscription.

A Calcutta High Court advocate, Saadulla had quickly risen in the League to become prime minister of Assam in 1937. Despite being bed-ridden and reeling with flu much of the time, he held the premiership for seven of the ten years to Partition, only losing his wafer-thin majority to Bordoloi briefly in 1938 and then permanently in 1946, both occasions when his colleagues defected to the Congress, which more generously doled out ministries. After the war, Saadulla played his cards badly—twice so, proving to be an intransigent Leaguer the first time, and a similarly stubborn nationalist Muslim the second. His policy of Islamising Assam proved counterproductive. 'In the four lower districts of the Assam Valley … Bengali immigrant Moslems have quadrupled the Moslem population during the last twenty years', he had gleefully written Liaquat Ali Khan in the summer of 1945, suggesting that his state was quickly becoming a Muslim Garden of Eden.[48]

But by February the next year, he was no longer prime minister. What's more, he had virtually lost control of the party, which decided to abstain from the assembly in protest against the Congress' 'eviction policy'. Migrants were being deported wholesale. Saadulla was caught between a rock and a hard place. His party wanted more Muslim migration into Assam, but his former coalition partners, the Assam United Party and those representing the functional

constituencies, would not have it. Islamisation was also alienating
voters, who had shown Saadulla the boot.

Reluctantly, he came to terms with reality. The 'political
situation', he wrote to Jinnah in April 1947, was quite 'hopeless
from any point of view'. He advised caution. With Bordoloi in power
and widespread support for India, he suggested it best for the Assam
League to desist from the Pakistan demand, even join the Indian
Constituent Assembly. In any case, Saadulla argued, the odds were
stacked in its favour, because Assam would inevitably become a part
of Pakistan. With the 'whip hand over Assam', Bengal could force
the province to merge into it—and a united Bengal, of course, was
destined to become a Pakistani province—for Assam's '400 million
pounds of tea' had to go through either the port of Calcutta or
Chittagong, the conduits of all seaborne trade.[49]

As it was, when the Partition plan was announced, it became clear
that a united Bengal was not going to take Assam with it. Stranded in
the Indian Union, the Assam League dissolved itself on 30 May 1948,
donating its newly replenished coffers to a trust board for the 'social,
economic, religious, and cultural upliftment of the Muslim public'.[50]
In a fitting triumph for the nationalist Muslim, Saadulla, who still
commanded a following among the state's Bengali Muslims and jute
producers, joined the Assam Provincial Congress Committee.

Saadulla had burned his fingers once, supporting an unpopular
policy. In his Congress avatar, he would do so again. He refused
to play the part of the self-effacing nationalist Muslim. And he
refused to conflate party and nation. Far from it. In the Constituent
Assembly, he routinely attacked the Oligarchy for marginalising
minority voices. He called for separate electorates and reserved
seats. Damning intraparty collegiality, he locked horns with the
Hindu leadership. Hoping to secure greater representation for
Muslims on the eve of the 1951 election, he demanded proportional
quotas. The Congress had reserved eighteen tickets in the assembly
of 108 for 'hill people'. It made sense, then, to hand out twenty of
the remaining ninety seats to Muslim candidates—in keeping with
their numbers, some 22 per cent of Assam's population. He went
on to accuse delimitation authorities of gerrymandering to deprive
Muslims a substantial majority in any constituency. Still, eleven

seats had an absolute Muslim majority, and in another twelve, the *qaum* constituted over 35 per cent of the population. Likewise, in the Lok Sabha, Saadulla felt that Muslims were owed, proportionally speaking, at least two of the state's twelve seats; SCs and STs were reserved three.[51]

The PCC barely concealed its impatience with Saadulla. In the end, the Congress fielded only fourteen Muslims for the assembly, and one for Parliament.[52] For each rejection, the logic was set out by B. R. Medhi, who became chief minister. In Goalpara, in light of the 'communal disturbances'—riots—'there is no prospect ever of the Muslim candidates being returned'. Similarly, in North Salmara and North Lakhimpur, Muslims had 'no chance', apparently because it was a double-member constituency. The Hindu leaders of Bihpuria were 'veteran Congressmen of proven integrity' whereas their 'junior' Muslims counterparts were not. Riots had prompted an 'exodus' of Muslims in Barpeta; were a Muslim to be fielded, the 'strained feeling' between the two communities would most 'likely become aggravated'.[53] In a word, Medhi wanted Saadulla and his men to act more like nationalist Muslims, while what they wanted was to be more like the Scheduled Castes.

Saadulla took matters up with Nehru. 'It may not be known to you that on my advice and guidance, 90 per cent of the Muslims of Assam has [sic] joined the Congress', he wrote. 'I am fired with the zeal of a new convert to see the Congress succeed', which he was certain it would, but for the 'narrow and communal outlook evinced by local Hindu Congress leaders'.[54] It appears from Nehru's correspondence with Sri Prakasa, governor of Assam, that he did not reply to Saadulla, deciding instead to heed the advice of Medhi, with whom he was in touch. The letters are a telling comment on what India's ruler thought of Saadulla, and, more generally, of the Muslims who had recently joined his party, which, on the face of it, had only been eager to accept them into its fold. 'I am entirely against Congress setting up as their [sic] candidate a Muslim who has played a leading communal part in the past, even though he formally joins the Congress now', Nehru wrote Prakasa on 11 October. 'If I cannot get a more suitable candidate, I would rather not run a candidate for a seat and allow an independent Muslim to stand for it'.[55]

Dispelling the taint of 'communalism' was harder than it seemed. Still, Saadulla and his team of League defectors were not entirely unwanted in the Congress. As Nehru acknowledged, they had their uses. They helped the party appear more Muslim-friendly. They were, then, to be tolerated so long as they knew their station. So, Nehru cynically advised more tickets for Muslims, lest it seem a 'poor bargain' to the *qaum*. 'Saadullah [*sic*] is not at all a safe man, and yet, in all the circumstances, I do not very well see how we can leave him out. Outside [the Congress], he might prove dangerous', Nehru cautioned Prakasa. 'The remaining Muslims should generally be chosen from the younger lot with progressive ideas. Their past association with the Muslim League need not by itself go against them unless they have been very active and aggressive'.[56]

As we have seen in the assembly and in the backroom back-and-forth of Assamese politics, 'active and aggressive' Saadulla most certainly was. He paid dearly for it. First, in November, ten candidates from his faction were purged for being 'communal-minded' and 'disloyal to the state'. In the revision of the rolls supervised by Azad and Kidwai, both more exemplary nationalist Muslims, they were replaced with more obviously 'nationalist' Muslims. At this point, Saadulla was the sole Congress Muslim candidate for the Lok Sabha standing from Assam.[57] But within weeks, he, too, was deselected. Decrying 'communal bias', Saadulla finally tendered his resignation.[58] When the results were announced a couple of months later, they were at least in part a vindication for him. While the Congress won seventy-six of the ninety-two seats it contested, Muslims kept at arm's length from it. To the eight Congress Muslims elected, there were seven Muslim independents. Further, the only Muslim representing the state in Parliament was a Socialist, Jonab Amjad Ali, who beat the Congress' Hindu candidate in Goalpara, where, in Medhi's estimation, apparently no Muslim could win. But schadenfreude, of course, was no substitute for power. Sad-eyed, sullen, and a spent force, Saadulla died four years later.

'A Graveyard for Politicians'

If Saadulla was not the right kind of nationalist Muslim, and Mahmud and Kabir drifted away from the party, the question arises: who were the uncritical figures who stayed true to the Congress?

These were often politicians a rung lower in the pecking order: local, not state, bosses who, lacking a constituency of their own, were more plainly given to acts of fealty, and for this reason, a better fit with the politics of circumscription that the Congress favoured. By virtue of their lesser status, many of these sanguine nationalist Muslims were also people who left behind fewer traces in the dailies. But evidence of them in the archives is not to be found wanting. For our purposes here, two instances from the Home Ministry papers will suffice.

Given the kind of forelock-tugging encouraged in Nehru's India, it should scarcely be surprising to learn that self-effacing nationalist Muslims who had rendered service to the party were often recipients of Home Ministry awards. Through the fifties and sixties, a number of minor political actors applied for an allowance as 'political sufferers'. All that was needed was evidence of detention during the Raj or proof that one was a relative of someone killed by the police. As a political sufferer, one was entitled to a one-off grant, a stipend, or a children's scholarship.

Unsurprisingly, the list of its Muslim recipients was a roll-call of nationalist Muslims. One such figure was Anis Ahmad Abbasi, editor of the *Daily Haqiqat,* a Lucknow Urdu publication fallen on hard times. In his claim, he highlighted his role as a Khilafatist alongside 'Mahatamaji' [*sic*]; the harassment he faced as a JUH man; his unfortunate defeat at the hands of a Leaguer when he stood in Sitapur in 1946; the 'sacrifice' he made two years later when he stood down as an independent in Lucknow—Khaliquzzaman's seat in the UP assembly until his resignation—to better the Congress candidate's chances. Standing as an independent for the Constituent Assembly and Parliament, he withdrew from both races 'on the advice of the late Mr Kidwai'.[59] For his troubles, he earned for himself the status of 'political sufferer'. The award came with a prize of Rs 2,000 in 1957, enough in those days to purchase a second-hand Standard 10.

Another self-denying figure was Abdul Ghani Chauhan, a Mathura notable, who was awarded Rs 1,000 after being vouched for by a Congress MLA: he 'belongs to that calibre of nationalist Muslims who stood the acid test of Partition'. A second recommendation was of the same tenor: 'Even during those days when the muslim league [sic] was bitterly opposed to [sic] Indian National Congress, he never was deflected from the right path'.[60]

As the Home Ministry files suggest, such transactions were not uncommon, and certainly not the preserve of Muslims, but Muslim cases were the only ones that made explicit mention of religion, as if the award was solely for the right kind of—Congress—Muslim. Simply put, the recognition of Muslims as 'political sufferers' was, as it were, *baksheesh* for delivering the Muslim vote to the Congress.

A cut above the nationalist Muslim political sufferers, but below state leaders, one finds a set of nationalist Muslim politicians who were—deliberately it appears—given onerous portfolios, which they tolerated though not without resentment. Surely it was no accident that at a time of rampant and seemingly intractable food crises, many of them wound up with the food ministry—in the words of S. K. Patil, who held the unfortunate job at the centre, 'a graveyard for many [politicians] cleverer and more imaginative than I'.[61] In the late fifties and early sixties, it was invariably Muslims—A. Q. Siddiqi, Moinul Haq Choudhuri, and Syed Ali Zaheer, the food ministers of Madhya Pradesh, Assam, and Uttar Pradesh; and G. S. Kazi, Bombay's civil supplies and housing minister—who were tasked with the politically sensitive business of importing food grain, a thankless job for which they invited ridicule and criticism.[62] The union minister of irrigation and power, Hafiz Mohammad Ibrahim, more plainly recognised that he was 'helpless' when it came to the agrarian problem. Indeed, failing compulsory procurement, ceiling legislation, and greater interventionism in yield-enhancing technology and supply chains— all above his pay grade—there was little he could do. Rumours abounded of their divided loyalties: Choudhuri, in one account, was painted as a traitorous saboteur, encouraging Muslims to flee to Pakistan and hoping to do the same himself.[63]

While the great offices of state remained out of reach for Muslims, their ranks were disproportionally represented as

135

education ministers. The inaugural office holder was Azad (1947–58), the next but one Kabir (1963), who was followed by Chagla (1963–6) and Fakhruddin Ahmed (1966–7); after a brief spell, the ministry fell to Zaheer's nephew, Nurul Hasan (1972–7). Here, one surmises a similar logic at work. If food was a difficult ministry, education was a neglected one. Indeed, the cheese-paring education budgets of the early postcolonial state were a testament to the ministry's priority: 0.8 per cent of national income at the time of independence, rising to 2.4 per cent in 1963.[64] Not only paltry in world-historical perspective—at the close of Macmillan's premiership, the corresponding figure for the metropole was 4.2 per cent—it was meagre by the standards of the ministers themselves.[65] Azad was of the opinion that expenditure in government schools ought to be met entirely by the state. Still, there was a concerted effort by Nehru and Shastri to make schools and universities leaner (eliminating 'wastage' was the watchword) and more autarkic (schools were expected to take up 'economic activities' such as producing yarn and cloth to make ends meet). Already a low priority in public spending—between the First and Second Five-Year Plans, total outlays grew by 132 per cent, for education 40 per cent—after the Sino-Indian War, education became even less of a state concern, compelling Chagla to forgo his plans for expansion and instead focus on 'consolidation and quality', a vision which rested on the hope that a few great public institutions of learning would spur many private ones eager to emulate them. Wishful thinking, of course.[66]

Elsewhere, nationalist Muslims struggled to be taken seriously. Zaheer, for instance, was summoned in 1965 by Sucheta Kripalani, the chief minister, who in a 'friendly gesture' invited him to become the state's 'finance minister within certain limits' [sic]. In this improvised competency-sharing arrangement, he was to be reduced to 'an understudy of the chief minister', his powers even less than the finance department secretary's. All decisions were to be referred to her, she was emphatic. Seeing the bargain for what it was—that he would have to shoulder the blame for all that went wrong while she got to arrogate power without responsibility—Zaheer, then a veteran minister of twelve years, turned down the offer, preferring no portfolio to 'such humiliating conditions'.[67] It is possible, though only conjecture, that Mrs Kripalani felt that Zaheer was in some sense undeserving on account of his dishonourable past. We know enough about attitudes in the party to appreciate that Zaheer's history as a Leaguer, who had only left his Oxford friend Liaquat Ali Khan's party in 1937 when he was defeated by a mere twenty-one votes in Azamgarh—to say nothing of his family: his brother Sajjad migrated to Pakistan to start a communist movement there; their father Sir Syed Wazir Hasan was once a League president—must have been a handicap for him.[68]

All in all, the fifties and sixties were a time of frustration for the eminent Nehruvians. Few of them would not have, in darker moments, looked on enviously at their 'communal' *confrères*, seemingly freer to air their views and to act on their convictions. But was the grass really greener on the other side?

PART II

'COMMUNALISTS'

4

LOYAL OPPOSITION

'Communalism'. Less a description than an imputation, contempt drips from every mention of the word. So much so that, until fairly recently, Muslim political formations were seen as unworthy subjects of research. Anachronistically irrelevant, ideologically bankrupt, electorally nugatory—there was, in Gertrude Stein's famous dictum, 'no there there'.

Such a view, of course, was more a reflection of the predilections of the Indian liberal academy than Muslim politics per se, and there is no reason why such *partis pris* need to be perpetuated today. In Mushirul Hasan's opus on Muslim India since independence, for example, Muslim parties and associations receive a scarce dozen pages of consideration. The compression appears, at first blush, illogical. But from his vantage point, it is eminently reasonable. Cataloguing the failures of the Muslim parties, and contrasting them to the painstaking successes of the nationalist Muslims, Hasan concludes with evident satisfaction: 'These trends refute popular notions of communal consciousness as a strong element in voting behaviour'.[1]

Another clue to his historical method lies in his preface to David Lelyveld's monograph on *Aligarh's First Generation*. In it, he laments the agendas of a 'generation tutored in Marxism-

Leninism'—mesmerised by 'economic, agrarian, and institutional' but not confessional history, and uninterested in laundering Muslim reputations, blighted as they were by Hindu nationalist invective. The way forward was clear. Historians 'need to situate prominent political and religious figures with a perspective that would enlarge our appreciation of their role'.[2] In other words, the historian's task is to make idols, not break them. So, taking 'communalists' seriously was tantamount to iconoclasm.

Truth be told, however, 'communalists' were no different from their 'nationalist' brethren. Indeed, when placed under the microscope, it becomes clear that the binary is a false one, which, by dint of repetition and amplification, has acquired a life of its own. A closer look at the League's manifestoes of the fifties, for instance, reveals that the 'communalist' party simply rehearsed the promises of the 'secular' Congress, which, at all events, were common currency at the time: *inter alia*, socialist nostrums, industrialisation, prohibition, 'Harijan uplift', anti-corruption measures.[3]

Nor is it entirely apposite, it will be argued in these pages, to write off Muslim formations as inconsequential. They were not, as popular discourse has it, relics from Jinnah's time, banging on about separate electorates. In the South, especially, they were an electoral force to be reckoned with, often holding the balance of power in the states, at times supporting 'secular' parties, at others 'chauvinist' ones. The communalists, of course, demanded a pound of flesh for these machinations, which came in the form of blunting the atheistic ardour of the Communists and the Kazhagam, pork-barrel funds for the Muslim poor, and greater representation on councils and assemblies thanks to seat-sharing arrangements, not least with the Congress.

In what follows, I chart the various strategies adopted by Muslim parties in Nehru's India.[4] Above all, there were two of them: the 'long march through the institutions' and 'entryism *sui generis*'— Muslims furthering their sectional interests by capturing the levers of state power in their own name, and by embedding themselves in the Congress to effect meaningful change from within.

To these could be added two political phenomena, for they were not strategies as such: 'the protest vote', which found Muslim political operators undermining the Congress in all possible ways, even to their detriment, in order to register their disaffection with the status quo; and associationalism, with its grammar of self-help and Tocquevillian promise of working around the party-political system.

On the whole, the political mobilisation of Muslim parties had an unintended upshot: the 'Green Scare'. By threatening the Congress with their success, Muslim parties indirectly prompted it to mend its ways. Delhi's neglect, it was widely understood, had resulted in Muslim voters falling prey to crafty communal operators. As a result, it became much harder to ignore Muslims. Funds, sinecures, and parleys followed in short order, which, after a fashion, was precisely what the Muslims were after in the first place.

'A Snake Without Fangs'

To the constellation of Muslim parties clustered in the South and West, the riposte to Islamophobia was a long march through the institutions. A strategy of West German derivation coined by Rudi Dutschke initially as a student slogan of the Left and later applied in different world-historical settings, its broad thrust was simple enough: 'working against the established institutions while working in them', in Marcuse's famous description.[5] In concrete terms, for Muslims this meant embracing rather than eschewing state apparatuses by winning power locally and regionally.

The foremost party to deploy this strategy was the Indian Union Muslim League. Very early on, its leaders militated in favour of battling what they saw to be the greatest social ailments of the time—rampant Islamophobia; insurgent secularism; the flattening of linguistic and cultural identities—with greater, not lesser, political participation. This, it hardly needs telling, was quite a distance from the ever-depoliticising world of the nationalist Muslims. Parliamentary participation and alliance-making were deemed essential to forestall the ascendancy of the godless communists in Kerala and Dravida Munnetra Kazhagam in Tamil Nadu. Indeed, it was the incipient threat of these two atheist movements—for they were both much more than just political parties—that provided the impetus for mobilisation.

On 14 December 1947 in Karachi, the League resolved to split into two national branches. It was widely understood that its Indian chapter was to be wound down in the following weeks. But on 10 March the next year, at Rajaji Hall in Madras, the Indian League decided against dissolution, not so much on account of burgeoning political ambitions, but rather on sufferance. A political 'vacuum', its leaders felt, would have had produced the most deleterious results for the *qaum*.[6] Against Jinnah's wishes, the *fez*-sporting Madrasi Mohammed Ismail, *quaid-e-millat* ('leader of the community') to his followers, was elected president.

Unsurprisingly, the League's centre of gravity had shifted southward. Nineteen of the thirty delegates in attendance at Rajaji Hall were Madrasis. Another eight were from Bombay and Mysore. The changing of the guard represented not only the takeover of the party by southerners, but also by radicals. Their experience in the constituent assembly was formative, but so, too, was their confrontation with Congress majoritarianism. For in 1950, Delhi's new rulers decided to strip all 'dual parliamentarians', those who sat in both the national and a state legislature, of their place in the former. The casualties were overwhelmingly non-Congressmen. This was by design. 'It was a device by which the Congress tried to keep away from the future interim legislative assembly such members as had political differences with the party in power', Mohamed Raza Khan, a League stalwart from Madras, would later observe in his memoirs.[7] In the by-elections that followed, MPs were chosen by simple plurality voting, whereas the incumbents had been elected through proportional representation. For the League, the upshot was that all of its Madrasi MPs—Ismail, Pocker, Ibrahim, Baig—lost their seats in the Lok Sabha.

Adversity is a remarkable stimulus. Certainly, it helped Ismail consolidate a consensus around a politics of assertion. Thanks to the somewhat more representative, if complex, electoral system that obtained at the council level—a legacy of the Raj—the League was able to control a few levers of state power in the fifties and sixties. In 1961, on account of cumulative voting, nearly as many League as nationalist Muslim councillors—four to the latter's six—were elected to the Bombay Municipal Corporation. Similarly, the

Muslim political class more generally, if not Leaguers in particular, benefited from the peculiar system of communal rotation for the Madras mayoralty, put in place by the Justice Party in 1923, as well as the existence of functional constituencies—guaranteeing business interests parliamentary representation, as in contemporary Hong Kong—until both were done away with in 1959. In the eight-year cycle, a non-Brahmin caste Hindu would serve as mayor for the first and every second year after; and a Muslim, Christian, Dalit, and Brahmin in the second, fourth, sixth, and eighth years, respectively. Among the functional constituencies were the Muslim Chamber of Commerce and the Hides and Leather Merchants Association, both of which returned Muslims in the fifties.[8]

Reservations helped, too. Between 1946 and 1949, the League won five by-elections in the Madras assembly: all were reserved seats. In 1952, after reservations were scrapped, it managed to retain only two. Gerrymandering compounded its problems. When, nearly a decade after independence, Nehru set about reorganising the states of the Union in order to forestall the rising tide of nativism, the Madras League wound up an inadvertent casualty. Two of its most important redoubts, the Muslim oases of Kozhikode and Palghat, were hived off to the new state of Kerala.

The Leaguers sought greener pastures. Carpetbagging seemed to work for the Madrasi party president Ismail, who, in 1962, became MP for Manjeri—a constituency four-fifths Muslim—in Malabar despite not speaking a word of Malayalam. He was joined in Parliament by one of his mates, C. H. Mohammed Koya, who, too, was handsomely returned on the back of Moplah support from a Malabar constituency. Their runaway success despite the odds was testament to Muslim disaffection, which, for obvious reasons, only registered electorally in demographically atypical constituencies— those with significant Muslim populations. Leaguers ably rode the waves of Muslim disquiet in Madras as well. A. K. A. Abdus Samad became the first League councillor in Madras since independence when he was returned from the state's only Muslim-majority constituency, Harbour Division, in 1959.[9]

For all that, the League's long march through the institutions was more than a numbers game. Above all, it entailed mainstreaming its brand of minority politics. To this end, the party adopted a two-pronged strategy. On the one hand, Leaguers endeavoured to suffuse the press with nationalist declamations of every kind. Their name notwithstanding, they went to great lengths to demonstrate their recantation of separatism. The party president's *curriculum vitae* suggests that he was well-positioned to make the case for League patriotism. A young Ismail had once been a Congressman, wearing *khaddar* to his wedding in 1923. He defected to the League only in 1936, when the Congress' T. T. Krishnamachari beat the local Muslim candidate, Jamal Mohammed, after running a brazenly Islamophobic campaign. Once a reluctant Leaguer, after independence he remained a willing nationalist. Under his leadership, the IUML supported Nehru's 'police action' in—invasion of—Hyderabad in September 1948, which left some 40,000 Muslims dead. A decade later, his Keralite party colleague Baffaky Thangal could be found promising Delhi's rulers that the League would 'stand united in India's defence' were a war to erupt over 'the fate of Kashmir'.[10] For his part, Ismail not only championed the cause of the Tamil language, remaining mostly indifferent to Urdu, but also was ever on the lookout for opportunities to display his unimpeachable nationalist credentials. When the Sino-Indian War broke out, he 'offered his only son' to the armed forces, topping up the Abrahamic sacrifice with a Rs 200 contribution to the war fund.[11]

On the other hand, Ismail hoped to turn the patriotic ingratiation to good account by mass mobilisation. In the early sixties, when ties between India and Pakistan appeared to be improving—in September 1960, Nehru met his counterpart in Karachi to ink the Indus Waters Treaty—the League put on a 'grand show of Muslim political power', calculating that the thaw in relations meant greater latitude for the *qaum*. Orchestrated by Ismail, and uniting the Muslim peasants from the backwaters of Ramnad and Tinnevelly and the Muslim working classes of the northern districts, the September 1960 rally in Madras was, perhaps, the largest Muslim protest of the early postcolonial period. Shipped to the state capital in over fifty buses with four days' worth of supplies, peasant and proletarian marched shoulder to shoulder. 'Are we not a mighty force?' they cried. 'Do we not count?'[12]

Ismail's penchant for parliamentary and street politics, however, was not universally shared in his party. Effectively in power since Partition without ever having his mandate officially renewed, he was faced with a coup for the first time in 1961. Led by Mohamed Raza Khan, two hundred League rebels denounced him as a 'communalist' and demanded his ouster. He was too assertive, his style too aggressive, they felt. For his part, Ismail accused the rebels in his Urdu weekly *Nusrat* for having 'sold the religion', leaving behind a 'depoliticised League', 'a snake without fangs'.[13]

The chief certainly understood his opponents better than they let on. For behind closed doors, Khan had as early as 1956 gone over to the Congressman Kamaraj Nadar, bad-mouthing his party leader and charting a new course for the League: 'our policy should be simply to support the Congress and leave it at that. Do not ask anything in return. Let us not also stand for election' [*sic*].[14] The 1961 coup, then, was a long time coming. When it failed to defenestrate Ismail, Khan and his men struck out on their own, forming the All-India Muslim League (AIML, as distinct from Ismail's IUML).

If the League was plagued by the question of politics proper, linguistic anxieties intruded as well. The Madras League, especially, was riven with factions. Madras in the fifties, it will be recalled, included not just the areas that make up present-day Tamil Nadu, but also parts of Malabar, South Canara, and the Andhra region. The latter for the better part went unnoticed by the state League. Similarly, the Malayalam-speaking Malabar leaders couldn't care less about the Tamil capital. Urdu and Tamil speakers in Madras city, too, wanted nothing to do with one another. The party's decentralised structure—'two-anna members' could set up 'primary Leagues', local branches—exacerbated these differences.[15] In 1950, Madras Leaguers left to form the left-wing United People's Party, and seven years later, when the Kerala League aligned itself with the PSP, the tut-tutting party *pur et dur* parted ways to form the All Kerala State Muslim League.[16] Undeniably, on account of all the bickering and infighting, Muslim League politics in postcolonial India had a rather Monty Pythonesque quality to it, all very People's Front of Judea and Judean People's Front.

The cleavage *par excellence* was the North-South divide. Time and again, plans were made to merge the Muslim Jamaat of Uttar Pradesh and the IUML—yoking together, as it were, the two Muslim League heirs of the North and South into a single, powerful, pan-Indian Muslim party—but these, for some reason or other, never went through. The two parties were divided, foremost, on their reception of the Left, the IUML opposing it tooth and nail and the MJ being more sanguine. Regional cadences accounted for this. In the North, the communists, thanks in large part to the efforts of the formidable organiser Z. A. Ahmed, commanded a significant following among the Muslim working classes, whereas in the South, the Left was a militant force whose irreligious zeal made Leaguers squirm.[17]

There were, then, many long marches through the institutions. But when one steps back, it becomes clear that only two tesserae in the League mosaic were of any account: the IUML in Madras and Malabar. Both, after a fashion, proved successful. Their top priority was to carve a place for Islam in public life in settings singularly hostile to religion. The southern context, of course, was distinctive because the CPI in Kerala and the DMK in Tamil Nadu had no real northern equivalents. Marx and Periyar's progeny and Gandhi's heirs were chalk and cheese. Indeed, the former's was not the 'secularism' of the latter, but instead—to the League at least—secularisation proper: to the Communists and the Kazhagam, religion was evil, and needed to be erased from society. Truth be told, on the hustings and in power, the DMK 'soft-pedalled' its atheism, godlessness being fundamentally inimical to its supporters.[18] Much the same could be said about Kerala's communists, few of whom were intractable atheists; many in fact saw the Muslim question through Leninist lenses, viewing minoritarian aspirations with sympathy.[19] But none of this really mattered to the League, which tended to, first, take Communist and Kazhagam rhetoric far too seriously, and second, exaggerate its own role in putting a damper on the unholy crusades. But this should not detract from its real, albeit limited, contribution to changing the balance of opinion in both parties.

It is undeniable that the League strived hard, by turns, to block the ascent of the two 'atheist' parties, and to co-opt them and enfeeble their heretical agenda. In 1957, the IUML snubbed a pre-electoral alliance with the DMK, demanding an end to its atheistic crusade. At first, when the unreconstructed Kazhagam proved unobliging, the League promptly let the talks collapse, letting on that it would rather the Congress coast to victory with a divided opposition than enter a Faustian bargain. But then, desperate as the DMK was, it caved in to the demand. A seat-sharing arrangement ensued. The DMK stood down in two parliamentary constituencies and a few in the assembly to further League prospects.[20] And in 1962, the two parties entered into a pact—more forcefully this time around—to contain the Congress. While the League returned only a single MP to Delhi, according to Theodore P. Wright Jr, it nevertheless facilitated 'the election of fifty DMK legislators', for which the Kazhagam returned the favour by sending one Leaguer each to the national and state upper houses. Two years later, the League swept the seats it contested in the Madras municipal elections, winning five even as the nationalist Muslims took none, with DMK support. The League's Habibullah Baig was sworn in as deputy mayor.

In Kerala, meanwhile, the League was busy campaigning against the state's communist rulers. It demanded the redaction of blasphemous textbooks; restoration of religious education in state schools; reservations to the tune of 10 per cent (they were at 7.5 per cent) for Muslims in public services; and the reinstatement of the right to limitless construction of mosques and *madrasas* in Malabar, where old Madras rules capping religious construction still applied, the reorganisation of states notwithstanding. Happily, the League was able to turn most of these demands to good account: mosque and *madrasa* permits were liberalised, Communist plans to scrap religious reservations jettisoned, and offensive textbooks suitably bowdlerised.[21]

What is more, Leaguers played a part in seeing off the Communist government itself. Setting off the cascade of events was their decision to join hands with their enemy's enemy, the Christian clerical and political elite, in opposing the Communist-sponsored Kerala Education Bill. The two peoples of the book had apparently not seen eye to eye since the 'blasphemous' publication of *Thirusabha Charithram*, lit. *The History of the Church*, in 1950 by the local clergy. But in 1957, faced with a greater adversary, the two sides quickly buried the hatchet. The League was promised a redacted edition by Christian authorities, who duly published the assurance in the pages of *Deepika*, a leading Catholic daily based in Kottayam.[22] Now, a third element, the Congress, manifested itself in the coalition against the godless communists, in effect sealing the fate of the bill.

In truth, of course, there was nothing about the education reform that was decidedly atheistic. In fact, chief minister E. M. S. Namboodiripad was at pains to clarify that it was aimed at 'eliminating malpractices' and standardising the education system, not threatening minority faiths as such.[23] But that was precisely how the Church and *ulama*, supported foremost by the Congress and the League, saw the matter. In particular, two of the bill's clauses offended them: one providing for the nationalisation of schools whose managements betrayed signs of neglect, and the other the requisitioning of school premises for the purposes of land reform.[24] After the failed stab at undoing the bill in the courts, they took to the streets. Extraparliamentary action reached a crescendo in the summer of 1959, when, clashes between the police and protestors providing for convenient cover, Nehru decided to call time on communist rule in Kerala. Namboodiripad was thrown out of office, and President's Rule imposed.[25]

The Communists took the lesson to heart. That the League was ready to endure isolation and Congress rule rather than reach a *modus vivendi* with them was certainly instructive. The CPI never returned to its anti-quota position of the fifties. Its volte-face served it well, as it did the League, whose left-wing 'Young Turks' were quick to sense an opportunity.[26] A year later, in 1960, the two parties went so far as to contest the Trivandrum elections as a team, winning M. Bavutty Haji two years at the mayoralty. The improbable had thus happened. For the first time, a Leaguer had been handed control of an Indian city. Moreover, not only had Haji overcome Islamophobia, but he had done so with support from the Left, now reconciled to communal quotas.[27]

The red-green combine was not without its sequels. To the horror of Congressmen, a number of Leaguers stood as independents with CPM backing in the 1965 assembly election.[28] Five of them won, after which they simply 'defected' back to the League. As it was, though, the League, the Marxists, and the new Kerala Congress—the party of the *savarna* and Syrian Christian gentry—were denied power by Delhi. Twenty-nine CPM parliamentarians were placed under preventive detention and President's Rule extended for another two years in Kerala. The League, which polled nearly 4 per cent of the popular vote and was due a few cabinet positions, would have to wait half a decade before it could enter government as—and here was the unlikeliest of unions—a junior partner in a Congress- and Communist-dominated coalition. In the mid-sixties, Ismail had no truck with the Congress: 'eighteen years of absolute power has corrupted the Congress absolutely'.[29]

But by 1970, much had changed. For one thing, Ismail was a different man. Despite, or perhaps because of, his advanced age—he was seventy-four—he was at the top of his game. That year, new branches pullulated in Bihar and Assam, the Progressive Muslim League of West Bengal affiliated itself to the League, which crossed the half-million mark for membership; that figure, multiplied by the fee of 12 *paise*, also pointed to the fact that it was now flush.[30] The party did fairly well at the hustings in Kerala, while, for unrelated reasons, the incumbent Marxists did not. With no clear winner, the fate of Trivandrum was up in the air. All of a sudden, the League found itself kingmaker, and the Congress its passport to government and greater respectability. Ismail obliged.

Curiously, Ismail's belated appreciation of political realities—two years before his passing—mirrored that of his northern colleagues. A decade earlier, the League residuum in Uttar Pradesh had resolved in Allahabad to abandon its overtures to Nehru's party. The 'Congress has become incompetent to solve our problems', the censure read. All the same, Mufti Fakarul Islam's men were forced to sullenly admit, not long after, that building bridges with the PSP and CPI had failed as well.[31] Here was a truism. No minority party could keep at arm's length from the Congress behemoth for too long. At some point or other, usually sooner rather than later, Muslim parties felt compelled to come to terms with the Congress, either joining its ranks or backing it from without—whether uncritically or resignedly made little difference in practice. The Congress was, after all, the only game in town.

'Against the League, Not Leaguers'

If the course charted by Leaguers recalls Dutschke's long march through the institutions, the strategy deployed by some of their brethren brings to mind a postwar Trotskyist tactic: entryism *sui generis*.[32] The adjective is crucial here, a reflection of the extent of the marginalisation of the actors in question—the Western European Left; Indian Muslims—who, had they been more aware of each other's existence, would certainly have discovered much to commiserate over. Both *in extremis* and confronted by unvanquishable hegemons—Christian and social democracy; the Congress—there was little either could do to dislodge the powers that be. Equally, entryism proper was not an option. Briefly infiltrating parties to upend years of ideological work was wishful thinking. Neither the centrist consensus in Western Europe nor Islamophobia in India could be defeated in a heartbeat. Better to prepare for the long haul. This, then, was 'deep entry', entryism *sui generis*, entryism 'of a special type'.[33] Leaguers would embed themselves in the Congress—not so much in the manner of a conspiratorial sleeper cell, waiting in dormancy before engaging in rapid action, but of seasoned political operators in a hostile climate, bringing about slow, incremental change without jeopardising their *métier*.

Drawing up the balance sheet of League entryism produces a striking contrast. Rather counterintuitively, it appears that the entryists in the North—where the effects of Partition were more fully registered—fared better than their cousins in the South, where yesterday's Leaguers struggled to find legitimacy as today's Congressmen. We have already met some of our friends in the North—Saadulla, Rasul, Karimuddin, Hussain—in the previous chapter, and a sustained account of their careers need not detain us here. As we have seen, they managed to establish a passable, if precarious, foothold in the Republic. Saadulla secured a temporary sinecure, which, in the event, he only lost because he went for broke. Rasul rose steadily through the ranks, winning office and acclamation, a Rajya Sabha seat and a Padma Bhushan. Karimuddin became paterfamilias to a large nationalist Muslim clan, a dynasty not unlike the ICS families of the Raj, junior members in perpetual hock to the senior sectaries of the ruling caste. Hussain had himself nominated to two Rajya Sabhas.

The Congress was happy to have them. As an AICC general secretary, Sadiq Ali, put it: 'we are against the League, not Leaguers'.[34] Ahead of the 1951 polls, nineteen of the 225 League incumbents in Parliament, most of them from Bihar, Uttar Pradesh, and West Bengal, were given Congress tickets. Remarkably, all but one were returned. What is more, so smooth was the entryism that lifelong nationalist Muslims suddenly found themselves surplus to requirements. Opening its doors to the League produced an auxiliary exodus. Nationalist Muslims deserted the Congress *en masse* to join the KMPP and the Socialist Party.

The South, as ever, was a world away from the North. Here, entryism proved ruinous. The survival of the League saw to that. In the first election, both entryist incumbents—that is, those who won in 1946 on a League ticket but then contested as Congressmen in 1951—in Madras were defeated by Leaguers. More generally, too, Madrasi Leaguers fared better than Muslim Congressmen. In sum, six of the former but a mere two of the latter were returned to the Union and state legislatures. As in Madras, so in Kerala. In 1953, the Kerala Muslim Jama'at Federation, a splinter from the League, too, hitched its wagons to the Congress—also to no avail. Likewise, the merger of the Travancore-Cochin branch of the League into the Congress in 1949 achieved little, excepting the elevation of its local president, T. A. Abdulla, to the provincial cabinet. Not long after, demands were made 'from some quarters' to reduce the number of ministers in the name of austerity. Three Congressmen were made to resign, one of whom was Abdulla, no longer needed now that the Congress had gone through the motions of signalling its secular credentials.[35]

What of the entryism of the Fourth Party in Bombay? Here, too, the same trajectory: first, a brief stab at independent Muslim politics, 'the long march'; then, a period of wracking doubts, dilemmas, and internal tensions; next, unbridled support for the Congress at a time of notional independence; finally, the ineluctable merger, welcomed initially and later regretted. Formed in the late forties, the unimaginatively titled Fourth Party was the renegade offshoot of the League that had come to the conclusion that its brand name had been rendered odious by Partition.

Its very anodyne appellation was intended to express its essentially depoliticised character. It was not, for instance, the 'Muslim' or 'Workers" or 'People's' or 'Peasants" or 'Minorities" Party. But, in fact, what it did was cloak what were incontrovertibly strongly held convictions. For the Fourth was, to all intents and purposes, an arm of the 'first' party, as it were. So much so that two of the four Fourth Party MPs ran on Congress tickets in 1951. Both won. The other two contested as independents, and both lost. Lesson learned, one of the losers, Jukaku Shamsuddin, then defected to the Congress and earned himself a deputy ministership in Mysore. His party colleague and close friend A. K. M. Hafizka, a fellow Canarite Navayat Muslim, too, found success as a Congressman, becoming a Bombay MLA. The message was clear. The Fourth Party desperately needed the Congress to secure funds, legitimacy, and reelection.

Entryism, then, made sense. Indeed, there was much to be gained from absorption in the Congress. Primarily, it held the possibility of shaking off communal untouchability. For, in 1952, even as the Bombay PCC president S. K. Patil courted his Fourth Party opposite Hasanji P. Ebrahim, in public he dismissed reports of his overtures as 'malicious propaganda'.[36] Such strenuous denials would surely have stung. *Faute de mieux*, the Fourth Party would have felt the need to change tack. This it ultimately did in 1955, folding into the Congress. More than a merger, it was complete submission. For even on the very day it took place, Ebrahim and Hafizka felt it necessary to apologise to the chief minister, Morarji Desai, for their tragic 'mistake', the original sin of establishing the Fourth Party in the first place instead of simply joining the Congress at independence.[37]

For a brief instant, the Fourth Party had spelled trouble for the Congress. In 1950, it had set alarm bells ringing when it beat a Congress-sponsored independent—even Muslim Congressmen knew that, locally, affiliation to Nehru's party was a liability—in the Bombay City South Mohammedan assembly by-election.[38] But by mid-decade, however, it was hard to tell apart a nationalist Muslim from a Fourth Party man. For their preoccupations were, like those of Muslim Congressmen, in the main cultural, not socioeconomic:

the banning of an issue of *Life* magazine that depicted the Prophet; separation of *halal* and *jhatka* meat in slaughterhouses; more public holidays to mark Muslim festivals.[39]

The brigading, however, came at a high cost. Exacting Congressmen were quick to demand their pound of flesh in the form of deference and overall slavishness. For the Congress, entryists like Hafizka certainly had their uses, such as when he assumed the position of Bombay PCC president—becoming, in 1967, only the second Muslim to do so—in a highly choreographed spectacle: 'a large numbers of Muslims gathered at Congress House', with 'garlands galore', to greet the man of the moment, who, wearing wayfarers, descended the steps with folded hands to frenzied cheers. Introducing him, the former mayor Patil explained the choice candidly, but not without litotes. Hafizka, he said, had been recommended 'in the interest of minorities', especially since 'the Muslims had not gone the whole hog with the Congress in the general election'. (In fact, what the Congress had on its hands was nothing short of Muslim desertion.) For good measure, in his own address, Hafizka 'made special mention about the special problems of minorities', though, tellingly, 'without naming them'.[40]

Indeed, in Pitkin's terms, descriptive representation was one thing, substantive representation quite another. Hafizka discovered this the hard way when he was ticked off for having the temerity to rebuke the Congress for its ham-fisted response to—in truth, also complicity in—the Ahmedabad riots of 1969 that left 400 Muslims dead. He was sternly advised against breaking party ranks: 'such a statement did not further the interests of the party at all'.[41] A *mea culpa* followed in short order, one probably scripted for him from on high. The misgivings of his colleagues were unwarranted, he wrote, for his original remark—'a section of minorities feel that there is a systematic effort to annihilate them and ruin them economically'— was made, we are told, not so much with Ahmedabad in mind as with Al-Aqsa, the Jerusalem mosque torched by a Christian radical in August.[42] The Nehru jacket had turned out to be a straitjacket.

Oddly enough, the Bombay Leaguers who rejected entryism came to adopt a strategy that, in its own tangential way, came to resemble it. More independent on paper, these men were also, paradoxically, more dependent on the Congress. When the Fourth Party was wound down, many felt betrayed—but many also felt powerless, helpless even. The Congress was only ready to accommodate a few entryists on the Bombay Municipal Corporation. Elsewhere, where the balance of power was less precarious and the Muslim presence negligible, Muslims could safely be ignored. Unsurprisingly, Fourth Party bosses in Poona, Surat, and Ahmedabad pronounced the *mésalliance* ill-judged.

But going it alone was easier said than done. In Bombay, Ghulam M. Banatwalla, the local League's leading light and later seven-time MP, was defeated by the PCC general secretary in the 1962 assembly election. A tough hand became even tougher in 1967 when cumulative voting in multi-member constituencies was scrapped.[43] Leaguers tried to prevent the Congress from ramming the electoral reform through the Lower House. Ismail pointed out that with a 'minority of 45 per cent', the Congress had sustained artificial majorities of '75 per cent of the seats in Parliament'. To this a livid Congressman replied that 'those members of legislative bodies who persistently defied the chair', opposition parliamentarians such as Ismail, ought to be 'debarred from elections'.[44] Here G. N. Dixit betrayed a not uncommon sentiment: an unease with democracy and pluralism widely shared in Mrs Gandhi's Congress; even the premier herself was not above it. But there was little Leaguers could do. Banatwalla's partisans, who had rejected absorption into the Congress, suddenly found themselves forced to seek out questionable allies. Desperation prompted the League to partner up with the Sampoorna Maharashtra Samiti, itself an unconvincing amalgam of Socialists, the Peasants' and Workers' Party, two communist parties, the sugar-lobby vehicle Janata Aghadi, and ... the Hindu Mahasabha.

Rapid decline took root. Testament to this was the fact that, from 1977 on, even Banatwalla did not seek election from Bombay, but rather from the safe seat of Ponnani in Kerala. Four in five of its residents were Muslim. He did not have Malayalam, but then again, this was hardly an insuperable problem in the rotten borough, where he was wont to campaign 'door to door in breathless English ... Everyone listens attentively except they do not understand a word of what he says'. But this mattered little, for, as *India Today*'s reporter wryly noted by way of explanation, 'incomprehension has nothing to do with faith'.[45]

In the event, while Banatwalla may not have joined the Congress, his political élan was, for all his independence, more Congressman and less Leaguer. His obituary in the London *Times* reflects on his supremely 'careful style', his studied 'reluctance to use belligerent language', his stoical refusal to condemn 'Hindu fanatics anxious to heap more misery on an already downtrodden people'. Like most Congressmen, Banatwalla preferred the culture wars to political concerns, attracting press coverage for condemning the national song, Vande Mataram, as 'anti-Muslim', and hitting out at Taslima Nasrin, the *émigré* free speech activist exiled from her native Bangladesh—later banished from India as well—for the same reason. More obviously political matters were another matter. On his account, nothing was to be gained from deploring the flattening of the Babri Masjid. Accordingly, he tiptoed around what was indisputably a watershed in interfaith relations, if not the most important development in the religious life of the Republic.[46]

The Banatwalla line was, in effect, a parody of Fourth Party entryism: strategically its obverse, but teleologically of a piece with it. Where it merged into the Congress to influence it from within, Banatwalla steadfastly held his own even as he became a virtual understudy to the nationalist Muslim. They were both, after a fashion, biddable, quietist, depoliticised, and culturally inclined—in other words, carbon copies of the nationalist Muslims. The Fourth Party surrendered political autonomy to the Congress party apparatus; Banatwalla, to the Congress worldview.

An analogous strategy was deployed by the All-India Muslim League, albeit with one crucial difference: it was less interested in mimesis than collaboration. More important to it was being in the Congress' good books. A breakaway from the IUML, the IAML was formed in October 1961 by Mohamed Raza Khan after his failed coup to defenestrate Ismail.

Now, Khan and Ismail had form. Interestingly, it was the former who had facilitated the latter's rise. When Jamal Mohammad, the most powerful man in the Madras League, had stepped down in 1939 to attend to the financial difficulties plaguing his business empire,

Khan had connived with other party notables to block the ascent of his apprentice Abdul Hamid Khan, a former mayor of Madras. Probably cursing himself for it later, Raza Khan had gone on to egg the presumably more malleable Ismail into running against the rising star. As it was, Ismail not only won the leadership but also ruthlessly set about consolidating power in his own name. In 1945, when Raza Khan's clique tried to prevent him from assuming the presidency, it was too late. By then, he had packed the parliamentary party with allies, and with a vote of 5 to 4, installed himself as party leader.[47]

Soon after its formation, the AIML pledged support to the 'secular national leadership', denouncing the League's promiscuity; at the time, Ismail was busy shopping around for allies, striking deals with the DMK in the South, RPI in the West, and SAD in the North. An early statement appealed to the better nature of Congressmen, imploring them 'to treat the Muslim community with sympathy'.[48] Here, then, was the petitioning élan that *fin-de-siècle* Congressmen had adopted to influence Raj policy. It was also just as ineffective.

This was because, ideologically speaking, there was little that the AIML had to offer. Simultaneously making its pitch to the Congress and the ordinary Muslim, it ultimately appealed to neither. Voters felt they were in hock to Congressmen, who, for their part, bristled at Khan's suggestion that the nationalist Muslims 'sat in an ivory tower, pampered by their admirers in the majority community'.[49] Even so, eager as ever to divide a foe, Kamaraj readily bankrolled Khan's League and its English fortnightly *Tarjuman*, a rival organ to Ismail's *Siraat*.

But funds alone proved a poor substitute for a political programme. There was little to Khan's platform beyond 'patriotism', a quality which he felt Muslims were deficient in. There was only so much that could be achieved by tearing into the DMK for burning copies of the Indian Constitution, extolling the armed forces every time the country went to war, and calling for the extension of the reservations enjoyed by the Lebbais to the rest of the community.

In his memoirs, Khan gloomily reflected that the love for the Congress was unrequited. 'We were misunderstood. We were not able to do much'. The moment of realisation had been his defeat in the Madras election of 1964. Further confirmation came with his crack at rapprochement between the two Leagues the next year, which he abandoned after a few combined rallies in which it became apparent that all the future held for him was a repeat of his Boswellian past, years spent playing second fiddle to Ismail. If the Congress was the devil, Ismail was the deep sea. So, the career politician decided to withdraw from politics proper, venting his grievances in the pages of *Tarjuman* instead.[50] As for the AIML itself, it ambled along under M. S. A. Majid, a nondescript nonentity still wedded to Delhi's rulers, until its eventual absorption into the IUML in 1985.

The IUML itself, it must be said, was not above cutting deals with the Congress. Indeed, their late colonial rivalry, and the reductive contrast between Congress secularism and League communalism, have obscured what is in fact a much more complex picture. For even as it pursued its long march through the institutions, the League nevertheless sought, every so often, to associate with Delhi's rulers, entering into electoral pacts and serving cheek by jowl with Congressmen in government. For their part, Congress regional leaderships were quite content with such shotgun weddings. Green or red, communal or secular, an ally was an ally; and sometimes, one simply needed allies. Delhi, however, was less sanguine.

When, for instance, the Madras Congress struck a deal with the League ahead of the 1952 municipal election, the high command was anything but amenable. Standing down in constituencies with sizeable Muslim population was not only unpalatable, it was a vindication of Jinnah's argument. The Muslim League 'is a pernicious organisation. I wish to give it no quarter', Nehru wrote the Madras PCC president P. Subbaroyan, architect of the pact. There was, undoubtedly, a touch of Northern, perhaps even Kashmiri *pandit*, disdain for the Madrasi Muslim in Nehru's missive. For, it seems, it was not merely the League that was worthy of contempt, it was the ordinary Muslim of that province, too. 'Why have we failed in Madras in regard to the Muslims?' he asked:

> I think there has been too much softness shown to them … It may, of course, be possible to win a few seats with their help. But I would sooner lose those seats than seek their help … Muslims in Madras, if I may say so with all respect, are singularly ignorant of what goes by the name [*sic*] Muslim culture.[51]

159

He went on to note that he found risible the Madrasi Muslim usage of the Urdu honorific *janab*—lit. 'sir', but closer to 'Your Excellency'—which was both dated and alien. 'It would be perfectly absurd to use that appellation in North India'. Needless to say, the identitarian import of what he dismissed as a contrivance, that it was a way to mobilise the Muslim community—not very different, in fact, from his own stab at playing native, what with his carefully cultivated sartorial choices: the over-thought *dhoti*, *kurta*, jacket, and cap—seems to have completely eluded him.

Accordingly, the central leadership vetoed the deal. As it was, though, Subbaroyan surreptitiously disobeyed Delhi's directive in Tiruchirappalli and a handful of other municipal constituencies, to the benefit of both the local Congress and the League. Similarly, two years later, when the Scheduled Caste leader Kamaraj Nadar replaced the Brahmin C. Rajagopalachari as Madras chief minister in order to thwart the anti-*savarna* DMK, he was only able to win his by-election in Muslim-heavy Gudiyattam thanks to League support.[52]

The logic of Congress-League solidarity was underscored *à l'envers* as well. In next-door Kerala, it was only because Nehru vetoed the triple alliance with the League and the PSP that the Communists swept to power in 1957. Likewise, in 1961, Delhi's distaste for the 'communal' League cost it an important by-election. At first, the Congress in Kerala had been prepared to let the League's Mohsin bin Ahmed run unchallenged for the late K. M. Seethi Sahib's seat, which had freed on account of the long-running IUML general secretary's death. Delhi, however, was disinclined to take the view that this was sportsmanship. So a suitable candidate, K. Kunhi Mohammed, was flown in from on high. When the state Congress went so far as to expel him from the party, the centre saw to it that he ran as an independent. The League had the last laugh. Ahmed trounced Mohammed.

All the fractiousness notwithstanding, the League and the Congress did cooperate on occasion. In Kerala, the Congress could not ignore the League for long, given the sheer instability of politics there. In the seventeen years to 1965, the state saw seven elections, nine ministries, and three spells of President's Rule. The ever-tottering balance of power ensured that every party, the

League included, found itself sought after at some point. Happily, party-political support more or less mapped onto primordial social cleavages. The CPI was effectively the party of ex-Untouchables and the Ezhavas, the toddy-tappers.[53] The Congress was a Christian-Nair affair. The League alone stood for Muslim interests. Inevitably, the Congress had to from time to time seek out the League. Such deals, of course, were ephemeral and entailed, on the part of the Muslims, much propitiatory hand-wringing.

Still, Leaguers felt it was worth it. After teaming up in Kerala to foment the extra-parliamentary overthrow of the Communist government in 1959, in the election that followed, the League ran on a platform of 'communism is *haram*', declaring a vote for the three-party—Congress, League, Socialist—alliance a 'religious duty' for Muslims. The confidence of Leaguers was growing by the day. Illustrative was the boast of one of its notables: 'Nehru had to seek our assistance to defeat the Communists in Kerala'.[54] There was more than just braggadocio. In West Bengal and Madhya Pradesh, League units were sprouting like mushrooms after the rain. The world was going its way.

Not for long. After the election, the Congress at once turned hostile. Thanks to its strong showing—its seat share increased by nearly 50 per cent thanks to League and Socialist support, even as it lost a tenth of its vote share—its ally had become perfectly dispensable. Now branding the League 'communal', the Congress essayed to keep it out of government. All it offered was the assembly speakership and a Rajya Sabha seat, scraps spurned by Ismail.[55] Beggars, however, cannot be choosers. Operating from a position of weakness, what with a mere eleven seats, the League offered unconditional support to the Congress-PSP government, hoping to influence policy without portfolios.[56]

But propping up Trivandrum's rulers failed to end the untouchability of Muslim politics. As before, after every riot, Congressmen renewed their threats to ban the League, the alliance notwithstanding. Moreover, when Sahib broached the subject of electoral reform, calling for an end to the gerrymandering of Muslim-heavy constituencies and demanding proportional representation in multi-member constituencies, the reply he received was unequivocal:

161

no dice.[57] The *coup de grâce* came when he died in April 1961. The Congress agreed to let a Leaguer, C. H. Mohammed Koya, fill his shoes as speaker only after he resigned from the party. Only as an 'independent' was he palatable to Kerala's nationalist Muslims, who were lobbying for one of their own, Nafeesath Beevi, to replace the deceased Leaguer. Once again, Ismail took this in his stride, believing that, on balance, working with the Congress was better than working against it.

Taking a long view of the strained partnership, it becomes clear that the League did profit from it after all. Slowly but surely, the Congress at the centre reconciled itself to local imperatives. Indira Gandhi gave her blessings to the United Front government, a coalition of Congressmen, Communists, and Leaguers which ruled Trivandrum for nine years until 1979, even as it put her in a tight spot. Symptomatic were the flights of oratory on display in the CWC meetings of the early seventies, one of which had her admonishing the League for 'spreading communal poison' in Uttar Pradesh even as she defended in the next breath her alliance with the very same communalists in Kerala.[58] By the end of the decade, even these inhibitions had been cast away. Koya secured the Congress' support to become the first and only Muslim League chief minister in the history of the Republic in 1979. Admittedly, his government lasted a mere fifty days. He lost his majority when A. K. Antony's Congress (Urs) stabbed him in the back.[59]

Where once, in the early fifties, the League had to contend with the taint of communalism, three decades on it had become a 'normal' party, worthy of association and alliance. To be sure, the passage of time had played a part in its mainstreaming—Jinnah fading from public memory—and so had circumstances, on account of the dramatic tenor of Keralite politics. But undeniably, so, too, had the League itself, craftily strategising, biding its time, swallowing its pride, by turns appealing to and appeasing Congressmen, all the while building on its strengths, making its presence more acceptable in the febrile political landscape, and, in the process, destigmatising Muslim politics.

'The Protest Vote'

The long march was wrecked on the shoals of Congress hegemony. Entryism foundered on the rocks of inaction. To many Muslim political actors of the day, the costs of both far outweighed the gains. They were, then, unwilling to steer a course between the Scylla and Charybdis of go-it-alone assertive Muslim politics and near-slavish alignment with the Congress. That they had nothing, and so nothing to lose, was their original insight. Politically, this translated into a most improbable tactic: the protest vote. The objective was to undermine the nationalist Muslims at any cost, even self-harm, such as when they enabled a Hindu nationalist candidate to defeat a Congressman.

As a phenomenon, the protest vote was rare. But of its existence there can be little doubt. Moreover, it is important to us because it speaks volumes about the quandaries of the *qaum*, its sorry condition, which made Muslims ready, not unlike the child who slashes his wrists to evince his dissatisfaction with life to his parents, to countenance self-harm simply in order to be seen by the state. Even the League, at times, was not above self-destructive revanchism. Emblematic was Ismail's negotiating position with the Congress in 1951: either accept the League as the sole representative of the *qaum* by agreeing not to field Muslim candidates or risk its wrath. The proposition, of course, was unacceptable to the Congress. The upshot? The League withdrew its offer, expending its energies instead on stymieing the efforts of Congressmen seeking election.

The Congress' comportment in office only confirmed its suspicions. For one thing, Delhi set about gerrymandering constituencies, skewing contests against the League. The reorganisation of states similarly took the wind out of its sails. First, in 1953, coastal Andhra was detached from Madras to weaken Communist influence, reducing as a result the bargaining power of the League, now perfectly superfluous to the revitalised Congress. Three years later came a second scission, this time severing Malabar from Madras and combining it with Travancore-Cochin to create Kerala. Again, the League was thrown into disarray, its centre of gravity shifting to the new state. Ismail had to go through the motions of co-opting Malayalam-speaking elites in Kerala and Tamil-speaking Lebbais in Madras, which traded English for Tamil as the state's official language.

The fifties were a low point for Congress-League relations. Rare were instances of cooperation, such as when Rajagopalachari enlisted League support to survive a vote of confidence in 1952. Here, again, the League availed itself of the protest vote—after a fashion. In exchange for its backing, it demanded a guarantee from Rajagopalachari—which he provided without missing a beat—that no nationalist Muslim would be inducted into his ministry. Discrediting Congress Muslims took precedence over augmenting Muslim representation in the League's calculus. Party trumped communitarian interest.[60]

Five years later came a re-enactment, albeit with a twist. Ahead of the 1957 election, in yet another slapdash effort to court Muslims, Kamaraj offered the League a dozen tickets. This, it should be said, was the best he could come up with, for his hands were tied on account of the squeamishness of his colleagues in Delhi, who wanted nothing—nothing in plain sight, at any rate—to do with a 'communal' party. Ismail turned down the offer. As it was, eighteen Keralite Leaguers ran as independents because the Election Commission refused to recognise the party. Nine won. True, the League worked hard to win, but it worked even harder to see Congressmen bite the dust. So much so that party workers actively campaigned for Hindu candidates most likely to beat Congress Muslims.

A few months on, the League could look back at its handiwork with some satisfaction. For one thing, Congressmen were seething with fury. C. K. Govindan Nair, the local PCC president, blamed the drubbing on Muslims. The Communists won a comfortable victory. A mere six nationalist Muslims took their seats into the bargain. But the protest vote came at a bloody price. For weeks into the new administration, sectarian violence broke out in Cannanore, a coastal town in North Malabar with a large Muslim presence. Sunnis and Wahabis clobbered one another, and the police looked the other way. Kerala's new Communist rulers, it appears, saw it as none of their business to interfere in what was purely a religious matter.[61] This raises a counterfactual question: if ensconced in Trivandrum with the help of the League, would the Congress have taken an equally detached view?

More generally as well, the same dilemma obtained. To have friends in high places or to register a protest vote? The League tried, by turns, to take power in its own name; curry favour with the revolving cast of rulers in Trivandrum, Madras, and Delhi, variously the DMK, CPI, and INC; and record protest votes against them. If the former two strategies produced unspectacular results, the latter tactic was no better. Frustrating Congress Muslims was one thing, furthering the League's prospects another. Smarting from the League's wiles to pull them down, livid Congressmen time and again dealt with it by deploying the punitive might of the state, as ever at their service in early postcolonial India, the happy product of permanent incumbency. Leaguers were detained in Aligarh and Lucknow on the flimsiest of charges. The party's Calcutta offices were sequestrated. The editor of its mouthpiece *Nai Duniya*, Maulana Abdul Waheed Siddiqui, was locked up for having the temerity to propose a new branch in the capital.[62]

The League's reaction was yet another protest vote. In 1964, it cajoled the Christian leadership of the Congress into defecting from the party, bringing down the R. Sankar government in the process. Now, had the eleven Leaguers in the assembly refused to play Iago to K. M. George's Othello, the Congress' Christians most certainly would never have had the nerve to create the Kerala Congress; in the event, they did, assured of League support in a confidence motion, which duly arrived in autumn. The elation, however, was short-lived. If Trivandrum had been a terror, the toppling of Sankar's government brought a commensurate, perhaps greater, monster to the state. The League now had to face up to much more vigilance and mistrust, since Kerala had been placed under President's Rule— in other words, under the watchful eyes of Delhi. Another wave of arrests, detentions, and sequestrations ensued.

Protest voting, of course, was not the preserve of the League. Another brief example should suffice for our purposes here. In 1967, in Chandni Chowk, an overcrowded and impoverished inner-city Muslim ghetto in Delhi that was once the commercial heart of the Mughal Empire, a group of politically minded 'Muslim teenagers'

165

decided to revolt against their condition. Tired of the Congress, whose candidates had been returned to Parliament from the bowels of Chandni Chowk with scarce contest for two decades, the striplings struck out on their own. On the hustings, then, two bands of Muslim entrepreneurs were to be found out and about: one supporting the local Hindu Congressman, Sham Nath, who had signed up to a Muslim-friendly 'pledge' imposed on him by local notables; the other the Anjuman Naujawan-e-Millat [lit. the Community Youth Association] candidate, Hafiza Ali Bahadur. Surprising even her own associates, the tyro carried a sixth of the vote, undercutting—first-past-the-post being what it is—the Congressman's majority and allowing a Jana Sanghi, no less, to wrest the seat from the incumbent. In effect, the protest vote of the radical Muslim youths had helped send, if only unwittingly, a Hindu nationalist to Parliament from Chandni Chowk.[63]

Agentic and damaging in equal measure, the protest vote ultimately had an import that could not be gauged in purely material terms. Here was a politics of dignity. It did not matter that acts of self-preservation contained in them the seeds of self-destruction; as Freud tell us, Eros and Thanatos, the life and death instincts, are Siamese twins. To the Muslim political elites engineering protest votes, incrementalism would not do. Having no say, then, was better than having some say in Muslim affairs, so long as it meant being seen and heard, considerations that were in short supply for Muslims in postcolonial India.

'Refrain from Being Cantankerous'

The long march showed that beating the Congress at its game was impossible. Entryism entailed a near-complete loss of communitarian identity. The protest vote was self-defeating. Small wonder, then, a section of the Muslim political class was prepared to reject party politics *tout court*. Such a worldview naturally inclined them towards the Tocquevillian promise of voluntarism, premised on spontaneity and self-interest, so celebrated by the Frenchman. But democracy in India was a world removed from *Democracy in America*, whose passages describe a people singularly taken up by associationalism:

'In the United States, people associate for purposes pertaining to public security, commerce and industry, morality and religion. There is nothing the human will despairs of achieving through the free action of the collective power of individuals'.[64]

Such a cheerful view of the power of associations was unthinkable in the early postcolonial Indian setting, where suspicion of any kind of extraparliamentary political activity was the norm. A whole lexicon—'sedition', 'foreign hand', 'anti-national', and, above all, 'communal'—served to discredit sectional groups, none of which, by definition, could measure up to the rhetorical sleight of hand perfected by the Congress to present its own interests as the common good. If associations in general were thought to be potentially dangerous, needless to say, minority associations—especially Muslim ones—were even more suspect. To be sure, Nehru's and then Mrs Gandhi's five-year plans waxed lyrical about their transformative and emancipatory power.[65] But even so, in practice, neither the state nor the public warmed to them. 'Indians suffer from too narrow a definition of politics', Theodore P. Wright Jr would rightly complain.[66]

Advancing Muslims interests through associations, then, was always going to be a tough ask. Indeed, many found the very prospect discomfiting. Soliciting votes in God's name was perfectly acceptable, of a piece with the grammar of Indian politics as it was, but any deeper imbrication of faith and politics warranted caution. So many Leaguers put up stiff resistance to the associational turn championed by hard-line elements of the party, who argued that electoral considerations detracted from larger issues: it was time the League redirected attention to strengthening Islamic identity, organising 'training camps' and running Quranic groups. When these began springing up across the Malabar coast, nervous Leaguers made for the door, some, such as M. K. Ummer, secretary of the Mattancherry branch, going so far as to protest against them alongside nationalist Muslims.[67]

Added to apprehension about Hindu reaction were more practical concerns. Militating against associationalism was the simple fact that India was (and is) a partocracy. Indeed, from the highest reaches of political life in the land to the lowest, the values of partocracy prevail. Power and pork barrels, clients and contracts, even jobs and the justice system—all course, in some shape or form, through the sinews of party politics. Where parties commanded the loyalties of the teeming masses—the Congress boasted 11 million members in 1967; the League half a million in 1971—civil society organisations, with the honourable exception of the Sangh Parivar nebula, barely left a mark.[68] The corresponding figure for the Islamist charity Jama'at-i-Islami, one of the largest Muslim organisations, offers some sobering perspective: 2,000 members at the close of the sixties.[69] Simply put, associations had been crowded out by parties.

Their parlous financial condition added to their woes. All told, their achievements were modest, pale in comparison to those of their world-historical contemporaries, say, the Edhi Foundation in Pakistan or the Aga Khan Foundation, to think of two obvious examples. Both the latter possessed large networks of volunteers conducting relief operations, running schools, funding businesses, and disbursing aid. To many, they were nothing less than a parallel welfare state. Meanwhile, Muslim associations in India could only look on in envy. Even the largest of them had to make do with social provision on the cheap. For the Jama'at, largesse was not an option, hence, its focus on pedagogy—libraries, reading rooms, printing presses and the like.

Smaller, more regional Muslim outfits tended to be even more starved of funds. In Assam, for instance, the Shillong Muslim Union—established in 1905 and once the throbbing heart of philanthropic activity in the province, enjoying a considerable rentier income, not to mention the patronage of Saadulla and Fakhruddin Ali Ahmed—was in dire straits. In 1962, a frustrated *maktab*, primary school, teacher could be found lamenting the absence of assistance after the devastating floods as well as the plight of his employers, who had been unable to pay his salary for fifteen months. In better days, he wrote, the SMU would have stepped in.[70]

Such a shambles was not unusual. The Tameer-e-Millat, one of the largest Muslim associations in Hyderabad, too, struggled to branch out beyond educational activity. Penniless and plagued by malfeasance—every so often its managers were caught with their hand in the till—it had just about enough funds to put together a few 'study circles and educational meetings' and organise the occasional 'social event'. But little else. The National Integration and Spiritual Rearmament Congress, another Hyderabadi association, found itself in a similar predicament. A lack of pecuniary means induced, as recompense, a penchant for abstraction. Unusually for a minority association, it 'focused not on political and economic striving, but on higher, spiritual principle'. Its constitution was, in essence, a miscellany of lofty and lyrical New Age nostrums. Its aim, we are told, was to 'humanise, universalise, and divinise the social behaviour of men'. More practically, this translated into encouraging Muslims to conduct *yagnas*, sacrifices, and pray alongside people of other faiths at churches, temples, and *gurudwaras*. In the event, it had 'no appreciable success in achieving these goals'.[71]

For all that—government suspicions, monetary limitations—it must be said that for Muslims, associationalism had an undeniably seductive logic. The Indian state, as we have seen *passim*, was often an Islamophobic agency. Changing state behaviour from within was not really an option. For one thing, the bureaucracy was closed to them. In the early Nehru years, Muslims were removed *en masse* from public positions amidst fears of Pakistani 'fifth columnists' that had it in for India. Muslims, perforce, had to sidestep the state.

An early indication of the efficacy of civil society came in 1952, when campaigners petitioning for the recognition of Urdu as a second language in Uttar Pradesh managed to collect a staggering 2.2 million signatures, which were forwarded, doubtless on untold reams of paper, to the president of the Republic.[72] Admittedly, at the time, the activism was of little account. To the chagrin of Muslims, the UP Official Languages Act only recognised Hindi, providing cover for the suspension of state aid to Urdu schools. Still, given the preference of the Hindu Congress elite, the associational option was the only sound one. Dr Sampurnanand's view on the matter is illustrative. A Sanskritist and one of the state's longest-serving chief ministers, he did not mince his words. Urdu, he wrote in his *Memories and Reflections*, was a 'language of the *bazaar*, un-national if not anti-national'.[73]

Muslims hardly had any reason to rejoice when the Kripalani Committee of 1961, ostensibly constituted to inquire into the grievances of Urdu speakers, delivered its stern verdict. Muslims were advised to 'refrain from being cantankerous', and Lucknow warned against 'creating special vested interests' that would later prove hard to 'dislodge'.[74]

As weapons of the weak went, then, popular pressure was as good as it got for Muslims. The Anjuman Taraqqi-e-Urdu took up the cudgels for the tongue in the sixties, passing the baton to the publicly funded Urdu Academy in the seventies. Ultimately, associational activity dovetailed with party-political action. For it was in the competitive electoral environment of eighties Uttar Pradesh that Muslims were able to turn their lobbying to account. In its 1980 manifesto, the Congress—now frailer, so readier to heed Muslim opinion—made its first explicit promise to recognise Urdu as a second language, a pledge it finally fulfilled ahead of the 1989 election.[75]

Muslim associations, then, were subject to party-political co-option, and ultimately Congress domination. There is an irony here, for the very promise of associationalism—its distance from party politics—was subverted.

All the same, associationalism could just as well produce depoliticisation, vacuity even, vociferous proclamations of nationalism taking precedence over all else. Two of the largest Muslim civil society organisations of the early postcolonial period, the Muslim Convention and the—unrelated—Muslim Convention of South India, are cases in point.

Right from the outset, the MCSI was an arm of the party in power. Indeed, the list of the attendees of its first session read like a Who's Who of the Congress. As if to disabuse Muslims of lingering doubts about where its loyalties lay, it made clear ahead of its first meeting, in December 1956, that it hoped to 'give a lead to Muslims of South India to abandon its concept [sic] of separate entity and to advise them to join forces with progressive political elements'.[76] Now, which were these? Syed Mahmud, its president, who, as we saw in Chapter 3, was not above likening himself to Nehru's loyal mutt, helpfully supplied an answer, making clear that the use of the plural—'progressive political elements'—was unmerited: 'Muslims must throw in their lot with the Congress, the best organisation from all points of view'.[77] Speaking after Mahmud, the well-upholstered Mohammed Usman, a Justice Party stalwart and former Madras governor, went further: 'to vote against the Congress at this juncture' was 'an un-Islamic act', no less.[78] Nationalist Muslims had come to acquire, in the language of military strategists, full-spectrum dominance in this notionally unattached association.

The League was the MCSI's foil. In fact, it was its very existence that had provoked the creation of the Convention, even if its convenors often made light of it. So, while, on the one hand, it could self-assuredly conclude that 'the Muslims have been steadily adjusting themselves', leaving only a few 'League die-hards' in Coimbatore and Fort Cochin occupied with the Sisyphean task of opposing the Congress, on the other it felt explicit disavowal was in order, the dreaded party in question even warranting scare quotes, as if its very existence was a matter of conjecture: the MCSI 'abjured communal political organisations like the "All-India Muslim League", regarding their activities as detrimental to their true interests'.[79]

If the MCSI was a creature of the Congress, its élan was that of the nationalist Muslims. The occasional plea for reservations apart, all it offered was nationalist guff, flag hoisting and patriotic sermonising being standard fare at its congresses. 'Let Mussalmans of India beware, let us not become a caste of untouchables', Mahmud declared.[80] But how, more prosaically, was the *qaum* to escape its bleak condition? 'The remedy is to belong truly to the great organism of India so that we should circulate freely in its blood stream'. Platitude for platitude.[81]

Motivational talk, of course, made a poor proxy for associational activity proper. Nor did it help that the Convention did not want to wade into the 'Urdu-Hindi controversy': it 'had no meaning today'. It appears that the MCSI notables were more exercised about foreign affairs than their poorer brethren at home. At one of its meetings, the *nawab* of Chhatari broke into a harangue about Pakistan, whose rulers, for admittedly cynical purposes, had raised the alarm over India's treatment of its Muslims: 'it is not the concern of those people to be concerned about us'. Usman looked further west, thanking Nehruvian benevolence for letting Indian Muslims publicly support Nasser's nationalisation of the Suez Canal, an 'Islamic cause', he quaintly declared, imperilled by the Israeli invasion under Anglo-French aegis of the Sinai.[82]

For all that, the MCSI still appeared too 'political' for some, a reflection of the general odium attached to associationalism. Indeed, its failure to persuade Mirza Ismail, a former secretary to the Mysore *maharaja* and Hyderabad Nizam, to take up the presidency makes for an instructive, if melancholy, episode.[83]

Now, on the face of it, the toffee-nosed Ismail appeared a perfect fit with the Convention. To begin with it, he was no radical. In the raging language wars of the fifties, he had sought a *via media*: Hindi, because 'it is so highly Sanskritised', was 'quite alien' beyond the. Hindi belt, and Urdu equally arcane on account of 'its Persianised quality'. A nationwide imposition of either would only betray 'provincialism'. English was the way out.[84] A similar pragmatism guided his concern for 'the wretched Kashmir quarrel'. Along with B. N. Rau, Ismail counselled Nehru to turn the Valley into an autonomous region, holding on to Ladakh and Jammu but conceding Azad Kashmir and Poonch to Pakistan. 'The prime minister would not hear of it'.[85]

Ismail not only shared in the Convention's spirit of compromise, but also its superciliousness. Its prescription for emancipation was entirely apolitical, rooted in a language of self-help and nationalist declamation. Here, there was no room for the gritty world of marches and hustings. Indeed, the business of the MCSI was entirely transacted at elite conclaves. Likewise, the mandarin, in true technocratic fashion, felt that it was the responsibility of elites, figures such as himself, to 'raise the spirit of unity and tolerance' in the country. Even so, mass education was unwholesome: the whole 'scheme smacked of aboriginality', he noted in the *Leader*, feigning incomprehension at 'the nation's new-fangled enthusiasm for the common man'.[86] As he saw it, 'the best form of government' was 'one in which democracy is tempered with might be called "elitocracy" or the rule of the best elements of the community'.[87]

The synergies notwithstanding, *plus royalistes que le roi*, Ismail turned down the presidency. 'We should avoid having a separate political organisation as it is bound to arouse distrust in the minds of our fellow-countrymen'.[88] The remark underscored the discomfiture of many Muslims, who felt that, for all its external trappings, associationalism was not entirely dissimilar to party politics, and, for this reason, equally *haram*. Ismail's maxim from his memoirs, 'it is never safe or wise to project religion into politics and allow politics to masquerade in the guise of religion' was a widely shared one.[89]

As with the MCSI, so with the Muslim Convention. Here, too, the twin characteristics of Congress dominance and depoliticisation were on display. Formed in June 1961 at the instigation of the JUH's Maulana Hifzur Rahman, the MC was to act as a brake on the League, which had made strides in the municipal elections of Bombay, Bhopal, and Ahmadabad that followed the riots of February.[90] A harbinger was the Muslim Convention of 1960, also chaired by Mahmud. Nothing had come of that venture. Jama'at-i-Islami leaders and Congressmen learnt the hard way that faith made for a poor sealant. Some ideological differences were simply unsurmountable. The same discovery was made when pan-Islamic parleys resumed in May 1961. Rahman's catchphrase, 'the national integration of Muslims', was not merely objectionable to the Jama'at, it was beyond the pale. The Islamists were working towards an 'Islamic revolution' in which Indian Muslims had no option but to play 'the historical role of the leadership of mankind'.[91] As it was, both the Jama'at and League were kept out.

No effort was made to cloak Congress hegemony or conceal its fundamentally anti-political agenda. Muslim business interests managed to throw out the demand for parliamentary quotas. Meanwhile, the call for reservations for Muslim industrialists in government advisory committees—on trade, finance, banking, and insurance—was left in. Yusuf Shirazi, speaking for capital, suggested that the Convention's first order of business ought to be the creation of Muslim chambers of commerce and industry across the country. As for the ostensible excuse for the meeting, putting together relief aid for the victims of the Jabalpur riots, it barely cropped up. Clearly, capital was in the driving seat, leaving the clergy and career politicians to carp about the appropriation of the MC by 'Muslim business interests, this group of successors of the Ispahanis and Suhrawardys'.[92] Most of its meetings, it seems, were whiled away discussing definitions of secularism. Unsurprisingly, little came of it in the end.

All in all, the experience of the MC and MCSI suggests that to be a leading Muslim association in early postcolonial India was to walk a tight-rope, and ultimately do very little. Associationalism, moreover, was beset by the same dilemmas faced by the practitioners of party politics proper. Unsurprisingly. The leading nationalist Muslims of the day were also the movers and shakers of Muslim civil society. Partocracy and civil society parsimony saw to that.

Lacking funds and mass cadres, Muslim associations in India also lacked the reach of their peers in the Muslim world, outfits such as the Edhi and Aga Khan Foundations. But then again, they were cast in a different mould. As elite concerns, more interested in summitry than charity, they were more akin to lobbying groups than developmental agencies. As such, they fared no better. Muslim associationalism ultimately was a flight to nowhere. With little clout—financial or moral—and little interest in carrying out sustained, issue-based campaigns, let alone shaping national discourse, the MC and MCSI did not hold a candle to, say, the NAACP or the Board of Deputies, to take two obvious world-historical parallels.

'Judged by its Potentialities'

Strategically, both party politics and associationalism let down Indian Muslims. Teleologically, however, both achieved more than what is apparent at first blush. For, collectively, if unintentionally, the long march, protest vote, entryism, and associationalism produced an ambience of disaffection whose cumulative effect was a deafening crescendo, one the Congress could ill-afford to ignore. The upshot was panic at the highest levels of power in Delhi and the state capitals, productive for Muslims as it was perturbing for Congressmen. Analogous to the Red Scare in the advanced capitalist world, this was, as it were, a Green Scare.

Just as the threat of communism altered North Atlantic state and society—through welfarism, social democracy, statism—without the red flag ever flying over Western capitals, the coeval threat of 'communalism' in the Indian setting equally indirectly ameliorated the lives of ordinary Muslims. The bugbear of a largely imaginary communalism, in short, produced a veritable affirmative action programme for Muslim India.

It is useful to recall here Rajni Kothari's landmark essay on the 'Congress system' in India, wherein 'political competition was internalised and carried on within the Congress'. On this account, in the fifties and sixties, non-Congress formations acted not as opposition parties as such, but as 'parties of pressure', changing the balance of opinion within the Congress rather than presenting a serious alternative to it. This is true, but not in the sense that he meant it.

Kothari was not only a formidable institution builder, but also an eminent Nehruvian. Something of the panegyrist remained in his oeuvre, traces of an exculpatory temptation he found difficult to resist appearing in more places than one. Indeed, the essay in question is best read as an astute work of Nehruvian propaganda. The 'Congress system', in effect, put a liberal spin on one-party democracy. Despite having achieved hegemony, we are told, the Congress showed 'great sensitivity on the question of respect for minorities'.[93]

On closer inspection, the Congress system appears as one whose ordering principle was not accommodation but fear: namely that which Kothari's parties of pressure instilled in the Congress. The sops came on sufferance. Tangible benefits flowed to Muslims not because of Nehruvian benevolence, but the fear induced by the prospect of electoral defeat, a reversal of the regime of permanent incumbency. I have argued elsewhere that the Congress adopted the language of the Left when its position was threatened by socialists and communists alike, putting together some semblance of a welfare state and instituting land reform in order to tranquilise the restive *mofussil*, brimming as it was with dangerous ideas.[94] Likewise, the incipient success of Muslim parties and associations dictated that they be nipped in the bud and the community's interests heeded.

The case of Hyderabad is instructive. Here, Muslim politics had a late start. Resolved to snuff out dissent in the unruly Deccan princely state—ruled since the early eighteenth century by the Nizam—Delhi dispatched its armed forces in September 1948 to subdue the twin threats posed by the Muslim Razakar militia

175

and peasant-led communist insurgency. The crushing of both also killed off Muslim politics. For quashing the militia also entailed overwhelming the All-India Majlis Ittihad-ul-Muslimin, the political corollary to the paramilitary Razakars, formed in 1927 and forced into administration upon Hyderabad's annexation. Its leader Kasim Razvi, a votary of Hyderabadi sovereignty, was sent packing to prison for *dacoity*, brigandage. Hyderabad's Muslims, then, had little option but to throw in their lot with either the Congress or the communist People's Democratic Front, now cleaned up and shorn of its anti-parliamentary radicalism.

The Congress only permitted, so to speak, Muslim politics in Hyderabad in the late fifties—at a time and on terms of its choosing. The AIMIM leadership was released from prison in 1957, when the Congress, cynically enough, felt it could benefit from a counterweight to the PDF, whose socialist platform was winning it considerable subaltern Muslim support. The decision the previous year to hive off parts of Hyderabad state to Bombay and Mysore, reducing by 40 per cent the Muslim proportion of the population in the rump Andhra Pradesh, cushioned the potential blow. Nehru's thoughts of his legacy must not be discounted. A decade in power and soon to enter his eighth, the premier released not only Razvi, but also, a few months later, another recalcitrant Muslim, Jammu and Kashmir's Sheikh Abdullah, from his prisons.

Appointing Abdul Wahid Owaisi as his successor, Razvi decided to vote with his feet. From the safety of his retirement in Karachi, he could reflect on his prescience. For Owaisi, quickly making up for the lost decade, at once found himself the victim of a smear campaign. Accusations flew in from every shade of nationalist Muslim opinion: Congress MPs and MLAs, councillors and JUH clerics, the All-India Shia and All-India Momin Conferences. The objective was not to oppose but to obliterate the Majlis, as if it were a foreign foe. The 'communalists [of] the AIMIM will be shown their place', V. K. Krishna Menon, the defence minister declared in February 1958.[95]

Clearly, Owaisi had rattled some nerves. In March, he was placed under preventive detention. *Habeas corpus* was promptly denied. Disinclined to present even a fig leaf of judicial independence, the courts fully supported the government's decision, ruling that while Owaisi's offending speech was in itself 'unobjectionable, the spirit behind it' was not. 'The speech is to be judged by its potentialities', not its contents. But a year in jail did little to dent Owaisi's popularity.[96] On the contrary, it turned him into an object of sympathy. For when the AIMIM made its electoral debut in the council elections of June 1960, it won eighteen of the thirty seats it contested. The nationalist Muslim tally was four. The AIMIM's strides, moreover, came at the Congress' expense, not the PDF's. Nehru had fallen into a trap of his own making.

Regret was followed by alarm. The Congress, after all, had been trounced by Islamist upstarts. Indeed, behind the AIMIM's routine affirmations of secularism was an unyielding fundamentalism. Take its manifesto of 1961, a paean to a Muslim *imperium in imperio*: mandatory religious instruction in schools; a compulsory charity levy for the *qaum*; the repeal of interfaith marriages; revocation of the ban on polygamy; collective fines, paid communally, to foot the bill for riot damage; state funding for the restoration of mosques damaged during the police action; better relations with the Muslim world; and, possibly, Muslim quotas in legislatures—all grist to the Green Scare mill.[97]

The Congress response was threefold. First, to manufacture a greater majority, it merged Hyderabad and Secunderabad to water down the Muslim presence, reducing, as a result, the Majlis' strength from nearly three-tenths to just under a fifth in the city corporation. Second, overwrought Congressmen set about disbursing sweeteners in the form of pork barrels. Rs 1,000,000 was allotted to a dole specifically for unemployed Muslims. Another million was promised to pump capital into 'small industrial units' set up by Muslims. It was also no accident that the Andhra Pradesh government was the first in the country to recognise Urdu. Third, Majlis councillors were persuaded to defect to the Congress, a development hastened in no small part by Owaisi's peremptory management. By all accounts, he ran his party like a fiefdom, spurning the League's overtures for a merger. Selection and deselection were autocratic affairs, typically favouring Owaisi kith and kin. Nine councillors jumped ship.[98]

Gerrymandering, pork barrels, douceurs. None of these, of course, bespoke integrity. But more important for our purposes, all three marked a break with the old settlement, wherein Muslims were simply ignored. The Congress' concerted efforts to wean *petit-bourgeois* Muslims off the Majlis meant only one thing: the *qaum* was indispensable for it. This was not political representation in the conventional sense. But representation it nevertheless was—only a step removed from an orthodox understanding of it. A vote for the Majlis was, perversely, a vote for Congress renewal. The AIMIM promised funds, seats, and a voice for Muslims, but ultimately and ironically, it was the INC that delivered them.

Such were the lineaments of the Green Scare. What transpired in Hyderabad, of course, was not unique. The League's strides in Kerala, too, forced the Congress into confronting its 'Muslim problem' head on. Prompted by the 'growing anti-Congress feeling among the Muslim community', Mrs Gandhi opened parleys with 'some non-party Muslim leaders of Kerala' during her first year as premier. Time was when 'communalists' warranted a quick, imperious dismissal.[99]

Across the border in Madras, even nationalist Muslims felt obliged to make barbed remarks about the Congress. This may well have been calculated self-flagellation. Even so, that an important figure such as the Madrasi Rajya Sabha MP N. Mohammed Anwar could demand separate electorates and unabashedly declare that Congress Muslims like him were only 'show boys', and that 'there is no political party of the Muslim community in this country excepting the Muslim League', spoke volumes.[100]

* * *

Famously for Bismarck, politics was 'the art of the possible': by definition, then, a chaotic affair. If, at first blush, one might be tempted to give the lie to the Iron Chancellor's cynicism, our survey above might serve to correct misperceptions. Indeed, the dictum appears to be fundamentally sound. By casting an eye over the largest Muslim parties and associations of the Nehruvian period, we have seen sectional interest and ideological imperative, solidarity and enmity, structure and agency, scrupulousness and opportunism by turns coincide in uneasy symbiosis. Contradictory impulses abounded. Conflicting strategies found a way of co-existing.

Muslim outfits experimented, at once, with long marches and protest votes, entryism and associationalism. All to mixed results. The Congress proved too powerful. This was a battle where it paid to be Goliath. Here, there were too many Davids, all of whom had broken slings, tiny stones, and poor aim. The Congress was able to fend off the Muslim challenge with remarkable facility, co-opting rivals, gerrymandering constituencies, taking up Muslim *causes célèbres*, striking deals, incarcerating enemies, declaring states of emergency, changing laws, and channelling funds. All the same, the Green Scare was not without a silver lining. For fears of 'communalism'—more accurately, of Muslim disillusionment with Congress rule—rekindled the incumbents' interest in the affairs of the *qaum*.

But was this as far as Muslim politics could go? Many Muslims did not think so. Indeed, many of the Congress' *bêtes noires* correctly identified their disunity as their Achilles' heel. Too many small Muslim parties dotted the Indian political landscape, and there was scarce cooperation between them. What was needed was a pressure group to coordinate their activities, and put together a minimum programme.

Progress on this front came in fits and starts, ultimately leading to the creation of the Majlis-e-Mushāwarat in August 1964, three months after Nehru's quietus and six after postcolonial India's bloodiest riots. It is to this strange beast we now turn.

5

PRESSURE POLITICS

One for all and all for one? If disunity had been the Achilles' heel of Muslim politics throughout the Nehruvian period, at its close Congressmen and Leaguers, clerics and lay politicians, nationalists and Islamists, all concluded that the chasms between them, in fact, counted for very little. More united than divided them. The nationalist Muslims were beginning to grow impatient with the Hindu leadership; Leaguers were never particularly hot-headed to begin with. The *maulanas* and career politicians were agreed on the need to protect the *sharia*. India's Islamists were in fact rather conventional nationalists; nationalist Muslims were not above exceptionalist pretentions. They all broadly shared in what could be called an Indian Muslim ideology.

A concatenation of crises accelerated this belated appreciation. The most important was Nehru's death in May 1964, which led many Muslim notables to reassess the political conjuncture. But even before that, disaffection was growing. The nationalist Muslims had started to chafe at Hindu prejudice. They tried, to little avail, to draw attention to the trouble brewing in the borderlands, where Muslims were being deported *en masse* to Pakistan; the underrepresentation of Muslims in the services; the short shrift given to Urdu and Muslim personal law; and the sharp increase in violence against Muslims, several thousands of whom perished in the 1964 riots, prompting 800,000 to emigrate to Pakistan.

Indeed, the existence of the implausibly inclusive Mushāwarat was only made possible by the character of Nehruvian rule. In particular, it was the hypocrisy of secularist discourse and confessional praxis perceived by Muslim elites across the board, in conjunction with a realisation of their helplessness before Congress hegemony, that prompted the parleys between Islamists and Muslim secularists, Shias and Sunnis, Muslims of the North and South, the Congress' auxiliaries and enemies that culminated in the Mushāwarat's formation. Impulses towards unity came on sufferance.

Rumblings

We have seen the frustrations that beset the *qaum* in the early Nehru years in the previous chapters. At the time, however, many guilt-wracked Muslims were ready to give Delhi's rulers the benefit of the doubt.[1] Partition was typically explained away as an inexplicable and collective 'madness'. As it turned out, though, while the madness abated, Islamophobia did not. We get a glimpse of the zeitgeist in the Home Ministry Papers. The loyalties of Indian Muslims remained open to question.

Today, the securitisation of Islam is typically seen as a recent phenomenon—of a piece with the world of 9/11 and BJP rule. But Nehru's age was not very different. Illustrative of the misgivings about Muslims were commonplace fears of Pakistani saboteurs and spies smuggling themselves into the country, of Indian Muslims harbouring them.

In 1963, for instance, a complaint was received by the Home Ministry about the activities of Irshad Ali Khan, a six-foot-tall Pakistani sub-inspector 'with a scar on his nose' who had, 'through the connivance of his relations', crossed into India without a visa.[2] Allegedly 'on a mission of spying', he had found a safe haven in a 'purely Mohammedan *mohalla*' of Malerkotla. Following the tip-off, extensive inquiries were made, but the allegation of his 1961 romp across the Punjab 'could not be substantiated'. This was because the reality was rather more prosaic. Khan was no illegal alien. A migrant on a Category C visa, he had returned to retire in the company of his father, a former army major. Evidence to the contrary notwithstanding, the charge of spying stuck, and the ministry rejected his resettlement application on account of 'the possibility of his collecting military intelligence'.[3]

There are a number of striking aspects to this bizarre affair. First, the fact that what ought to have been an open and shut case of repatriation assumed a sinister significance when a nebulous connection was made between the Muslim within and the Muslim without. In other words, a conspiracy was born. Second, that the state acted as an Islamophobic agency, deciding against the migrant based on 'evidence' that was untrustworthy at worst, tenuous at best. And third, that state paranoia dovetailed with—and fed on—that of society. For the complainant was not a public employee, but was nevertheless humoured by the ministry's functionaries.

Lest it appear that too much is being read into an unrepresentative case, a brief sketch of the migration crisis in the North-East should amply confirm the imbrication between the securitising logic of border-making and stigmatisation of the Indian Muslim. Here, too, popular memory has erased earlier chapters of an older history. The discourse around the 'illegal immigration' of Bangladeshi Muslims into the Assamese plains and beyond, widely understood as an Islamophobic dog whistle, is conventionally seen as a product of the pogrom orchestrated by East Pakistani generals in 1971, which provoked a wave of migration into India. Later, in 1983, more than 2,000 Muslims perished at the hands of Hindu Assamese nativists, and in 2019, the BJP set about amending citizenship laws to, effectively, render Muslims stateless.

But Nehru's India was much of a muchness. As early as 1956, a Home Ministry under-secretary could be found sounding the tocsin on the infiltration of 'Pakistani nationals' into Tripura, where free movement obtained; passports were checked only on crossing the 'Inner Line' into Assam.[4] Anxieties stemmed not so much from the prospect of migrants soaking up jobs but instead converting locals to Islam. 'We have a sufficiency of *mullahs* and *peshimams* [Muslim prayer leaders] of our own', an Agartala administrator noted contemptuously, 'and, of late, it has been observed that there has been a great deal of activity within the state for the building of mosques ... one can only surmise this is pro-Pakistan propaganda'.[5]

With a view to curbing Islamic activity, the state in due course turned on the *qaum* itself. At the close of the Nehruvian period, Pakistan's Jabbar Khan Commission could report that in the five months to October 1962 alone, some 17,500 Indian Muslims from Tripura and Assam had been expelled from their homeland, unwelcome exiles 'returned' to East Pakistan. A random sample pointed to the Indian origin of 92 per cent of them.[6]

True, the Commission was not a disinterested agency. Still, it is clear, even from Indian records, that the deportation campaign was a ham-fisted affair. As Table 1 illustrates, in Nehru's second and third terms in office, over 35,000 'Pakistani nationals' in Assam were either deported or given notice to leave the country. Likewise, some 23,500 were deported from Tripura, 40,500 from West Bengal.[7]

The same transpired in other parts of the country, if in less systematic fashion. Outside the North-East, it appears, bureaucratic obduracy counted for more than intentional malice. A number of Muslim businessmen from Bombay, for instance, returned from a business trip to Pakistan in 1958 only to discover that they had been stripped of citizenship. Now, a 'permit system' had taken effect in July 1948 to facilitate travel, but few availed of it. Even after 15 October 1952, when Indians in Pakistan were offered Indian citizenship, there remained an element of unregulated porosity. These, after all, were paper laws that assumed significance only if one had the misfortune to get caught in the dragnet of the state. Few did, because the desert lands connecting West Pakistan and India were for the better part wild country, the presence of the state sparse like its vegetation. More than an encumbrance, borders were an abstraction. So, when the Bombay businessmen found that Indian authorities were stalling in issuing them return permits, they returned on Pakistani passports. There was 'no other way', they later insisted, adding that they attached little value to the piece of documentation. The Home Ministry felt otherwise. Their fate, then, was sealed.[8]

Table 1: The Deportation of 'Pakistani Nationals' from Assam, 1952–1962

Year	Detected	Prosecuted	Deported	Voluntarily left, or intending to leave, for Pakistan
1952	66	66	65	
1953	1,210	1,210	1,148	
1954	1,345	1,345	1,259	
1955	1,407	1,407	1,328	
1956	5,966	5,966	5,334	
1957	3,638	3,463	2,970	100
1958	3,384	1,671	1,398	1,713
1959	2,092	1,786	1,373	306
1960	2,621	2,421	2,232	200
1961	5,146	3,624	2,119	1,412
1962	14,616	3,164	1,148	11,297
Total	**41,491**	**26,123**	**20,374**	**15,028**

Source: Annexure I: Pakistani Nationals Detected, Prosecuted, and Deported, NAI, MHAP, File 20/78/62-F.III. Note that the third and fourth columns effectively collapse into one another, suggesting that the trials were in all likelihood held in kangaroo courts: 78 per cent of those prosecuted were deported.

The borderlands, though, had it worst. Indian Muslims, according to eyewitness accounts, were driven out of their homes 'like herds of cattle', made under duress to 'sign papers declaring falsely that they were Pakistanis', and sent packing to makeshift camps on the border. Many of them not only had the right papers, but also appeared on Indian electoral registers. Not that it mattered. It was their faith that marked them as suspect.[9] The descriptions of the police raids make disturbing reading, officers gleefully killing cocks and hens, looting cattle and crops, deploying hired tribal hands to destroy Muslim homes, and packing Muslims in motor buses like sardines, only to abandon them at the border.[10]

Even the JUH saw fit to criticise the deportations. But its damning report never saw the light of day. For as nationalist Muslims, its leaders were—by definition—good nationalists. Alluding to India's disastrous China war, they felt its publication would have been politically inopportune. The JUH general secretary publicly kept his counsel, expressing his displeasure only in a missive to Nehru, decrying the 'inhuman and ruthless manner' in which the Foreigners Act was being implemented.[11] The Muslim chief secretary to the government of Assam, A. N. Kidwai, too, advised caution privately, even as he closed ranks publicly, putting on air that 'India looked after her nationals very well. Therefore there was no question of deporting any Indian national, Muslim or otherwise'.[12] Clearly, Congress Muslims were tiring of the Congress.

Ultimately, it took Nehru's intervention in December 1962 to suspend deportations under the Foreigners Act.[13] It was, of course, too little, too late. The premier, moreover, was not opposed to deportation per se. It was, instead, only its unedifying optics that offended his sensibilities. Stern inveigling was better than outright coercion: 'send notices to proved [sic] illegal immigrants and ask them to leave'.[14] The logic of securitisation, and the attendant Islamophobia brought on by it, went unchallenged. 'Infiltration' was the watchword, and a punitive mindset accompanied it. A 'shoot at sight policy' was contemplated, but in the end vetoed by the MEA—not so much on account of pangs of conscience, but because of the watchful eyes of the international community: 'Pakistan would certainly raise a hue and cry, and even bring the UN into the picture'.[15] Even six months after Nehru's feeble calls to desist, his government was still evicting 'one Muslim every three minutes'.[16]

Securitising discourse was infectious. Societal suspicion and state action fed off each other, mutually reinforcing prejudice. On the lookout for Muslim immigrants, marauding gangs of 'Hindu volunteers' bearing 'deadly weapons' and chanting '*bandemataram*' could be found marching across the Tripuri countryside. A Congress lawmaker, Kali Babu, was once spotted in the ranks of just such a vigilante group. Reports emerged of abductions of 'teenaged Muslim girls' on the banks of the Feni River, and of Muslims receiving 'fatal injuries' at the hands of Hindu mobs.[17]

The press was not far behind. *Janmabhoomi,* a Jorhat weekly, reported that the Muslims of Goalpara were 'mixing beef' in the milk they were selling Hindus (how exactly we don't know; the mind boggles).[18] Likewise, the *Assam Tribune* reproduced verbatim the Congress chief minister's unsubstantiated claims without comment or editorialising: 'About Three *Lakh* Pak Infiltrators Living in Assam', screamed one of its headlines.[19] In truth, less than 15,000 were 'detected', the bulk of whom were probably unsuspecting Indian Muslims. A few weeks later, the Hindu nationalist *Organiser* told of 'not three *lakhs*, but over one million Pak infiltrators in Assam', quoting a cabinet minister.[20] Congressman Siddhinath Sarma himself went on to rail against 'Pakistan infiltrators' and their Indian Muslim 'collaborators' in an opinion piece for the *Nagpur Times*.[21] In the Assam assembly, his colleague Motiram Bora denounced the Muslim 'political adventurists', who, 'during the day time, play the role of true Congressmen, but during the night', reveal their true colours as 'closeted' Pakistanis, 'holding secret conferences with *maulvis* and *mullahs*'.[22]

By the close of the Nehruvian period, nationalist Muslim patience was wearing thin. The deportations were only the tip of the iceberg. There was also the underrepresentation of Muslims in government. In 1961, Muslims accounted for 10.7 per cent of India's population. There was not a single Muslim to be found, though, among the Home Ministry's fifty-five joint, deputy, and under-secretaries in the year of Nehru's passing.[23] The All-India Radio did not have a single Muslim in a senior managerial role. Neither did the All-India Institute of Medical Sciences.[24] Three decades into Congress rule, Muslims accounted for only 4.5 per cent of the country's judges, 4.4 per cent of the Union's civil servants.[25]

Urdu politics, meanwhile, had hit a *cul-de-sac*. By the unwritten rules of Indian politics, mobilising around language was *halal*, around religion *haram*. Muslims had to be prudent because the Cassandras in government, Nehru included, worried endlessly about the prospect of balkanisation. The anti-secession amendments of 1963, which promised paramilitary fire and fury to those threatening the territorial integrity of the homeland, reflected this sentiment.

As Paul Brass argues, with enough mobilisation—and enough damage to the Congress' electoral prospects—demands for a new state were usually met. So, where Maithili failed, Tamil, Marathi, and Punjabi succeeded. The latter case, in particular, was instructive.

What was under Master Tara Singh's leadership a confessional crusade—Sikh separatism—was initially met with state repression. But when it mellowed into a linguistic movement for a separate Punjabi state under Sant Fateh Singh, it was met with less resistance, even relief. Tamil Nadu, Maharashtra, and the Punjab achieved statehood in 1956, 1960, and 1966, respectively. Urdu, however, went the way of Maithili.[26]

Why? First and foremost because enlisting mass support for an elite concern was a tough ask. In the early twentieth century, obtaining Muslim support for a very specific, not to mention elite, demand—jobs for the well-heeled—made sense. Then, politics had been the preserve of the influential. But when the small, propertied franchise gave way to universal suffrage, Urdu at once became a harder sell. Now, Urdu mattered to the Muslim elite because it was a metaphor of Muslimness, redolent of *ashraf* literary *hauteur* and a reminder of a past when Muslims lorded over the Subcontinent. But nostalgia was a finite resource. Worse, it was the nostalgia of a minority of a minority.

The Muslim elite, moreover, had flogged Urdu as far as it could go. In the 1951 census, 6.8 per cent each of the respondents in Uttar Pradesh and Bihar had returned themselves as Urdu speakers. A decade on, the figures stood at 10.7 and 9.8 per cent, a reflection not so much of the exponential spurt in Urdu learning as of the growing elision between faith and tongue.[27] So much so that all that was left was to carp, as the Anjuman Taraqqi-e-Urdu did, about the 'suppression' of the 'true' figures by the government. Census authorities, however, were at pains to suggest that such claims were unfounded, and there is indeed reason to disbelieve the Anjuman. For one thing, the figures make sense. Some 92 per cent of urban Muslims in UP and Bihar identified as Urdu speakers in 1961. Arguably, in early postcolonial India, Urdu was more truly a plebeian language than it had ever been, shorn of its *belle-lettrist* connotations. But this also meant that Urdu mobilisation had reached the end of the road.

In any case, Muslims could not appear too forceful. The tight-rope act entailed, by turns, convincing Muslims to view Urdu as 'their' language and denying that it was a 'Muslim' language to begin with. Some campaigners went as far as to suggest that, outside the rarefied world of the Hindi intelligentsia, all northerners who purported to speak Hindi in truth actually spoke Urdu—the real homespun language of the commoner. But as Gopal Mittal, editor of the Urdu *Tehreek* and a Hindu, pointed out in *Radiance*, therein lay the rub. On his account, stressing Urdu's heritage of 'secularism and composite culture' was counterproductive. It won plaudits from those least invested in it—Hindus—and, conversely, did a disservice to those with the biggest stake in it—Muslims. Better, then, to call a spade a spade, and defend Urdu as the 'language of the Muslim community', worthy of statist protection as per the Constitution's fundamental rights.[28] It was easier said than done. As a newspaperman writing for an Islamist weekly, Mittal was unencumbered by *bien-pensant* opinion. Career politicians, of course, were denied this luxury.

Then there was the practical problem of having a widely spoken language that was, alas, not spoken widely enough in any part of the country. Indeed, the thin distribution of its speakers was Urdu's greatest obstacle. This was clear from the outset. While constitutionally protected as one of the fifteen recognised languages in the Eighth Schedule, Urdu was not, for the purposes of administration, an official language, the honour falling to English and Hindi at the centre and the latter alone in Bihar and Uttar Pradesh. The other fourteen, however, found official use as state languages. But Urdu never found its place in the sun. 'Urdu, poor thing, has no region', A. J. Faridi, a Socialist lawmaker and one of the Mushāwarat's prime movers, would later lament.[29]

Hindi, then, enjoyed untrammelled hegemony. All that the Muslim political classes could aspire to was to have Urdu recognised as a 'second official language' in Uttar Pradesh and Bihar. But when, in March 1959, Faridi introduced a bill in UP to this effect, he sent alarm bells ringing. 'Such an arrangement will obviously create a permanent and distinctive class of citizens, which is against the very spirit of a single nationality for all citizens of India', the Language Department declared in forthright tones, interpreting the Geist, as was common at the time, in strictly monolithic terms. 'It will encourage separatist tendencies'.[30]

The rebuff was accompanied by character assassination. To Govind Narain, chief secretary, Faridi was a provocateur, not a parliamentarian. Moreover, most of his desiderata were already in place. So long as there were 'forty prospective pupils in a school', and at least ten in every class, keen on learning Urdu, arrangements could be made for instruction in the tongue. The trouble was—as Faridi time and again pointed out, not that it mattered to Narain—that the *qaum* was an atomised community, everywhere but preponderant nowhere. Furthermore, the chief secretary noted, the Information Department translated all public notices into Urdu. Libraries were encouraged to purchase Urdu titles. 'Generous grants-in-aid' were given to government schools and *madrasas* alike. Urdu departments were established in higher institutions of learning. What more did Faridi want?[31]

Still, there was no denying neglect. Even as late as 1964, when 10.7 per cent identified as Urdu speakers, a mere 2.8 per cent of students in primary education were enrolled in Urdu classes. Certainly, the contrast with Bihar was striking. There, there was no mismatch: both the corresponding figures stood at 9.8 per cent. Unlike in Bihar, public examinations in UP included a compulsory paper in Hindi. Where Patna provided instruction in mother tongues to minorities in primary schools, Lucknow did not. Why was this the case? Paul Brass adduces three reasons: the relative weakness of the Pakistan movement in Bihar, and hence of confessional attachment; Bihar's linguistic heterogeneity—Maithili, Bengali, Oriya, Santali— which allowed Urdu to clamber onto the minoritarian bandwagon; and the greater presence of Muslims in government, the upshot of fewer lay-offs at independence. [32]

Faridi, then, had good reasons to introduce his bill. But in the sterile debate that followed, it became clear that he never had a fighting chance. Led by the leader of the house, Hukum Singh Visen, Congressmen saw off the bill in no time. Completely depoliticised, the matter was seen entirely in constitutional terms. Here, Visen—'I happen unfortunately to be a lawyer'—was on home turf. Faridi's demand for the publication of public notices in Urdu went against the letter of the law, he noted, trotting out Article 348(b)(iii), which, in his admittedly perverse reading, called for 'orders, rules, and regulations, and byelaws' to only be issued 'in the English language'. This required a sleight of hand. Visen insisted throughout the debate that Faridi's bill sought to substitute Urdu for Hindi and English. Faridi was at pains to correct what was a grotesque caricature of his plea, but in the end it mattered little. Much of the 'debate' in fact was taken up by procedural objections raised by Congressmen bent on silencing him. The little dialogue that there was suggested asymmetric information. Faridi commanded few facts, whereas Visen appeared to rehearse arguments familiar to us from the Language Department document—discussed above—suggesting a liaison of some kind between party and government, a coupling if not illegal, then certainly at the furthest reaches of legality. The bill was shot down twenty-two to nine.[33]

Two years later came another blow. At first blush, the 'three language formula' was a perfect solution. Its premise, certainly, betrayed a utopian spirit: the construction of a strong national sentiment through the fitting agency of language exchange. Muslims were to be schooled in *devanagari*, and Hindus *nastaliq*. Southerners were to learn Hindi, and the *doab*'s denizens the Deccan tongues. But this was wishful thinking. Resources turned out to be woefully inadequate, the upshot of years of propaedeutic neglect on the part of the Congress since education devolved into Indian hands in 1919. Public recruiters struggled in vain to find teachers who had some command of both Hindi and a southern tongue.

Improvising frantically, it was then decided to mollify local religious fears than foist alien tongues that few were willing to learn, and even fewer able to teach. So, in Uttar Pradesh and Bihar, students were to be schooled in English, Hindi, and a third language of their choice. Hindus, it was assumed, would plump for Sanskrit, Muslims Urdu. Ironically, then, the third tongue came to be a tool for forging not unity, but confessional pride. One can imagine Nehru with his head in his hands, his utopian intentions crumbling on the rocks of hard realities. Even this proved wildly optimistic. In the end, Muslims were forced to learn Sanskrit. Urdu instruction was only available in government schools where fifteen pupils per class, and a minimum of sixty pupils across classes, put in a specific request to that end. This ruled out most Muslims who lived outside the *qasbati* ghettoes. Congressmen realised that the formula was failing the *qaum*. Minority students, it was suggested, were to be offered an elective fourth language, the impracticability of the policy underscored by the brute fact that few Indians had any facility in even one tongue. Nothing came of the proposal.

An attendant anxiety was the question of Muslim personal law. While the common code had been consigned to a corner of the Constitution that contained mere counsel to the coming rulers of the country, suspicion of the state's secularising impulses stayed strong. To many Muslim leaders, Article 44—'the state shall endeavour to secure for the citizens a uniform civil code'—had to go lock, stock, and barrel. That the prospect of *sharia* reform kept raising its ugly head in Nehruvian India only confirmed Muslim fears. Not only did Congressmen and pressmen time and time again issue calls to ban polygamy, Nehru himself pushed for, as the discourse then went, 'modernising' Muslim laws. In July 1963, Muslims took to the streets in protest. Some 100,000 marched in Bombay. Similar crowds were seen in Kanpur. As a result, even the old nationalist Muslim position—of not opposing reform *tout court*, but insisting that it would, one day, come from 'within the community'—was no longer tenable. Zakir Husain and Humayun Kabir backtracked on their calls for gradual reform, instead calling, 'in view of the changed circumstances', only for the convergence of Muslim personal laws across the Union. Standardisation, as distinct from modernisation, was the new watchword. No government could 'take the initiative' when it came to changing personal laws, Kabir argued. Such matters were to be 'left exclusively' to figures who understood 'the principles of the Koran and the *hadith*'—the *ulama*.[34]

Closely aligned was the preoccupation with cultural erasure. It was argued, most forcefully by Faridi in 1961, that Uttar Pradesh's history textbooks contained paeans to idolatry. Worse, while Hindu kings were written about in hagiographic tones, Muslim rulers were written off as villains of the piece. In a land in which the study of epics had not yet undergone a secularising process, he argued, the inclusion of extracts of the *Ramayana* and *Mahabharata*, but not the Quran and *hadith*, was a concession to Hindu sentiment. Even a Hindu revivalist such as Sampurnanand, chief minister of Uttar

Pradesh, conceded that there were 'derogatory' references to the Prophet in textbooks. Even so, he went on to defend the canonisation of the Hindu classics, necessary as they were to conjuring nationalist loyalties. Aurangzeb's seventeenth-century poll tax on Hindus and Mahmud of Ghazni's marauding of temples in the eleventh century, he added, could not be expunged from history. 'Admiration for Rama and Krishna, Arjun and Bhim, Ashoka and Harsh Vardhan' ought to be truly universal; these were not, in his retroactive appropriations, Hindu mythological characters and kings, but Indian ones. Faridi's protestations—Hindu rulers destroyed temples, too; it was quaint to annex Ashoka to Hinduism—fell on deaf ears. Here, again, a more forceful approach was needed.[35]

Such was the state of affairs that even lifelong nationalist Muslims were ready to jettison their circumspect ways. The second half of Nehru's premiership, especially, was punctuated by evidence of their alienation. In 1957, the Congress established a ten-member Minority Committee. It was time for a new Mass Contact Campaign, its first report announced. Just like its predecessor, it proved a desultory affair. Its findings were presented in exonerative fashion: 'it was difficult to give adequate representation to the minorities in the services' because, apparently, 'whenever posts were advertised', few Muslims bothered applying. Better, then, to let 'Muslim social organisations set up private employment exchanges'. Other suggestions included excluding Hindi marks from aggregates for Muslims in higher education; rehabilitating Muslims dispossessed by Partition; pumping out 'vigorous propaganda' to call out some of the 'purely imaginery [sic] grievances of the community'.[36]

The nationalist Muslims were unimpressed. Along with Ambedkar's *protégé* P. S. Deshmukh, presumably chosen only to deflect the charge of communalism, Kabir and Azad privately circulated a note in February 1958 declaring the exclusion of Muslims from affirmative action 'a matter of utter shame'. Given Azad's record and Kabir's élan, this may have been disingenuous. But the fact that these very figures could point to the inequity of the reservations regime only went to show how ever-so-slightly more assertive nationalist Muslims had become.[37] Unfortunately for Azad, it was a belated realisation. A few days later he was dead. A second 'secret letter' on the 'minorities problem' followed in August, this time singly authored by Kabir, again meant solely for cabinet consumption.[38] He once again railed against reservations, demanding, as was to be expected from a nationalist Muslim of his day, not the inclusion of subaltern Muslims among the backward castes, but an end to affirmative action for Dalits and tribesmen. They would have to 'take their chances along with other communities on grounds of merit and competence'.[39]

The preoccupation with reservations was purely epiphenomenal. Behind the Olympics of minoritarian one-upmanship—was the Dalit the more deserving subaltern or the Muslim?—was a broader comment on Muslim disaffection. Feeding into their growing disillusionment was the realisation that the Congress was no longer the only path to electoral success. In the 1962 general election, for example, five Congress Muslims lost to independents in Andhra Pradesh. The next year saw the union minister of irrigation and power, Hafiz Mohammed Ibrahim, one of Uttar Pradesh's most powerful Muslim politicians, defeated in a by-election. In any case, Muslims were struggling to secure nominations. In 1957, it is true, the CWC had resolved in favour of proportional representation or 'at least 15 per cent of nominations' for minorities, whichever was greater. In practice, though, few state, district, municipality, and corporation boards followed its guidelines.[40]

They were already casting around for other parties. On the Right, the Swatantra seemed promising, for the better part 'steadfastly secular' and 'solicitous of the interests of Muslims' in the words of its contemporary chronicler.[41] Likewise, on the Left were the CPI and the Praja Socialist Party to which the physician Faridi was drawn, leaving the former for the latter in 1959.[42] None of these, of course, were Muslim parties. In short, the Mushāwarat was a long time coming.

Riots

Nehru's India isn't usually associated with riots. But riots galore there were. And Muslims were only too aware of this. Accounting for just under a tenth of the national population, they made up 82 per cent

Table 2: Riots in Nehruvian India, 1954–1963

'Cause'	Number of incidents	Number of people killed			Number of people injured		
		Hindus	Muslims	Not Known	Hindus	Muslims	Not Known
Music before mosques	74	7	23	8	598	418	135
Desecration of places of worship	24	2	0	4	87	43	3
Molestation of women	51	11	73	0	96	195	20
Cow slaughter	59	6	33	0	72	961	48
Throwing of *gulal* on Holi	41	3	12	0	219	214	11
Quarrels at religious processions	46	2	27	7	129	162	16
Assaults	67	7	51	6	174	259	37
Accidents	19	2	1	0	45	25	12
Feuds	8	1	3	0	8	24	0
Pro-Pakistan activities	8	0	7	0	51	85	0
Land disputes	31	2	13	0	61	90	8
Altercations	86	5	11	0	260	215	15
Miscellaneous	63	12	22	0	187	190	66
Total	**577**	**60**	**276**	**25**	**1,987**	**2,881**	**371**

Source: 'Secret Annexure III: Communal incidents during 1954–1963', NAI, MHAP, File 19/26/64-Poll IA.

of the fatalities, and 59 per cent of the injured in the riots of 1954–63 (see Table 2). So, while Nehru's India has gone down in popular history as an halcyon era of communal peace, the contemporary record strikes a very different note. Early postcolonial riots may have lacked the ferocity, forethought, and fatality associated with later communal violence, but they were nevertheless planned and bloody affairs. Much ink has been spilled in trying to suss out the causes of riots, considerations that need not detain us here. For our purposes, a few preliminary observations should suffice.

First, it is important to recognise that riots are not—as is often made out in the press—spontaneous moments of savage frenzy. Rather they are put together, almost with the precision of a watchmaker, by cynical actors all too aware of the political capital to be made from confessional polarisation. Indeed, of the existence of what Paul Brass calls 'institutionalised riot systems' there can be little doubt. It takes a certain skill to transform seemingly innocuous occurrences—a pig wandering into a Muslim gathering, a *tazia* knocking over a holy tree—into full-blown riots. It is in the micro-politics of neighbourhoods, his preferred unit of analysis, that we find Brass' *agents provocateurs*, instigating their followers to run riot in order to demonstrate their indispensability to their clientele by, ironically, protecting them from the very violence that they provoked in the first place.[43]

A gentle critique comes from Ward Berenschot, who asks, after Donald Horowitz, 'why the followers follow', to argue that riots are as much the work of—if not more so—'instigatees', as it were, as instigators. Riots, on this account, are the natural upshot of the 'mediated state', which, attenuated by definition, requires go-betweens to carry out the business of government: neighbourhood political entrepreneurs who broker deals, disburse funds, engage in underhand activities, and *also* orchestrate communal riots. What animates them is the prospect of state capture, the attendant spoils of office and sway over pork barrels. Rioting is not their *raison d'être*. Theirs is the mundane world of drainage and water supplies, ration cards and hospital beds, roads and railways, permits and licenses. These are, then, not so much institutionalised riot as patronage systems.[44]

Brass' contention, Berenschot seems to suggest, is perhaps too conspiratorial. To be sure, rioting comes with the territory, but only because local entrepreneurs require such grisly episodes to generate a sense of persecution. A siege mentality, of course, has its uses, translating into the kind of blind loyalty that makes the ordinary citizen beholden—thanks to the absence of a welfare state—to the go-between. The result is a mutually reinforcing cycle: more loyalty; more violence; more clientelism. Lather, rinse, repeat. Here, then, is the making—in common parlance—of the 'riot-prone town', places such as Ahmadabad and Aligarh, Meerut and Moradabad, where a feedback loop of violence and vengeance, rage and revenge, obtains.[45]

A range of related interventions confirm the causal link between deprivation and state neglect on the one hand and the work of intermediaries and business of rioting on the other. For Asghar Ali Engineer, in a land where communities, not individuals, are the building blocks of society, interfaith violence is merely economic competition by proxy. In an ethnically divided labour market, the faithful inevitably vie for greater confessional market shares. Indeed, once sublimated into a confessional register, *déclassé* resentments, natural enough, fix on industries with ample scope for religious rivalry—ones with significant Muslim participation, as in the manufacture of *bidis*, brassware, handicrafts, textiles, silk, woodwork. This is class conflict played for high stakes. Defeat can mean dispossession, even death. Indeed, it is no accident that rioters, in the main, tend to come from the ranks of the precariat in deindustrialising towns. The poor kill the poor. Ahmedabad's frequent riots are a case in point: typically, they concentrate on its eastern and southern parts, the setting of the sunset textile industry, leaving the city's leafier, western half untouched. In Aligarh, too, violence is the preserve of town, not gown.[46]

In the final analysis, however, the ubiquity of riots is best explained in electoral terms: the unholy, if not singularly Indian, union of, in Steven Wilkinson's telling, *Votes and Violence*, by far the most persuasive account of the subject. At the outset, he quickly sets about eliminating rival explanations. Economic explanations, *à la* Engineer? These warrant quick dismissal. Riots don't make business sense. Indeed, they kill businesses and affect supply chains. The relationship between the Hindu moneylender and Muslim artisan, or, say, the Muslim employer and Scheduled Castes employee, is one of mutual dependence. Empirically, too, it is clear that wrecking and ransacking follow rioting and rampaging, and not the other way around. Local businesses are rarely the *fons et origo* of riots. Quite the opposite, in fact. *Petit-bourgeois* violence is, instead, the product of the lawlessness that accompanies riots. Ecological theories, premised on the assumption that large minority populations and mass migration prompt interfaith violence? Here, again, objectively little points to the fact that confessional parity in itself exacerbates tension—an essentialist reading that finds little purchase today. Seventeen of the 219 largest cities in the country boast a greater than 40 per cent Muslim population, few of which are riot-prone. Institutional decay theories, in which ethnic violence is seen as an upshot of the decline in state capacity? Too general to account for the wide variation across space and time, not to mention oblivious to political agency.

Short work, too, is made of Ashutosh Varshney's influential, but ultimately tautological, thesis: the more the dialogue between faiths in civil society, the less likely riots. Turning Brass' analysis inside out, Varshney points to the existence of 'institutionalised peace systems'.[47] Troublemakers, on his account, are spectacularly unsuccessful in settings where communal sentiment cuts little ice. A contrast follows between the peaceable towns of Calicut, Surat, and Lucknow, all overflowing with associational activity, and their unruly antipodes: Aligarh, Ahmedabad, and Hyderabad, all with scarce civic life. At the heart of this contention, however, is a contradiction succinctly captured by Brass' *précis*: 'where there is extensive civic engagement between Hindus and Muslims, there is peace; which amounts to saying where there is peace, there is peace'.[48] What's more, a number of methodological curiousities and a preference for giving Hindu nationalists the benefit of the doubt—a harbinger of the pieces on Modi that would appear in 2014—compound Varshney's original sin of wishful thinking.[49] Wilkinson, for his part, focusses on the ahistorical character of his generalisations. For associational mixing and tolerance cannot, in themselves, prevent communal violence. Thirties Punjab, just such an eirenic polity under the Unionists, could effortlessly slide into violence at Partition. Likewise, temporally closer to us, multi-ethnic and tolerant Yugoslavia quickly shaded into civil war and balkanisation after communism.

Communal violence, *in nuce*, is the product of electoral competition. As such, riots are best viewed as little more than *danses macabres* meant to woo the marginal seat swing voter. Accordingly, in states with close contests—a *de facto* two-party system—the incentive to stoke riots is greater.[50] For in such environments—first-past-the-post as ever the handmaiden of majoritarianism—there is a strong premium on creating a consolidated Hindu constituency. This, of course, requires flattening other cleavages. It is here that the stigmatisation of the Muslim comes to the fore. The unpopular minority *par excellence*, the *qaum* makes for the perfect Other. This is a truth politicians know only too well. Interfaith violence goes a long way in turning attention away from intercaste tensions.[51]

The *fin-de-siècle* famously and brutally brought this home. Following the fallout of the extension of reservations to 'other backward castes' along the lines of the Mandal Commission came the levelling of the Babri Masjid in 1992 by Hindu nationalists bent on building a temple on its ruins. Some 2,000, almost all Muslims, perished in the riots that ensued. Cashing in on Hindu radicalisation, the BJP successfully traded in its upper caste image for a pan-Hindu one. Electorally, mounting an attack on Mandal with *mandir* made perfect sense. Polling at 11 per cent in 1989, a year before the government announced its intention to implement the Mandal report, the BJP doubled its vote share in 1991, riding to power five years later.

The early nineties, of course, have received ample scholarly attention. The early sixties less so. But the two periods are much of a muchness. In Uttar Pradesh, for instance, the Jana Sangh polled 10 per cent in 1957, 17 per cent in 1962, and 22 per cent in 1967; the Congress, meanwhile, at 32 per cent was not much ahead. Congress hegemony was loosening, and the Sangh's prospects brightening. A two-party system was taking hold. For both parties, then, the *qaum* was simply not worth it. If uniting Hindus meant vilifying Muslims, so be it. So it was that the Congress let riots run their course. Here it might be apposite to cite a UP senior police officer's maxim, arrived at after a careful study of 'ten major riots' and corroborating Brass' own conclusion, independently reached: 'no riot can last for more than twenty-four hours unless the state administration wants it to'.[52]

In the spirit of recapitulation: riots are planned (Brass); riots are about patronage (Berenschot); riots are caused by deprivation (Engineer); riots are shaped by electoral exigencies (Wilkinson); riots are abetted by the state (*passim*). Equally, riots in the Indian setting are practically pogroms, its perpetrators in the main Hindu and victims Muslim. These are incontrovertible verities reached with the convenience of hindsight, but also painful truths that were known to contemporary Muslims. Indeed, this was the stuff of lived experience.

The Gorakhpur riot of May 1965, for instance, bears out all of these. Planning: troublemakers made a minor dispute the trigger of something bigger. The immediate cause, if it can be called that, was the discovery that a Scheduled Caste girl and a Momin boy had eloped, leaving locals furious. This set the tone for the ructions that ensued two days later, when a thirteen-year-old Muslim cyclist accidentally knocked down a middle-aged Hindu woman, who promptly gave him a thrashing before a growing crowd. As it happened, he gave her the slip, only to return with his mates bent on revenge. What started as a slanging match descended into a full-blown riot, crowds swelling and brickbats flying. So far so spontaneous. It took less than two hours, however, for the fracas to acquire an altogether different character, betraying precision as much as preparation. Two hundred houses, mostly owned by Muslims, were ransacked. The streets turned into a sea of men bearing 'spears, swords, and daggers'.[53]

Patronage: not long after, *Link* speculated that the rioters in all likelihood would go unpunished—which they did—for they were acting on the orders of the Mahant Digvijayanath, the powerful chief cleric of the Gorakhnath temple who had famously done time for exhorting 'Hindu militants to kill the Mahatma' and, equally notoriously, called for the disenfranchisement of Muslims.[54] The riot, then, was to serve as a reminder to Gorakhpuris that his shock troops were the only force of law and order in town. Economic logic: the violence, targeting Muslim houses and industries, undeniably was aimed at showing the *qaum* its station. Electoral considerations: three years later, Digvijayanath became

MP for Gorakhpur, a seat that would later fall to his successors, the Mahants Avaidyanath and Adityanath, both of whom were to become prominent BJP politicians.

State neglect and complicity: policemen were spotted in the company of the mobs. The rest of the force had absented itself from the scene, *Link* reported on the authority of a Muslim notable. All the ninety-eight taken into custody for arson and murder were set free for want of evidence. Authorities, it appears, were loath to punish the agitators on account of their connection to Digvijayanath, already much more than a *mahant*. A powerbroker who had a say in public appointments and an army of toughs at his beck and call, the cleric was, as Gorakhpur's functionaries were well aware, a man one would be foolish to cross.[55]

Gorakhpur was not an aberration. Riots were routine. And there was little the nationalist Muslims could do about it. When the Bihar PCC president, A. Q. Ansari, called for an investigation into the Sitamarhi riots of April 1959, for instance, he was repeatedly stonewalled. Two of his colleagues, Abdul Ghafoor and Fazlur Rahman, both members of a 'Muslim ginger group' in the UP assembly, threatened to resign over the matter. Again, to little effect. Case closed, without closure, of course.[56]

Such episodes can be indefinitely multiplied. The 1961 riot in Jabalpur, one of the bloodiest of the sixties, wedded, as it were, Engineer and Wilkinson, the economic and electoral. It began as a purely personal affair—the suicide of a Hindu girl, who killed herself after being spurned by an old flame, a Muslim; he was her rapist in another version of the tale—before turning into a confessional one. It later transpired that the incident was not unrelated to developments in the local *bidi* industry, the bailiwick of Hindu manufacturers increasingly threatened by Muslim *arrivistes*. The boy who drove the girl to her death may have been an agent of the latter, put almost clinically to the task to deliver a stern message to the Hindu entrepreneur who was her father. A demonstration ensued, which the ABVP and RSS promptly hijacked. A riot then unfolded, and the army was called in, bringing a swift end to the violence, but not before nearly 200 people had perished, few of whom were Hindu. Hindu houses had been marked, and, for this reason, spared.[57]

The state was missing in action. Again, the rioters failed to get their just deserts.

Nehru responded by lambasting his Bhopal government, whose leaders, he angrily noted, were to be found 'sitting inside their houses like *purdah* ladies during the riots'.[58] But his sense of urgency was only met with indifference. State politics had different cadences, other priorities. Here, political pragmatism trumped forthright secularism. On this view, a few dead Muslims could easily be shrugged off as collateral damage. Elections were just a year away, and the Congress simply could not be seen 'appeasing' Muslims so close to hustings season. Over the coming months, the riots spread like wildfire. Everywhere, it was the same story of accidie and acquittals. Time and again, electoral concerns were invoked and Muslim concerns ignored.

All the same, for better or worse, nationalist Muslims stuck to the only party they deemed fit to rule. But then came the final straw, Hazratbal. That this metonym means little to the reader should hardly be surprising. There is no accounting for the caprices of historical memory. Not without justification do Nellie, Blue Star, Ayodhya, Godhra—the anti-minority pogroms of 1983, 1984, 1992, and 2002—conjure vivid mental images. Hazratbal, by contrast, more often than not draws a blank. But of its significance, by any criterion, there can be doubt. Contemporary reports speculated that the death toll topped 1,300.[59] The French academic Violette Graff puts the figure even higher at 'several thousands'.[60] Fatalities were topped up with a diminution of another kind, a step towards finishing the incomplete business of Partition, as it were. Fearing for their lives, more than 800,000 Indian Muslims left the country for a more strenuous but also safer life in Pakistan. Likewise, when retaliatory anti-Hindu riots broke out in East Pakistan, some 693,000 crossed the border into India.[61] Very simply, Hazratbal can lay claim to being the most violent Hindu-Muslim conflagration in postcolonial India. And for Muslim politics, too, Hazratbal was a watershed. Pithily put: no Hazratbal, no Mushāwarat.

The facts are these. On the night of 27 December 1963, the *moi muqaddas*, a strand of hair that had once supposedly nestled in the Prophet Mohammad's beard, disappeared from the Hazratbal

Shrine, lit. the Prophet's riverine abode, situated on Srinagar's Dal Lake. Worshipped since 1699, when a Kashmiri merchant had purchased it from the heavily indebted managers of the Prophet's tomb—on the run from Medina having incurred the wrath of the Ottoman sultan—the solitary strand had served as a kind of surrogate *hajj* for penurious locals. Like the Holy Places but cheaper and closer, it was almost as if the proverbial mountain had come to Mohammad.[62]

Twentieth-century relevance came with the National Conference's appropriation of the shrine, adding political import to its already abundant spiritual significance. It was, of course, a deeply symbiotic relationship. For one thing, it raised Hazratbal's heretofore high profile even further. For another, it allowed the 'secular' NC, a vehicle for Sheikh Abdullah's political aspirations, to posture as a thoroughly pious party. Formed in 1941, the NC was a breakaway from the Muslim Conference opposed to Dogra rule and tenuously aligned with the Congress. The MC, for its part, was increasingly drawn to the League. Here, then, was the making of the epic *sher-bakra* rivalry, pitching, as it were, the NC's lions against the MC's sheep, which animated late colonial Kashmiri politics.

The NC very quickly became the hegemonic force in the kingdom on the back of its calls for land reform (which cost its leadership, most of it drawn from the professions, nothing) and its undeniable religious tenor (which amounted to more than just a residual Islam unthinkingly retained from its MC past). This was just as well, because Kashmir's Muslims were, indeed, second-class citizens in their homeland, subject to special taxes and *corvée* labour and denied jobs in the services, practically the preserve of Kashmiri Pandits. Brahmin mandarins; Rajput rulers; immiserated Muslims. It was easy to see why the Sheikh needed Hazratbal. As religious symbols went, it also fulfilled a counterweighing function. The MC—now a party merely of the old gentry, in the main Sufi landlords, and the Srinagar *vieux riches*—was in the hands of the Mirwaiz of Kashmir, head priest of the Valley.[63]

When the *moi muqaddas* went missing, Kashmir exploded in violence. Lal Chowk turned into a sea of black flags. 'Hundreds' died in combat. There appeared no end in sight. Still, an end there miraculously came, when the relic mysteriously resurfaced on 4 January—in the very spot where it had always been, as if untouched.[64]

Who stole the *moi muqaddas*? Who returned it? Who triggered the riots? Who called them off? There are no simple answers. There is, however, a more profitable line of inquiry than the immediate question of whodunnit: namely, *cui bono*? The Congress, it appears. The gains were threefold.

First and foremost, the Hazratbal incident paved the way for Congress hegemony in Kashmir, ending a sixteen-year spell of NC rule. Here, a brief excursus into the labyrinthine world of Kashmiri politics is necessary. Since its contentious accession to the Indian Union, secured through military intervention and backchannel pressure, Jammu and Kashmir enjoyed, on paper at any rate, a degree of autonomy denied to the other states of the Republic. Its chief minister was a 'prime minister'. Sovereignty was pooled. The Union's competencies were restricted to foreign affairs, defence, and communications under Article 370. On everything else, the Kashmiri parliament had the final say. In practice, of course, Delhi called the shots. Sheikh Abdullah, premier from 1948 to 1953, had been consigned to prison by Nehru for protesting Delhi's decision to backtrack on the promised plebiscite that would have given Kashmiris the choice to plump for either India or Pakistan. His successor, Bakshi Ghulam Mohammad, who ruled for a decade to 1963, had been more to Delhi's liking. To begin with, he had no truck with Kashmiri self-determination. His flagship Naya Kashmir programme, a 'new Kashmir' built on mass education, cheap rations, and public infrastructure, was also one Delhi could get behind.[65]

Even so, Bakshi was an embarrassment. First there was the appalling human rights record. He had introduced the death penalty for those 'suspected of pro-Pakistan leanings', agreeable enough to Delhi were it not for regular international condemnation. Then there was his militia, the Peace Brigade, given to all kinds of nastiness, imprisoning and torturing political opponents, branding them with hot irons, subjecting them to the strappado, and making them walk barefoot on ice. Preventive detention was common. There was a blanket ban on political gatherings. Government spies hovered around college campuses. In short, he ran a police state.

'Bakshi uses unscrupulous methods', Nehru conceded in a rare candid moment to a Jammu journalist, but then again, 'democracy and morality can wait. India's case in Kashmir now revolves around him, and despite all its shortcomings, the Bakshi government has to be strengthened'.[66]

There was another issue. Namely, that elections in Kashmir had more of a nineteenth century British quality to it than anything contemporary or Indian. The majority of candidates were returned unopposed from pocket boroughs. Potential challengers routinely found their nomination papers rejected on technical grounds. As for the results, they could put Ceaușescu to shame. The NC took every seat in the assembly in 1951, carrying 92 per cent of the house in 1957 and 1962. 'It would strengthen your position much more if you lost a few seats to *bona fide* opponents', Nehru nervously wrote Bakshi.[67]

Very reluctantly, Kashmir's premier came around to his Delhi counterpart's view. Accordingly, he was 'Kamaraj'd' in October the next year, purged, along with eleven cabinet and chief ministers, in an attempt to breathe new life into the Congress after a series of by-election débâcles and the defeat the Chinese handed the Indians. Khwaja Shamsuddin, a little-known minister, landed the Kashmir premiership in short order. Essentially jobbed into power by Bakshi to block the ascent of G. M. Sadiq, a creature of the Congress, Shamsuddin's elevation was both an affirmation of the Conference's subordination to Delhi as well as a reflection of the limits of its servitude. The Congress could get rid of Bakshi but could not prevent him from choosing his own replacement.[68]

The tables were to turn very quickly. For in two months came the *deus ex machina* of Hazratbal. Unable to subdue the violence, Shamsuddin was gone in a hundred days and Sadiq sworn in as premier. Finally, the Congress had its man in Srinagar. For nearly a decade now, it had been sedulously courting him. The wager paid off. In January 1965, less than a year into his term, Sadiq abruptly defected to it, becoming, as it were, the first 'Congress' prime minister of Jammu and Kashmir. His entire cabinet and working committee followed suit. For long either a bit player or backstage puppeteer, the Congress at a stroke found itself in the driving seat.[69]

This pre-eminence it turned to good account. The NC had won seventy of the seventy-five seats in 1962. Fast-forward five years and the Congress won sixty-one. Sadiq's elevation also shifted the balance of opinion in the Kashmir Congress, thus far amenable to demands for greater autonomy, to a hard-line unionist position that was Delhi's preference. Time was when Sadiq himself had advocated great power or Security Council mediation and a plebiscite. No more. A month into his term in March 1964, he could be found promising closer 'integration' with the Union, even the scrapping of Article 370 so long as the decision was made by an impartial arbiter and not him. Between Sadiq and his successor, the Congress would enjoy ten uninterrupted years in power.[70]

The second way in which Hazratbal benefited the Congress was by weakening the secessionist movement. At the time, two organisations best represented this tendency, both attached to the Action Committee set up by the Mirwaiz to recover the relic. One was the Political Conference, established by Mohiuddin Kara. A home for former NC communists as well as the Pandit gentry opposed to land reform, it was the most powerful outfit in the Valley clamouring for Kashmir's accession to Pakistan. Mirza Afzal Beg's Plebiscite Front, on the other hand, was after self-determination.[71]

Both were a nuisance to Delhi—until Hazratbal. The unrest served as the perfect cover to lock up Kara, who was blamed for the large crowds massing on Lal Chowk. By a stroke of luck, he was replaced in the Action Committee by Maulana Masoodi, who walked a fine line between its radical and moderate elements, earning plaudits from Sadiq and Shastri, at the time Delhi's emissary in Kashmir.[72] The result was that the Political Conference effectively recanted its hard-line pro-Pakistan posture. The 1962 election, meanwhile, was the last one the Front boycotted. The Congress repaid the gesture by declaring it illegal soon after. When the Kashmir Accord was inked between Indira Gandhi and Sheikh Abdullah in February 1975—the former disbanding the Congress government in Kashmir and releasing the latter from prison to anoint him chief minister in exchange for never bringing up the plebiscite again—a defeated Front leadership resigned itself to absorption into the NC. The upshot, of course, was entirely agreeable to the Congress. Virtually unique in world-historical terms, state repression had weakened secessionists, turning fiery idealists into weary pragmatists.

Sadiq successfully neutralised the parliamentary opposition as well. At first, during the early days of tenure in which rulers generally succumb to a spirit of statesmanship, he attempted a change of tack. Hoping to ease tensions, he released Abdullah from prison. History called into question the wisdom of his gambit. The Sheikh had been released once before, in 1958, to uproarious celebration by his people. He had gone on to deliver an animated speech at Hazratbal to a crowd of 200,000 that ended in violence. After a kangaroo trial, he was promptly rearrested. As it was, 1964 proved to be a repeat of 1958. Abdullah once again seized his brief moment in the sun, dismissing Kashmir's accession to India as only 'provisional' at Hazratbal. Accordingly, he met Nehru and then the Pakistan president, Ayub Khan, in Rawalpindi, ruffling feathers in Delhi by insisting that all three 'nations'—J&K and 'our neighbours'—had to strive together for peace.[73] The Sheikh, it is true, did not set out to scandalise Delhi. He simply had to take the line he did to forestall the Mirwaiz from turning his insurgent appeal to good account.[74]

But Delhi was disinclined to take a dispassionate view of his speech. For Bakshi was plotting Sadiq's downfall with Abdullah. A motion of no confidence was on the cards. Sensing a pincer movement, Sadiq resolved that now was not the time to champion a constructive opposition. Bakshi was sent to prison in September 1964. Abdullah followed him there in May the following year. There they both remained until the former retired from politics, securing his release in June, and the latter relinquished all claims to autonomy, finding himself a free man a decade later.

Third and finally, Hazratbal hastened Kashmir's integration into the Indian Union, long a Nehruvian desideratum. On taking office, Sadiq's first order of business was to move an amendment making, in line with convention, Kashmir's prime minister just another chief minister. Likewise, directly elected representatives replaced the assembly's nominees in Parliament. Already Delhi had granted itself the ability to dismiss at will the government in Kashmir, essentially demonstrating that Article 356, governing relations between the Union and the states, counted for more than Article 370, which accorded Kashmir special status. Already, too, in 1954, the jurisdiction of the Supreme Court had been extended to Kashmir.[75]

On the whole, then, Hazratbal was a blessing for the Congress. First, National Conference hegemony gave way to Congress rule. Second, secessionists suffered setbacks. Third, Kashmir was brigaded into an ever-closer relationship with the Union. What's more, the violence quickly blew over once the hairy situation was resolved.

But, for all that, there was little the Congress could do to contain the blowback across the border. The streets returned to silence in Srinagar, but daggers were being drawn in Dacca. There, in a retaliatory logic familiar since Partition, Hindus—guilty by association for the theft of the relic—were slaughtered wholesale in January, provoking, in turn, riots on the Indian side, the upshot no doubt of furies fanned by fleeing Pakistani Hindus who brought harrowing tales of violence with them. As a perspicacious *Times* reporter observed, 'refugees are always the plague carriers of communal violence'. By 9 January, all of Calcutta was ablaze. The violence was avenged on the other side, necessitating yet more reprisals. For the rest of the winter, 'the grim pendulum of communal killings' swung endlessly between India and Pakistan.[76]

Already a poor state, West Bengal was completely overwhelmed. Unsurprisingly, many refugees decided to vote with their feet, making their way into the *mofussil*. So it was that, as if in a relay race, the baton of violence passed to the Hindi belt. All it seemed to take was the arrival of 'trainloads of destitute refugees', teeming with tales of savagery and sadism, for a town to erupt into riot. This, at any rate, was the case in the three industrial towns that witnessed the worst of the violence: Jamshedpur, Rourkela, and Raigarh. If these were by far India's bloodiest riots, they were also, in another sense, archetypal ones. Indeed, they conformed to all the generalisations about riots seen above. They certainly had a pogrom-like quality to begin with. Here's the *New York Times*: 'virtually all known victims have been Moslem'.[77]

Premeditation? A clue lies in the skewed death toll. We also know that it was the Hindus, bearing all the marks of Brass' death-dealing political entrepreneurs, who sparked off the riot in Jamshedpur. The RSS *sarsanghchalak* M. S. Golwalkar, no less, was arrested in Bihar on 23 March for his role in stoking the violence. In Agra, the Jana Sangh's city president was to be found amidst the rioters, providing direction and morale.[78] It was only later that Muslims, resorting to frontier justice in default of remedial justice, responded in kind.[79]

Deprivation? It was no accident that the three main flashpoints were all industrial towns. Jamshedpur was the site of the Tata steel works; Rourkela, of one of the publicly owned Steel Authority of India's largest plants; Raigarh, of one of the densest concentrations of jute mills in the Republic. Those who worked in these were the aristocracy of labour: organised and unionised, earning respectable wages, working reasonable hours, and enjoying regular benefits. They were, in other words, the envy of the working poor. It was from this stratum, variously 'tribal people' and '*goonda* elements' to the press, that 'the Hindu organisations' drew their rioting recruits, tasking them with 'the killing of Moslems' employed in the factories.[80] Of their resentment there can be little doubt. We know, for one thing, that Jamshedpur was a land of housing shortages and high indebtedness. There is also the character of the kind of Muslims who found employment in these mammoth enterprises. Theirs was, in the main, a first-generation mobility brought on by early postcolonial urbanisation. Envy, then, was only to be expected.[81]

Electoral logic? This, too, was not found wanting. As Steven Wilkinson has it, riots go a long way in recalibrating fault lines. Is it unreasonable to suggest that a class cleavage gave way to a confessional one? In 1962, Communists beat Congress candidates by comfortable margins in Jamshedpur. Five years later, the Congresswoman who had lost by over a quarter of the vote improved her share of it by half, defeating the Communist in a stunning upset. Crucially, the collapse of the Left came at a time when the Hindu nationalists gained a foothold in the town. Before the riot, they couldn't even field a candidate. Post-riot, they took over a tenth of the vote. Where there was once a working class, there now were communalists and secularists, those who looked to the Sangh to protect them from violent Muslims and those who turned to the Congress to protect them from Hindu rabble-rousers.

What of the Congress? The communal peace threatened, it fashioned itself as a secular redoubt. If absent at the time of the riot, it later went into overdrive. The Prime Minister's National Relief Fund stepped in with a Rs 100,000 cheque for the Muslims of Rourkela.[82] Congress ministers set about 'helping members of the minority community return home' under police protection. All of a sudden, there appeared no end to the resources the state had at its disposal.[83]

Muslim despair? What pained the *qaum* most was the virtual absence of the state when it was most needed. The Indian state, of course, has always been a greater punitive than redistributive agency, more in its element deploying police and paramilitary personnel than its nugatory welfarist resources. That it disingenuously, if also tragically, struck a *laissez-faire* note, letting the riots rip through the three industrial towns for four full days before intervening, only went to show Muslims that the government did not have their interests at heart.[84]

Unsurprisingly, a certain defeatism overtook Muslims. Many recent migrants abandoned their new industrial jobs to return to the countryside. Others left their homes to ghettoise in new, unequivocally 'Muslim' neighbourhoods such as Jamshedpur's Azad Nagar. Still others took to the Islamist Jama'at-i-Islami, which raised its profile fighting *pro bono* cases defending Muslims dispossessed by emboldened Hindus.[85]

Another sore point was the handling of the aftermath. Funds were forthcoming. Justice was another matter. In Orissa, the chief minister, Biren Mitra, overruled a judicial inquiry into the Rourkela riot. Later, his cabinet managed to stave off debate on the subject for twelve days by endlessly moving procedural adjournment motions. Tiring of their games, the opposition then tabled two motions of no confidence, deploying 'the last weapon in their parliamentary armoury'. The Congress' unassailable majority saw both defeated.[86]

As in Orissa, so in Bihar. When the nationalist Muslims under Ansari's leadership set up the Bihar Congress Muslim Front on 7 May demanding an inquiry into the riots, they were stonewalled by their colleagues. As a ginger group, there was only so much it could do. Even while laying into the government for its indolence, the Front was forced to feign forbearance. Indeed, its spokesmen emphasised that it was principally concerned with 'inculcating a true spirit of nationalism' among Indian Muslims, as if the lack thereof had brought on the riots that were the proximate cause of its founding. More concretely, this meant seeing Indian Muslims 'shed their last drop of blood for the sake of Kashmir in order to foil the evil designs of Pakistan'.[87]

Perhaps the prudence was purposeful. Loud admonitions only served to rile up the press, whose displeasure few Muslim politicians were ready to incur. Small newspapers—with circulations of five to ten thousand, such as the Marathi weeklies *Sobat* and *Vivek* or the Assamese *Janmabhoomi*—were particularly feared on account of their ability to elude national attention, hence print hate speech and stoke violence.[88] Better then to quietly go about the business of reform and rehabilitation than stir resentment. Unfortunately, though, there was no escaping unwanted attention. Kabir may have shown exceptional restraint in focussing his energies on helping Muslims rebuild their lives rather than bringing the rioters to book, but this did not stop the Bengali *Ananda Bazar Patrika* from running a smear campaign against him for, apparently, raising Rs 100 million for the Muslims of Khulna. The implication was that Kabir, 'basically a Pakistani', wanted to perversely reward the Muslims who massacred Hindus.[89]

For all their self-discipline, of nationalist Muslim dissatisfaction there can be no doubt. As early as 13 March, when the rioting in Bengal was yet to spill over into the Hindi belt, Mahmud gave an interview to *Dawat,* the Jama'at-i-Islami's Urdu organ, in which he vividly described the post-riot scenes he witnessed in Calcutta, hinting *en passant* at a break with the nationalist Muslim élan:

> Complaining every time before the Hindus and the government should not become our habit. We have made enough complaints. But the world does not help those who only make complaints. It rather honours activity and dynamism.[90]

At long last, then, the nationalist Muslims were ready to embrace agency and cast away the self-imposed crutches of comportment that had debilitated them for so long.

Rebirth

'Activity and dynamism' there finally came, if only through the unconventional agency of the Majlis-e-Mushāwarat. It took, it bears repeating, a cascade of slights and grievances accumulated over seventeen years of Congress rule for the nationalist Muslims to make good their extremely qualified break with the party. After Hazratbal, no longer would it suffice to dismiss political violence as inevitable, and interfaith relations inherently inimical, as many a defeatist Congressman and pressman once did.

On 9 August 1964, independent Muslim politics took wing. Meeting at the palatial headquarters of the Nadwatul Ulama in Lucknow, the Who's Who of Muslim India set up the Majlis-e-Mushāwarat, lit. 'consultative assembly', an appellation that, anodyne enough, was an honest reflection of both its ecumenical and informal character. It was not, in the first instance, a political party: its members did not discard their older affiliations. As for its all-inclusive character, it cannot be stressed enough. Among its conveners were Congressmen Mahmud and Kidwai on one side, and Leaguers Ismail and Sait on the other. It included clerics of every stripe: modernists of the Nadwatul Ulama and JUH as well as Islamists of the JI. There were figures from Sunni centres of learning and Shia lobbying outfits.[91]

What had brought them together was, as Madani put it, the 'lesson' of Hazratbal. The time to put aside differences and close ranks was now. The Islamists at *Radiance* had been arguing much the same since April: what was needed was a 'non-denominational *shura* of the whole *umma*'.[92]

Of equal moment was the passing of India's first premier on 27 May. In one of its first resolutions, the Mushāwarat deplored his death as 'an extremely tragic event for India'.[93] Now that the secular colossus who for long had been the only glue holding Hindu nationalists and nationalist Muslims together—restraining the former, indulging the latter—was no more, it was a foregone conclusion that the scarce influence of Muslim Congressmen was to dwindle further. Having one foot out the door was a sensible hedge.

The plan, as laid out by its first president Mahmud, was to first organise Muslims and then build a mammoth subaltern alliance.[94]

Reversing convention, his ambitions were growing with age. No longer would he have identified, it appears, with his youthful self-description as 'Nehru's dog'. Ironically, he had become more cynical (lit. 'doglike'). Already in 1963, he was busy courting the country's premier Islamist organisation, hoping for a historic JI-JUH compact. In this he had been helped by the reconfiguration in the JUH provoked by the deaths of the nationalist Muslims of old—Maulanas Madani, Aseer, and Rahman, all unwavering Congress loyalists. The newer generation was decidedly bolder. After Hazratbal, Mahmud's advances became more urgent, to which the JI *amir* replied reassuringly: 'I abide by the Constitution. We are not opposed to secularism' but rather 'atheism'.[95]

Theirs was a politics of stealth. Short of a full-blown party, a pressure group could escape the charge of sectionalism, not to mention operate almost invisibly on the political scene, as if under a radar. But it was not only the stigma of communalism that prompted it to adopt its singular style. For there was, in a sense, no alternative for an outfit that had so brazenly brigaded Left and Right, 'secularists' and Islamists, modernists and revivalists together. Such eclecticism by definition precluded sectional interest. *Radiance* recognised this: it was 'impossible for the Mushāwarat to act as a common platform of all groups and organisations of the Indian Muslims'.[96]

The adoption of such a style may have been convenient, and perhaps inevitable, but it was not without its defects. The most damaging, certainly, was its inability to shape the national conversation, a direct upshot of its discordant character. All it did was strike deals. It was, foremost, an elite agency. Accordingly, it had no ideology, no cadres, no mass following. It took a good two years, in fact, for it to acquire a press organ, the Urdu daily *Qaed*. It took still another two for the Hilal-e-Ahmer, its 'volunteer organisation', to come into existence. Meant to be an answer to the shock troops of the Sangh Parivar, its activities barely registered after its formation.[97]

In partocratic India, these were major shortcomings. In another polity, one less apprehensive about lobbying, such as the United States or the European Union—both lands where such activity is not only legal *sensu stricto* but also encouraged *sensu lato*—the Mushāwarat would have happily described itself as a lobbying outfit without compunction. As it happened, in India the word was *haram*. So, the Mushāwarat had to be more prolix: its business, in its own words, was to seek out potential candidates and have them sign up to its charter, agreeing to 'work for the adoption [of Muslim-friendly policies] in the Legislature and Government if I am elected to Parliament or Assembly'.[98]

In practice, though, the charter counted for much less than all manner of pragmatic considerations, Mushāwarat organisers holding their noses and picking the least bad of the bunch. The downside was that a lawmaker could simply renege on the gentleman's agreement, as so many indeed did. The risks of retraction were negligible. A paper organisation, it was hardly in a position to apply popular pressure on parliamentarians. Equally, its press presence was non-existent. The biggest weapon in its arsenal was the far from formidable threat of withholding support when the uncooperative lawmaker stood for re-election.

A second defect lay in its incontrovertible *ashraf* character, which, in itself, would not have been a serious limitation. Only that the *sharif* of the Mushāwarat were not particularly attentive to the concerns of the common Muslim. After the initial jolt of 1964, riots ceased to be the centre of attention. Over the next two years, it seems, its leaders buried their heads in the manicured lawns of the Aligarh Muslim University, attempting to stave off state interference in its affairs.

Perhaps this was inescapable. Its leading lights were all men of letters. Their honorifics said it all: Prof Humayun Kabir, Dr A. J. Faridi, Dr Syed Mahmud. They were not nature's populists. Kabir, for instance, was to Myrdal the 'Indian philosopher and administrator' best known for his singular defence of central planning—seen in his oeuvre as a bottom-up, and not top-down, process, reflecting for this reason not state interest but the will of the people. He was also an early, probably the first of, Kant's Asian translators into English; an accomplished novelist; a populariser noted for his book-length essays on the Bengali novel; and a commentator on foreign affairs. With such intellectual demands on his time, it is hardly surprising that he had so little of it to dedicate to his political vocation.[99]

Mufti Atiqur Rehman, who straddled the JUH and Deoband and succeeded Mahmud as Mushāwarat president in 1968, was another scholar who had strayed into politics. Born into 'an eminent family of *ulama*', he followed in the footsteps of his forebears, becoming a sermoniser at Calcutta's Coolootola Mosque, setting up a theological press, editing the monthly *Burhan*, and translating Ibn Taymiyyah and Ibn al-Jawzi into Urdu. When he left the JUH to join the Mushāwarat, he was, unsurprisingly, unable to break with his *déformation professionnelle*. As before, the learned cleric remained absorbed by religious and pedagogic, not so much social and political, matters. Rehman kept his seat at Deoband. The causes that he championed, too, betrayed a greater concern for Islam than for Muslims, for the faith than the faithful. He sat on the boards of the Hajj Committee, overseeing the state subsidy to pilgrims making the *hajj* to Mecca, and the Central Wakf Council, which was tasked with the monitoring of the *waqf* regime that enabled Muslim rentiers to avoid taxes and expropriation. Later, he went on to co-found the All-India Muslim Personal Law Board to protest secularisation. None of these were issues that elicited mass enthusiasm. The ordinary Muslim could not care less about the 15,000 or so annual peregrinations to the Holy Places. In other words, a mere 0.0002 per cent of Indian Muslims made the *hajj* every year. Equally, *waqf* property trustees and men opposed to adoption and adequate alimonies for Muslim divorcées were hardly the widest of constituencies.[100]

Sayyid Abul Hasan Ali Nadwi combined Kabir's academic temperament with Rehman's pietistic worldview. Author of fifty books, including an *autobiographie-fleuve* of seven volumes, *Karawane Zindagi*, and a multi-tome compilation of 'stories of the Prophets', Nadwi also penned 'thousands of papers, articles, and speeches', taking time out to edit the Urdu *Tameer-e-Hayat* and the Arabic *al-Bathul Islami* and tour the Middle Eastern lecture circuit. He was also an inexhaustible font of institution building, serving as Nadwatul Ulama rector and setting up the Deeni Talimi Council, a network of religious primary schools that doubled as a textbook watchdog. All of this left little time for lawmaking and lobbying.[101]

Another founding member, his near namesake Maulana Abul Lais Islahi Nadwi, chief of the Islamist Jama'at-i-Islami from 1948 to 1972, too, was more interested in religious than socioeconomic affairs. Educated at Nadwatul Ulama as well—hence the toponymic surname—he worked as a staffer at the Urdu biweekly *Madinah* in Bijnore and taught at a *madrasa* in Akola. Just like the other Nadwi, he was also among the founder members of the Deeni Talimi Council and AIMPLB. Mass politics was not his forte. The common man's struggle not his. Indeed, his pronouncements suggest that he operated on a different plane, where *ashraf* piety was of greater import than bread-and-butter issues.

His colleague Maulana Muhammad Muslim, editor of *Dawat*, was of an even more anti-political bent. A brief glance at his *curriculum vitae* can create the opposite impression. He spent at least five spells in prison for criticising the Congress regime: in 1948, 1950, 1964—when Nasser visited India—during the 1971 war, and for the entire duration of the Emergency of 1975–1977. But this was more a reflection of the Congress' insecurities than Muslim's opinions. Indeed, one gets a sense of an endlessly anachronistic man from his son's reminiscences, not only not a threat to Delhi but deeply allergic to collective action of any kind. A poor politician, in other words.

He delighted in charitable causes, 'fasting for days' to feed his guests and forcing his family—'wife and eleven children'—to sleep rough in order to accommodate the homeless in his rented '10 x 10 room'. He was also a rather intense character. Indeed, he could have stepped out of a Russian novel. 'There were [times] when we saw him standing up late at night praying alone, crying. There were mornings when we saw him focusing on a page of the Quran gazing into the horizon for hours not responding to our questions'. He had a heightened sense of interiority that came with a general hostility to the social world: yes, 'it was impossible to change the world', he would concede to his critics, but 'one has the capacity to change oneself ... The Quran and the one who introduced the Quran to humanity are the sources to acquire basic traits of character. Building character is a lifelong process'. Such a reflexive worldview, premised on *ashraf* paternalism and the valorisation of austerity, was hardly conducive to the world of mass politics.[102]

Even the career politicians of the Mushāwarat were, after a fashion, apolitical. Mahmud held his *métier* in disdain. So much so that he regarded it as a term of abuse. He left the outfit in 1968, 'accusing its leaders in Uttar Pradesh of reverting to politics'.[103] But then again, trained as a barrister-at-law, it would have been surprising if he had felt otherwise. The 'primary organiser' of the Mushāwarat in his native Bihar, the hotelier Mohammed Yakub Younus, too, was an unlikely man of the people.[104]

A third defect—the upshot of its second—lay in the Mushāwarat's embrace of Islamic exceptionalism. For a lobbying outfit keen to appeal to Hindu voters, its superciliousness no doubt was deleterious, giving ammunition to its critics to denounce it as Jinnah's League *redivivus*. Missing in Ali Nadwi's *ashraf* pitch at the group's first meeting was any reference to inequality or injustice. Insofar as a comparison between the Hindus and Muslims was apposite, it was not to point to the discrimination and difficulties faced by Muslims—objectionable on account of the secular pretensions of the postcolonial regime but more generally as well—but to stake a claim to Muslim supremacy. Muslims deserved better because they were smarter, more tolerant, and better nationalists than the Hindus. In India, Muslims

> are distinguished as compared to the majority or any other community so far as their diverse Islamic practical, administrative, and intellectual capabilities are concerned. Thanks to the creed of monotheism, Islamic ethics, the Islamic concepts of social justice and equity, large-heartedness and liberality of outlook and that fundamental attitude with regard to the universe, the brotherhood of man, and the worth and sacrosance [*sic*] of human life which Islam has bestowed upon them, they possess greater creative spirit and the capacity to cooperate and to live according to the principle of give and take than the others—and these qualities have contributed a great deal towards making them more tolerant, more humane, more earnestly devoted to the welfare of all mankind, and endued them with greater feeling of gratitude and patriotism. They initiated the struggle for national freedom, and took a leading part in it and their sacrifices were greater than those of any other community, if one judged them in proportion to their numerical positions.[105]

And here's Mahmud: 'we are brothers in religion. We believe in one god, in one prophet, and regard the Holy Quran as the fountain spring of all righteousness and virtues. This unity of faith calls for a closer tie'.[106] Not a hair's breadth separated the layman from the clergyman. Remarks such as these cannot be dismissed as early concessions to mass appeal. A good three years later, when the Mushāwarat drafted its constitution, at the top of its 'list of objectives' came its resolve 'to participate in the [sic] social and national issues in a manner befitting the status of a chosen community (khair-e-ummat)'.[107] Such an arch-ashraf worldview was, by its very nature, incompatible with mass politics. For the 'chosenness', as it were, of the chosen people inevitably implied some degree of exclusion, which, when prosecuted in the de haut en bas style of the Muslim political class, precluded the kind of alliance-building and give-and-take on which modern political life was premised.

Factionalism was its fourth defect. This was clear even before its founding. Madani, who participated in the proceedings of August 1964, had in fact been highly critical of Muslim political formations of any kind, excepting the JUH of course. Indeed, in July, he had filed a writ to the Supreme Court to block the formation of the Mushāwarat. There is little doubt, then, that there was an element of insincerity to his volte-face later that summer. And sure enough, in November, he had already thrown in his lot with the National Democratic Convention, 'which was staged as a counterpoise to the Mushāwarat'.[108] The somersaults betrayed an inconvenient truth. The Mushāwarat meant many different things to its moving spirits. If for some it was a gambit to weaken the Congress and force it to take notice of Muslims, for others—more firmly in the Congress camp—it was simply a bargaining chip.

In nuce: no following; ashraf character; confessional fixation; uncertain ambitions. In all, then, it could be said that the Mushāwarat was a failure foretold.

Resolutions

Even so, it proved to be a surprisingly enduring political experiment. It still exists today, if in an attenuated form. What's more, it demonstrated—in its early days, at any rate—a remarkable ability for reinvention. Indeed, within two years of its founding it had ceased to be a recorder of Muslim grievances, morphing instead into an electoral machine.

Perhaps this owed to a growing realisation that reform required representation in Parliament. The Mushāwarat had spent its first biennium doing little except reassuring Delhi that it was a 'secular' outfit, not too different, intellectually speaking, from the Congress. After riots, its 'fact-finding missions' took the form of 'joint appeals' co-signed by Hindu and Muslim 'VIPs'. The statements themselves tended to be insipid, to a less charitable eye even willing to make light of, if not condone, interfaith violence. Witness one from September 1964: 'the Muslims in India have been [*sic*] target of much unkindness ... But for the prompt and firm measures taken by the government, the situation in Calcutta, Jamshedpur, Rourkela, and other places would have become perilous'.[109] Unkindness? Most Muslims in these towns would have been struck by the inappropriateness of the remark. Unperilous? That was one way of describing the bloodiest riots in postcolonial Indian history.

Appearing unthreatening also meant drawing a careful distinction between the—worthy—Indian Muslim in the borderlands and the—unworthy—migrant from beyond. Scapegoating the latter served, of course, to shield the former from the not uncommon slippage between the two. The Mushāwarat's first resolution 'expressed its deep concern over the influx of uprooted Hindus from East Pakistan', even as it berated the government for its inability to create 'peaceful and satisfactory conditions' for the *qaum*.[110] It was not, then, the unyielding logic of borders so much as the hypocrisy—receiving Hindu migrants, expelling Muslim natives; both in national interest—that rankled.

Not for nothing was the document called the 'National Integration resolution'—ostensibly after the *sine qua non* of nationalism found sorely lacking in the Republic. 'It is necessary to remove the fancied grievances and mistrust of that section of the majority so that the motherland may have internal peace', it read.[111] The choice of words was revealing: 'mistrust', not Islamophobia, connoting almost an error of judgement rather than deep-seated hostility; 'motherland', nodding in the direction of the Hindu traditionalists whose ranks dominated the ruling class.

219

The National Integration resolution of August 1964 was in July 1966 superseded by the nine-point People's Manifesto.[112] The focus was now explicitly electoral. Prescriptive policies took the place of didactic generalities. No one could fault it for lacking ambition. The Mushāwarat demanded the revision of textbooks; recognition of Urdu; use of the epithet 'anti-national' to be made a 'cognisable offence'; creation of a minority board; a welfare state worthy of the name; compensation for riot victims; proportional representation in legislatures; vigilance in combatting 'moral degradation', beginning with a ban on alcohol, 'obscene literature', and 'immoral films'; and non-interference in the affairs of the AMU, *auqaf*, and Muslim personal law.[113]

Some of these might appear unrealistic to contemporary readers but were, in fact, eminently reasonable propositions at the time. The aspiration to full employment, for one thing, was of a piece with mid-century Keynesianism. The electoral system, for another, was still in a state of flux: separate electorates and multi-member constituencies had been abolished at the Union level only in May 1949 and March 1961, respectively, and even later at the council level. Proportional representation was no pipe dream.

But the extent to which the People's Manifesto constituted a minimum programme is unclear. It is possible that the paper certitudes were little more than a smokescreen to paper over internal contradictions. As such, it was only an exercise in public relations. For any semblance of a united front was undermined by the reality before it. The Mushāwarat's cadres were in fact the League's, so absent north of the Vindhyas. Its ideology was a medley of the nationalist Muslim position—tempered by the impatience produced by watching riot after riot fly by—and the more assertive Jama'at's. Capital and a national presence came from the JUH and Muslim Congressmen.

This division of labour determined the shape of things to come. It certainly informed its style of politics, premised on pledges and charters rather than parties and cadres. For it was essentially a compromise between the Lohiaite line that Faridi represented— 'anti-Congressism' above all—and Mahmud's nationalist Muslim tendency, reprising, in effect, Ayesha Jalal's 'bargaining counter'.

Whatever Mahmud did, one eye was always on the Congress, whose premier was forwarded, without fail, every Mushāwarat resolution.[114] So much so that in his correspondence with Shastri, Mahmud almost sounded like a mole in the Mushāwarat:

> I know some of your colleagues do not approve of my recent activities in organising the Muslims, but they forget that I have been a Congressman for almost fifty years and the Congress is in my blood and bones. If I can rally the Muslims, it means an addition to the strength of the Congress ... But for my efforts, the chances are that a majority of Muslims would have been attracted to sectarian and militant organisations.[115]

Mahmud was playing a double game. Bestriding two worlds helped him raise his profile in both. The Mushāwarat benefited from having a Congressman as its chief, bespeaking legitimacy and public recognition; the Congress, an extramural barometer of Muslim disaffection. Mahmud, for his part, used his new platform to press for sinecures, demanding a seat on the cabinet's emergency committee.

As it was, the tension—to influence the Congress or oppose it?—was never quite resolved. In the 1967 elections, the Mushāwarat would do both. In a sense, then, the nine-point People's Manifesto collapsed into a one-point programme: to get as many promising candidates, Congressmen or otherwise, to sign its charter as possible. The manifesto itself, signalling a semblance of coherence, was only a means to that end. Much the same could be said of the effort from March 1966 on—nineteen months into its existence—to organise state-level meetings and build cadres.[116] It took another six months for it to pass a resolution in favour of electoral participation, the Jama'at's Islamists only reluctantly agreeing to the impious proposition—and only tacitly at that by abstaining on the vote. The polls were two months away.

What of the slate that the Mushāwarat finally settled on? On paper, they had one thing in common: they had all signed its charter, a mimeographed copy of which was sent to its Delhi headquarters, agreeing to advance Muslim interests. In practice, of course, they did no such thing, not least on account of the woolliness of its formulation. It was all a shot in the dark. Practically speaking, there was little the Mushāwarat could do to tie its legislators to their promises. As many an opportunistic candidate realised, its canvassing came cheap.

The Mushāwarat was more or less indifferent to ideology, and agnostic to confession, in its choice of candidates. Those seeking office, especially in marginals, were eager to capture 'the Muslim vote'. It was a marriage of interests that generated a potpourri like no other. Congressmen accounted for a mere 12 per cent of Mushāwarat endorsements, Muslims a paltry 15 per cent. This was Muslim politics as it had never been before. It was predominantly Hindus who were to represent Muslims. In party-political terms, too, the Mushāwarat cast a wide net.

In six of the eight states that mattered to it, Congress incumbency was a given. In these, it sought out Congressmen and socialists. Peace with the Left did not rule out an arrangement with the Right. It endorsed Swatantra candidates in Mysore and Uttar Pradesh. In Maharashtra, a number of its recruits belonged to the Republican Party of India, hinting at some kind of Dalit-Muslim subaltern solidarity. In Uttar Pradesh and West Bengal, where Delhi's rulers were in dire straits, it was able to conceive a fuller break with the Congress. Here, it was no bit player. Without its involvement in Muslim-heavy marginals, the winning coalitions in both states—the Samyukta Vidhayak Dal and United Front—would have ended up with smaller majorities. In Tamil Nadu and Kerala, the League was left to its own devices. Jammu and Kashmir was ignored for fear of Hindu backlash.[117]

The results make for uneven reading. The numbers offer a rather roseate view. About a third of its candidates—forty-two (seven Muslims) out of 135 (twenty-one)—wound up in Parliament. Nearly one in ten parliamentarians had committed themselves to improving the Muslim condition. Stepping back from the statistics, however, one gets a very different picture. Far from heralding a new kind of politician, the Mushāwarat merely recycled old wine in new bottles. Its main leader in West Bengal, for instance, was notionally not a Congressman. But little less than a year had elapsed since Humayun Kabir had joined the Bangla Congress. Elsewhere, too, the Mushāwarat was not spoilt for choice. In Rajasthan, it was left with no option but to back the Congress. Supporting any other party risked bringing the Jana Sangh to power.

The impracticability of its style of politics was underscored by the new SVD government's mammoth 'thirty-four-point programme' in Bihar. The Mushāwarat managed to get a word in edgeways, but so did the more powerful Jana Sangh, whose presence in the alliance allowed it to 'maintain an independent stand'—a veto—on Urdu. It also struggled to whip 'its' MPs to back or reject this or that legislation.

The Uttar Pradesh Mushāwarat, too, had its hopes raised and dashed. Under Faridi's direction, it had taken the bold decision to endorse only non-Congressmen. The gamble had paid off. Thirty-nine signatories were returned to the 425-stong assembly. And as luck would have it, the Congress' days were numbered. Two eleventh-hour defections helped Charan Singh replace C. B. Gupta in Lucknow. Weaker, so more dependent on sectional interests, the kulak chief promptly cut a deal with the Mushāwarat, swearing in six of its MLAs as ministers. But it was all downhill after that. This points to a peculiarity of the Muslim political classes. They have always excelled at counting heads and securing sinecures. Equally, they have always failed at directing policy. Spectacularly so. Only one figure in this sextet, the Swatantra's Akhtar Ali Khan, made some muted sounds about the pressure group's programme, protestations that were quickly brushed aside. As for the Mushāwarat's hopes for Urdu, they were stillborn. Incredibly, the committee to look into the question was placed in the hands of a Jana Sanghi, the education minister Ram Prakash. The recommendations practically wrote themselves: having two official languages was inadvisable and impractical.[118]

Another eye-opener came later that spring in the form of the Six-Day War. Fired by the turn of events in the *umma*—Israel had invaded the Sinai, conducting airstrikes on Egyptian positions and overrunning the peninsula—the Mushāwarat pledged resources to Palestine, eulogising the Khartoum Resolution that committed the Arab states to 'three noes': 'no peace with Israel, no recognition of Israel, no negotiations with Israel'. Opinions in the parliamentary wing of the Mushāwarat, however, were diametrically opposed to the

223

central leadership. To its non-Muslim legislators, the byzantine world of Middle Eastern geopolitics was a distant concern. To its Muslim ones, of course, it was anything but. The trouble was in convincing their indifferent party colleagues. Because the Mushāwarat men belonged, in the main, to parties other than the Congress, its leaders inevitably had to contend with lawmakers cast in opposition mode. If the Congress, its well-worn bromides about non-alignment notwithstanding, was favourably disposed to the Arab states, then the opposition parties, in a spirit of instinctive contrarianism, had to appear sympathetic to Israel. When four Swatantra MLAs— all Mushāwarat men—tried persuading their party to reverse its position in light of the Six-Day War, all of them were suspended. The Swatantra's stand remained unchanged.[119]

To Faridi and those temperamentally like him, the Mushāwarat had reached the end of the road: 'these parties lost no time in turning their back on the gentleman's agreement. The SVD government proved no better than the Congress government'. A year on from the polls, his fundamental criticism made eminent sense. How could the Mushāwarat expect to be taken seriously when it shied away from conflict of any kind? Politics was about taking sides. What was needed, then, was not a pressure group but a party. As Faridi saw it, it was time the Muslims stopped whingeing and asserted their agency: 'we have to stand on our own legs ... no other group or political party is going to protect us'.[120]

Early intimations of a party-political turn came in February 1968, when Faridi, displaying remarkable flexibility, enlisted the Congress' support to bring down the Singh government in a vote of no confidence. Uttar Pradesh was placed under President's Rule. The *mariage de convenance* did not deter him from having Maulana Muslim, whom we have met earlier, set up a meeting with Ram Prakash, the Jana Sangh's top man in the state, a mere three months later. Clearly, he enjoyed the rough and tumble of politics. Stealth was not his style.[121]

And so North India's first Muslim party, the Muslim Majlis, was born. Its arrival in June came with a renunciation of the élan of old. Muslims had tired of their role as 'a cat's paw [of other parties] in the game of politics', Faridi held. The very name, in its unblushing use of the M-word, too, signalled a break. 'We practise what we profess'. It was a curious argument, for Faridi himself had ruled out a merger with the Muslim League because Hindus were 'psychologically allergic to the name'.[122]

In any case, the name never caught on, probably on account of its near-eponymous parent organisation. Alert to political realities, Faridi was clear from the outset that the UP Majlis, as it came to be known, was to be more than a Muslim party. A subaltern alliance between Muslims and Dalits thus came into being on the strength of this reasoning. Both communities, its founding document held, shared in a 'feeling of inferiority'. That the one owed to *déclassé ashraf* rancour and the other to centuries of oppression did not matter. Forged on practicality, not solidarity, it was a *mariage blanc*. Majlis candidates were to field Muslims to court the *qaum*; Republican Party ones, Dalits to woo the Scheduled Castes. Never were the twain to commingle.[123]

This changed in 1969, when fresh elections in Uttar Pradesh were announced. The UP Majlis was going to go it alone, but then a crisis intervened. Its undeniably religious election symbol, a half-moon and star, was peremptorily withdrawn by the Election Commission after protests from 'certain political parties' (which these quarters were—powerful enough to have it bend over backwards—is not hard to guess). Now, election symbols in the early postcolonial Indian setting were of especial salience. In a land in which over half the world's illiterates lived and *a fortiori* voted, there was no real substitute for simple pictorial representation. It made the business of soliciting votes easier for parties, just as it did the business of deciphering ballots for analphabetic voters. The Majlis' already grim electoral prospects had worsened at a stroke. Necessity being the mother of invention, it entered into an alliance with the Republican Party. Together, they ran a slate of ninety on a 'Federation' platform, this time with an uncontroversial election symbol, the suitably secular dromedary. Faridi held the reins, as its programme made clear: proportional representation; socialism; textbook reform.

But the eleventh-hour alliance failed to save the day. By its own admission, the Majlis ran a desultory campaign, poorly funded and poorly organised. It did not help that its small membership—some

40,000—was also not particularly dedicated. Only five candidates were returned, four of whom cannily defected to the Congress ahead of the 'Indira waves' of 1971–2 that swept away the opposition.

Mrs Gandhi's popularity since her populist turn—promises of land reform; slogans of socialism; nationalisations galore—appeared to be growing with every passing day. If the Congress had been floundering in 1967, it was flourishing as never before in 1971. Sensibly, Faridi swallowed his pride and cut a deal with the premier, pledging unstinting support on the hustings. In return, she promised to put in place an outreach scheme to drum up Muslim applications to the police, standardise syllabi, and create an 'Urdu university' in Rampur. More immediately, the Congress stood down in five constituencies, all Muslim enclaves, in order to improve the Majlis' chances. But it need scarcely have bothered. All five went down in defeat. Faridi himself withdrew from the contest in Rampur, closing ranks behind the nationalist Muslim Zulfiqar Ali Khan, apparently threatened by an insurgent Sanghi. Only he wasn't. Khan won with a comfortable majority of 18 percentage points. Faridi's well-meaning gesture, then, was not only entirely superfluous, but also counterproductive, giving credence to the view that the Congress was the only force standing between Muslims and the Sangh.[124]

What's more, Faridi had been had. After the polls, the Congress was quick to renege on its promises, undermining—as the Majlis saw it—the autonomy of the AMU and tabling in Parliament heretical reforms to allow childless Muslim couples to adopt, a prelude to a common code, many felt. As for the Urdu university, it was never heard of again. Police reform, too, was forgotten. Personally as well, Faridi felt hoisted by his own petard. He was arrested for his week-long *satyagraha* protesting the AMU Act. Time and again, emergency laws were invoked to prevent the Majlis from holding meetings and using loudspeakers. Its mail was routinely censored and held up.[125]

It was not long before it was put out of its misery. Two developments in 1974 hastened its demise: the state election of February and Faridi's death in May. Once again disenchanted with Congress rule, the Majlis had, with pendular precision, swung to the opposite end. Charan Singh, whose BKD the Majlis had only a few years earlier helped topple, cut Faridi a generous deal. All but four of the twenty-six Majlis candidates ran on Dal tickets. But the Majlis was a spent force. The BKD as a whole fared rather well, winning a quarter of the seats. Its Majlis Muslims, however, were defeated in all but three of them.

If the Majlis had ploughed on year after year despite its record of failure, it had been able to do so only because Faridi was a man of independent means. For one thing, its unruly district branches, which collected an annual fee of 50p from the rank and file, hardly ever paid into the party coffers. For another, party membership had stagnated. The Majlis, then, was only able to overcome its parlous finances thanks to Faridi, who time and again tided it over, not to mention paid for the running of the party headquarters out of his own pocket. When Faridi, a sprightly sixty, suffered a fatal heart attack in May, it was a foregone conclusion that his party would follow in his footsteps. The quietus of *Qaed* ensued. Acephalous and insolvent, the Majlis withered away.[126]

* * *

What are we to make of this unorthodox political experiment? Admittedly, in the mid-sixties, the 'conditions'—in the old-fashioned teleological sense—were ripe for Muslim mobilisation. All the same, the Mushāwarat ended up being a road to nowhere.

Why was this the case? In part, of course, because of simple plurality voting, relentless factionalism, and the general *ashraf* tenor of Muslim politics. But *a fortiori* because neither the party nor pressure group fully broke with the nationalist Muslim political élan. For all their novelty, they still operated in a thoroughly circumscribed political space. The juridical always trumped the political, the constitutional the sectional. Here's Faridi at the UP Majlis' first annual conference: 'we want only those rights which are promised by the Constitution to the minorities'.[127]

The Majlis' Urdu campaign was similarly presented in the depoliticised language of constitutionalism. The objectives, variously, were to make the tongue a 'regional language under Article 347' (by which the president could direct state governments to recognise languages of 'substantial' minorities); 'the second official language of UP, *vide* Article 345'; a language of instruction even in schools where

227

'there is only one student to study it, in consonance with Article 350(A)' (another presidential prerogative).[128] There was something quaint about its faith in the discretionary powers of the president, and in the letter of the law more generally. To begin with, the Indian presidency—more akin to the British constitutional monarchy than the imperial American presidency—was largely a ribbon-cutting affair, an office uniquely unsuited to bring about meaningful change. Likewise, the *Rechtsstaat* was only what the Congress made of it. Preventive detention, torture, emergency rule, and states of exception made quick work of legal niceties.

There was, then, no substitute to mass mobilisation and collective action. Such painstaking endeavours the Mushāwarat men found distasteful. In an audit of its first decade of existence in March 1974, when large parts of the country were convulsed by the JP Movement, its general secretary laid the blame for its failures on its 'agitational politics', which, apparently, had 'confused the whole Muslim community'.[129] If its leaders took such a dim view of the restrained deal-making it engaged in, was it any surprise that assembling cadres, taking to the streets, and fielding its own slate were not for it?

Ultimately, if Muslims were weaned away from the Congress, it was not because of the Majlis, still less the Mushāwarat, but rather the Congress itself. The decisive break came in 1977, by which time the Majlis had ceased to exist and the Mushāwarat had fallen dormant, in the polls that were effectively a referendum on India's first dictatorship. In particular, it was the mass sterilisation and gentrification—both discharged in a thoroughly coercive and Islamophobic fashion—overseen by Mrs Gandhi's son that caused resentment. As an all-too-visible minority given to inner-city ghettoisation, with greater rates of urban poverty and fertility at that, the *qaum* sadly but not surprisingly attracted the attention of every zealous and quota-minded apparatchik in the country. Gunning for Muslims was a sure-fire way of getting into the good books of the Gandhis.

For its part, the Congress only went into damage control when the snap election was announced.[130] Too late. Only a quarter of the eighty constituencies with significant Muslim populations returned

Congressmen.[131] The 'Muslim vote' went instead to the Janata Party, the heteroclite coalition of Socialists and Sanghis, ex-Congressmen and ex-Untouchables, princes and the proletariat that swept to power. Nineteen seventy-seven marked the beginning of a new chapter in Muslim politics. The Congress was no longer the only game in town. The Mushāwarat experiment, as such, was over. Shown to work, tactical voting was the way forward for Muslims.

In the final analysis, the Mushāwarat promised more than it delivered. Even so, it would be unfair to write it off completely. The last word, perhaps, ought to go to Sayyid Abul Hasan Ali Nadwi:

> It was necessary for Muslims to realise the weight and importance of their position. This was, in itself, a big gain. To make a child realise that he could stand on his feet and walk, it would be worthwhile to take the risk of his falling down or even getting hurt. But if for fear of injury, he is not allowed to use his legs, he can never be expected to move about properly all his life.[132]

In this limited sense, it achieved its objective. Of course, on account of the diversity—ideological; sectarian; temperamental—within its ranks, it was never meant to last. Still, on the hustings at least, Muslim voices were heard. Promises were made to the community. These, in the event, turned out to be but politicians' empty promises. Influencing policymaking through whispers and nudges proved to be harder than expected.

Nearly a half-century on, the Mushāwarat still exists. In the summer of 2018, I made a trip to its derelict—and virtually unpeopled—headquarters in Okhla, hoping to find a private archive to base the reconstruction contained in these pages. I had no luck. The trip would have been entirely otiose but for a conversation with its amiable president, who, over postprandial tea and biscuits, informed me that the organisation had moved office five times since its inception, relocations in which no papers had survived. Perhaps there was a metaphor for the Mushāwarat itself here. Flitting about from one alliance to another, from one election to the next, it ultimately left behind no lasting legacy. It was caught, as it were, in a permanent interim, a halfway house between the Nehruvian nationalist Muslims, walking on eggshells, and Syed Shahabuddin's generation, taking to the streets.

Unsurprisingly, both the nationalist Muslims and Islamists were deeply dissatisfied with their participation in the Mushāwarat. But what, indeed, did India's Islamists want?

6

ALMOST LIBERAL

India's early postcolonial years, the heyday of statist nationalism, were a hard time to be an international Islamist. This the Jama'at-i-Islami Hind, the Republic's premier organisation of this persuasion, was to learn in a hard school.

Indeed, the Jama'at was subject to endless obloquy. In the fifties, Bihar had banned its members from the public services.[1] A decade on, little had changed. The dismissal of twenty bureaucrats who were card-carrying Jama'atis earned plaudits from the home minister, Lal Bahadur Shastri: 'the JI is an anti-national organisation, which helps in spreading subversive activity', he asseverated in Parliament to cheers of 'correct policy', 'weed out every single one of them'. The Jama'at was banned in Pakistan, he added, as his colleague Harish Chandra Heda hinted wistfully at deportation: 'so they cannot go there also'.[2] Nor was this the last time the Jama'at elicited parliamentary interest. Time and again, lawmakers would lay into it. 'Its cadres refuse to stand when the national anthem is sung'. 'Its chief is a Pakistani citizen [sic]'. 'Its literature refers to our prime minister as a superficial thinker' (quelle horreur). 'It is receiving foreign money'. As an 'extreme section', it must have, no evidence needed, had a hand in riots, and therefore ought to be banned.[3]

231

To be sure, the Jama'at was not alone in being on the receiving end of state power in this period. In Nehru's India, 'anti-national' forces of all stripes were subdued. The RSS, for instance, was banned in 1948, some 20,000 jailed. On the opposite end of the spectrum, India's communists, both militant and democratic, were not infrequently placed behind bars, most notably in 1950 and 1962. Naga sovereigntists routinely found their demands rejected by Nehru; their homelands overrun by paramilitaries. Opposition parties had to contend with executive fiat as well. Between 1953 and 1961, all five state governments that were run by, or were coalitions that depended on, parties other than the Congress were dismissed by Delhi. The upshot was that 'no non-Congress chief minister lasted his full term of office in the Nehru era'.[4]

While, over the years, scholarly attention has focused on each of these groups, it appears that the mid-century crisis of Islamism has fallen through the cracks. Writing on the Jama'at has focussed on the thought-world of its founder Maududi and his epigoni, and, as a recent set of largely sympathetic authors have it, the newfound liberalism of the various South Asian Jama'ats, all of which, through charity,[5] dialogue,[6] and, incredibly, feminism,[7] are busy battling the evils of our time. Of these, there are many: in India, Hindu nationalism in one account[8] and 'neoliberalism' in another,[9] 'Western' secularism—here seen as a Christian ruse—in Pakistan.[10]

'Islam Is Not Democracy'

Given the growing historical interest in twentieth-century Islamism since its recrudescence since 9/11, it is surprising that, while the lineages of virtually every global Islamist current have attracted academic comment, the early days of the Jama'at have spurred so little of it. But the reasons for this elision are not hard to discern. Politically, it carried little weight, counting only 240 members at independence, and just under a thousand a decade later.[11] Materially, sources on it are hard to come by. Mentions in the *Times of India*, the newspaper of record, and in government papers are scarce. The archives of its house organ, *Radiance*, are similarly elusive, as indeed are its pamphlets.[12] And academically, the liberal doyens of postcolonial Indian history have long held its politics odious, and hence unworthy of research. Emblematic is Mushirul Hasan's off-the-cuff dismissal in his *Legacy of a Divided Nation*: the Jama'at 'did not share Nehru's vision of a socially emancipated, forward-looking India'.[13] One suspects that for Hasan and historians like him, the JI serves but as a useful foil to make the nationalist Muslims look good.

Such accounts, of course, also make for convenient history, the kind with neat moral endings. During the halcyon days of 'secularism', so the argument goes, India's Islamists were frozen in time, trying unsuccessfully to bring into existence an Islamic state. But as Hindu nationalism picked up steam, Islamism acquired a novel urgency. After years of stasis, its intellectual tectonic plates were set into motion. The result, as one commentator puts it, was 'the transformation of the Jama'at'.[14] In the eighties and nineties, its defiance mellowed. In its place came a growing preoccupation with practical pursuits: literacy, charity, community. Secularism, democracy, liberal education, transactions with non-Islamist outfits—all that was once *haram* became *halal*. Here, one witnesses an inversion of heroes. The state, now cast as villain, was decimating Muslims whereas the Jama'at, shorn of its fundamentalist elements, emerged from its peripeteia as a champion of liberal values, casuistically extolling its founding father's oeuvre as a defence of the 'secular democratic system' in 1997, and opening up its *shura,* executive body, to women in 1999.

This view has only been sustained thanks to the mid-century lacuna in the Jama'at's history. Indeed, it was in the fifties itself that it came to question the central tenets of Maududi's corpus, the bedrock of its beliefs. So far, most scholarly interventions on the Jama'at have either completely disregarded this period or, at any rate, been incurious to it. M. S. Agwani's foray into *Islamic Fundamentalism in India*—one of the earliest—for one, betrays both disregard and incuriosity. All we get is a single withering judgment: 'Since independence, [the JI has demonstrated] little evidence of intellectual creativity or dynamism'.[15]

Three and a half decades on, his verdict remains more or less unchallenged. Channelling the consensus, Jan-Peter Hartung notes that in Nehru's India, secularism 'remained the organisation's enemy number one'. It was only 'with Maududi's demise in 1979' that it 'became more autonomous'. Hindu nationalists had to flatten the Babri Masjid for its cadres to 'transform [into] ardent defenders of democracy'.[16]

Likewise, two recent accounts, one from Irfan Ahmad, an anthropologist, and the other from Maidul Islam, a political scientist, too, appear guilty of the charge of presentism. Both frame recent developments as novel ones. To Ahmad, again, it was the surge of Hindu nationalism that prompted the Jama'at to reinvent itself as a secular bulwark against the Sangh Parivar, just as it turned a mutinous section towards a more radical kind of Islamism, premised on *jihad*. So, by contrast, Nehruvian India became a period of toleration. 'The Muslim public's disavowal' of its ideology and 'secular democracy played a key role in the moderation of the Jama'at'.[17] On the contrary, it was state suppression that the Jama'at worried about, not so much its lacklustre following. Vanguardist *hauteur* precluded such populist concerns. Contra Ahmad, then, moderation was not the upshot of a growing appreciation for 'secular democracy' but a tactical response to the heavy-handedness of the early postcolonial state.

For Maidul Islam, meanwhile, it is another development of the eighties, the onset of economic liberalisation, that prompted the transformation of the Jama'at. Here, the lure of Islamism owes to its fledgling critique—even if seriously compromised—of the 'neoliberal consensus', the entrenchment of which was coeval with Hindu nationalist ascendancy.[18] It was the twin threats of the Parivar and privatisation that provoked the recantation of Maududi, we are told.

Pace Islam, it was as early as the fifties and sixties that the Jama'at reinvented itself. In negotiating the meridian of statism with a series of volte-faces, it was not unlike its counterparts elsewhere in the *umma*. Indeed, Islamist movements everywhere were plagued by ascendant nationalists. The Muslim Brotherhood and the Masyumi, for instance, were banned in Egypt and Indonesia in 1948 and 1960, respectively. The Libyan Muslim Brotherhood met the same fate in 1973. Pakistan's Jama'at-i-Islami, too, was subject to repeated censure. *In extremis*, Islamists honed the age-old Islamic art of *ijtihad*, creative interpretation. These weren't merely questions of strategy, but ideology as well. The aspiration of Egyptian Islamists to create an 'Islamic order', for one thing, gave way to a glacial incrementalism.[19] Their Indonesian equivalents came to terms with the insufficiently Islamic constitution of 1945.[20] Their Pakistani peers not only made peace with but actively campaigned for a 'secular' female candidate— doubly *haram*—in the 1965 presidential elections.[21]

Confronted with the majoritarian instincts of the Nehruvian state, the JI, too, watered down its Islamism, internalising the language of liberalism that it had once railed against, one which in its very essence was inimical to an Islamic social order. Its mutation was admittedly in bad faith. Even so, it reveals volumes about the character of the postcolonial state. The Golden Age of secularism was not too dissimilar to the years of Hindu nationalist ascendancy, we learn from *Radiance*. There is an element of irony here. For as inadvertent, even if imperfect, liberals holding up a mirror to the state, India's Islamists unexpectedly shone a light on the illiberalism of the secular, tolerant Congress regime. It is not unreasonable, then, to see in the limits of Islamism also, as it were, the limits of pluralism in postcolonial India.

'I Am a New Muslim'

The Jama'at's was, foremost, a utopian project. 'We admit', an early pamphlet read, that 'the ideology of Islam and its practical implications ... are hardly corroborated by a study of existing societies'. That ideology was its founder's, Syed Abul Ala Maududi.[22] Right from its birth in 1941, it was an iconoclastic concern, reflecting his intellectual imprimatur. A 'Muslim' organisation, it drew the ire of the *ulama*—Sayyid Abul Hasan Ali Nadwi and the Deobandi cleric Muhammad Manzur Nomani railed against it—and plaudits from Gandhi, who only a few months before his murder in 1948 was spotted at a Jama'at gathering in Patna.[23]

Maududi's Islamism was a strange beast indeed, a product of his experiences and the intellectual currents of India's interwar years. He traced his roots to an eponymous Chishti Sufi notable of the twelfth century. It followed that as a *sayyid*, descendant of the

Prophet, he belonged to the ruling class, and as such, had a right to rule. This he tirelessly reminded his readers in his writings. Being *déclassé* accentuated such sentiments. His grandfather was a *pir*, saint, close to Bahadur Shah Zafar's court, his father a law graduate who dropped out of the 'un-Islamic' AMU to become an ascetic. Maududi had been young enough to witness his family's immiseration. Growing up in the Deccan—where he proudly maintained his Delhi Urdu accent, uncorrupted by local inflections—he trained as a Deobandi cleric only to strike out as a journalist in the early twenties, writing for Congress-friendly papers. An autodidact, he was drawn to Marx and Lenin, but also to Comte, Darwin, Fichte, Goethe, Hegel, Paine, Rousseau, Smith, and Voltaire. Equally he was fascinated by *taraqqi-pasand*, a modernist literary movement in Urdu letters, as well as *nechari*, naturalist, thought, which welded Western science with Islamic culture, the latter legitimising the former, occasioning, as it were, an Islamic modernity.[24]

As it was, Maududi would reject all of these influences. Two formative set-pieces provoked the rethink. First, the growing influence of Hindu traditionalists in the Congress convinced him that the nationalists were less tolerant than he imagined. The assassination of Swami Shraddhanand, a revivalist Hindu cleric, in 1926 by a Muslim, and the attendant revulsion against the *qaum* that swept society, were instructive in this regard. Second, his marriage in 1937 to Mahmudah Begum, a cousin born into the Bukhari family, the hereditary *imams* of Jama Masjid, freed him from having to fend for himself. Hereafter, a man of independent means, he became a full-time publicist. The same year, the exalted poet Iqbal handed him his estates in Pathankot, tasking him with the running of his new *madrasa*, the Dar-ul Islam.[25]

Here, Maududi developed his life-long interest in pedagogy. He found his calling. Four years later, putting his uxorial wealth to good use, he set up the Jama'at-i-Islami in Attock, Punjab, a spitting image of the Dar-ul Islam. Confounding his expectations, though, it scarcely registered on the national scene, its exhortations to shun the League and boycott the postwar polls falling on deaf ears. Indeed, it was only after Partition when he threw in his lot with Pakistan that he acquired a modest degree of influence. Still, in 1979, when he breathed his last in Buffalo, he could only look back on a wasted life. All the Jama'at had ever done was take drubbing after drubbing at the polls.[26]

If Maududi's life was a comment on his mediocre skills as a political operator, the same, however, cannot be said of his prolific output as a social commentator. There was little under the sun he did not have an opinion about. It is too easy to pigeon-hole him as a traditional Muslim conservative. His preoccupation with state authority—even he was not immune from the infectiousness of statism—for a start, set him apart from other revivalists. This he synthesised with Islamist thought. 'The Islamic system of law needs for its enforcement the coercive power of the state'.[27] This, moreover, was an absolutist state:

> In such a state, no one can regard any of his affairs as personal and private. Considered from this aspect, the Islamic State bears a resemblance to fascist and communist regimes. But despite its totalitarianism, it is something vastly different … [For] such a balanced system could not have been framed by anyone but the Omniscient and All-Wise God.[28]

Consequently, his accent was on political power, not personal piety. Power ultimately rested with God. It is for this reason that Maududi rejected the Muslim League, which, he felt, on account of its claptrap about democracy and representation, had little time for divine sovereignty, so necessary in an Islamic state. The odds that it would change when territories were bequeathed to it were low: a lemon tree rarely begat mangoes, he noted ruefully in a critique of nationalism.[29]

So, while he prized state power, Maududi was no nationalist. The Islamic state was not to be 'a nation-state' but 'a world-state'. For nationalism, which had taken hold of the 'world like parasitic lianas', could only result in failure, just as the French and Russian Revolutions apparently had.[30] 'Muslim nationalists'—Leaguers—and 'nationalist Muslims' were, then, both contradictions in terms, not unlike 'communist fascists', 'socialist capitalists', or 'chaste prostitutes'.[31] This was a vision that was at once radical and deeply conservative. For, on the one hand, it was not merely the 'well-being of a class or a nation' that mattered, 'but of humanity as a whole'.[32] Still, on the other, it was a classless society in that every class was depoliticised, having surrendered every vestige of agency to God. So Maududi opposed even the meagre land reforms of Liaquat Ali Khan in the fifties. Islam protected property rights, he argued anachronistically. His disapproval of Kaukab Siddiq's 'Marxist' translation of his oeuvre into English, which took classlessness a step too far, should hardly come as a surprise.[33] Equally unsurprising was his view that 'immediate revolution is neither possible nor desirable'. What was needed was 'gradual change, replicating the prophetic era', he wrote in *Tarjuman*, reminiscing the splendours of the Rashidun Caliphate.[34]

His views on democracy were par for the course. 'Islam is not democracy; for democracy is that particular form of government in which sovereignty ultimately rests with the people', not the 'Kingdom of God'.[35] Such a view, as Faisal Devji points out, was fraught with tension. For the political was, in Maududiesque thought, a category shot through with antinomies. The exercise of human sovereignty, taken to its extreme in Maududi's caricature, would inevitably imperil humanity, given the tendency of regimes founded on popular consent to slide into dictatorship, or at the very least produce class conflict, which at any rate was equally abhorrent.[36] Sovereignty belonged to God. This, paradoxically, was more democratic. After all, only a divine authority, understood *sub specie aeternitatis* as the only kind of authority that rejects sectional interest, can ensure that the will of the people is respected. So Maududi came to champion a kind of anti-politics, an Islamic state deprived of agency.[37] As a publicist of the armchair variety, he could ignore its impracticality. But not for long. As it was, a decade living in Pakistan was enough to reconcile him to electoral democracy. A spell in prison for inciting riots had a sobering effect. In 1957, he went so far as to suggest that 'transforming the political system can only be done through constitutional means: elections. Transformation of the political order through unconstitutional means is forbidden by the *sharia* [*sic*]'.[38]

His views on secularism showed greater consistency. He simply had no time for it. In May 1947, arguing with remarkable self-assurance, he recommended Indians to organise society around Hindu scriptures, rejecting the 'secular democratic' system of the 'deviant nations' of the West.[39] The counsel stemmed from a cocksure belief in the inherent ability of India's caste contradictions to crumble any Hindu political project in the Subcontinent. In good time, Maududi felt, Indians would feel compelled to have a crack at an Islamic state.

Inevitably, in such a depoliticised society the burden of socialisation was to fall on pedagogy. Here, the Jama'at chief was on firm ground, having penned the propaedeutic *Towards Understanding Islam* for Hyderabad's director of education in 1932, the year he was born again ('in reality, I am a new Muslim', he had declared, forsaking 'Western' clothing and—less wisely—razor blades).[40] He was hostile to clerical education despite having himself trained as a Deobandi *alim*. Instead, he preferred a hybrid education. At the Dar-ul Islam in Pathankot, students received at the hands of martinets a training that was a blend of 'modern'—scientific—and 'traditional'—Islamic—learning. By all accounts, the atmosphere was less classroom, more cadre.

To recapitulate, Maududi's, and metonymically the Jama'at's—it was pretty much a one-man show—was a statist project averse to nationalism and secularism that in extolling a depoliticised polity, rejected elections and favoured a most uncritical schooling system. But this *nizam-i zindagi*, 'complete system of life', as the JI chief had it, was to come adrift.[41] For ideas, of course, are products of their milieux, and, for this reason, rarely emerge unscathed from changes in circumstances. In postcolonial India, virtually every tenet of Maududi's ideology was to be turned upside down. Life under Congress hegemony would force the Jama'at to rethink completely its positions on statism, nationalism, secularism, education, and democracy.

'Democracy Is Preferable to Dictatorship'

Little can be learned about the Jama'at from India's leading dailies, public records, and intelligence reports. For in all of these, portrayals of it scarcely rise above caricature: by turns seditious, dangerous, and reactionary, but also marginal, unserious, even absurd. It is only in the pages of *Radiance*, its in-house journal published from Okhla since 1963, then, that one finds a fuller treatment of the injustices suffered by the Jama'at, its changing worldview.

For an organ of a small organisation, *Radiance* cut a rather unprovincial look in the sixties. Its correspondents, if poor writers, nevertheless appear well-travelled and well-read. Reports were typically filed from the capital, but were anything but parochial. A typical issue could take its readers on a journey, spatially, from the Middle East to India's northeast; temporally, from pre-Islamic Arabia to yesterday; thematically, from Islamic finance to the fine arts. Priced at 25p—on a par with its Hindu nationalist contemporary, *Organiser*—and with a circulation of 10,200 at its peak in the early seventies, *Radiance* commanded a small but global readership.[42] Copies were airmailed to Nepal, Ceylon, Britain, the United States.[43]

Aesthetically, the paper sported a Spartan design. Apart from the green masthead, nothing else was in colour. Images were rare. So were by-lines, most in any case pseudonymous: 'the Critic', 'Observer', 'Non-Entity', 'Son of India', 'Statesman', 'Aligarian'. In terms of content, *Radiance* stuck to a regular format: national news on the front page; three editorials on the second; news, letters, skits, jokes, poems, agony columns, clippings from the Urdu and English press, and profiles of Muslim notables, past and present, in the inner pages; and political tittle-tattle on the last.

Financially, *Radiance* was perennially in poor shape, regularly soliciting funds from its readers.[44] Advertisements from local *petit-bourgeois* concerns, such as a 'hen egg *halwa* shop' that sold a cheap confection 'with precious ingredients for virile power', point to low ad rates, hence low revenues, and a significant Delhi readership.[45] Still, when push came to shove, Mohammad Yousuf Siddiqi, *Radiance*'s well-networked and respected editor, could put his friendships to work and keep the printing presses greased and running. Astonishingly, Syed Mahmud—Nehru's 'dog'—was one of the paper's patrons. Taking a rather capacious view of *zakat* in his retirement, he donated Rs 115,000 into its coffers. The JUH's Mufti Atiqur Rehman, too, was willing to sponsor the house journal of his sometime rivals.[46]

On the whole, on account of its regularity—it is still in print, and, excepting the Emergency when it was banned, it has produced numbers with remarkable consistency—and fairly large readership, it could well be described as the premier journal of Muslim India. Certainly, it was better read than its Urdu peers: the JUH's *al-Jamiat* had a circulation of 5,500 in 1972; the JI's own *Dawat*, 6,700; the Lucknow weekly *Nida-e-Millat*, 5,800. Even as some regional Urdu papers boasted better sales—the Bangalore *Nasheman* (46,600) and the Patna *Sangam* (10,600), for instance—*Radiance*'s eclectic coverage and national readership meant that it was a cut above its competitors.[47]

It was also, perhaps, the only paper in English to unwaveringly platform, and document the lives of, marginalised Muslims from across the Republic in its pages, issue after issue. A letter it published in one of its early numbers, for example, documented the travails of a Bareilly activist, who, for distributing leaflets on Muslim personal law, found himself detained without trial. When he tried to secure bail, he was warned that the lawyer working his case would wind up the way he did, yet another hapless figure languishing in India's carceral world. The magistracy meant business. His counsel was briefly jailed soon after. Six months would pass before he emerged a free and bitter man, ready to 'quit the country' and 'go away anywhere in the world except Pakistan'.[48]

It was under such circumstances—the Nehruvian settlement, what with the premier himself with one foot in the grave, never looking more uncertain—that the Jama'at underwent its postcolonial reinvention. Its leaders came to appreciate that its survival turned on its ability to attune itself to the sensibilities of the new regime. When *Radiance* published its very first issue in 1963, it included an 'eight-point agenda' that read more like the manifesto of a mid-century social democratic party than an Islamist call to arms: 'championing the just cause of the downtrodden sections of society'; 'eradicating moral laxity, corruption, and other social evils'; promoting 'religious and social reform'; 'educating public opinion to discard communal prejudice in favour of a humanitarian and national outlook'. The last item in this enumeration, in particular, betrayed how far behind it had left Maududi: 'strengthening the democratic forces in the country against the totalitarian and the fascist, and protecting against any violation of the fundamental rights granted by the Constitution'.[49]

No Islamic state, then. Still, this was not a blanket repudiation of the past. Rather it was a creative adaptation to the present. As its 1956 constitution had it, its *raison d'être* was no longer the pursuit of Islamic principles in political life but in 'the individual and social aspects of man's life'.[50] In this shift in accent, as it were an inward turn, was to be discerned a scaling down of ambition. Indeed, no longer was the Jama'at interested in supplanting the Indian state. Instead, it now hoped to work around it, accepting, if only on sufferance, its authority, while it waged its war of position. This is clear from one of its pamphlets, a surprisingly honest document, published in 1960:

> Some people raise the alarm that the Jama'at is out to establish a theocratic Islamic state ... [But it] is basically a peaceful, non-communal party [*sic*] working democratically for a moral and spiritual re-orientation of outlook ... It is only when the principles of the Jama'at find favour with the majority of the Indian people that the idea of social and political reorganisation can be entertained ... [Until that time] it would hardly be worthwhile for the Jama'at to take part in parliamentary activity or the general political life of the country.[51]

On the question of democracy, too, the Jama'at appeared willing to betray Maududi: 'this democracy is essentially of the Western type in which the status and position that should rightfully belong to God in human affairs is assigned to the people'. So far so Maududiesque. 'Yet, in so far as its general practical manifestations and impact on life are concerned, it is by large preferable to monarchy, totalitarianism, or dictatorship'.[52] *In nuce*: given real-world constraints, depoliticisation was preferable to state capture, democracy to its alternatives. Reading *Radiance* from across the border, Maududi must have turned purple with rage.

But its revisionism, seen from any angle, served it well. At independence, it must be remembered, the Jama'at was a rather small organisation, counting but 240 souls, the bulk of its total membership of 999 having left for the Muslim Zion. The ensuing decades were kind to it. Already in 1957, it set about expanding its base—until then largely clerical, landed, and *petit-bourgeois*—

to include industrial workers through an outreach programme.[53] The same year, it launched as part of a 'four-year plan' (a sign of its undying contrarianism?) an ambitious literacy drive. Its female leadership, meanwhile, got to work on repairing the imbalance between the sexes in its ranks.[54]

By 1960, it counted 981 members, and in 1981, some 36,000 'sympathisers' who had 'informal contacts' with 310,000 Muslims. This was accompanied by a commensurate achievement in infrastructure: over 1,100 libraries and reading rooms, 600 schools and twenty-three colleges, topped up with a presence in 700 mosques; a mosaic of magazines and newspapers flying off the shelves in metropolises in literally every corner of the country: New Delhi, Guwahati, Madras, Ahmedabad.[55]

It was an unlikely achievement: an Islamist organisation had established itself in a secular, democratic state. How had this come to pass? Through pragmatic acculturation, it will be argued below.

'The Real Function of the State'

To begin with, the new Jama'at, quite unlike the old, came to believe in a small state. Still, its allergy to statism did not translate into a simple forsaking of it. An unlikely understanding of the role of the state is to be found, for instance, in a column by the 'Critic', a *Radiance* regular. Essentially a diatribe against Delhi's *hajj* policy, the piece begins by noting a fall in the number of *hajjis*, pilgrims to Mecca, sponsored by the Indian government. Once footing the bill for some 23,000 pilgrims every year, the state by 1962 was sponsoring only around 15,000 journeys, fewer than Pakistan.[56] Demand, however, was growing. There were by then more than 30,000 applicants every year. True, the cheese-paring cuts owed not to discrimination against Muslims, as was insinuated, but to a foreign exchange reserves crisis.[57] But whatever the reason, it stung all the same. If Rawalpindi could set aside funds for 20,000 peregrinations, surely the richer Indian state could shell out much more, the 'Critic' wondered. To show little interest in the affairs of Muslims was to shirk governmental duties. For 'the real function of the state in a democratic set-up is to provide facilities for the observance of these [religious] principles and creeds'.[58] The state, in effect, was a force for good when it was pressed into the service of the faithful, but otherwise, as a logic unto itself, pursuing its socio-economic imperatives, it was a contemptible agency. Here, then, was a curious logic: more state intervention was desirable but also—as we will see below—less statism.

On similar lines, in 1963, against the backdrop of a bill banning polygamy in Maharashtra, *Radiance* endorsed the views of a Delhi special judge, S. Aziz Shafi, who welcomed the new law. It would benefit a 'lot of poor women'. In tailoring its ideology to fit postcolonial specifications, the Jama'at was letting its vanguardism take a back seat. To be sure, Shafi's piece was written in a spirit of compromise. He was prepared to countenance a government with greater juridical power. But in return he expected two things. One, a discretionary right: that judges be allowed the final word, for if a man could provide for two wives, he ought not to be denied the opportunity merely on account of the letter of the law. And two, residual judicial autonomy: wherever 'it is not possible to have Muslim judges ... the government should appoint tribunals of *ulama* to allow or disallow a second marriage'.[59] For the JI, this was an unorthodox view on at least two counts: first, in the legitimacy it bestowed on the clergy so detested by Maududi, and second, in its ambiguous acceptance of state interference in the institution of marriage.

All the same, the broad thrust was clear. Even in measured lurches to the state (the 'Critic') or in hard bargains with it (Shafi), a thoroughgoing scepticism towards statism there remained. On one level, such a view was, of course, of a piece with other non-statist conceptions that were common currency at the time, not too dissimilar, say, to the Socialist party chief Ram Manohar Lohia's notions of rural communitarianism, where the work of the state was left to decentralised, self-governing villages; the Sarvodaya movement leaders Vinoba Bhave and Jayaprakash Narayan's of trusteeship, where in place of the state it was the rich who were supposed to be have an obligation to the poor; or even Nehru's of, for want of a better phrase, pull-yourself-up-by-the-bootstraps socialism, where self-help counted for more than state intervention.[60]

The upshot was a shift from Maududi's top-down strategy of training an Islamist leadership and letting *dawa*, God's call, eventually trickle down to a bottom-up strategy of moving conveniently into the interstices left by the government to create a parallel welfare state. So, while the postcolonial Jama'at drew, albeit unavowedly, on socialist themes, it remained opposed to socialism proper. Indeed, it was not uncommon to find in *Radiance* reproductions of essays and cartoons printed in *Swarajya*, the journal of India's libertarian Right. One panel, for instance, anthropomorphically depicted the State with a chisel in one hand, clasping with the other the feet of the Constitution, here represented as a pair of legs, which were obviously too large to fit into the tiny pair of slippers, labelled Socialist Pattern, that lay in front of it; the implication, of course, being that cack-handed socialists were about to draw blood.[61]

Yet on another level, it was a view unique to the Jama'at, which had belatedly concluded that a Maududiesque state capture was not on the cards. A greater presence of the state, then, meant a reduced role for Islam. So, *Radiance* came to rail against 'governmental interference' in the governing of *auqaf*, Muslim endowments, which had resulted in embezzlement to the tune of millions.[62] What was left unsaid was that state oversight—'excess of state authority'—was, in fact, a response to the wholesale appropriation of endowment monies for private gain. *Radiance* had mistaken cause and effect.[63]

That was not all. *Radiance* writers called for exempting *auqaf* from land reform and ceiling legislation. Urban land, likewise, had to be made immune from rent control acts to facilitate greater rentier income. Moreover, it was suggested that *waqf*-funded 'scholarships be made repayable when students start earning'.[64] Usury, of course, was un-Islamic, but Muslims had to move with the times. It was thanks in part to the Jama'at's lobbying that Parliament passed the Wakf Act of 1954, which—while bringing the state in—kept government oversight to a bare minimum. The JI, in essence, was as much a shaper as it was the product of early postcolonial anti-statism.[65]

On its view, statism was not only irreconcilable with Islam but also tantamount to Hinduism. The Seerat-e-Hussain's Salahuddin Tayabji refuted in *Radiance* Donald Eugene Smith's claim in *India as a Secular State*—which was widely hate-read and biblically quoted in Jama'at circles—that there was no 'legal connection' between state and religion in India. What better evidence than the presence, in the 500-strong Lok Sabha, of '450 Hindu MPs, the fact of their large majority a sufficient guarantee of their politico-religious position?' If lawmakers were confessional, by extension so was the state. The 'privileged treatment given to Hindus' in riots was no accident.[66]

The same could be said of calumnies against the *qaum* written by senior Congress figures. Take, for instance, a 1964 column— extracts from which were carried in *Radiance*—by N. V. Gadgil, former governor of the Punjab, thundering with denunciations and brimming with angst:

> Indian cities today are full of spies. They are welcome guests in masjids and many of them get help from some Indian Muslims. A permanent solution has to be found out [sic]. It can be one of the two: one, India should cease to welcome any immigrants from Pakistan. The other one is migration and exchange of population through international agencies, as was done after the First World War.[67]

Both the historical familiarity and phrasing hinted at another Shoah, the implications of which were not lost on the *Radiance* writer reporting on the philippic: 'he meant nothing but to banish the Indian Muslim to Pakistan'. A population transfer was 'no solution ... It is permissible on no level—international, political, moral, social, and democratic'. Here was the writer of an Islamist paper propounding the principles of liberal democracy to a genocidal notable of Nehru's purportedly secular party. Alice had entered the looking-glass.

But there was more to *Radiance* than its endless exposés of Congress villainy. There were times when Delhi's rulers were praised in no uncertain terms. After the Jamshedpur riots, it was apparently Congress party workers who 'brought back sanity' by 'rescuing' the town 'from the hideous grip' of '*goonda* gangs acting in league with the RSS'.[68] Ironically, it was the persistence of riots under Congress rule that, after a fashion, made the Islamists look kindly on it. But convince the Jama'at to respond in kind it did not. Indeed, it never felt the need to create an all-out militia, say, on the lines of the interwar Khaksars. But for it being a 'Muslim' organisation, such a development would not have been in the least remarkable. And this is crucial, for it speaks volumes about the limits of Muslim politics in postcolonial India. The Congress, for one, had a stormtrooper force in the Youth Congress, an extortionate lumpen army that secured votes and raised funds. The Jana Sangh, for another, counted on *karsevaks* of the RSS for muscle. For the Jama'at to have a private army of its own, however, was unthinkable.

It was on account of such constraints that it came to distrust state power. While it preferred to subject the Congress to scathing critiques, the Jama'at was nevertheless alive to the fact that it depended on its tender mercies.

'Send Back Illegal Migrants'

On the question of nationalism, the chasm between Nadwi's and Maududi's Jama'at was even greater. When, in 1951, Maududi characterised India as a *dar al-kufr*, 'house of unbelief', and Pakistan a *dar al-Islam*, 'house of Islam', his Indian counterpart was quick to issue an acid rebuttal in the pages of *Zindagi*: the founder's was not the last word on *fiqh*, jurisprudence.[69] Two years later, Maududi again earned the opprobrium of the JI when he coolly suggested that were Muslims to be persecuted in India in the manner that the Ahmadis were by the Pakistani Jama'at—he was soon to wind up in prison for spurring violence against the sect—he would 'have no objection; even if the Muslims in India are treated as *shudras* [lower castes] and *malishes* [outcastes] and Manu's laws are applied to them'.[70]

But the JI's nationalist pronouncements were not simply reactions to Maududi's gaffes from across the border. Nor were they lacking in positive content. Nadwi's consolidation of power as Jama'at *amir*, in fact, owed in no small measure to his exhortations in *Zindagi* to Indian Muslims to do their 'duty' and 'stay in their country'.[71] It is hardly a stretch, then, to find one of *Radiance*'s writers singing the praises of Azad: 'this learned man of the east for nearly fifty years stood as a champion of nationalism'.[72] This was, of course, a term of approbation. The break with Maududi was clear.

As the Nehruvian years rolled by, the Jama'at doubled down on its nationalism. In 1957, it snubbed the overtures of its Pakistani counterpart, which, in the name of *qaumi tabligh*, proselytisation, tried to convince it to support its position on Kashmir—that as a 'Muslim' region it rightfully belonged to Pakistan.[73] But Gholam Rasool, the Pakistani emissary, returned from Patna a disappointed man. The Indian JI could not possibly support Pakistan, which was an un-Islamic state, he was told. Instead, it would 'stay neutral'.[74]

Nation trumped *umma* on both sides. National loyalty counted for more than pan-Islamic solidarity. Five years later, the JI exchanged its neutrality for an unflinching embrace of Indian irredentism. There was no question of accepting the status quo, let alone carving up Kashmir or calling for its independence. By then, those who dissented from this line had at any rate walked over to the Jama'at-i-Islami of Jammu and Kashmir, set up in 1952.[75] Now, the JI was on the same page as the nationalist Muslims, one of whose speeches, emphatically declaring that 'Kashmir must belong to India', was reproduced verbatim in *Radiance* with an approving headline: 'Mr Anwar Explains Muslim Viewpoint: Stirring Speech in Rajya Sabha'.[76] What greater evidence of the affirmation of nationalism could there be than the internalisation of the logic of borders?

As with Kashmir, so with Assam. When the Congress escalated tensions over immigration, the 'Critic' clarified that 'sending back illegal migrants' to East Pakistan was kosher. The burr in his saddle was just that it so happened that more than a few Assamese Muslims were being deported as well.[77] It was only a month earlier that *Radiance* had applauded Madani, the JUH general secretary, for demanding 'all Indian Muslims to discharge their duties and responsibilities' by 'not giving any quarter to any infiltrator. Rather they should help the authorities in detecting such persons'.[78]

In 1960, a pamphlet explicitly laid out the JI's reversal on nationalism: 'the whole history of the Jama'at is eloquent proof of the fact that it has served the best interests of the nation'. It then expressly disavowed any cosmopolitan ambitions:

> The fact that not only in India but in other Eastern countries like Pakistan, Egypt, Indonesia, Ceylon, and Malaya, other parties

are engaged in propagating the Islamic way of life, and that there exists some similarity between their outlook, activities, and programmes, may give an innocent outsider the impression that the Jama'at has international connections ... This is a conclusion arrived at in ignorance of the real nature of this party ... It would suffice for us to declare that the Jama'at has no organisational links with any party outside India.[79]

Maududi's Islamist internationalism, in a word, lay in ruins.

'Make Them Really Secular'

If on nationalism the Jama'at was playing catch-up with the Congress, on the question of secularism it was a step ahead. In 1970, it went so far as to proclaim that 'in the present circumstances, the Jama'at wants, in contrast to other totalitarian and fascist modes of government, the secular democratic mode of government to endure'. This, it hardly needs saying, was a far cry from the Islamic totalitarianism of Maududi's 'Omniscient and All-Wise God'.[80]

But even before that, there were efforts to out-secular the Congress. To an extent the Jama'at's hands were tied. It simply had to adopt secularism as its creed. To begin with, it was confronted with a government that had more than its fair share of Hindu nationalists—Mookerjee, Patel, Prasad. Furthermore, Partition and older communalisms, of which the Jama'at was a product, had seen to it that civil society, the state, and the citizenry—above all, but not only, on account of Hindu preponderance in all three—all looked askance at Islamism, and even at Islam itself.

Perhaps it was an acknowledgment of this reality that prompted it to join the Mushāwarat. Its participation certainly helped deflect criticism. When, for instance, some nationalist Muslims convened the Secular Muslims Conference in response to the 'Islamist' Mushāwarat, *Radiance* feigned bafflement: 'It is unclear what actually they are going to counteract'. The Mushāwarat, after all, 'opposed neither secularism nor the Congress'. How could it? 'The representatives of the Congress Muslims' were very much a part of the pressure group. Its president, Syed Mahmud, was 'himself a

Congressite'.[81] At other times, *Radiance* gleefully bent the stick in the opposite direction: it was the Congress that was not secular. In 1963, reacting to the Law Ministry's decision to set up a commission to propose changes to Muslim personal law, *Radiance* denounced the 'government's anti-secular act'. A common code went against the spirit of secular democracy.[82] More secularism was needed. Syllabi in state-funded schools had to be revised in order 'to make them really secular'.[83]

It would not be absurd, then, to describe the Jama'at's worldview as liberal, even if it does not bring to mind one of liberalism's more familiar individualist strains, but instead its communitarian ones. Thus, taking a dig at the recent 'assertion of a Hindu Punjabi that his mother is not Punjabi' enough, a *Radiance* contributor could contrast such a 'silly, wild, and funny' instance of 'non-integration' with the 'misfortunes' of Muslims, who through forced conversion were being coerced into 'assimilation'. Some could afford not to integrate; others were forced to assimilate. There was a critical distinction, one of agency, and in it could be read traces of a liberal spirit, a defence of communitarian pluralism quite at odds with Maududiesque Islamism.[84]

'The Muslim Way of Life'

If, as Maududi intended, an uncritical education system could produce Islamists *en masse*, so, too, could state schooling biddable youth nourished on a steady diet of nationalist ideology. Diagnosing the contemporary 'problem of education', the JI chief noted in 1960 that 'impressionable young minds are being indoctrinated with the beliefs of the majority community'. 'Islamic traditions' and the Muslim 'way of life' were under imminent siege.[85]

Similarly, as a 1964 resolution of the Jama'at's Hyderabad branch had it, it was because Muslim leaders had lowered their guard by ignoring *deeni talim-o-tarbiat*, religious education, that they were faced with this 'crisis' of faith, 'the increasing trend against the observance of *purdah* among the [*sic*] Muslim girls, their free movements and half-nakedness in dressing'. It was time to take back control. '*Deeni talimi* schools must be run at every place', the resolution read, adding sententiously that 'girls' schools must also be run to train up better wives and mothers [*sic*]'.[86]

As it was, the Jama'at adopted a two-pronged strategy to stave off the threat of secular schooling. On the one hand, it strove to carve a space for itself in the education market where it could maintain a semblance of curricular autonomy, and on the other, it sought to influence state education to make it, as we have seen, 'really secular'.

In the early fifties, considerable effort was expended demonising 'secular' education, which, in the Jama'at's expansive definition, included not only state-funded centres of learning but also the AMU and most *madrasas*. These it deemed un-Islamic and boycotted. In *Zindagi*, such institutions were stigmatised as 'slaughterhouses' that made quick work of the Muslim mind. Co-education, 'Western dress', and the movies were similarly subject to censure: good Muslim youths were to steer clear from such temptations.[87]

But this received image of inveterate Islamism is an incomplete picture, occluding the rapid rethinking that we get a glimpse of in the Jama'at's resolutions and in *Radiance*, pragmatic nooks and recesses expediently hidden from view by the all-encompassing façade of Islamism. In 1957, in fact, the JI lifted the ban on studying at the AMU for its 'sympathisers', and a decade later for its card-carrying members as well. Six years later, it went so far as to defend the AMU's status as a minority institution.[88] And in 1965, when the winds of student protest blew from Aligarh carrying the message of Muslim solidarity, its gusts carried the Jama'at along with it, stiffening its commitment to confessional autonomy in education.[89] As part of the Mushāwarat, the JI defended the 'varsity's special character', railing against the 'unnecessary, undesirable, undemocratic, and unwarranted' ordinance that extended government oversight.[90]

It is also clear from its communiqués that the Jama'at intended to reform, rather than reject, state education. At a *shura* meeting in September 1963, for example, its leaders appeared rather pleased with Nehru's three-language formula and hoped that the government would follow through with it.[91] Likewise, at the close of the decade, *Radiance* goaded the government to revise syllabi by stripping textbooks of confessional content. The Islamic quotient of learning—the Quran, *hadith*, theology—could well be left, it was argued, to private institutions such as the Deeni Talimi Council, which could operate night schools, topping up the heathen education acquired during the day.[92] Such a private-public balance was necessary, the secretary of the UP Deeni Talimi Council argued a couple of months later, for 'the absolute nationalisation of education without exempting minority institutions would in effect amount to endorsing the policy of the Jana Sangh to Indianise the Indian minorities'. The spirit of secularism meant letting 'sub-nationalities'—minorities—carve a niche in the education marketplace.[93]

In essence, it was a two-pronged strategy: reforming public education and revitalising private instruction, secularising the one and Islamising the other. Where Maududi hoped to forge a vanguard equal to the task of fomenting insurrectionary action, his successors aspired merely to make Muslim youths more observant.

'Responsible Leaders of the RSS'

What of the realm of electoral politics? *Prima facie*, Maududi's conceptualisation and Nadwi's execution had much in common. Both were firmly grounded in anti-political thinking: 'theodemocracy' in the founder's case, resting on a singular defence of the Quran and conforming all activity to it; and, for his Indian successors, a similar legalist espousal, but of a different holy book, the Indian Constitution, every article of which had to be followed to the letter: there could be no politics outside it.[94] Central to both imaginaries was the firm belief that political action—collective bargaining, debate, dissension, protests by unions, parties, and civil society—counted for nothing. It was no accident, then, that the postcolonial Jama'at decided to keep off elections. They were 'non-Islamic in concept'.[95]

The organisation hierarchy, too, betrayed a deeply depoliticised style. At first glance, the Jama'at displays all the trappings of internal democracy, but on closer examination, these reveal as mere artifices. Its main decision-making body, the fifteen-member *shura*, advisory council, as the name suggests, could do no more than counsel. The *amir* had a veto on all matters. In any case dissent was rare. The advisory council and *amir*—both elected by the fifty-member *majlis-e-numaindagan*, council of representatives, in turn elected by the membership—typically worked in unison, making decisions unanimously. In case of deadlock, a largely hypothetical scenario, the *amir* needed to carry a mere third of the advisory council with him—a *de facto* veto—in order to prevail.[96] Ironically, then, it was in almost Hindu terms that the JI understood politics, seeing the purity of its cadres, not political success, as paramount. The moral trumped the material.

This, again, is an incomplete picture. For such a view—which, for obvious propaganda reasons, *Radiance* preferred to foreground—cloaks the gradual rethink underway at the Jama'at headquarters. This was the revenge of the political. The Jama'at, it is true, boycotted the 1951–2 and 1957 elections, but it came to question the wisdom of the interdiction soon after. In 1961, it paved the way for a makeover, sending fifteen *ulama* a questionnaire to determine if electoral participation was permissible under *sharia* law. Twelve answered in the affirmative. With this as cover, the *shura* resolved that voting was *halal* so long as it helped move the country away from its 'ungodly' conjuncture. The next year, Nadwi spiritedly called on Muslims in *Pas che bayad kard?*—'What Is To Be Done?', a pamphlet of Leninist inspiration—to march to the polling stations, even as he forbade Jama'at members, who were to be held to a higher standard, from doing the same.[97]

But even this caveat came undone in 1967, when the JI formally allowed its cadres to vote, notionally under the following three conditions: first, that Muslims were faced with the threat of a full-blown Hindu dictatorship; second, that the local candidate considered anti-*sharia* legislation *haram*; and third, that he promised to address Muslim concerns.[98] The next year, a resolution was moved to lift the ban *tout court*, no conditions attached. But it failed to carry the *shura*, where a three-fourths majority was necessary—instead it was a tie—and was then sent to the *majlis*, which shot it down. Nadwi, who by then had turned coat, was disappointed by the turn of events. All the same, he was gone in four years and replaced by his secretary, Muhammad Yusuf, an arch-conservative rather ill-disposed to democracy.[99]

Three years later in 1975, Delhi declared a state of emergency, banning and driving underground those it deemed enemies of the state, the JI included. After the *autogolpe*, the presses of *Radiance* were immediately shuttered. They were to remain under lock and key for nineteen months, leaving us in the dark about its activities. What we do know, however, is that for the Jama'at, the Emergency was a turning point that brought the illiberalism and Islamophobia of the Indian state in fuller relief. Its properties were impounded and Yusuf was thrown in prison along with 700 Jama'at members.[100]

More generally, too, evidence piled up pointing to Islamophobia. And for once, it was not just *Radiance* reporting on it. The entire fourth estate was. Famously, in the villages of Gurgaon, 8,000 mostly illiterate Muslim Meos were browbeaten and forcibly sterilised under the watchful eye of the police, amid gunshots and tear-gas.[101] Next-door in the capital, Delhi's gentrifier-in-chief had inner-city Muslim ghettoes bulldozed and its residents evenly distributed along the city's peripheries so as not to have, in his words, 'destroyed one Pakistan to create another Pakistan'.[102] When the Emergency was called off in 1977, the Jama'at naturally enough campaigned for the Congress' ouster. When that was achieved, a *majlis* poll settled the political question for good: 1,046 favoured lifting the ban on voting to 277 who did not. Democracy was *halal*.[103]

So much for high politics. But politics intruded in other, subtler ways, too, subverting Maududi. The knots that Sayyid Anwar Ali, a Jama'at ideologue, tied himself into nicely captured its inescapability. Even as he argued against reservations, hoping that his brethren would, rather than carp about representation, choose instead to simply live as good Muslims, inspiring by example others to defect to Islam, he nevertheless felt obliged to rail against the Congress for doing away with separate electorates and distorting the 'true representation of Muslims'.[104]

Democratic politics was infectious. The Jama'at's new élan lent itself to all manner of alliances. In the fifties, it backed the Buddhist Dalit demand for university and government job quotas, the kind enjoyed by Hindu Dalits. Still, external support was one thing, more organic connections another. These took longer. A catalyst was the realisation, in the early sixties, of its growing irrelevance, spurred by a wedge in its ranks that turned on two questions.[105]

First, whether the time had come to throw open its doors to non-Muslims. The organisation's objective, after all, the 'progressives' argued, was to fight for *ghaleb-e-islam*, Islamic rule, and not *ghaleb-e-muslimeen*, rule by Muslims. In any case, everyone was a Muslim: 'All men are born Muslims. But then the foolish and the wicked ones stray away'. In the event, nothing came of such contortions. The proposal to roll out the red carpet for, as it were, non-Muslim Muslims was shot down by the *majlis*.

Second, whether the time had come to seek out representation in Parliament. The RSS had the Jana Sangh. Where, then, was the Jama'at's equivalent? To this end, an entryist putsch was proposed: the Swatantra Party could become its vehicle. Few could fault it for ambition. But this, too, was aborted. Sure, C. Rajagopalachari was 'tolerable', the *majlis* felt, 'but how could a former *akhand* [irredentist] Hindu [such as K. M. Munshi] be tolerated?'[106]

In the end, the reformers won out. By the mid-sixties, the Jama'at had made its peace with the League. *Radiance* happily carried its president's speeches in its pages. What mattered was that they had a common enemy in the Congress, bent not only on defeating Muslim parties on the hustings, but on annihilating them by hook or by crook. When, in 1964, Nehru's education minister, M. C. Chagla, crisscrossed the South setting out the case for banning the League, *Radiance* gave a full page to the story.[107] When riots rocked western Uttar Pradesh in the summer of 1963, the Jama'at leadership opened talks with nationalist Muslims. In September, when the Deobandi cleric Maulana Syed Asad Madani was sworn in as the new JUH chief, his inaugural address received a laudatory notice in *Radiance*. There seemed to be no limits to the Jama'at's newfound promiscuity.[108]

These were the opening salvos that culminated in the Majlis-e-Mushāwarat. Toleration, not vanguardism, was the requisite of the hour, and the Jama'at gamely rose to the task. The conviviality was attractive to both sides. The Islamists lost some of their characteristic impatience. The nationalist Muslims, meanwhile, learned to live with them, admire them even. Ultimately, when cracks emerged in the Mushāwarat coalition, it was not the JI but the JUH that, probably under pressure from the Congress, pulled out from the pressure group in November 1965, leaving Nadwi's followers fuming.[109]

It was now, ironically, the cool-headed moderates of the JUH who came in for a tongue-lashing from the stiff-necked Islamists of the JI for their uncompromising, holier-than-thou attitude: 'how we wish Madani realises that he is at present the general secretary of a respectable organisation with a glorious past'.[110] An inattentive reader would be forgiven for thinking that the columnist was writing about a caliphal institution rather than a Congress affiliate. The real reason the Jama'at was so keen to see the Mushāwarat succeed, it is fair to speculate, lay in the eminently respectable cast of notables attached to it. Some of the stardust sooner rather than later was to rub off on it. Its own strategy, moreover, was marked as much by its belated ecumenicism as a latent entryism. By the mid-seventies, it was clear that the Mushāwarat had fallen into Jama'at hands. In 1995, Shafi Monis, the number two in the JI hierarchy, was to become its general secretary.

More surprising was the Jama'at's sanguine attitude towards Hindu fundamentalism. In 1964, for instance, *Radiance* deemed the overtures of the Jana Sangh to the Mushāwarat 'a good augury'. An element of expediency to their incipient alliance there certainly was across the board. In the triangular contest for Phulpur, the Muslim vote had at once become a coveted prize, sought even by the Sangh. Noting its past record, but nevertheless warming towards to it, *Radiance* 'hoped this appreciation will not end with the by-election'.[111]

It did not. A decade later, vestigial inhibitions sloughed off, the Jama'at was to be found undertaking social work with the Arya Samaj, a Hindu revivalist group.[112] And after the Emergency, even Yusuf, the new *amir* and hard-liner, was willing to countenance a 'new relationship with the RSS'. It had helped that when Mrs Gandhi had him banged up in prison, he had shared a cell with Sanghis. During the dark months of dictatorship, Hindu nationalists became a known quantity to him, no longer abstract villains but friendly faces. 'Physical proximity' made him see the Sangh in a new light, he later said to the *Times*. It also altered Sanghis: 'responsible leaders of the RSS are now adopting a non-communal attitude'.[113] But the rapprochement was not to be. It was only a matter of months before disillusionment set in on both sides, and the bouquets were replaced with brickbats once again.[114]

'A Concession to the Males'

Olivier Roy has observed that it is on the hill of politics where Islamists go to die.[115] For their accent on individual piety typically comes at the expense of social aggregation. The Holy Book and the *sharia* are given pride of place, but unions, parties, civil society—the stuff of the modern state—no place at all. Such a juridical, anti-political, anti-majoritarian worldview ultimately condemns most Islamist movements to failure. Modest reinvention saved the Jama'at from this fate.

Still, its revisionism should not detract from its essentially Islamist character. Nor should its liberal rhetoric be taken at face value. What better way to bring into sharper focus the limits of its renovated liberalism than *Radiance*'s running war of words with its 'secular' nemesis, the *Secularist*? What so riled up the Islamists was that the organ of A. B. Shah's Bombay-based Indian Secular Society envisaged secularism in the strictest sense of the word: the separation of state and religion. In this, the *Secularist* was quite at odds with what for the better part of the twentieth century passed for secularism on Indian soil, variously tolerance and the state's equidistance from, and equal appreciation of, all faiths, a consensus that ran from Nehru to Nadwi. *Radiance* was, as it were, the Charles Taylor to the *Secularist*'s Steve Bruce.[116]

To put it mildly, then, the Jama'at's understanding of secularism sat uncomfortably with the Society's. In one of its first broadsides against the *Secularist*, *Radiance* took umbrage at Shah's objection, apparently motivated by Islamophobia, to 'the Jama'at's call for *jihad*' in the wake of a Christian fundamentalist's attempt to torch the Al-Aqsa Mosque in 1969. 'Religious fights', *Radiance* editorialised, had their uses. And so did secular hypocrisy, for Shah and his ilk were 'misguided secularists', or worse, incorrigible Islamophobes. Hamid Dalwai, a Maharashtrian Muslim and associate of Shah's, supposedly was of the latter sort, having provocatively written in *Muslim Politics in India* that he would 'force' Muslims to shave their beards were he to become 'the dictator of India'.[117] Then came the clincher: 'can Mr Dalwai or Mr Shah say the same thing about the beards of the Sikhs?' Of course, they could not, it was insinuated, for the *Secularist* set were not social reformers as such, but instead *soi-disant* 'modernisers' of Islam, especially when it came at the *qaum*'s discomfort.[118]

A week later, *Radiance*'s A. Karim Shaikh laboured the same point, except with more hyperbole: 'the Indian Secular Society is the cultural extension of the Jana Sangh just as the Sangh is the political extension of the RSS'. As for Shah himself, he was a 'Western Orientalist' whose 'anti-Islamic zeal' owed in no small part to his desire to please his benefactors, which included—as Shah had indeed once admitted—the Ford Foundation and the CIA-funded Congress for Cultural Freedom. What followed, however, was less a critique of the *Secularist*'s illiberalism than a demonstration of the limits of its own Islamist liberalism: adultery apparently was unheard of in Islamic societies because the punishment for it 'according to Islamic jurisprudence', rightly, 'is death'. Muslims, then, for they inhabited a higher moral plane, were entitled to multiple wives, 'a concession to the males' that a common civil code had no right to jeopardise. That there was, in reality, no capital punishment for adultery in India mattered little. The parting shot said it all: 'it is a waste of time to persuade Muslims to substitute manmade laws for the universal and faultless laws given by God'.[119]

Radiance, undeniably, was on to something. Vindication came with Shah's response, which revealed the essentially Hindu character of his 'secularism' that lay behind the atheist edifice. He started out with a defence of president Sarvepalli Radhakrishnan's 1962 broadcast calling for a *dharmayuddha*, religious battle, albeit one with clear Hindu overtones, against China—it reflected national, not confessional, sentiment, Shah noted—and ended with a screed in uppercase:

THE HINDUS ARE LOSING PATIENCE NOW. UNLESS MUSLIMS REALISE THAT THEY ARE LIVING NOT IN THE SEVENTH CENTURY BUT IN THE SECOND HALF OF THE TWENTIETH, AND CHANGE THEIR ATTITUDES BEFORE IT IS TOO LATE, I AM AFRAID THEY ARE INVITING DISASTER FOR THEMSELVES.[120]

The problem, in short, turned entirely on Muslim intransigence. Elided was any mention of Hindu rage. If Shaikh, Shah continued, wanted to hold onto his beliefs—'polygamy, unilateral divorce without alimony, unequal inheritance'—'I would advise him to emigrate to Saudi Arabia'. In a sense, the rebooted postcolonial Jama'at was both vindicated and discredited: the former on account of Shah's reply, and the latter its evident Islamic supremacism.

For all its revisionism, then, its pragmatist excrescences never fully supplanted its ideological core. That remained the establishment of an Islamic state. As its ideologues put it in a propaganda pamphlet:

> The Jama'at's ideology demands a reorientation of outlook in light of the Divine Guidance available to us in the religious scriptures, of which the Quran is the final, most complete, and now the only authentic restatement. The Jama'at's message is, in short, a plea for the adoption of the Islamic way of life in practice.[121]

Its newfound secularism, moreover, was strictly a matter of convenience:

> Secularism as a state policy, which implies that there should be no discrimination or partiality on the basis of religious belief, can hardly be questioned and that too by a religious minority. But if, beyond this utilitarian expediency, some people have deeper philosophical connotations in mind, we beg to differ. These philosophical connotations are essentially Western in origin, and carry a spirit and a history which are totally foreign to our temper and needs.[122]

This was followed by disapproving comments on Western irreligiosity. The upshot of 'the new science' with its attendant atheism, both lubricated by the 'metaphysical gap' left by a regressive church whose 'cumbrous theology' had fallen 'foul of the pioneers of science and the leaders of the state', godlessness had produced 'many of the ills from which the modern age suffers'. There was, then, no better antidote to 'the falling standards of moral behaviour ... the evil, the corruption, the selfish pursuit of narrow parochial interests, the rapidly deteriorating norm of human relationship' than an Islamic state.[123]

The Jama'at's project, Nadwi suggested in 1960, entailed recasting 'the entire structure of individual and social life in the light of His guidance. Muslims can hardly succeed in living up to the precepts of the good life until they make their non-Muslim brethren partners and co-sharers in this venture'.[124] Via coercion or consent? Either way, the elision is in itself revelatory. The JI struck a similar note in its symposia, one of which was titled 'How to achieve Muslim domination in India'.[125] Maulana Mohammad Mustafa's despondent comment at another gathering confirmed the sentiment. The quandary of the *qaum* might never have arisen had early modern India's Mughal rulers 'followed Islamic principles rigidly'. Indeed, if they had, 'there would not have been a single non-Muslim in India'.[126]

Lurking beneath the sheen of its nationalism, likewise, was an enduring Muslim cosmopolitanism. The Jama'at's Bihar bosses spoke of revolution. Muslim flags, they said, would go up in all of the world's capitals. In the spring of 1957, they wired funds to Nepali Jama'at leaders in Morang to build a new branch to woo the Muslims of the Terai, and sent activists to Seoul to help Korean Muslims set up a chapter in the peninsula.[127]

The broad thrust of the Jama'at's thinking, then, like that of all religious fundamentalisms, was exclusionary. This should not surprise us. If precedent is any guide, the revivalist's defence of pluralism hardly stands on *terra firma*. As Farzana Shaikh persuasively shows in her study of Muslim politics in late colonial India, even such enlightened figures as Chaudhri Rahmat Ali and Mohammad Iqbal, both of whom broadly accepted representative politics, nevertheless rejected a multi-confessional federation on Islamic grounds.[128] Francis Robinson makes a similar point. Muslim notables—rulers; writers; clerics—have throughout the nineteenth and twentieth centuries responded to the crisis of modernity by, on the one hand, appropriating its terms—rationality; democratisation; constitutionalism—and, on the other, cultivating a fogeyishly overdeveloped sense of Muslim authority. The Muslim Self has always been defined in contradistinction to the Hindu Other. Toleration has been the casualty of such operations, exceptionalism the upshot.[129]

But if the course charted by the Jama'at is a comment on the limits of Islamism, it is also a comment on its obverse, the limits of

Nehruvian secularism and pluralism. For it was only in the absence of secularism and pluralism proper that the JI felt compelled to commandeer both principles and call out the state for its shortcomings.

In doing so, the Jama'at developed, after a fashion, a more radical critique of secularism than so many have from the perch of the liberal academy. On these accounts, Nehruvian secularism has been, by turns, celebrated as a singularly Indian answer to Western secularism and criticised for having no relevance to the Indian genius. From the ranks of the former camp, Amartya Sen, for one, has commended the early postcolonial state for tweaking secularism to suit 'Indian' sensibilities by giving religion greater latitude in matters of personal law.[130] Rajeev Bhargava, for another, has lauded it for heeding diversity and stopping short of a complete separation between religion and state, instead maintaining a 'principled distance' between the two.[131] Stanley Tambiah, too, has eulogised early postcolonial secularism, both as idea and practice: 'there was something large-hearted and genuinely accommodative in Nehru's attitude to Muslims in India'.[132]

From the ranks of the latter camp, meanwhile, T. N. Madan and Ashis Nandy have argued in their separate analyses that it was Nehru's interventionist secularism—the former placing an accent on its Christian (read: Occidental) origins, and hence improper graft onto Indian soil; the latter in a more outré intervention on, as it were, the 'intolerance' of godless modernity, alienating to the left-behinds—that inadvertently produced the conditions in which Hindu nationalism could thrive and flourish.[133] Likewise, Partha Chatterjee has depicted Nehruvian secularism as an interfering statist project aimed singularly at Hindu reform—the majority community being the only subject worthy of secularisation—leaving Muslims to be cosseted by its self-appointed custodians. This, then, was secularisation at different speeds, to Chatterjee a himalayan blunder, giving ammunition to Hindu nationalists to rail against 'pseudo-secularism'.[134]

It is important not to lose sight of Ariadne's thread in this thicket of opinions. What is common to both narratives is that the distinctiveness of such a thing as Nehruvian secularism is taken for granted, even if its success is contested on account of the Hindu nationalist backlash that denoted in its wake. Trading in ideal types such as 'Indian' and 'Western' secularism [*sic*] (what possibly unites French *laïcité*, the upshot of the *Loi de 1905*, and Christian Democracy in Italy, where the *otto per mille* still obtains, let alone Polish Catholicism and Greek Orthodoxy?) and pitching Nehruvian against contemporary rule (the former tolerant if prematurely secular, the latter forthrightly confessional), these accounts typically combine normative and comparative, but altogether ignore historical, reflection. So it is that both proponents and detractors of Nehruvian secularism, in jousting over its indigeneity, pass over questions of greater import. How did Indian secularism work in practice? How did it appear to India's minorities?

As we have seen in this chapter, some preliminary answers are to be found in *Radiance*, whose Muslim writers were responding, often in *ad hoc* fashion, to events as they unfolded, not to some rose-tinted myth of the Nehruvian regime reconstructed after the event. By bringing to the fore its authoritarian and Islamophobic impulses, *Radiance* drew attention to a rather different facet of the Congress regime, one quite at variance with the exnominated account of its hegemony in the fifties and sixties. It was Nehru's knee-jerk recourse to incarceration and suppression to silence dissent that led the Jama'at to become wary of state power. When the cost of coming across as even remotely critical of the country's rulers became clear, *Radiance* took to nationalism. The JI also came around to the then hegemonic discourse of secularism, laying every so often into the Congress for its failings on this front. Its willingness to come to an understanding even with Hindu nationalists, and to embrace democracy after India's first dictatorship, too, point to national conditions a world removed from the ones described in glowing accounts of Congress rule, by turns liberal, tolerant, and democratic. Here, instead, was a regime that was illiberal, intolerant, and undemocratic. Very simply, the Jama'at had no choice but to contend with it, playing on its turf even while opposing it, criticism of any kind strictly circumscribed by the regnant ideology of the time.

Nehruvian secularism, in the final analysis, was more a rhetorical strategy to legitimise Congress rule than a meaningful signifier in its own right. For it served primarily to police political activity in the

Republic, pushing to the periphery sectional interests anathema to it. 'Principled distance' in practice meant that the Jama'at, too, had to be banned when the RSS was, as in 1975, the brigading ostensibly a gesture of even-handedness. It did not matter that the influence the latter commanded through its cadres (some 3,000,000), ubiquity, and public acceptance when compared with the pitiful following of the former (2,831 members) put paid to any sense of proportionality. As the 'Critic' caustically noted in *Radiance*, theirs was 'the parity between the wolf and the lamb'.[135]

* * *

In these brief surveys of the League, Mushāwarat, and Jama'at—the subjects of Chapters 4 to 6—what we have, then, is not simply a chronicle of the trials and tribulations of India's Muslim minority, but rather a worm's-eye view of the age of Nehru. In these pages, I have tried not merely, as Walter Benjamin famously has it, to 'brush history against the grain'—as it were, empathise with, and recover the annals of, history's losers, hidden in plain sight.[136] I have tried instead, to paraphrase another astute theorist and practitioner of history, Carlo Ginzburg, to explore an anomaly to elucidate the rule—repurposing the minority question to reflect on the majoritarian character of Indian democracy.[137]

PART III

NOTABLES

7

CLASS ACTS

There was never a good time to be a Muslim in postcolonial India—not unless one was the right kind of Muslim. For there was, even in such a hostile landscape, a certain kind of elite Muslim figure who did rather well in this period. This was the world not so much of the career politician or cleric as of the noble and notable. We are in the land of *waqifs* and *wasiqadars*, princely pensioners and patricians, *mutawallis* and other men of independent means.

Partition, it is true, threatened their social standing just as it did the lives of their poorer *confrères*. Even so, on account of their class position, practical intelligence, and persuasive skills, they were able to resort to a creative set of strategies to protect their privileges, at times even inveigling the state into topping them up with annuities, loans, grants, and tax breaks.

Their sense of propriety served them well. They were quick to present themselves as representatives of Muslim India, and remarkably, to convince authorities of the validity of that claim. Time and again, an elision was made between their interests and the community's, submissions that Delhi's unsuspecting rulers took at face value. So, Muslim notables landed on their feet in postcolonial India, holding on to their wealth and the quaint laws they favoured.

In short, here a rather different picture emerges from the one in the foregoing chapters. But this should not surprise us. As will be argued at greater length in the conclusion, contrary to popular belief and indeed scholarly consensus, class has always counted for so much more than confession in postcolonial India.

Religious Rentiers

In the early hours of 2 February 1975, policemen armed with preventive detention papers showed up at Delhi's Jama Masjid, the heart of the capital's inner-city Muslim ghetto, and took off with the *imam*, Syed Abdullah Bukhari, who had only a while before led a protest outside the Delhi Wakf Board, a stone's throw from the mosque. A riot ensued.[1] The cleric's enraged votaries rampaged about the neighbourhood, setting shops ablaze and waylaying passersby. Ten were killed, some hundred injured, even as officers of the law merely 'stood by passively' as Muslim attacked Muslim.[2]

What are we to make of this bloody affair? The answer, it seems, is not the reassuringly familiar one. For this episode unsettles much that passes for common knowledge about *auqaf*. On the conventional account, as singularly 'Muslim' endowments, *auqaf* are cherished Muslim institutions, their autonomy apparently a cause dear to the community. Against this united front, we are expected to encounter the state, an Islamophobic agency bent on making life miserable for the *mutawallis*, its custodians. But oddly enough, here the police had absented itself from the scene. For its part, the Delhi Wakf Board hardly fit the bill of a faceless Islamophobic bureaucracy, controlled as it was by the local Muslim elite. Its chairman was a Muslim. So was his detractor, the *imam*. The victims of the riot, just as its perpetrators, were all Muslim.[3]

Pitching the state against the community will not do. A religious lens is perhaps not the best one. *Auqaf* are better seen as staging grounds for a purely economic struggle. On the one hand was the *waqf* board that managed the coffers of the mosque, paying the *imam*'s wages. Then controlled by Congressmen, it had challenged Bukhari's incumbency on account of his 'anti-Congress politics' and extortion rackets: his cronies collected protection money from local shops and fleeced tourists. On the other was the *imam* himself, who wanted to break away from the board, which at the time was subsidising the mosque to the tune of Rs 1.3 million a year. It was in the first instance the board's embezzling and mismanagement of mosque funds, he alleged, that had pushed it into the red, prompting the divestment of other assets in the capital. But Bukhari did not want to get rid of the board. Rather he sought co-option. It was simply a seat at the high table that he was after.[4]

Ultimately, controversy turned not so much on state interference but on the precise nature of state assistance. The opposition of Hindu state versus Muslim *mutawalli*, then, is misplaced. The *waqf* regime instead pitched one set of Muslim notables against another. But what exactly is a *waqf*?

A *waqf*—lit. 'stops'—quite literally 'halts' the alienation of property once it passes from *waqif*, owner, to *mutawalli*, the custodian responsible for the redirection of rentier income towards Islamic ends, however defined. Traditionally, endowment revenues served to dispense patronage and fund holy armies, festivals, charity, and the dependants of *waqifs*. Unquestionably, public largesse often cloaked private concerns. It helped that in Islam, the separation of the two realms was, to begin with, a rather tenuous affair.[5] As it was, 'halting' property forestalled expropriation. It should come as no surprise that *mutawallis* were often kin to *waqifs*.[6]

From the early second millennium on, *auqaf* mushroomed across the Muslim world, excepting perhaps in West Africa. In Mughal India, they enjoyed royal patronage. Famously, the upkeep of the Taj Mahal was financed through *waqf* rents.[7] With the coming of colonialism, *auqaf* received fresh impetus. The trigger was the new Muslim code, which called for the carve-up of property between heirs based on a literal, if seldom applied, interpretation of the Quran. Turning adversity into opportunity, Muslims circumvented the law by setting up *auqaf*. The advantages, then, were twofold. Endowments enjoyed lower tax rates and, because mortmain, were inoculated from partition.

The former perquisite, of course, proved a burr under the British saddle. The Muslim endowment, Calcutta decided, was an instrument for tax avoidance, if not outright tax evasion. Laws preventing abuse and facilitating expropriation followed in short order. The Privy Council confirmed that *auqaf* had to perform a public function. There was nothing altruistic about protecting familial wealth. This had an unintended consequence. *Auqaf* increasingly became religious institutions. *Mutawallis* scrambled to set up *madrassas*. Spending on religious ceremonies, *eidgahs*, and *imambaras* shot up.[8]

Therein lay the prodromes of the entanglement of endowments and Muslim politics. With the expansion of the franchise, outlays on Quranic education and Islamic pomp were doubly useful. *Mutawallis* became influential public figures.[9] Devolution eventually allowed Muslim notables to push through the Mussalman Wakf Validating Act in 1913, restoring the use of *auqaf* for private purposes, in effect returning to the *status quo ante*.[10]

When the Congress Raj superseded the British Raj, Delhi hoped, just as Calcutta once had, to render *auqaf* 'legible', in Scott's memorable metaphor, to taxation.[11] Nehru's mandarins, of course, had in mind Mammon, not God. This was a case of mid-century fiscal nationalism, not religious majoritarianism. *Waqf* reform had nothing to do with Islamophobia and everything to do with state capacity. Turkey, Egypt, and Iran, too, were reining in *auqaf*.

This has been forgotten, perhaps deliberately by historians keen to subsume *auqaf* into a narrative of state 'interference'. The word choice, an uncritical regurgitation of an emic perspective, is telling. S. Khalid Rashid, for one, writes of the 'crippling operation of laws of estate duty, income tax, wealth tax, gift tax, land reform, ceiling, and rent control' that did in *auqaf*.[12] His own evidence, though, belies the *mutawallis*' ample room for manoeuvre. In Uttar Pradesh, for example, private endowments could reserve as much as 75 per cent of income for *waqif* heirs and still be considered tax-exempt public *waqf*. Under land reform rules, custodians were allowed enough land to refashion themselves as rentiers. They were also issued land bonds as recompense for dispossession. What of rent controls? A number of *waqf* boards granted endowments exemptions from such undesirable distortions of the free market.[13]

In the fifties, it was Muslims themselves leading the reforming effort in Parliament, whereas Hindu lawmakers were at best indifferent. Far from railing against state interference, they were instead courting state protection. Outsourcing management to the state, they argued, was simply cheaper than leaving it to individual custodians. Indeed, the passage of the Wakf Act of 1954—later seen as the *ne plus ultra* of interference—was met with broad approval, necessary to stave off 'encroachments' by Hindu migrants pouring in from Pakistan. What better guarantor of property rights than government?[14]

The final bill paid heed to virtually every note of dissent struck by the nationalist Muslims. *Waqf* boards were made nominated, not elected, bodies, so insulated from the vagaries of populism, what with the disconcerting prospect, all too real in a world of representative government, of the Muslim riff-raff taking the boards by storm and dispossessing the rentiers. They were frank. With elections, they said, there was no telling who could be in charge. But the reservations of their critics—how could such an arrangement secure 'proper representation for all classes of people?'—could not be put away quite so easily.[15]

As at the centre, so in the states. Sparring apart—sectarian wrangling and personal beefs galore—when the dust settled, the Uttar Pradesh *auqaf* bill of 1951 left more or less the entirety of the Muslim establishment content.[16] True, the Sunni Wakf Board was at first divided on its merits. On the one hand, there were those who objected to government control on principle: no good could come from investing the state with the power to dissolve *waqf* boards. On the other were those who took a more sanguine view: precedent dictated that compromise was the best course of action; rejecting the bill lock, stock, and barrel risked a repeat of 1936, when opposition *à l'outrance* counterintuitively ended up delegitimising the board's position altogether. As it was, the bill had been rammed through the assembly with scarce consideration of Sunni opinion. But there was a critical difference between 1936 and 1951. Then, a joint Shia and Sunni board that bore no sectarian stamp could well mask the discontent of one branch of Islam. This time around, however, there were two *waqf* boards. Counterbalancing was no longer on the cards.[17]

Then there was the question of private endowments. Were they *auqaf* proper? A member of the group felt that all endowments that spent 10 per cent of their income on charitable endeavours were *auqaf*. Another member declared himself opposed to thresholds of any kind. Then there was the question of disputes: what if a *mutawalli* found himself at loggerheads with a *waqif*? Some suggested state arbitration, others an independent tribunal. The former, of course, was the more economical, if also more intrusive, option; the latter the obverse in both respects.[18]

None of these debates were decisively resolved. Still, board members found some common ground. It was unanimously agreed, not least because it was a shot in the arm for the board itself, that *waqf* boards were to be the final authority on the transfer and sale of property. Such an arrangement also benefited the *mutawallis*, keeping things within the community, as it were, Muslim boards being infinitely preferable to secular courts. It was also decided to increase the levy on rentier income by a percentage point. This sum, it must be said, was not a 'tax'. The 6 per cent of rents collected by the boards ultimately wound up back in *auqaf* themselves, funding upkeep, all the more necessary since so many *waqf* properties had gone to rack and ruin on account of neglect.[19]

On the final day of parleys, the Sunnis were at each other's throats once again. The debate turned on whether a *waqif* could fire a crooked *mutawalli* without judicial intervention. More than a few recoiled at the prospect of a secular judiciary pronouncing judgment on so Muslim a matter. But then again, their critics pointed out, setting up Islamic tribunals would be prohibitive. In the end, deadlock was averted. The penny pinchers persuaded the pious. Due process was left to the courts. The *pur et dur* held their noses. So much for state interference. The second sticking point was the manner of election to the boards. Was it, in keeping with democratic spirit, to be an 'election' at all? Some suggested an indirect one, based on a small electoral college, which would return the best clerics. Others of a more conservative stamp preferred the older system wherein 'institutions of established reputation' each sent a representative. No decision was at hand, and consultations came to a grinding halt.[20]

The Shia, too, were divided. The All-India Shia Conference, a vehicle of the clergy and gentry, and Shia parliamentarians, typically men of commerce and the professions, had for some time been at daggers drawn. Luckily for the former, there were not very many of the latter in the forties. So it was that the AISC chief was reduced to apoplexy when he 'got wind of the real object behind the amending bill'. Shia lawmakers were set to give themselves more power to appoint board members. Parliament was treading on the Conference's toes. Angry missives to Nehru followed.[21]

Still, the outrage was far from unanimous. A note of dissent was sounded by the Conference's UP branch in Amroha: 'the circular issued by [the AISC chief] Syed Kalbe Abbas ... is misleading and is wrong and does not deserve any attention. It is only reasonable' to expect Shia parliamentarians to represent Shias. The AISC did not take the insubordination lightly, declaring the UPSC 'an unconstitutional Shia Conference'.[22]

The sectional contretemps cloaked what was in fact a clash of personalities. Abbas felt that Amroha's revolt had been orchestrated by the *nawab* of Rampur, who had fallen out of favour with Lucknow. Zaheer, who had only recently been ousted as AISC president, argued that endowments had to be made answerable to the people. He had had it with the deplorably incompetent *mutawallis*. The rebellion spread to the Bihar Shia Conference, which, too, declared in favour of lawmakers. This Abbas blamed on the blood ties between the *nawabs* of Patna and Rampur, chiefs of the Bihar and UP Shia Conferences, respectively.[23]

With such wide support for 'state interference', both in the assemblies and the state conferences, there was little the AISC could do to stop an idea whose time had come. Even so, it was still able to influence the regulatory regime to good effect. Alerting the assembly to the predicament of the *waqf* boards, slipping into arrears on their payments to endowments even as properties fell into disrepair, it had the law amended in 1952. *Auqaf* 'affected' by the abolition of *zamindari* were granted a fixed annuity to tide them over.[24] The fiscally emaciated Indian state, whose rulers were on the one hand pressing for land reform, on the other allocated Rs 61,000 for the UP *waqf* boards.[25] It could be said, then, that parliamentary oversight was the price the Conference, as the vehicle of the gentry, paid to secure concessions for its class. Put in other words, the *waqf* regime spoke to the AISC's class interest just as did to the Shia parliamentarians' sectional interest; all in all, a satisfactory outcome.

What of the *mutawallis* themselves, missing from our account so far? They, too, had reason to rejoice. The new legislation may have beefed up the *waqf* boards, but nowhere nearly enough to constitute a threat to them. In fact, the law was on their side. The UP *waqf* act of 1960, for instance, made it well-nigh impossible for boards to dismiss bent *mutawallis*. Until 1971, a *waqf* tribunal had to first give the green light before a board could take over the management of a *waqf*. Typically, tribunals 'took not less than three years' to come to a decision, giving custodians ample time to get their act together. If endowments forestalled expropriation, voluntary alienation—'gift and sale'—nevertheless remained possible under certain conditions. A testament to the spectacular weakness of the boards was their instant dispensability. The UP Sunni Wakf Board, for instance, 'was sent into hibernation' for six years in 1968 by the high court for failing to resolve a disputed election. *Mutawallis*, moreover, found representation on *waqf* boards—the overseer also the overseen, as it were. In UP, for instance, the board comprised two government nominees, a *mutawalli*, and eight elected officials. The latter often happened to be *mutawallis* or their marionettes. So much for the opposition between private *auqaf* and *waqf* boards.[26]

In any case, *waqf* boards were pinched affairs. In Uttar Pradesh, they managed to audit only one in seven Sunni, and one in fifty Shia, endowments annually in the seventies. With a team of twenty-one to supervise thousands of *auqaf*, such a state of affairs was only to be expected. Footing the bill for *waqf* boards, *mutawallis* naturally wanted supervisory authorities to be as lean as possible. But cutting corners came at a price. Board functionaries were poorly paid, even denied social security. No insurance was made available, for instance, to an employee who lost his eyesight in the line of duty. They were generally staffed by retired public servants who tended to 'accept a lesser remuneration' than workers in their prime. Underfunding was compounded by outstanding debt. In 1974, *mutawallis* were in arrears to the boards to the tune of Rs 8 million.[27]

If *mutawallis* were spared the worst of board scrutiny, the boards themselves were let off with scarce oversight. Delhi's watchdogs were essentially toothless agencies. The Central Wakf Council, for one, was only an advisory body whose recommendations were mostly honoured in the breach. Similarly, the Wakf Section, established to facilitate inter-board dialogue, had its hands tied. Its queries and findings were unflinchingly ignored. Underfunded and understaffed, District Wakf Committees likewise found themselves unable to stand up to the boards.[28]

All the same, the trope of 'state interference' dies hard. Even if *mutawallis* got a word in edgeways in shaping the *waqf* regime, we are told, there is no denying expropriation, encroachment, and mismanagement; all, to varying extents, the product of state action, complicity, and neglect. But here again, in this version of events, Muslim agency is at a discount.

It is also important to register the imperatives of the Indian state, committed as it was at the time, at least rhetorically, to redistribution. As the Rudolphs remind us, the Indian state was a fairly autonomous actor, a sectional interest in its own right, a reality that has been obscured—alas—by the overdetermination of identity politics in the Indian setting.[29] Put differently, the state had a logic of its own. The construal of statist imperatives as guided by confession, of course, suited Muslim political actors rather well. A more dispassionate reading, however, suggests that reform was simply the order of the day. During his early years in power, Nehru transferred 14 million acres to the peasantry. Likewise Mao, the ruler next-door, redistributed 111 million. Japan, South Korea, Taiwan, and Vietnam, too, turned over land to the tiller. Like many other self-respecting mid-century states, then, the Indian one was simply flexing its muscles by expanding its tax base and flattening arrant inequities. Such activities, inevitably, entailed getting caught in the crosshairs of traditional elites—Hindu, Muslim, or otherwise.

The case of Lucknow's Husainabad Trust is instructive. Here Muslims in government defended 'state interference', Muslim trustees decried it. Ultimately the latter won out. The interferers, then, were not particularly interfering. In 1949, Lucknow hoped to declare the Trust a private *waqf*, so an appropriate target for expropriation. To this end, it recruited a number of Shia jurists to make its case. But the plan backfired. Husainabad, they held, was a public trust, used since its founding in 1839—with cash flows from interest paid by the East India Company for money lent to it by the *nawab* of Awadh—to patronise clerics and sponsor festivals.[30] In 1960, Lucknow made another attempt to take over the Trust, which Awadh's royal descendants promptly frustrated in the courts.[31]

The same transpired when the state tried to attach land owned by the Shia College, 'the most important Shia institution in India'. Here, again, religion had very little to do with the dispute. Its hostel, the additional director of education argued, sat on prime land. Now, as it happened, the Government Constructive Training College next-door was at the time casting around for a hostel of its own. Why not simply hand it over, in keeping with the statist zeitgeist, to the state-owned college?[32] In any case, the land belonged to the state, which had let it out to the college for the nominal rent of a rupee a year. The ten-year lease expired in 1948.

But for the massive lobbying effort of the Shia College, Lucknow would have had its way. As it was, it was forced to concede defeat. It was, in part, the government's own men that did for the education department's plans. The college board included retired functionaries such as the former president of the Court of Wards Saiyid Abdul Hasan and director of education I. R. Khan, both of whom wrote letters to friends on high.[33] The display of elite Muslim solidarity secured the College another ten-year lease. As for the state-owned college, plans were made to relegate it to Rae Bareilly.[34]

Another tussle ensued in 1955, when the lease came up for renewal. Lucknow's mandarins made a last-ditch attempt to rescue the hostel for the polytechnic, in its death throes. 'Vacate the building', read the curt message sent to the college management.[35] The Shia notables were equally adamant, demanding a ninety-year extension.[36] They prevailed. Six days after the warning, a Shia deputation of landlords, advocates, and jurists descended on the chief minister's office, where they received a 'sympathetic hearing'.[37] Soon after, formidable pressure was brought to bear on the bureaucrats, who had little option but to back down. In the end, the vocational college was sent packing to Varanasi. The Shia College hostel remained in place. This time for good.[38]

Other instances of 'state interference' were equally guided by *raison d'état* rather than religious prejudice. In the fifties, Lucknow was understandably wary of letting Islamic trusts press-gang students into Quranic learning in state-recognised schools. So, in 1952, it demanded that the Anjuman Islahul-Muslimin in Hamirpur desist from foisting Sunni theology on the pupils of the Islamia Higher Secondary School.[39] The letter sparked a lively debate, giving the lie to a straightforward, confessional reading of the state's motives. Who deliberated on charity endowments? The competency was a hot potato that no one wanted to hold. The education department passed the case on to the municipal department, which sent it right back, as if a boomerang. For five years, the file then shuttled to and fro between Finance and Education, case officers of both puzzling over whether it was indeed a trust to begin with. Throughout, the Anjuman unhelpfully declined a 'free audit'.[40] What is clear from the unhurried pace of the proceedings, and the eschewal of confessional language of any kind on the part of functionaries, is the complete absence of any vindictive sentiment. In the end, the Anjuman had its way.

Perhaps the biggest threat to the *mutawallis* came from the evacuee property regime. In part derived from wartime legislation to curb German interests in the Subcontinent, it was inaugurated in July 1949 with the creation of an all-powerful Custodian of Evacuee Property, who at once set about expropriating Muslims who had left for Pakistan as well as their relatives. At a stroke, hundreds of thousands of Muslims lost the right to alienate their lands. By all accounts, the Custodian was an implacable agency. Even as it cautioned against bringing Muslim homes and businesses 'to a standstill', it nevertheless did precisely that, sequestrating everything from land to firearms to bullion.[41]

Here, then, lay untrammelled executive power. Checks and balances were sacrificed on the altar of efficacy. Less than a week into the expropriations, the UP Custodian could boast of having overseen 'transfers of evacuee property on a rather extensive scale'.[42] Dispossessed 'evacuees' tried disputing the Custodians' right to attach property. To pre-empt this, they were given *carte blanche* to use government staff and bookkeepers to ensure implementation.[43]

At first sight, the reasons for creating the new authority were plain enough. At Partition, departing Muslims left behind some 5.5 million acres of land in India, their Hindus counterparts nearly 67 million in Pakistan. On both sides of the Radcliffe Line, governments had moved swiftly to entrust these assets to a Custodian, ostensibly for caretaking. Somewhere along the way, *raison d'être* was replaced with *raison d'état*. Indian Muslims returning home were now seen as Pakistani spies. Making matters worse, they had no means of redress. For the Custodian was also vested with juridical powers, not to mention exempt from having to comply with the right to property, one of the most important pillars of the Indian Constitution. Often acting on dubious tip-offs from refugee informants, the Custodians would swoop down on lands owned by minorities—Muslims in India, Hindus in Pakistan—promptly declaring them evacuee property.[44]

In theory, both states compensated evacuees with government bonds and cash. But in practice, restitution was rare. The paperwork was impossible to navigate, the authority of Custodians impervious to challenge. Once it came into existence, the category of 'intending evacuee' created ample room for the state's worst instincts to manifest. All it took were the misgivings of a single local bureaucrat for a Muslim to have his assets attached. Under pressure from refugees, whose confessional impulses were second to none, both governments began parcelling out evacuee property to them.[45]

Waqf custodians were marked men in the eyes of Evacuee Property Custodians, the one quintessentially Muslim and the other undeniably Islamophobic. In Bihar in 1955, some 400 villages fell into the hands of the Custodian in one fell swoop.[46] By 1962, around 20,000 *auqaf* across India had been confiscated as evacuee property.[47]

But *mutawallis* negotiated the difficult conjuncture with aplomb. First, in Uttar Pradesh, and perhaps elsewhere too, Muslims successfully lobbied the government to allow evacuees to sell their lands ahead of the abolition of *zamindari*. Timely sales saved many families from financial ruin.[48]

Second, the *nawab* of Chhatari turned his rapport with the Congress leadership to good account by getting Achhru Ram, the Union Custodian, fired in 1951. Apparently a reputed Islamophobe with concern, in his own words, only 'for our displaced brethren'—

Hindus and Sikhs—Ram had declared the *nawab* an evacuee. It was, admittedly, the inconsistency of having ruled the exact opposite just a year earlier that cost him his job, not so much his dim view of Muslims.[49]

Third, individual Muslims surreptitiously set about undermining the evacuee regime by prising open some wiggle room for themselves. Colonel B. H. Zaidi, Aligarh vice-chancellor, for example, inveigled the Custodian into handing back the endowment provided by the late Sir Ziauddin Ahmad, his predecessor at the university, to his heirs.[50]

Fourth, Muslim notables also had the ear of the country's ruler, who readily acknowledged in his correspondence the pain that Custodians were causing them. True, Nehru defended the authority in 1953, maintaining that the baby ought not to be thrown out with the bathwater. But even so, he hoped Muslims would bring ill-intentioned confiscations to his attention. The advantages of such a rough and ready policy, while unstated, were obvious. Short of jettisoning the evacuee property regime *tout court*, encouraging Muslim elites to depend on him allowed Nehru to cultivate an image of magnanimity, not to mention also press on with land reform and refugee rehabilitation. Repealing the act would take another three years.[51]

Fifth, and *a fortiori*, the cumulative pressure ultimately convinced Delhi, in September 1960, to return all Custodian-held endowments to 'non-evacuee beneficiaries'. The deadline to 'institute legal proceedings for their recovery' was extended to 1967.[52] Sixth, to top it all, the state agreed to release the interest that had accrued on the assets, even permitting 'beneficiaries' to forward money to *mutawallis* now settled in Pakistan, so long as the remittances complied with exchange control regulations.[53] Taken together, the lobbying efforts of Muslim notables were nothing if not an impressive demonstration of political agency that helped the *mutawallis* see off the biggest threat to their existence in postcolonial India.

A more sustained, if less severe, threat came from 'encroachments', a term of art that conceals an essentially intra-communal class struggle behind a confessional cloak. Now, the most celebrated instances of 'encroachment' are unrepresentative. But their atypicality does not, in any sense, detract from what is at stake here. In two of these, one encounters a collision between the forces of rentier and luxury capitalism: the construction of The Ashok, the sky-scraping, state-owned five-star hotel, erected on a *waqf* graveyard, in the capital in 1956, and, many worlds removed, of Antilia, the $2 billion residence of the Ambani *ménage*, built in 2010 on *waqf* land that allegedly once housed an orphanage.[54] The average 'encroacher', of course, did not exude such glamour. Most of them belonged to the Muslim lumpenproletariat, eking out an existence in decaying settings. It was these poor and omnipresent Muslims who were the bugbears of *mutawallis*, not so much the stray billionaire. A survey in 1985 revealed that some 9,000 mosques and 900 graveyards in *auqaf* were in 'disputed possession'.[55]

Curiously, the 'encroacher' sometimes was the state. In the capital, for instance, nearly 250 *auqaf* were locked in dispute with the Delhi Development Authority, which was in charge of council housing. If we are to trust the government's version of events, local authorities had acquired hundreds of *waqf* properties during Lutyens' rebuilding of Delhi in the 1910s. In 1940, however, at a time of heightened religious fervour, the DDA had felt compelled to lease them back to *mutawallis* for 'religious purposes'. So, in 1970, the DDA could, noting that the custodians had overstayed their welcome, confidently demand restitution. Litigation ensued. Eleven years on, both sides were still at sixes and sevens. Complicating matters was the fact that some of the disputed sites were mere cartographic constructs with no corresponding existence in the real world. The question of reimbursement, too, remained unsettled. The dispute was never resolved. But, paradoxically, therein lay the *mutawallis'* victory. It was testament to their dexterity at lawfare, lobbying, and conciliation that, three decades into independent rule, the show was still on the road. In the eighties, most *mutawallis* could look back with a sense of immense satisfaction at how well they had weathered the heyday of land reform.[56]

Delhi's functionaries, meanwhile, came to regret having leased out land to *auqaf* and other 'recognised religious institutions': the Sanatan Dharam Sabha, Gurudwara Prabandhak Committee, and the like (Muslim endowments were not alone). The *mutawallis*, a bureaucrat noted at the time, were corrupt, craven men who wore their religious habits lightly. They most certainly 'did not care' for the properties they managed, 'allowing them to be misused' in so cavalier a fashion. Many had become 'squatting grounds'.[57]

All of this Delhi's bureaucrats found intolerable. But tolerate it they did. The severity of the city's housing crisis, worsened by endless waves of refugees, dictated that their lawbreaking had to be condoned. By the government's estimates, conservative at best, there were about 600,000 homeless souls in the capital. But public housing, which came with a price tag of Rs 500 million, was a proposition few mandarins were ready to countenance. Schools and surgeries were set to cost another Rs 400 million. Annual DDA budgets 'for re-housing purposes' meanwhile hovered around Rs 15 million, enough to provide for 12,500 families—in other words, less than one in fifteen destitute Delhiites.[58]

When in 1958 some sixty Madrasi weavers and their families descended upon the Karol Bagh Kabristan—graveyard—in the capital, they provided administrators with an all-too-graphic illustration of the problem. Here was a picture that cold statistics could not capture. As the months rolled by, waterborne diseases whittled down their numbers, even as the migrants adamantly stayed put, any predicament preferable to the prospect of facing up to the protracted decline of the handloom industry back home. Local authorities contemplated serving eviction notices, but baulked at providing alternative housing. As it was, the matter was settled on the cheap. Delhi seeded enough capital—Rs 1,000—for the establishment of a weavers' cooperative and recognised the graveyard shanties as permanent homes.[59]

It was compromises such as these that had *mutawallis* up in arms. State interference was wrecking *auqaf*. Public authorities always sided with encroachers, never encroachees. The next year, a compromise was brokered by Hifzur Rahman, who was rather favourably disposed to *mutawalli* landlords. For some time now, he had argued that evicting refugees was necessary, reasonable even.[60] But Delhi made it clear that it would not take the lead. Bad press was best avoided. So it was that endowments were empowered to evict people with a parliamentary act.[61]

The new law had its Muslim detractors. The Delhi secretary of the JUH, for one, felt it was out of touch with general Muslim opinion. On his account, it was the work of unbelievers, Deobandi *maulvis* who neither celebrated *urs*, saints' days, nor cared for *durgahs*. The Sunni Wakf Board had apparently called the police on Muslims praying at a mosque and had them booked for trespassing. *Mutawallis* and board members, then, were 'torturers and hypocrites', putting private property and profit above everything. Luckily for the custodians, caretaking was not a popularity contest. The partial defeat at the hands of one 'encroacher' (the state), then, was more than compensated for by triumph over another (the squatter).[62]

More than state interference, it seems, it was their own enormities that were undermining endowments. Indeed, what of the enemy within: embezzlement? Much is made of the malversations of the *waqf* boards, whose members were time and again caught with their hands in the till. And sure enough, by 1981, some Rs 5 billion had been stashed away in *waqf* boards across the country, ready to be channelled to *auqaf* in disrepair but kept away from them all the same. Board members had other designs, personal enrichment foremost among them.[63]

But *mutawallis* were on the take too. When the head of the Madhya Pradesh Wakf Board resigned in 1987, he pointed the finger at custodians running amok 'fattening themselves on *waqf* proceeds'.[64] Their rentier incomes had a way of disappearing into a thicket of oblivion. A wide range of malversations was available at their disposal: the illegal sale of *waqf* land and land bonds; the extraction of *pugrees* from tenants; in the case of private *auqaf*, the underdeclaration of rent to evade taxation.[65]

But there was little the state could do to rein them in. Fines were an option. But then again, they were only a rap on the knuckles— and someone else's at that. The few financial penalties that were put in place were simply passed on to renters. As the Wakf Inquiry Committee of 1976 noted helplessly, *waqf* boards were legally prevented from deposing *mutawallis* or taking over mismanaged *auqaf*.[66] If boards embezzled funds, the fact of the matter is that very little money wound up in them in the first place. *Mutawallis* were almost always behind with their payments. In 1988, for example, the impecunious Karnataka Wakf Board was owed Rs 8.2 million from the 20,700 endowments under its jurisdiction.[67]

More important, and seldom remarked upon, is the fact that board income derived entirely from the absurdly low 'tax' rate of 6 per cent of endowment revenue: 5 per cent for the state *waqf* board and 1 per cent for the Central Wakf Council. As charities, *auqaf* were exempt from taxation proper. The numbers don't add up. What of the remaining 94 per cent? Evidently, little of it went into upkeep. Managerial overheads were nominal. Almost all of it simply disappeared into the hands of *mutawallis*, who, by all accounts, did rather well. While the 6 per cent that wound up with the boards— for schooling, healthcare, food banks, and, indeed, *waqf* repairs—was the subject of endless carping, the rest was spent on trivial pursuits. A Madhya Pradesh *mutawalli*, for instance, spent more on 'costly marble floors' than on charity, an Uttar Pradesh *confrère* more on *urs* than on electricity. Hence S. Khalid Rashid's damning indictment of the custodian interest: '*mutawallis* hardly ever think of conserving surplus income, and instead spend it frivolously'.[68]

Given the sad state of affairs, reform was inevitable. The most sustained bid to shake things up came during Indira Gandhi's final term, when she made the rehabilitation of *auqaf* a pillar of her fifteen-point programme. The result was the Gopal Singh Report of 1980, which, in surveying the predicament of subaltern groups, sought recommendations on all manner of Muslim issues. The most detailed counsel was the one set out by the credulous journalist A. R. Sherwani, who suggested reconstituting *waqf* boards by inducting only the wealthy into them in order to proof them against pilfering. The understanding, of course, was that rich men are disinclined to line their pockets. He also suggested opening balance sheets to state inspection. Less control, more scrutiny, extra costs. This is what custodians were asked to get behind. Predictably the plan found few takers.[69]

Another set of recommendations came from the AMU's working group on economic development.[70] It proposed a new body, the Wakf Development Corporation, to bring Islamic finance in line with the tenets of market capitalism. Shares were to be issued, relaying equity capital into projects run by Muslim entrepreneurs after 'suitable feasibility studies'. *Waqf* boards were to be made answerable to shareholders. But why invest in Muslim charities? Colossal profits came the riposte. The corporation was to be exempted from a raft of laws shackling Indian capitalism—ceiling laws, rent control, and so on. Further, 'suitable', and no doubt stern, legislation was recommended to throw out tenants.[71]

Both suggestions made it to the Gopal Singh Report.[72] As luck would have it, though, despite being meant for lawmakers, the report was never tabled in Parliament. When Mrs Gandhi was confronted by Rafiq Zakaria, one of its authors, she simply said, 'Post mortem does not help. Forget [*sic*] past and let us look for [*sic*] future'.[73] And that was that.

There matters stood for a quarter-century, until they were revisited by the Sachar Committee in 2006. Its report was much of a muchness, reiterating the need to create a new regulatory body along the lines of the WDC. Again, market-oriented solutions predominated. Pointing to the low returns on capital that obtained, Sachar rather optimistically called for—in his neoliberal argot—the 'optimal utilisation' of *waqf* resources, which, apparently, could push up the rent-to-price ratio to 10 per cent.[74] He was delusional. Even private properties in the noughties struggled to extract 3 per cent.[75] In absolute terms, the figure made even less sense, premised as it was on a 7,400 per cent jump in revenues, from Rs 1.6 to Rs 120 billion.

To expect charities to outperform landlords, let alone by a magnitude of three times, was a tough ask. But Sachar had a plan. *Auqaf* were unfairly hobbled by rent control legislation, which 'provided protection to the tenants in such a way that owners lost the incentive to develop and maintain properties. The application of the Rent Control Act is damaging the noble interests of *auqaf*, hurting as it does the entitlements of the beneficiaries'.[76] He could have put it with greater brevity: spare a thought for the landlords.

The plan, then, was to turn Muslim endowments into a tool for rent extraction. Here was an unforgiving rentier capitalism of the type that left even private landlords looking positively paternal. Marketisation was accompanied by a studied silence on taxation. The state had paid, and continues to pay, dearly for the elision. Literally so. A crude calculation can help us gauge the loss to the public exchequer. Sachar expected an annual revenue of Rs 120 billion from *auqaf*. State capacity, that is, taxes as a proportion of the domestic product, at the time of the report was in the region of 11 per cent according to the World Bank. By its own admission, then, were the Committee's findings implemented, it would cost the state around Rs 13.2 billion a year in lost tax revenue.

If Singh's report was buried after scarce discussion, Sachar's fared markedly better. In January 2014, the National Waqf Development Corporation came into existence with a capitalisation of Rs 5 billion.[77] Continuing the work of Manmohan Singh, his successor Narendra Modi brought in Deloitte consultants to streamline *waqf* administration.[78] Other consultancies, investment banks, and real estate developers have not missed a beat in becoming involved. The roll-call is a long one: PwC, Knight Frank, Jones Lang LaSalle, and Darashaw, famously brokers for the Nizam of Hyderabad when he was the richest man in the world.[79]

Whether it will deliver remains to be seen. *Mutawallis* have been involved in the process from the outset, a Deloitte staffer has reassured the readers of *Islamic Voice*. As if to disabuse anyone still in doubt about the real antagonism here, the NAWADCO chief has in no uncertain terms identified the real villains of the piece: '90 per cent of the encroachers and illegal occupants on *waqf* estates are Muslims only [*sic*] ... Tenants insist on meagre rents ... If the rents were fixed commensurate to market trends', it could, at the very least, triple rental incomes at a stroke.[80]

If there was a cleavage, this was it: lumpen Muslim tenants on the one hand and Muslim rentier *mutawallis* on the other. Indeed, it is not difficult to discern the class character of the residents. The bourgeois reflexes of press opinion serve as a useful index of their place in the world. 'Encroachers' reduced 'beautiful' neighbourhoods to 'shanty towns'. They were, variously, 'a menace', 'local criminals', 'grave squatters', 'slum dwellers', 'vandals' given to 'hooch and gambling dens'.[81] It was equally clear which side the state was on. Emblematic of official opinion were the reflections of the minister of state for minority affairs, Mukhtar Abbas Naqvi, who in 2017 descried a 'criminal conspiracy' between encroaching scroungers and 'the mafia'.[82] Time and again, the state declared open season on squatters, moving legislation, mobilising the courts, and marshalling the police to summarily evict citizens *en masse*.[83]

In the event, it is impossible to sustain the narrative of *mutawalli* victimhood that so many historians have unsuspectingly presented. Muslim notables were, on balance, ambivalent about the state, courting it when state protection held the possibility of benefiting custodians, and rejecting it when regulation had the potential to threaten their autonomy. *Mutawallis* succeeded in keeping overheads low, expropriation at arm's length, and encroachers on the run. It is no accident that they are, collectively, after the Indian Railways and Armed Forces, the country's largest landowners today, owning between them some 572,000 acres, or nearly 1 per cent of India's total land area. Postcolonial India may have been an inhospitable place for ordinary Muslims. But the Muslim rentier perhaps had never had it so good.

Eloquent Aristocrats

For Muslim aristocrats, too, class privilege acted as a prophylactic against the worst of Hindu majoritarianism. But this should not surprise us. Throughout the age of high imperialism, even when beholden to their Residents, royal houses had been able to exercise considerable agency.

It was only towards the *fin-de-siècle* that the princely states were forced to part with some of their sovereignty. Railways fell to the Raj, foreign travel came to depend on British approval, trade restrictions kicked in, seigniorage rights disappeared. Even so, even after devolution in the provinces in 1909, it was the princes who had greater autonomy. Indeed, in Princely India, a so-called '*laissez-faire* policy' obtained. Whereas Raj staffers had a vice-like grip on the fledgling native elite of the provinces, Residents were instructed to, in the words of the *Political Department Manual*, take over the reins only when aristocratic misrule reached 'a pitch which violates the elementary laws of civilisation'.[84]

The Raj had to make allowances for princes. They were, after all, an important prop for empire, having helped the British subdue the Revolt of 1857, stamp out popular protest during the world wars, and in general maintain stability in the intervening period. In the thirties, especially, the princes—barring the *gaekwar* of Baroda, to a man—acted as a bulwark against the rising tide of Congress nationalism. Indeed, outside parts of Orissa and the Punjab, nationalist sentiment—torpidly spurred by the *praja mandals*—was at a discount. True, there were a few hiccups under Curzon and Reading, but on balance, the princes had an ally in the viceroyalty, even if the political department and secretary of state on occasion conspired against them.

Power, prosperity, patronage. These were, then, some of the most privileged men on the Subcontinent. And there were many Muslims among them, quite a few of whom sat atop the pecking order of what was, in Ian Copland's words, a *darbari* oligarchy: Sultana Jahan Begum and Nawab Hamidullah (Bhopal), Liaquat Hyet Khan (Patiala), Nizam Mir Osman Ali Khan and his finance minister Sir Akbar Hydari (Hyderabad), and the *dewan* Mirza Ismail (Mysore).

In pole position in this sea of autocracies was, unquestionably, the Nizam of Hyderabad, who ruled an empire whose revenues and outlays matched Belgium's. And he ruled with a heavy hand. In diametric opposition to Mysore, where by the 1910s electoral experiments were well under way, Hyderabad had, as late as the mid-century, remained an authoritarian stronghold. When the Chamber of Princes—as it were, India's third chamber in parliament—came into existence in 1921, rather than mix with the minor nobility the Nizam absented himself from its founding. He could afford to. A further indication of his standing was his ability to secretly keep tabs on the communications of the viceroy and political secretary through his obliging Resident. He felt no inhibition in lining his own pockets. His wealth, in one analysis, was the product of 'a morass of corruption, nepotism, arbitrary decision-making, illegal exactions and confiscations, and general inefficiency'. His eccentricities, too, bespoke power, wealth, and confidence. One of his 'favourite pastimes' was to snap nudes of 'his European guests with hidden cameras', another to check in on the *zenana*, 'where his two hundred wives and concubines were said to cumulatively procreate at the rate of one offspring every four months'.[85]

The protracted decline of the aristocracy notwithstanding, the transfer of power came as a far from cataclysmic comedown. This is not to deny that the princes came down in the world. They did, not least because they had, right until the very end, remained loyal to the colonial regime. It was the fortuitous coincidence of three developments that did for them. First, the withdrawal of the League from the Constituent Assembly in January 1947, which tilted the balance in those halls to Congressmen, who did not suffer monarchs gladly. Second, the arrival of Mountbatten, the penultimate viceroy, who, while going out of his way to impress upon princes that he had their backs, when push came to shove readily dispensed with their paramountcy powers, prohibitive and pointless for the British to uphold once power had been transferred to the provincial leadership. And third, the volte-faces of Congressmen, notably Nehru's, who reneged on promises of a painless transition.[86]

But for all that, all the princes—some 600 of them—were happily pensioned off. Delhi deftly steered clear of confrontation, saving its firepower to put down subaltern uprisings instead. So, while 40,000 Muslims perished during the 'police action' of September 1948, in which Union forces stormed Hyderabad to put down communist peasants and Islamist militias alike, the Nizam found himself deposed with the utmost civility.

For the *qaum*, then, to echo Dickens, it was the best of times, it was the worst of times. Indeed, deposition did not mean dispossession. This was as intended. Here is Brigadier Rajinder Singh, proffering advice to Hyderabad's military governor:

> Look. Whatever position we put the Nizam into, don't forget he is a prince and that he did rule Hyderabad and that seven ancestors before him ruled it. So even if you want to be tough with him, it should be the velvet glove business, not the mailed fist.[87]

And 'velvet glove business' it most certainly was. The Nizam was spared expropriation. There was, then, one set of rules for the gentry and another for royalty. In 1950, he proceeded to dispose of his entire gold holdings—barring 425 kg of coins, which were sold to the state for their numismatic value—on the open market, investing the proceeds in government securities and personal trusts. What's more, he was handed a handsome pension of Rs 5 million a year, over and above a matching 'allowance' for maintaining his 'many wives', who, in the words of a functionary, 'led a life of leisured boredom'.[88] This was untaxed income. When the Hyderabad Municipal Corporation protested the arrangement, the Nizam agreed, with a touch of *noblesse oblige*, to 'donate' 0.5 per cent of his allowance to it. In council taxes alone, the waiver had resulted in a 'sustained loss of Rs 4,279,634' to the exchequer.[89]

That was not all. In 1950, the Nizam secured additional state funds to support the Turkish royal Mihisti Hanım and Dürrüsehvar Sultan, her daughter and Osman Ali's daughter-in-law, the Princess of Berar who divided her time between London, the Middle East, and Hyderabad. Because they needed gargantuan amounts of foreign exchange to support their lifestyles, and because the Nizam could no longer dip into his pound assets after being locked out of his Westminster Bank—now NatWest—account, he agreed to invest a portion of his pension in a government trust for the 'very low interest rate' of 1 per cent (bond yields at the time were in the region of 3 per cent). In return, Delhi paid in precious foreign exchange sums far in excess to what it allowed ordinary Indians to withdraw under the exchange control regime: sterling worth Rs 210,000 a year for Hanım and Sultan—in other words some £17,500, enough in the fifties to buy half a dozen houses 'in the heart of gentrified Islington'. Curiously, the sum came from the trust itself. Put differently, Nehru's government was borrowing money from the Nizam only in order to sponsor his kin.[90]

A decade on, the former ruler still had the government's ear. In 1964, seventy-nine and dying of tuberculosis, Osman Ali took up the question of succession. He wrote Nehru suggesting that they skip over his sons, the Prince of Berar Azam Jah (an alcoholic who had 'developed sadistic tastes', led 'a profligate life') and Prince Moazzam Jah (in general 'not acceptable to the people') and instead crown his grandson, Prince Mukarram Jah (a 'friendly but dignified' and 'sporty' youth with a 'sound education': Cambridge through Harrow and Sandhurst).[91] There was one snag, however. The dying wish contravened Muslim personal law. All the same, an exception was made, much to the dismay of the local Congress MP, who angrily noted that according to the *sharia*, 'a grandson has no rights':

> Mukarram Jah, as it happens, is hardly a Hyderabadi. His accent of Urdu is not Hyderabadi. Most of his life he has spent in foreign countries. On top of this, he has married a foreign lady. He does not inspire any confidence or affinity among the Hyderabad Muslims.[92]

But Osman Ali had his way. The *sharia* was cast aside, and Mukarram recognised as heir apparent. In February 1967, he acceded to the throne as Nizam VIII.[93]

On his way out, Osman Ali managed to secure yet another concession. This time he convinced Delhi's rulers that slashing his pension to a fifth of its value after his death—as had originally been agreed—was unfair. Worse, it would prompt him to economise, which was a bad thing, because the 'disbanding of his entourage' would cause 'considerable unemployment in Hyderabad'. He drove a hard bargain. In the event, his successor was left with a Rs 2 million pension—twice the figure negotiated at the time of Hyderabad's accession.[94]

Decolonisation and nationalisation, democracy and Islamophobia—all had proven to be empty threats. Osman Ali had imperturbably negotiated these troubled waters. His fortune told of a soft landing in postcolonial India. On his deathbed, he could take comfort from knowing that he was leaving behind enough assets to last at least a dozen generations of Nizams. He had approximately Rs 251 million tied in twenty-eight different trusts, including a 'religious endowments trust', a 'stepsisters trust', a 'grandsons pocket money [*sic*] trust', and a 'publication of poems trust', not to speak of his pre-Partition NatWest savings, some £35 million, which, after years of dispute, finally fell into the hands of his son in 2019.[95]

In using his wealth, authority, and suasive powers to extract concessions from the state, the Nizam was not alone. Wasif Ali Mirza, the *nawab* of Murshidabad, was another Muslim royal tolerated, even cossetted, by Delhi. In securing a lifetime tax exemption for him, the Finance Ministry averred that were he to contribute to state coffers like the rest of the citizenry, 'he would be reduced to a helpless and unenviable position'. Besides, it would be improper to tax him, for 'the *nawab* holds a very distinguished position in the Muslim community of West Bengal'.[96] His death in 1959 did not end the write-off. His agents inveigled the Finance Ministry into conceding a three-year tax holiday to tide over his son Waris Ali, the new *nawab*.[97]

Likewise, the Home Ministry accommodated Bhopal's former rulers because they happened to be prominent Muslims. Convention dictated that *nawabates* 'lapse for want of heirs'. This, indeed, had been the fate that befell the monarchies of Kuthar, Baudh, and Nandgaon. In 1960, Bhopal was to go the same way, since the first in line had taken up Pakistani citizenship. All the same, letting 'this *gaddi* lapse' was not an option. For, as the Home Ministry warned:

> We have to bear in mind that Bhopal is the second largest Muslim state in India, second only to Hyderabad. The lapse of the rulership of this important state may have undesirable consequences. The reactions of the Muslims in India may also be somewhat adverse.[98]

Here was a curious logic that spoke volumes of Delhi's thinking. Eleven years after Bhopal's merger into India, the Congress still felt unconfident representing its Muslim population without royal intermediaries. In the event, male primogeniture was abandoned and the dowager of Pataudi, Princess Sajida Sultan Begum, was sworn in as the *nawab begum*.

Yet a fourth figure was the *nawab* of Rampur, Raza Ali Khan Bahadur, who pulled off a land grab and got away with it. When in 1956, the Ministry of Railways accused him of occupying fourteen acres that belonged to it, he had a ready reply: the land was his. And sure enough, the sequence of events as he presented it, and the curious ways of the law, made his claim appear unanswerable. True, he had signed over his kingdom to the Union on 15 May 1949. But the physical transfer transpired only on 1 July, four weeks after the land grab, which had been duly entered into the 'civil ruler records' on 5 June by the *nawab* himself. Now, as Article 7 of the Merger Agreement had it, 'no enquiry should be made with respect to any of the *nawab*'s actions' from the time of his rule—which, of course, explains why he had been in such a terrific hurry to update land records two weeks after his deposition.[99] The Home Ministry coolly accepted the submission. Railways was asked to back off. The land was officially declared the 'private property of the Ruler [sic] of Rampur'. The *Rechtsstaat* trumped redistributive justice.[100]

The case of Ifthikar Ali Khan, the *nawab* of Malerkotla, a tiny North Indian kingdom of 166 square miles, too, bears out just how well Muslim princes handled the changing of the guard. He 'warmly welcomed' the annexation of his kingdom to the Punjab in March 1948, hoping, in a letter to the states department, that Malerkotla's new rulers would take good care of the Muslims in the army and administration. There were also other more pressing concerns he hoped Delhi would attend to. The annual pension of Rs 180,000 was hardly in keeping with his status, he complained. 'I would suggest that a provision be made to exclude my younger brothers, my uncle, and my mothers [sic]' from the pension. For their upkeep, he demanded an additional Rs 96,000.[101] Two more requests were put forth: that locally, the state recruit Muslims to the civil service and armed forces in proportion to their population—38.4 per cent—and that the army division retain its regal name—the unremarkable Malerkotla State Forces—to 'perpetuate their history of the unbroken chain of great services rendered from time to time'.[102]

As it happened, the latter demands soon receded from view, Khan's attention fixing on his pension. The task of convincing Muslim soldiers to stay on in India was left to his brother, who, it appears, wasn't terribly good at his job: 'I am sorry to say that our efforts have not borne much fruit'.[103] Demands of a personal nature, though, were relentlessly pursued. Khan held out for not only a fatter pension, but also a state-sponsored private jet and landing strip.[104] In the end, no guarantee was made to retain Muslims in the army and services, and the matter was dropped. Delhi pressed on with the accession, by all accounts a bloody affair. So we find the *nawab* writing to one of his royal peers, Kapurthala's Maharaja Sahib Bahadur, deploring the Hyderabad-style pogrom decimating his subjects—'harassment, mass murder, executions, persecution, general slaughter'—but avoiding any mention of it in his correspondence with government officials. Janus-faced, he was by turns assertive and relenting, depending on whether it was his pension or the fate of his former subjects in question.[105]

In the years to come, Khan was to continue to play—for a deposed royal—an outsized role in public life, *inter alia* lobbying for the Akalis, who were after a 'Sikh homeland'. In 1967, he coordinated an effort involving various Punjabi palaces to topple the United Front government. The coalition, he argued, had failed to curb 'lawlessness and the breach of peace in rural areas'.[106] The real reason for his fervent opposition surfaced soon enough in his flustered correspondence with Indira Gandhi. The Front—an alliance of the CPI, Jana Sangh, and Akali Dal—was set to 'further reduce land ceilings'. But no matter. What was more worrisome was that 'the communists' were making common cause with the 'Chinese and Pakistanis not very far away from our borders'.[107] His voice, of course, must have been one among many. Still, it may have been among the decisive ones. Defections ensued and the Front fell, to be replaced by a Congress-backed coalition.

All this goes to show just how persuasive the princes were, assertive in putting forth their demands yet, in equal measure, courteous and deferential to the republican elite. Theirs was the easy-going pragmatism of the upper crust. They had dealt with the Raj, internalising the *bienséances* of the ruling class. So they were able, just as amiably, to deal with Congressmen, speaking in the language of the greater good. Osman, Wasif, Raza, Sajida, and Ifthikar may have been Muslims, but above all they were monarchs.

Much the same could be said of the *wasiqadars*, whose class position insulated them from confessional conflict. Socially, they belonged to a more expansive category than did the princes, including not only Awadh's former royals but also their relatives and retainers. Over a few thousand at independence, not all were nobles. But all were notables. To keep a lid on discontent after it annexed Awadh in 1856, the East India Company had arranged a handsome pension for the *nawab* and his *ancien régime* administrators. These annuities, then, were different from the princely pensions only in a semantic sense: not for the cession of territories but for ending hostilities. Ninety years on, inflation had rendered them worthless. But what mattered in postcolonial India was not the figure itself, but the status *wasiqadari* conferred on the already well-heeled. It told of an aristocratic lineage, bespeaking pre-republican opulence and *tehzeeb*, a set of Persianate class markers.

At Partition, its retention was not a foregone conclusion. Were it not for a fortuitous set of circumstances, the state would in all likelihood have scrapped them. So it helped that, the odd personal beef aside, *wasiqadars* had for long been in possession of class solidarity. As early as 1912, they had found a voice in the Awadh Wasiqadars and Political Pensioners Association. It also helped that the bulk of them were Shia. To the Congress, they were, as it were, the good Muslims, loyal foils to the League-supporting Sunni. The All-India Shia Conference was practically a branch of the party. That the *wasiqadars* negotiated the transfer of power as ably—if not more so—as the princes should come as no surprise. Nehru left the arrangement untouched. A decade after independence, the Indian government was still paying the *nawab*'s descendants Rs 130,000 per year.[108]

But this did not prevent them from asking for more. At first, though, when the Calcutta-domiciled Prince Yousuf Mirza, who had, incredibly, crowned himself King of Oudh on 15 August 1947, demanded an additional Rs 3,000 a year, the Home Ministry proved reluctant to set a precedent for other royal offspring. But one prominent government voice appeared readier than others to entertain demands emanating from the House of Oudh. 'I agree with you generally', Nehru wrote the home minister, 'but, perhaps, we might agree to give some educational allowance to those who are studying in school or college'.[109]

The Ministry of Education, for its part, was disinclined to open its meagre purse for monarchs. 'Educational allowances', it suggested, were only for 'deserving students on the basis of merit. It will not, therefore, be appropriate' to use public funds for 'the children of the Oudh Family'. But Nehru had his way. Here, then, was a class solidarity of a different stamp, borne by the Harrow and Cambridge educated premier's fascination with the derelict glamour of the Indian aristocracy. There was, perhaps, an element of corruption, too. The prince and his family, it appears, had 'always held socialist views [*sic*] and had all along worked for the Congress, right up to the elections of 1957'.[110] The sweetener, then, did not owe entirely to epistolary flattery and royal prerogative, but to services rendered to the party in power as well. A 'special education scheme' was drawn up, its eligibility restricted to members of the 'ex-Royal Family of Oudh residing in West Bengal'.[111] In April 1958, Calcutta could be found informing Mirza that the allowance had come through—Rs 3,000 a year in convent fees and extracurricular tuition at a time when the premier could be found proudly proclaiming that per capita income had risen to Rs 281.[112]

The Mirzas were only the richest and most powerful of the *wasiqadars*. But the rest, with their smaller pensions, nevertheless belonged to the Muslim elite, and so were treated differently, as befitting their position. Some of them managed to hold on to their pensions despite residing abroad. Sajida Begum, a widow in Karbala, was one such figure. Before independence, her monthly *wasiqa*—issued in Lucknow—was generally wired to her by a private agent. The arrangement abruptly ended with the transfer of power, as foreign transactions and subjects came under scrutiny. But she wasn't devastated for long. Not long after she wrote a toe-curling letter to Nehru—'if you did not care to grant my request I shall only shed tears on my bad luck, smash my head on a rock, and pray for you [sic]'—her *wasiqa* was reinstated. What's more, thereafter it was sent directly to the Kingdom of Iraq.[113]

Many had their pensions reinstated by writing to '*wasiqa* officers'.[114] Qaiser Jehan Begum of Bareilly, for instance, managed to have her 'life grant', 'absolutely terminable on demise', converted into a 'heritable and transferable' pension.[115] In another case, Hakim Zafarul Haque, a Khairabad physician in receipt of 'Rs 150 *per mensem*' who was already two generations removed from the original *wasiqadar*—a bit player in the Revolt, his grandfather died in prison in the Andamans—coaxed Nehru into releasing a 'lump sum of Rs 1,000' to top up his pension.[116] In similar fashion, the state agreed to extend the *wasiqa* to the children of Qazi Abu Ahmad, whose death in 1958 in theory should have brought an end to the allowance. The Home Ministry took a more generous view. Ahmad, it was noted, had left behind a mere nine *bighas* (3.6 acres) for his family.[117] So the pension was continued. That two in five rural Indians were either landless or possessed less than 2.5 acres, so were perhaps more deserving, mattered little. For they were also, in the main, unlettered and lacked the literary adroitness and regal lineage that could have made them the fortunate beneficiaries of state largesse. There was, in short, one set of rules for men of means—Muslim or otherwise—and another for the rest.[118]

True, not all *wasiqadars* were able to extend their pensions with equal ease. For some, *raison d'état* got in the way. Qara Hussain Akther Mirza, for one, learned this the hard way when he returned to India after eight years in Karachi—'conditions in Pakistan did not suit me'—to find his *wasiqa* terminated.[119] Syed Raza, for another, found his pension suspended in 1961 after the Home Ministry came to 'suspect' that he was a Pakistani national. As it turned out, the suspicion was well founded. He had taken up Pakistani citizenship in 1959. Two years later, he acquired an Indian passport, and the pension was duly restored.[120]

Likewise, the Carnatic stipendiary Mohammad Sadath Hussain's *wasiqa* was halted when he left for Dacca. On his death three years later, his two widows and two daughters successfully sued for its reinstitution. As the law ministry saw it, 'it would not be fair to deprive the heirs, who are in India and who appear to be poor, of their right to the pension'. Only the arrears, on its account, were 'enemy property [*sic*]'.[121]

Syed Mohammad Mujtaba, too, was given the benefit of the doubt. A *wasiqadar* settled in Zahedan with an Iranian passport and a Pakistani partner, his discovery set alarm bells ringing in Delhi. He most certainly held 'pro-Pakistani views [*sic*]', the Home Ministry surmised, terminating his pension. The logic of securitisation would have meant that the matter rested there. But the *wasiqadars* were not to be dismissed so easily. As it was, the Indian embassy in Tehran concluded that stopping the *wasiqa* would prompt him to 'create disaffection' and stir 'bad feelings' towards Indians. The pension was reinstated.[122]

In the final analysis, the business of restoring pensions turned not so much on policies cast in stone as on effective correspondence. The Uttar Pradesh government acknowledged as much: 'our decision re: payment of *wasiqas* to persons who have settled in foreign countries is that payment should be made subject to good conduct and friendliness to India'.[123]

In other words, what counted was not nationality or residency but comportment. If adequately apologetic and suffused with nationalist rhetoric, a petitioner's letter could make functionaries see reason. In a setting where literacy was at a discount and hierarchical deference everywhere, what ultimately mattered was the possession of a rather scarce political resource, an epistolary fluency in effect the preserve of the upper class. Small wonder, then, that *wasiqadars* could extract thousands of rupees from a state that otherwise treated every Muslim as a potential enemy of the state, suspect until proven otherwise.

Aligarh's Oligarchs

It is surely no exaggeration to suggest that the Aligarh Muslim University has, for well over a century now, been one of the cynosures of Muslim politics—and perhaps the most important one. The *sharia*, *auqaf*, reservations, Urdu—interest in each has waxed and waned with changing dispensations, but attention accorded to the AMU has remained a constant, punctuating virtually every decade since the university's inception in 1875 with protest, outrage, and counterprotest.

Scholarly notice has mirrored the community's, if incommensurately. The late colonial years have piqued considerable interest on account the place of the university in the Pakistan movement.[124] The postcolonial period, by contrast, has received scant regard. Here, commentary has turned on its 'minority status', Aligarh's struggle to stave off—in the language of liberals—'state interference'.[125] A common, if implicit, assumption runs through much of this literature: an *a priori* supposition that the AMU's politics is Muslim politics, that the defence of the university's autonomy is, after a fashion, a defence of minority rights.

But is it? In what follows, I suggest that it emphatically is not. Nor could it have ever been, given its inherently elite character. That the university's affairs elicited little interest even in Aligarh town was par for the course. Its residents had problems of their own: riots, ghettoisation, deindustrialisation. 'The great divide between town and gown', as Mushirul Hasan has it in a sketch of his college years, was never bridged.[126]

But this is scarcely surprising. *Ashraf* elitism was hardwired into the AMU from day one. Indeed, the students that passed through it and the dons that taught and lived there on the one hand, and the ordinary Muslims of Aligarh town and the rest of the Subcontinent on the other, belonged to different species. The latter lived in society, as it were, and the former above it, as once Raj mandarins had.

We have a fine account of the *ashraf* milieu in David Lelyveld's social history of *Aligarh's First Generation*. Modelled after Cambridge and built with British patronage, the college that the peripatetic Company functionary Sir Syed Ahmad Khan set up in 1875 was founded with the aim of forging a new Muslim man—*homo aligus*—within its quadrangles.[127]

Khan has famously gone down in history for popularising the word *qaum* in its modern sense, understood not as 'tribe', 'caste', or 'family', but rather as the Indian Muslim community at large, an aggregation smaller than the *umma*—the global Muslim community—but larger than any *mazhab*, sect. Right from the outset, however, it was clear that his preoccupation was not so much with the *qaum tout court* but its *crème de la crème*, the ruling class of old. The college may have opened its doors to both Shias and Sunnis, but there was no space in it for bourgeois, let alone working-class, Muslims. Khan's contempt extended even to *parvenu* 'men of wealth'. Only 'men of respectable ancestry' mattered. His clients shared his worldview. The father of the college's first student, for instance, was candid when asked why he had decided to send his son there: so he wouldn't have to 'mix with vulgar people'.[128]

Tucked away in the Civil Lines, one of the Subcontinent's little Britains, its students were indeed cut off from the hoi-polloi. Their uniform was *ashraf* gear; first headmaster an Englishman; curricula a replica of the Cambridge Tripos. The milieu was Oxbridge and public-school England. Khan had visited the metropole during a period of advance in state education—the Elementary Education Act was passed in 1870—but what he had found more impressive was instead the Victorian public school, which had come under fire from the Clarendon Commission for corruption: religious, autonomous, elite, and not unlike the Indian *madrasa* in looking askance at the applied sciences and placing a premium on the classics. Aligarh ultimately adopted a hybrid pedagogy, reconciling Islamic theology with English empiricism. The purpose was twofold.[129]

First, to train a Muslim mandarin elite at a time when the services were becoming increasingly competitive. By 1903, there were over a million literates in the North-Western Provinces, and just over 1,500 in public employment. Traditional patterns of mobility were fast disappearing. Moving from *maktab* to government was no longer as easy as it once was. Equally, the pathway from the army to the services was closed off after the Revolt. Accordingly, Khan thought fit to throw his weight behind the British. In any case, he had for long been a loyalist, preferring, as he saw it, 'Company Raj to Hindu Raj'. On his view, the two distant Peoples of the Book had more in common with one another than did the more proximate adherents of the Subcontinent's two Great Traditions, one of which worshipped the cow whereas the other ate it.[130]

Second, to stem the inexorable decline of the *ashraf*. Their better days, undeniably, were behind them. Landholdings had become smaller with every passing generation. The lavish lives of the landlords had sunk many of them into debt. With the coming of the railways, and the rise of Hindu mercantile communities, a new elite had replaced the old. Inflation made quick work of *ashraf* wealth, and syncretism was dealt a blow by revivalism.[131] Concerted action was needed. Happily, Khan was up to the task. The *ashraf* had to modernise was it to maintain its station, he argued, and the Muslim University was to be the agent of modernisation. As in Tomasi di Lampedusa's famous formulation, if things had to stay as they were, things had to change. The response was unreservedly encouraging. By the *fin-de-siècle*, Aligarh was churning out Muslim graduates in droves, accounting for a quarter of all in the Subcontinent.[132]

Very simply, Khan's project was freighted with class interest. All the same, the import of class was quickly forgotten in the communal maelstrom of the forties. It was during this period that Aligarh acquired its reputation as a hotbed of Muslim radicalism, counterpointed by the moderation of the Jamia Millia Islamia, the dissenting university founded in 1920 by nationalist Muslims at the AMU.

On the face of it, the reputation was well-earned. The AMU was closely associated with the Pakistan movement. Some of the Congress' most trenchant critics had passed through it, figures such as the Ali brothers and the poet Hasrat Mohani, Congressman turned Leaguer turned Communist. But this is an incomplete picture. For Aligarh's alumni also included, *inter alios*, Ansari, Kidwai, Khan Abdul Ghaffar Khan, and Hafiz Mohammad Ibrahim—all figures (barring the latter, a League turncoat poached by the Congress) with splendid nationalist Muslim credentials. To these, a number of other names can be added: the *New Left Review* contributor Hamza Alavi, geographer Moonis Raza, and Urdu man of letters Rashid Ahmad Siddiqui. So much for its reactionary image. Further complicating the received account, the AMU drew the ire of Deoband, whose conservative clerics championed the more traditional, less Anglophone JMI.

After Partition, moreover, the AMU underwent a makeover. Lecturers from parts of the Subcontinent that became Pakistan were purged, prompting the vice-chancellor's resignation. Nawab Mohammed Ismail Khan's replacement, with fitting irony, was Zakir Husain, begetter of the JMI, who returned to Aligarh in 1948. An act of parliament in 1951 set in train a process of laicisation, opening the AMU 'to all persons irrespective of religion or caste' and making religious instruction optional.[133] Apostasy was encouraged. Hindu holidays were celebrated, dance and music endorsed, and coeducation introduced.[134] Syllabi, too, became less Islamic, more mainstream. Even in its late colonial prime, only two of its fifteen departments were, in some sense, confessional: Shia and Sunni theology. In the event, both were abolished in 1951. By the end of the fifties, the AMU and the JMI were comparable secular achievements, a testament to the ideological hegemony of the party in power.[135]

All of this went a long way in fuelling a *Kulturkampf*. The secularists lined up on one side, generally supportive of state intervention. The conservatives got together on the other, demanding greater autonomy. Still, until as late as March 1965, there was no hint of what was to come. Indeed, there was no indication at all of the botched assassination attempt that was to follow in April, triggering, as it were, Muslim India's May 68. For the AMU was, despite having made and broken Muslims careers over three generations, still a rather small institution in a parochial town. Indeed, it never quite overcame its insularity. 'Social life was restricted. There were no restaurants and no decent cinema halls', Mushirul Hasan remembers. Delhi, eighty kilometres away, was three hours by the Kalka Mail.[136]

Above all, Aligarh was a safe space for Muslims, who constituted three-fifths of its student and teacher bodies. A *tableau vivant* frozen in time, for Muslims, too, it was the back of beyond. Syed Mahmud, for one, came to regret retiring there, carping in his correspondence with Mrs Gandhi about the town's 'uncomfortable houses'. But this being Aligarh, 'I couldn't get a better one'. Sending her sympathies, the premier wrote to his daughter Hamida Naim, 'Mahmud Chacha tells me that you and the children have come to Aligarh. I can imagine how difficult it must be to reconcile yourself to the change. But you must be courageous for your own sake'.[137]

The arrival of Badruddin Tyabji at the Vice-Chancellery in 1962 awakened Aligarh's denizens from their slumberous state. A Bombay Bohra and former ambassador, he was determined to shake things up, developing 'fraternal ties' between the AMU and its Hindu counterpart, the Banaras Hindu University. The two communal universities were to be secularised through faculty exchanges and minority student quotas (for Muslims at the BHU and Hindus at the AMU) of 30 per cent, already a reality at Aligarh. It was a bold plan, but few cared for it. The only two people he could convince, it seems, were the UGC chairman D. S. Kothari and Nehru. His other planned reforms, food subsidies and an end to nepotistic appointments—the 'absolutely scandalous' principle of 'you scratch my back and I'll scratch yours'—too, stalled. Disappointed, he left Aligarh in February 1965 to return to diplomacy. In retrospect, his departure could not have been better timed.[138]

For on 25 April, his successor, Nawab Ali Yavar Jung, was the target of a failed hit by students. As it was, he only narrowly survived the attempt on his life. It took a week in hospital before he was back on his feet. Jung's election had been a controversial one. Accused, variously, of being an 'alcoholic', an 'atheist' afflicted with 'moral turpitude', he was despised by the staff, who were firmly behind the pro vice-chancellor, Dr Yusuf Husain Khan, Zakir Husain's brother and former Razakar, so Jung's nemesis from the 'troubled days of Hyderabad'. As VC, Jung had immediately set about making changes and, as a result, enemies. On 12 April, thirteen days before the assassination attempt, he had slashed the quota for home students from 75 to 50 per cent, in effect returning to the *status quo ante*; Tyabji had only just increased it. Since home students were in the main Muslim, and entrants at the graduate level Hindu, Jung had effectively undercut what was a minority quota. Protesting the decision, a self-styled 'action committee' was formed with the blessings of the Old Boys. Its comportment, however, was more befitting a militia. Less than a week into its existence, it had the union secretary beaten up. Meanwhile its weekly, *Shehr-e-Tamana*, carried threatening pieces promising violence. Around the same time, a Republican Party of India lawmaker and a retired Madras judge were arrested for inciting students to riot. On 24 April, a day before the assassination attempt, youths marched across the campus holding up placards that read '75 per cent or ?', the question mark in red, which they helpfully explained signified bloodshed.[139]

Calls to dispense with the university's 'minority character' came close on the heels of the assassination attempt. What was at stake was its 'Muslimness', the extent of which was contested. On the one hand, the AMU was formally recognised in 1920 as a 'central institution', entitled to public funding but also fair game for laicisation. Less Islamic curricula and more Hindu students was the price paid for government subsidy. On the other, Khan's college came with undeniable historical baggage. It had been established by and for Muslims. A commitment to minority rights necessarily meant upholding its minority character. Telegraphically put: state-sponsored or autonomous, secular or Muslim?

As things stood in 1965, a balance had been struck between the two positions to the advantage of the minoritarian view. Administrative power resided with the board of trustees, the preserve of the Muslim gentry. Hindu students had been admitted, albeit not commensurate to their numbers. The government, though, had been able to pack departments with non-Muslim staff and laicise syllabi, leaving a conservative professor of Persian carping about the *shuddhi*, purification, of the university underway. Hindu habits died hard, he could have quipped.[140]

The *via media* had left both sides dissatisfied. Now, with the assassination attempt, both the statists and minoritarians had an opportunity to alter the settlement to their benefit. For government, it was a chance to wrest control from reactionaries and obscurantists; for the board of trustees, from functionaries and secularists. Muslim politicians, then in their consensual heyday, were minoritarians to a man. Mahmud dismissed as 'ridiculous' the insinuation of a 'huge conspiracy between students and staff to kill the vice-chancellor', blaming instead the police, who shot at two students, injuring them. Similar 'protests have taken place in other places', he noted. But the police were never brought in. Nor was there talk of constitutional change to undermine the autonomy of those universities.[141] Maulana Biyabani Saheb, a Congress colleague, concurred: no attempt was made to erode the 'religious character' of the Banaras Hindu University when violence erupted there.[142]

The case of the BHU was certainly instructive. To begin with, its religious character was never in question. Here, the state's reforming ambitions were more modest. Few in government had the appetite to go head-to-head against the RSS, virtually in control of the university since around 1958. 'Progressive' staff had been hounded out, left-wing students prevented from campaigning at election time, and Sangh *shakhas* set up on campus. A mere 1 per cent of the BHU's students and staff were non-Hindu, even as around 40 per cent of the AMU's were non-Muslim.[143] In 1964, the education minister M. C. Chagla had introduced a bill in the Upper House to drop the confessional 'Hindu' from its name, a first step to rebranding it the Madan Mohan Malaviya Kashi University, after its Hindu revivalist founder.[144] He had Shastri's, and before him Nehru's, backing, but nevertheless felt compelled to back down before an RSS strike that brought the town to a halt. Starting on 17 November 1965, the tintinnabulation of 'gongs, bells, and conches' and Hindu chants—*Har Har Mahadev!*— went on for three interminable days.[145] By the end of it, Chagla was a broken man. As it was, he abstained on his own motion, hoping, incredibly, that the Lower House would take 'into consideration the views and feelings of the students and authorities of the university' and throw out the bill.[146] Neither House followed his lead, though both impaired the piece of legislation beyond recognition before passing it. The old name was retained. What's more, Chagla climbed down from his threat to appoint a non-Hindu vice-chancellor at the BHU, even as he remained determined to install a non-Muslim VC at the AMU.[147]

Indeed, in his handling of the Muslim University, M. C. Chagla was less timid. Why the differential treatment? A tentative answer lies in his biography. With Muslims, Chagla had an emic perspective. He was one of their own. A Khoja Muslim who went on to become chief justice of Bombay, he was cut from a different cloth than most Muslim politicians, who were of gentry and clerical backgrounds. As a young man, Mohammedali Currim Merchant rid his name of class and confessional markers and took on his childhood soubriquet, Chagla, Kutchi for 'favourite'. His last name, he later explained, had connoted 'filthy lucre', mercantilist origins being distasteful to the budding lawyer. More important was the endearment that reminded him that he was his father's best-loved son. The first and middle names betrayed his lapsed faith, so the ambiguous initials took their place.[148]

This youthful nonconformity he carried into adulthood. As a cabinet minister in the mid-sixties, he stayed an outsider, never formally joining the Congress. Pro-abortion and anti-*sharia*, he did not shy away from unpopular positions: 'it must follow as an inevitable corollary' of secularism 'that religion should play no part in our country as far public affairs are concerned', he declared to a largely Muslim university audience in Hyderabad. This, needless to say, was a far cry from the equidistance waffle of his cabinet peers. He was, quite simply, the perfect bugbear to conservative Muslims. If he had not existed, they would have invented him. Chagla had a tendency to describe Muslims in much the same terms as Hindu nationalists, with whom he often made common cause. In the same address, for instance, he excoriated the 'separatist tendencies' of Muslims, imploring them instead to 'join the mainstream of national life'.[149]

Rather unsurprisingly, he was a firm proponent of 'Urdu in *nagari*'—on grounds of 'national unity', of course. *Nastaliq* was the poor cousin. *Nagari*, 'which is the script of Sanskrit, the mother of most Indian languages', by contrast, was 'more scientific, with a capacity for reproducing all the sounds which are found in a language [*sic*]'. By becoming accessible to 'millions of non-Muslim admirers' in *nagari*, Urdu 'would receive a tremendous fillip'.[150] With views like these, and a penchant for quoting the *Bhagavad Gita* to boot, it was small wonder that *Radiance* reproached him for being a 'non-Muslim Muslim', 'more Hindu than the Hindus' even, whereas the RSS organ, *Organiser*, pronounced him 'a man of great initiative and drive'.[151]

In 1965, Aligarh's upheavals must have appeared to Chagla like manna from heaven. Taking umbrage at the protests, he laid the blame on two 'Urdu rags' and the climate of obscurantism. As he saw it, the path forward was clear: a CBI probe, new textbooks, and a parliamentary act to authorise government to fire staff 'whose loyalty is in doubt'.[152] Mahmud was having none of it. Chagla's actions were sure to 'have repercussions' in the 1967 elections, he warned. Nor was he doing the country any favours internationally. 'The Muslim world' was watching. The education czar, for his part, cautioned him against reading too much into 'a law-and-order issue'.[153]

It is easy to be wise after the event. Later, Chagla would acknowledge that Aligarh's May 68 was not 'purely a law-and-order problem'. It was equally fuelled by 'the non-utilisation of leisure' that pushed students to waste their spare hours on futile protest, the breakdown in 'dialogue between teachers and parents', and more broadly the disintegration of the 'traditional way of life', alienating students and creating a 'sense of insecurity and uncertainty about the new society'.[154]

But in the summer of 1965, such meditations were held in abeyance. Chagla was on a war footing. In May, the AMU constitution was suspended, and an ordinance passed transferring several competencies of the board of trustees—'the Court', as it was called—to government. Reduced in all but name to an advisory body of the Executive Council, the Court's strength was slashed from 115 to a lean fifty-one, thirty of whom were to be appointed by the Indian president. The Council was not spared either: revamped as a nine-member body headed by the VC, no less than seven were to be nominated by government. In September, the war with Pakistan as the backdrop, the ordinance was steamrolled through Parliament, the calls for 'harmony' more amplified than usual on account of the 'serious crisis on the border'.[155]

It was a dark day for the minoritarians. Autonomy had been seriously compromised. Were they ever to mount a defence of academic freedom, staff and students were certain to be met by stiff resistance now that government had seized managerial control. Moreover, the amendment had opened the door to a revision of the confessional balance at the university, frozen since 1961. The 'majority-minority ratio of 35:65 was very fair', it had then concluded. Now the prospect of an insurgency of Hindu students, well-heeled and better educated, arriving on campus threatened to throw positive discrimination out of the window.[156] Furthermore, Chagla's moves hinted at the possibility of a merger between the AMU and the other, largely Hindu, colleges of the district. Already, in the fifties, the Union's recognition of the university was the cause of considerable resentment among nearby institutions of higher learning, most of which were affiliated to the rather distant Agra University for no reason but to protect the minority character of what to the Sangh was 'an outpost of Pakistan'. In their common reading of the ordinance merged the hopes of Hindus and the misgivings of Muslims.[157]

Worse, Chagla had declared open season on the Court. Now the Court was more than just a board of trustees. It was, as Violette Graff has argued, *the* forum where that dying breed, 'the old Muslim elite of Uttar Pradesh, could meet and retain some of its past influence'.[158] Partition, land reform, and the displacement of the primary by the secondary and tertiary sectors of the economy had all made short work of their fortunes, leaving them clinging on to a vestigial pride in birth and rank. The Court, as if a veritable royal institution, allowed them to play-act as the ruling class.

In a rare moment of solidarity, Muslim leaders of all stripes closed ranks and came to the Court's defence. Their first target, of course, was Chagla. The JUH general secretary, Asad Madani, accused him of being 'opposed to the development of Muslim culture'.[159] The Urdu press parroted the charge, adding that the AMU's problem was that it was not Muslim enough; that its staff and students partook in Hindu festivals told of an 'inferiority complex'.[160] Some protestors, supported by the JUH, took out passports to travel to the Middle East 'to bring pressure to bear on the government'.[161] The Mushāwarat demanded the withdrawal of the ordinance, a judicial inquiry, a commitment to the AMU's 'Muslim character', independence in appointments to the Court, and Chagla's head on a platter.[162]

With the involvement of the Jama'at, Jamiat, and Mushāwarat, the assault on the Court very quickly came to be seen as an affront to the *qaum*. It was this sleight of hand that enabled UP's patricians to present their class interests as the concern of the community. Class privilege came to be dressed up as minority rights. The *Siasat Jadeed* in Kanpur pilloried the packing of the Court with Hindus as an 'undemocratic' attack on the community. Channelling 'anger and resentment', Bombay's *Khilafat* asserted that the ordinance 'will not satisfy any Muslim'. Patna's *Sangam* editorialised that the Congress had ceased to 'represent Muslims'. Delhi had abandoned 'its declared objective of safeguarding minority cultures', thundered the League's Calicut organ, *Chandrika*.[163]

Such was the outrage that even nationalist Muslims such as Colonel B. H. Zaidi, a former VC, and the barrister Akbar Ali Khan felt that they could not fully endorse Chagla. 'Outsiders on governing bodies should be kept to the minimum', they advised, giving 'qualified support' to the ordinance.[164] Clearly, Muslim Congressmen were under immense pressure. That the Congress was out of step with Muslim opinion was evident in the reception of the Bihar Congress Muslim Convention, whose thousand delegates met in Patna on 8 August to condemn Aligarh's millenarians. They were greeted by a 'jeering crowd of Muslims waving black flags' and 'hurling abuse'. The protestors lit a bonfire of pamphlets and waylaid delegates, 'snatching their belongings' and throwing their 'caps in the air'.[165] On the same day, as if to press home the message of Muslim dissatisfaction, a Mushāwarat conference opened in Lucknow to great fanfare. Jama'at and League luminaries rubbed shoulders with Aligarh Old Boys. In all, over a thousand notables descended on the state capital. In speech after speech, they laid into Congressmen— Chagla, Shastri, Nanda; none were spared.[166]

Enisled in the sea of Muslim dissent, Chagla stood virtually alone. Some support came from small enclaves with scarce influence: the self-professedly 'Congress-minded' All-India Seerat Committee and All-India Muslim Mutaheda Mahaz, the odd nationalist Muslim, Communist weeklies, leftist staff at Aligarh, and Jung—understandably after nearly being killed by students. None of them, for all their forthrightness, could hide from the fact that their Secular Forum, created to 'weed out communal elements from the university', was but a paper organisation.[167]

The precarious coalition was not to last. For in June, Jung and the JUH's Mufti Atiqur Rehman reached an agreement, sidestepping Chagla. Selling the education minister down the river, the vice-chancellor after conferring with the Old Boys' Association agreed that Aligarh's minority character was inviolable. In return, he was promised 'full support' to pursue 'firm and deterrent action' against students who had 'resorted to violent means'—to punish his would-be assassins in other words.[168]

All the same, the deal fell through when Rehman was defenestrated by Maulana Fakhruddin Ahmad. Aligarh had caused a rift in the ranks of the JUH. Things came to a head in July, when Rehman's enemies forced a vote of no confidence. After Ahmad's election, a purge ensued. Packing the Jamiat council with Congress loyalists, he proceeded to fully dissociate his organisation from the protests—and from the Mushāwarat as well.[169]

With no effort on his part, Chagla had scored an important victory. His luck was to stay with him. The minoritarians quickly ran out of steam. In September, students announced a strike over the AMU amendment—substantially the same as the ordinance—and warned the country's president in February the next year to pull out of a convocation or risk being torched on stage. Both proved empty threats. Around the same time, a *morcha* against the police presence on campus was called off.

When the university reopened, the Congress showed it was capable of ruthlessness. The geriatric editor of the *Nida-e-Millat* was sent to prison, his printing press raided and paper confiscated, for running a special issue commemorating the first anniversary of the protests. Likewise students celebrating a *yom-e-jung*—'day of war', but also perhaps a cruel pun on the vice-chancellor's name—to mark a 'year of struggle' that began with the attempt on Jung's life found themselves arrested for sedition. Forgotten as it fell from the headlines, by the end of the year it was clear that autonomy was a lost cause.[170]

Nineteen-sixty-five, in short, saw Chagla's statists defeat the Court's minoritarians. The education minister won the battle. Still, the government was ultimately to lose the war. Like the *mutawallis* and princes, the patricians of the Court turned adversity into opportunity. They had already drummed up considerable support for autonomy by wrapping their particularist demands in universalist casing. They had bet the house on popular protest and lost. Taking the defeat in their stride, they plumped for a change of tack. Thereafter, redress was no longer sought on the streets but in Parliament and the courts. Its high-political turn, as it were, was to serve the Court well. In the event, it took a mere sixteen years to turn the 1965 amendment on its head: in 1981, the Lok Sabha officially restored 'minority status' to the AMU.

How did this come to pass? Not through student campaigns. The real battle was instead fought behind closed doors. Success was not a foregone conclusion. An early setback came with *Azeez Basha v. Union of India*, in which the apex court affirmed Chagla's view that Aligarh 'was neither established nor maintained by the Muslim community'. Rather it was a 'national institution'. Article 30 of the Constitution, on 'the right to establish and administer educational institutions', therefore was irrelevant.[171]

The backlash from Muslim notables, though expected, turned out to be so fierce and sustained that Delhi could hardly sit back and hide behind the ruling. It felt compelled to first send an emissary, the Assamese Congressman—later president—Fakhruddin Ali Ahmed, to soften them up, then appoint the eight-member Beg Committee to sportingly try conclusions with them, and finally in 1968 succumb to a volte-face. The university, government agreed, was indeed established by Muslims.

If student protests tended to alienate Delhi's rulers, elite petitions seemed to persuade them. Still, the battle was far from over. For in 1972, Chagla's successor, the new education minister Nurul Hasan, a card-carrying Communist and former head of the AMU's history department, shepherded the passage of the AMU (Amendment) Act. Again, the Court's sympathisers were left fuming. True, the act strengthened the hand of the vice-chancellor and democratised the Court. But it was neither a concession to statist majoritarianism nor a betrayal of *Basha* and Beg. Attention, of course, fixed on the offensive clause that suggested, to complement the already popular courses on Muslim theology, the promotion of 'the study of religions, civilisation, and culture of India'—Hindu theology—as well. Hasan's rebarbative tone, all the railing against 'feudalists' and 'obscurantists', was of little help.[172]

The admonitory harangues, however, were misplaced. Above all, what the act did was not, as it were, de-Islamicise the AMU, but bring it in line with the Gajendragadkar Report, whose buzzwords, reflecting the Congress' corporatist sensibilities of the time, were efficiency and accountability. Indeed, similar amendments undermined the autonomy of the Osmania, Andhra, and Sri Venkateshwara Universities.[173] Hence the replacement of promotion by seniority with recommendation, appointment to student and staff committees by nomination rather than election, involvement of the president of the Republic in the selection of the vice-chancellor, and greater discretionary power for the VC at the Court's expense.[174] Equally, it was no accident that the government settled on a rotational system to appoint teachers to the Court. Elections, the act's authors argued, were 'expensive' and did not create 'consensus'. A similar corporatist impulse did for the elected treasurer, in whose place came an appointed finance officer.[175]

All of these changes were, quite justifiably, viewed by the Muslim elite as assaults on academic freedom—as yet another instance of the 'overbearing influence' of Mrs Gandhi's power-hungry government. Criticism came from all quarters. When the act was passed, Leaguers stormed out of Parliament. Communists decried its 'counterrevolutionary' thrust. Opposition also came from a familiar alphabet soup of organisations: the JI, JUH, IUML, AMU Students' Union, Old Boys, Mushāwarat, and UP Majlis.[176]

The *Secularist*'s A. B. Shah, the bugbear of conservative Muslims whom we met in the previous chapter, was quick to point out the incongruity of the alliance. Nadwi, on the one hand, had been on record defending the 'spiritual leader' of the 'Arab world', in whose name he acted. The gaggle of political parties, on the other, were struggling for temporal supremacy. 'One wonders whether the liberals in search of a stick to beat Mrs Gandhi with are aware of what they are bargaining for', he smugly noted.[177]

As it was, Muslim liberals and conservatives shared enough common ground. More than academic freedom, it was the state's attempts to lay waste to the Court, the residuary forum of the Muslim gentry, that rankled and united the Who's Who of Muslim India. Indeed, their objection to the amendment turned not on minority rights but on class snobbery. Here's A. J. Faridi's on the act:

> Care has been taken not to give any representation to [the] Muslim community as such. Class representation has been made the basis of representation in the Court. While, on the one hand, experts of Muslim culture and learning, the All-India Muslim Educational Conference, and the donors have been denied representation in this great seat of Muslim culture, on the other hand, representation has been given to trade unions, agriculturalists, and industrialists. The Beg Committee recommended that [sixteen] Muslim legislators should be included. This recommendation has not been accepted. Representation given to members of parliament has been increased to ten but the recommendation of the Beg Committee that they should be Muslim has been rejected. Thus, there is no guarantee that Muslims would remain in the majority in the Court.[178]

It was, in short, a lament for the *ancien régime*. Donors and 'experts of Muslim culture'—the gentry and clergy—were being replaced by trade unionists and agriculturalists, students and teachers. There was a veritable moral panic. India was 'going communist', Nadwi bemoaned. Basheer Ahmad Sayeed, a retired Madras judge, was on the same wavelength: 'this is socialism run amok. The Court is now overwhelmed by the paid officers of the university and its employees, young and immature [commoners] with a narrow vision'.[179]

But the patricians did not have to swallow their pride for long. Deliverance came through the discrediting of Mrs Gandhi's dictatorship. In the 1977 election, no party soliciting the 'Muslim vote' was willing to countenance alienating the notables so invested in the affairs of the AMU. Even the Jana Sangh promised minority status. After its incorporation into the Janata Party, the 'five-headed monster' formed by the union of Congressmen, Dalits, Hindu nationalists, socialists, and farmers, the new party leader Morarji Desai gave the same assurance. When it swept to power, the new coalition was quick to appoint a Minorities Commission, whose first order of business in January 1978 was to prepare a brief on Aligarh.

Pledges were one thing, policy another. The bill that reached Parliament in May 1979 was a compromise that pleased no one. If passed, it would have affirmed that it was not the state that 'established' the university. But then again, there was no mention that it was set up by the Muslim community either. The piece of legislation, then, did little to secure 'minority status'. The spectre of *Azeez Basha* haunted Desai. In any case, the damaging effects of the battle between the executive and judiciary fresh in memory, the post-authoritarian government had little interest in provoking a constitutional crisis.

The Congress, now for the first time on the opposition benches, meanwhile had little to lose by being reckless. Its sponsorship of a private member's bill unequivocally declaring that the AMU was 'established at the instance of the Muslims of India' was meant to be a clear signal to Muslims that it was on their side. Its gentrification and sterilisation programmes, which disproportionately targeted Muslims, apparently were water under the bridge.[180]

In 1980, the tables now turned, the Congress back in power and the Janata imploded, Mrs Gandhi tried for a brief moment to renege on the promise. Admonishing caution, she introduced a bill so byzantine that it was withdrawn almost immediately. But the Court's patricians did not have to wait long to get what they wanted. The AMU (Amendment) Act, unambiguously confirming the supremacy of the Court, Aligarh's indispensable role in the 'educational and cultural advancement' of Muslims, and most importantly, its establishment 'by the Muslims of India', was passed on 22 December 1981 after less than three hours of debate. At long last, the Court had regained its cherished minority status.

In the ensuing decade, it was able to turn its influence to good account, frustrating the best efforts of the two vice-chancellors, both reform-minded former IAS officers, who presided over the AMU for the better part of the eighties. Both Saiyid Hamid and Sayed Hashim Ali had little trouble crushing agitations and suspending student union elections when it suited them. Yet they remained unable to rein in the Court, whose splenetic members behaved as if they belonged to a debating society, thwarting new initiatives by picking at procedural errors and litigating over every last clause. Secularising the university had been a hard enough proposition in Chagla's time. In Hamid and Ali's, it became next to impossible. The two sides did little more than exchange insults for most of the decade. The VCs were 'communists' to their detractors, the Court's patricians 'obscurantists'.[181]

It had been a thirty-year-long struggle. But in the end, Aligarh's oligarchs came out on top. It was a remarkable achievement on at least two counts. First, it must be remembered that the university's matters were, perforce, a minority concern. Second, time was when the AMU produced a quarter of India's Muslim graduates. A quarter-century into independence, a mere five thousand of the quarter of a million Muslims enrolled in universities were to be found there.[182] Aligarh therefore had been up against considerable adversity. Mobilising support in such conditions, and in an environment uniquely hostile to Muslim politics at that, the Court's patricians showed themselves to be superlative political operators.

Their success, of course, owed a great deal to their class position. Aligarh town and gown make a telling contrast. Indeed, Aligarh's is a tale of two cities. One can be forgiven for thinking from the foregoing account that its problems were entirely pedagogic and patrician. But it would be remiss not to mention its unfortunate distinction as one of the most violent places in the Republic. According to Varshney and Wilkinson's dataset, with 388 dead in twenty-five riots between 1950 and 1993, Aligarh topped the grim league table. Brass, meanwhile, estimating the death toll at 176 in eighteen riots in that period, places the town marginally behind Meerut.[183] It was not always like that. David Lelyveld's somnolent, uneventful town of the late nineteenth and early twentieth century had generally been on the quieter side of the station, proofed from the periodic fracas that erupted on campus. In the half-century to 1949, it had witnessed a mere eleven deaths in four riots, trivial figures when compared to the violence unfolding in the rest of the Hindi belt.

In postcolonial India, town and gown swapped places. A perfect storm descended on its industrial neighbourhoods. In the Nehruvian period, pre-election riots were routine, occurring with quinquennial consistency: 1951, 1956, 1961, 1966. The Congress turned a blind eye to these. Nehru even made light of it. Despite evidence pointing to the state's complicity in the riot of October 1961, in which forty Muslims but no Hindus perished, he tried to deflect blame: 'Aligarh, representing to some extent the mind of the Muslim community in India as it is developing or has developed, has been going through these ordeals', he said to the press, highlighting the 'importance of text books in helping the student to develop a national outlook', as though rioters were in the main schoolboys nourished on an illiberal education.[184] In the years that followed, deindustrialisation dovetailed with growing confessional antagonism. Muslim labourers—locksmiths, metalworkers, weavers, butchers—increasingly came into conflict with Hindu traders.[185] By the eighties, the only Muslims left in the locksmith trade were blue-collar workers, as ownership, sales, and marketing were delivered into the hands of *bania* groups such as the Aggarwals and Varshneys.[186]

Throughout this period, the quadrangles remained insulated from communal violence. As Mushirul Hasan later recalled of his time there in the sixties: 'Hindu-Muslim tension in the city recurred, but this did not polarise our sentiments' at the AMU.[187] Indeed, the university witnessed its first communal riot, in Sir Syed Nagar where the professoriate lived, only in 1991. Reprisals in the town for trouble emanating from the university were another matter. It was a one-way street. Locals recognised this, not without bitterness. Here is Shahnawaz Hussain, a businessman in an interview with a sociologist:

Those who sacrifice themselves for the AMU ... never benefit from the AMU. In 1971, Aligarians, local people, agitated in favour of the AMU, against the government of India's plan. We were kept by the policemen and sent to jail for fifteen days. After this agitation, the AMU got its own authority. We sacrificed ourselves for this university but this university has done nothing for us.[188]

Quite justifiably, Aligarh's townsmen felt let down. Throughout the seventies, while the Court conducted its campaign for minority status, the denizens of the other Aligarh, a mere three kilometres southwest of the leafy campus, were embroiled in matters of life and death. Practically every year recorded a riot. In 1971, tumult followed the discovery of a young man committing voter fraud by casting his ballot disguised as a *burqa*-clad woman, RSS cadres setting fire to shops owned by Congress Muslims. The next year, on the eve of the state election, violence ensued when a Hindu child was hit by a Muslim scooterist. In 1978, riots broke out after the killing of the Sanghi wrestler Bhure Lal, as mourning Hindu demonstrators tried to force the town into lockdown. Bullets and bombs rained over the Old City. The turbulence in the Civil Lines, however, was confined to classroom contretemps.[189]

AMU students occasioned the major disturbance of the following year when they fought over train seats with Gujjars en route from Delhi. By the end of the day, the town was ablaze. The university emerged unscathed. A decade on, in 1989, little had changed. When students decided to conduct relief work in the aftermath of a riot and participate in a dialogue with the Hindu protestors campaigning to rename the town Harigarh, they were prevented from crossing the railway tracks by their circumspect vice-chancellor. Aligarh's townsmen were certainly on to something when they accused university students and staff of retreating into their ivory tower as soon as trouble struck on the other side. It is not surprising, then, that Shahnawaz Hussain's charge stuck.

The atomised attachments of town Muslims, too, were in marked contrast to the collective solidarity of the Muslim notables we encountered earlier. Here was another reason for their dire predicament. The Muslim community of the Old City was riven by caste divisions. It was almost as if the town's twenty-four important

Muslim *biradaris*—Momin Ansaris, Abbasis, Saifis, Qureishis—belonged to no common Great Tradition.[190]

Ghettoised and organised on *biradari anjumans*, caste associations, their lack of communal feeling beyond their immediate endogamic kinship group brings to mind Banfield's memorable characterisation of the peasants of Chiaromonte as a people rent asunder by 'amoral familism', incapable of overcoming their backwardness on account of their 'inability to act together for their common good, or indeed, for any good transcending the immediate, material interest of the nuclear family'.[191]

Switch family with local patrilineal networks and it is possible to talk of an 'amoral *biradari*ism', as it were. Even party politics evolved on *biradari* lines, the upper-caste Shamsis backing the League and making for Pakistan, leaving behind the Congress-supporting Ansaris, who were later to become beneficiaries of quotas, a kickback of sorts for their nationalism in Brass' conjecture.[192] Even decades after Partition, Aligarh's *biradaris* continued to inhabit different worlds. Sectarian, sartorial, exequial, and caste divisions were never fully overcome. When Elizabeth Mann visited the town in the late seventies for her ethnography, she found the prominent mosque at Upar Fort closely guarded to keep lower-caste Muslims out.[193]

In such conditions, no common 'Muslim' identity emerged. The upshot was that in the first six decades after independence, no Muslim ever became mayor of Aligarh. This in a town where two in five were Muslim. More generally, too, Muslims were—and remain—underrepresented in government. In 2010, the *qaum* accounted for only 5 and 7 per cent of the Aligarh Civil and Criminal Bar Associations, 5 and 3.5 per cent of the town's gazetted and non-gazetted police officers.[194]

Electorally, the community has fared no better. Muslims have represented Aligarh in Parliament only on two occasions, in 1957 and 1989. The lack of Muslim solidarity has certainly contributed to this state of affairs, but so has gerrymandering. Very early on, the delimitation commission separated the two Aligarhs, saddling the Koil constituency—sensibly reserved for the Scheduled Castes—with the Civil Lines. No Muslim, then, could ever hope to represent the district in which the university fell. Aligarh town, meanwhile, was fobbed off to a largely Hindu district. A small, urban Muslim oasis in a large, rural Hindu desert, the *qaum* at a stroke lost its local preponderance. At 18 per cent of the district population, there were fewer Muslims than Thakurs.[195]

Banias, in the main Varshneys, Aggarwals, and Maheshwaris, accounted for a fifth of its residents, and the Scheduled Castes, Jatav almost to a man, a seventh. In theory, a Muslim-Jatav combine could exercise a veto to keep out caste Hindus from office. The common front was only attempted once in 1962, when the Republican Party of India's Buddha Priya Maurya, *né* Bhagwati Prasad before his conversion, an AMU alum of working-class background, defeated the Congress candidate in a David and Goliath contest.[196]

But 'Jatav-Muslim *bhai-bhai*'—his brotherly slogan—was not the norm, but an aberration. In 1978 as in 1980, 1991, and 2006, riots pitted subaltern against subaltern. Everywhere, Dalits killed Muslims and Muslims killed Dalits. The most violent set-pieces took place in some of the poorest neighbourhoods, such as the ones around the Shah Jamal *durgah*. The Civil Lines, of course, remained untouched.[197]

* * *

In postcolonial India, Aligarh gown landed on its feet, town did not. Is it possible, then, to talk of two Muslim Indias? One, evidently, bore the brunt of Partition and Islamophobia. The other, by contrast, navigated these troubled waters with scarcely a scratch to show for it. For too long, historians have focused on the one at the expense of the other, documenting the plight of the postcolonial Muslim, contending with the caprices of successive governments that took scarce notice of them, risking deportation and dispossession, fearing death at the hands of Hindu mobs.

These, of course, are the kind of figures we have encountered in the foregoing chapters. But what of elite Muslims outside government, those who could pressure it—for they had the means to do so—without fearing for their careers and without consideration for popular sentiment? Muslim Congressmen, Leaguers, and Islamists were always in the public eye, not to mention also answerable to higher authorities, *inter alia*, party leaderships, memberships, the

317

electorate. Not so *waqifs* and *mutawallis*, princes and *wasiqadars*, Aligarh's oligarchs and patricians. Theirs were lives for the better part lived under the radar. True, they did come under press scrutiny time and again, but nowhere nearly as often as career politicians. They had the wherewithal to contend with the state as well as the luxury of being outside it.

In the event, two important aspects of this Muslim aristocracy stand out, both of which were flagged by a landmark report on the Muslim condition in 1977. First, that 'one of the major preoccupations of the Muslim elites has been the preservation of distinctive elements of Muslim culture in a non-Muslim environment'—the *sharia*, of course, but also Muslim institutions such as the *waqf* and *wasiqadari*, not to mention that epicentre of Muslim intellectual life, the Aligarh Muslim University. Second, that, on balance, 'the community's elites have done reasonably well'.[198]

Critical commentary in a land whose lettered class is consumed by its diversity, of course, tends to the confessional. Yet it appears, on this account, that class counted for more than confession as a predictor of easy existence in early postcolonial India. For obvious reasons, Muslim elites positioned themselves as representatives of the *qaum*. Yet it is not hard to come away with the impression that, for all their communitarian pretensions, it was their own class interests that they were defending. *Waqifs* and *mutawallis* spoke in the language of Muslim heritage and tradition to amass tidy fortunes even as they declared open season on their 'encroacher' *confrères*. Muslim princes and *wasiqadars* played on the tropes of decline and fall, as if characters in Satyajit Ray's *Jalsaghar*, to extract concessions from the state unavailable to poorer Muslims. Aligarh's Court, meanwhile, couched class privileges in the idiom of minority rights, even as those were at a discount in an all too real sense less than two miles away in Aligarh town.

Is it fair, then, to speak of an *ashraf* betrayal? It is to this question we now turn.

CONCLUSION
AN *ASHRAF* BETRAYAL?

'Muslim politics' in postcolonial India has been a politics *manqué*. It is not for nothing that general surveys of it turn into little more than chronicles of Muslim plight and victimhood. Agency is at a discount.

As the preceding pages bear witness, however, Muslims were far from passive actors in this period. We can say this with confidence because we have recovered in our survey the agency of a dizzying compendium of characters and organisations from the rise of the Khilafat movement to the fall of the Congress six decades later.

When it came to setting the nationalist agenda and managing interfaith relations, Bari and Ansari were second to none. Gandhi's consolidation of power, in fact, in no small part turned on their efforts. Ashraf, Husain, Kidwai, Kabir, Azad, Mahmud, too, had greater agency than they let on. The latter two, especially, often jousted with Nehru and Gandhi over tactics and competencies. True, Zaheer, Ali, and Khan were ciphers in the interim government. But they were playing a longer game, gradually winning the trust of their colleagues and compatriots in an age of acute ethnic conflict.

After Partition as well, the interventions of the 'communalist' and nationalist Muslims—Khaliquzzaman, Pocker, Ibrahim, Karimuddin, Mohani, Baig, Saadulla, Azad, Zaidi, Hussain, Rasul—in the Constituent Assembly give us a sense of agency, the one set exercised by political concerns, the other cultural safeguards.

Ultimately, the minority rights regime that emerged out of the constitutional settlement was the product of this division of labour.

As eminent Nehruvians, the nationalist Muslims may have struggled to have the ear of Delhi's rulers. Even so, Mahmud, Kabir, Saadulla, *inter alios*, leveraged their connections to secure personal sinecures and, on occasion, come to the aid of their unfortunate *confrères*.

More agentive at first blush, but operating under considerable constraints all the same, the 'communalists' resorted to a wide range of strategies and tactics to steer between the Scylla of Islamophobia and the Charybdis of capitulation to advance Muslim interests. Figures such as Ismail, Owaisi, Koya, Majid, Ebrahim, and Hafizka were, by turns, assertive and accommodative. Their actions, though, did not always produce the desired effect, impacting, as they so often did, the Muslim condition singularly through the inadvertent agency of the Congress.

It was the pressure politics of the Majlis-e-Mushāwarat that finally blew a hole through the Congress consensus, demonstrating, if tenuously and on sufferance, elite Muslim disaffection, solidarity, and agency. With it, Muslim politics in India came into its own. A common set of concerns crystallised, one which leaders as disparate as Mahmud, Madani, Muslim, Kabir, Rehman, Faridi, and the two Nadwis could get behind. Their common denominator was their collective refusal to fatalistically accept the *qaum*'s subalternity.

India's Islamists, too, contended with the *qaum*'s reduced position, rethinking key political questions by breaking with the central tenets of Maududi's corpus to discover that perhaps pluralism was not such a bad proposition after all. Here, then, was the birth of a postcolonial consensus that ran from Nehru to Nadwi.

Some wealthy and powerful Muslims, though, never had to contend with inferiority to begin with. In many ways the *waqifs* and *wasiqadars* and princes and patricians, all political animals a step removed from politics proper, never had it better. They navigated Nehru's regime *con brio*. *Mutawallis* made a Cayman Islands out of *auqaf*. Bahadur, Begum, Mirza, Osman and Ifthikar Ali Khan put Casanova to shame with their seductive correspondence. The camarilla of Aligarh's Court made comrades out of once combative Congressmen.

Minorities and Majorities

A recognition of Muslim agency, however, should not detract from an appreciation of its obvious limits. For, as we have seen, Indian democracy proved to be a rather unyielding straitjacket.

India's 'Muslim question', then, affords a window into the workings of Indian democracy. In a previous work, *India's First Dictatorship*, Christophe Jaffrelot and I considered what to many is an anomalous period, the Republic's twenty-one-month dark dalliance with authoritarianism. In this one, I have looked at the dark side of Indian democracy, the halcyon three decades—in the popular imagination—preceding and counterpointing the Emergency. The picture, rather counterintuitively, is much of a muchness: opposition leaders, from Abdullah in Kashmir to Owaisi in Hyderabad, wasting away in preventive detention; a mass pogrom in the Deccan in which tens of thousands of Muslims perished, the Sunderlal Report investigating the crimes of Delhi's proxies hastily buried by the premier; distortions of the popular will in the form of gerrymandering, plurality voting, President's Rule, and the purchase of lawmakers; wholesale deportation and dispossession of Muslims in the borderlands and beyond; suppression of civil society, outright bans and discrimination in public employment in the case of the Jama'at-i-Islami; censorship, from the bowdlerising of Azad's and Mahmud's memoirs under the personal aegis of Nehru to the interception of mail to damage the Majlis' electoral prospects; a culture of sycophancy in the Congress, leaving little room for nationalist Muslim agency; all against a backdrop of intermittent ethnic conflict, the *qaum*, forming a tenth of the national population, inequitably accounting for four in five fatalities in the fifties, and probably more in the mid-sixties, when nearly one in fifty Indian Muslims left for Pakistan.

It would be too simple to pin the blame for these on the Congress. Rather it appears to me that the party is best seen, in the words of Nehru himself, as a 'mirror of the nation'.[1] Accordingly, its style of rule reflected the conservative, confessional, conformist society it lorded over. In such a setting, an elision between *demos* and *ethnos* was inevitable. More so, of course, on account of India's

321

unfortunate distinction as a young democracy and a polity in which class consciousness had far from replaced primordial attachments.[2]

Democracy was never going to be much of a prophylactic against communalism. Religious discord has a long history on the Subcontinent, as Subrahmanyam and Bayly have persuasively shown. Decimation and desecration in the name of 'the Hindus' and 'the Muslims' were common enough between the eleventh and seventeenth centuries, contrary to the strenuous denials of the purblind secularists of the liberal academy that these were emic categories.[3] Even during the salad days of syncretism, Gaborieau tells us, co-existence was anything but peaceful, antagonisms playing out, if in low key, through 'rituals of segregation' and 'rituals of provocation'.[4]

These were latent sparks of conflict, scintillating through the *longue durée*. One worshipped the cow. The other ate it. One was given to idolatry. The other deemed it heresy. One partook in festive revelry. The other in commemorative mourning. And so on. Religious violence setting Hindu *qua* Hindu against Muslim *qua* Muslim reached new heights in the eighteenth century, the upshot of the kind of religious conformity promoted by figures such as Shah Waliullah and Shah Abdul Aziz among the Muslims and their Hindu coevals among the Ramanandis. Such provocateurs had a ready answer to the ecumenical spirit of Kabirpanthism and Vaishnavism.[5] Confessional impulses gained a further fillip at the following *fin-de-siècle*, the extension of the franchise setting the stage for religious revivalism.[6] The popular violence that accompanied Partition testifies to the fact that these were not merely elite ideologies; the vast majority of Indians seemed to share in them.[7]

Very simply, Hindus and Muslims have long been communities apart. Both, moreover, are totalising faiths. One need only think of the caste system and the *sharia*. Organising social life on their own terms, neither community had much time for the institutional superimposition of liberal democracy from on high. In any case, the graft was of little account beyond its expedience as a power-sharing arrangement between, on Bardhan's account, India's three 'dominant proprietary classes': capitalists, the bourgeoisie, and the gentry.[8] Beyond that, few ambitions fuelled postcolonial India's rulers. Nehru's phthisic welfare state, Myrdal reminds us, made even the advanced capitalist countries appear communist.[9] Likewise Nehruvian secularism was a far cry from secularisation proper, of the kind witnessed in, say, China, Turkey, East Germany, and the Soviet Union.[10]

So it was that confession was given pride of place in cultural and political life. *Sadhus* and *maulvis* found representation in Parliament. Religious codes and reservations were retained. Schools under religious control were lavished with state aid. Candidates courted clerical support and called on temples on the hustings. More disturbingly, riots came to be treated as routine, an integral if grim element of the grammar of Indian politics. True, efforts were made by Nehru to keep the barbarians at bay, but the Hindu nationalists could not be simply wished away. For time was on their side. The electoral, of course, was a majoritarian principle. And majoritarianism, of course, held the possibility not only of anti-minoritarianism but also, as it were, anti-minorityism. Here was the ruinous marriage of *demos* and *ethnos*.

Postcolonial India's 'Muslim question', then, was predestined to be a fractious affair. It was to this quandary that the Muslim political class addressed itself. The great challenge was to find a way out of the feedback loop of riots, ghettoisation, and religious polarisation by developing a Muslim political constituency, so also attending to the dilemmas thrown up by discrimination, disadvantage, and deindustrialisation, all of this with an eye to the sensibilities of an easily offended Hindu audience. It was a tall order. Was the *ashraf* elite up to the task?

Elites and Subalterns

Yes and no. This is because identity politics, Muslim or otherwise, obscures more than it illuminates.[11] For to speak of 'Muslim politics' in the Indian setting is to speak *sensu stricto* of *ashraf* politics. It could be said, then, that the story of Muslim politics in postcolonial India is a tale of elite capture. Indeed, the concerns that animated this class can hardly be described as the concerns of the *qaum* at large.

Consider the *waqf* regime, whose autonomy was apparently a *cri de coeur* for the whole community. Only that the fiction of believing that the two irreconcilable interests at the heart of it, the rentier and the 'encroacher', could be brigaded together became harder to maintain as time wore on. The same could be said of the Mushāwarat and its fixation with the Aligarh Muslim University. Even in Aligarh town, a stone's throw away, the ordinary Muslim couldn't care less about this symbol of the *sharif*. As one of its inhabitants put it: 'this university has done nothing for us ... Muslims are busy with their daily needs. They have no time; they have no money'.[12]

Muslim elites in early postcolonial India worried endlessly about the place of the *sharia* in society, the *hajj* subsidy, state recognition of Urdu. The Muslim masses were expected to get behind each of these demands. The results were mixed. True, the conservative clergy and the Muslim grandees backing them were able to convince thousands of outraged Muslim men to take to the streets to protest Indira Gandhi's reform of alimony laws in 1973 that entitled Muslim women to maintenance, the maelstrom from which the AIMPLB emerged. The *hajj* allowance probably mattered to the few tens of thousands of mostly *petit-bourgeois* Muslims in urban enclaves. Urdu found a wide constituency in the Hindi heartland, especially in Uttar Pradesh where as early as 1952 some 2.2 million signed a petition to recognise it as the state's second tongue.

Even so, there were serious limits to mobilising around a clutch of cultural concerns, all *ashraf* affairs at that. Great Tradition piety was a luxury few ordinary Muslims could afford. Indeed, all of it was of a piece with the ur-religious formation of the *ashraf*. We owe a coruscating analysis of the *ashraf* milieu and mind to Lelyveld. Ostensibly settled by lineage, *ashraf*ness, as it were, was in fact socially determined. For in practice, faking a fanciful genealogy was par for the course, obliging clerics always around the corner ready to supply the powers that be with illustrious pedigrees. It was all a class act. In common usage, '*ashraf*' and 'upper-class' are synonyms.

One could acquire *sharafat* by picking up the correct class markers: politesse and an interest in arts and letters, of course, but also by engaging in the pastimes of the well-heeled, such as the *mushaira* (poetry competition), *munazarah* (debate), and *mahfil* (musical extravaganza). Perfected persiflage, *hookahs*, and *paan* accompanied each of these. Women in this world spent their lives in *purdah*, from which they had respite only in the *zenana*, women's quarters. The typical *ashraf* household had an army of servants in its employ. Childhood was punctuated by a panoply of ceremonies and commitments: *bismillah*—the ritual involving the reading of the opening lines of the Quran—at the age of four, *hidiyah* on finishing the Holy Book, circumcision—'to tame a boy's impulses'—at age seven, the assumption of 'full religious obligation' after one's 'first nocturnal emission', *maktab* schooling under an *ustad*, the committing of Persian passages to memory, rigorous religious instruction at a *khanqah* under a learned *murshid*.[13]

This was the quaint world in which modern Muslim politics took shape. Reacting against the decline of their *qasbati* milieu and responding to the challenges of devolution in the second half of the nineteenth century, the *ashraf* took to a profoundly religious idiom to forge Muslim solidarity. *Madrasas*, *eidgahs*, and *imambaras* were erected, *fatwas* pronounced, Quranic learning encouraged. As a result, the very idea of Islam became *ashraf*ised, paralleling the Sanskritisation of Hinduism.[14]

A century on, the penchants of the *ashraf* still passed for Muslim politics *tout court*. By then, however, as the age of subaltern politics dawned in the wake of decolonisation and democratisation, what were once compelling symbols of mobilisation had become serious handicaps. The shortcomings of *ashraf* elitism in this period were clear and obvious. Their demands made little sense to the common Muslim, mired in existential struggle.

Muslim personal law? Furnishing Muslim men with a private fiefdom to do as they pleased was poor recompense for their despondent public existence in an Islamophobic society. At any rate, the images of jubilant *burqa*-clad women celebrating the criminalisation of triple *talaq* in 2019 bore powerful visual testimony to what the other half of the *qaum* thought of the *sharia*. The *hajj*? A long and arduous journey that only one in five thousand Muslims was prepared to undertake in Nehru's India, it was hardly the most salient of issues. The AMU's minority status? A life-and-death issue for the Court, not the *qaum*. *Auqaf*? A rentier's paradise, an occupant's hell. The revision of textbooks? The upshot of a misplaced conflation of casual prejudice and ethnic violence, so much more the product of electoral exigencies and state complicity. Urdu? Excepting in a few urban quarters, increasingly understood by Muslims as being incompatible with the late-century *idée fixe* of social mobility. The Mushāwarat's preoccupation with 'moral degradation'? Pharisaical cant to the *ajlaf* and *arzal* with little purchase. Azad himself was a dipsomaniac. Moreover, the interest elicited in 'obscene literature' and pornography suggests that, perhaps, Muslims enjoyed both just as much as their Hindu brethren. *Wasiqadari* pensions? By definition the preserve of the privileged few, not the malnourished many. The sanctity of 'living monuments'? A worthy reminder of historical Islamic *gloire* but little else. Better relations with the Muslim world? An *ashraf* parochialism masquerading as cosmopolitanism. Few Indian Muslims thought in terms of the *umma*. The repeal of interfaith marriages? Much ado about a statistically insignificant phenomenon, inter-*jati* unions were rare enough to begin with. Communal fines for rioters? Scarcely a deterrent.

Ultimately the cathexis on culture constituted nothing less than an *ashraf* betrayal. There was no room for trade unions, mass protests, anti-discrimination legislation, and subaltern solidarity in this version of Muslim politics. There was plenty, however, for high cultural totemic symbols such as the AMU, *auqaf*, Urdu, and the *sharia*. Small wonder, then, that the latter received press attention and constitutional protection, even as the Muslim political elite counselled depoliticisation.

Law and Politics

Wilde's quip about socialism, that the trouble with it was that it took up too many evenings, succinctly captures what Muslim elites thought of politics proper in the early postcolonial period. The streets were not for them. Nor for that matter were the hustings. Lobbying and backroom deals were their preferred *modus operandi*.

It all began with Bari's pact with Gandhi on 'the Mohamedan question', the fate of the Caliphate foremost on the former's mind. Similarly, the minoritarian veto on constitutional safeguards was mostly exercised not in the assembly but *in camera*. In government, nationalist Muslims strove to effect change privately in their correspondence, closing ranks with their party colleagues publicly. For its part, the Mushāwarat, too, tried to lobby its way out of its representational conundrum, preferring to commit existing candidates to its charter than field a slate in its own name.

True, stealth mattered. Invisibility was an appropriate rejoinder to Islamophobia. But even so, it is important to remember here was a consensus that stretched from the early Azad to the late Faridi. It was not so much strategic as characteristic. Put differently, its depoliticised, self-effacing style was simply a quirk of Indian Muslim politics. 'Politics' itself was a bad word.

This was by no means an élan unique to Indian Muslims. World-historically, Muslim societies have expressed a preference for the juridical over the political, the one immutable and sacred and the other precarious and profane. 'In principle, the Holy Law, in politics as in other matters, is based on revelation and is therefore not subject to change', Bernard Lewis observes of *The Political Language of Islam*.[15] In practice, of course, the 'gates of *ijtihad*', creative interpretation, never closed, as was believed to have happened *circa* 950.[16]

All the same, the broad anti-political thrust of Muslim political thought remained unaltered. In its original sense, the *sharia* refers to 'the way to a watering place'. The definite article admits of no alternatives. To take the road less travelled, then, is to 'stray from the right path'. The upshot is a submission to legal authority, in effect to the powers that be. 'Obey those in authority over you', reads the Quran. The message, 'amplified by exegesis and tradition, of this teaching is twofold—to the ruler, authoritarian; to the subject, quietist', Lewis tells us.[17]

Echoes of Calvinist predestination resonant, the abnegation of political agency came with the territory. In the Indian setting, the roots of the anti-political *shariatic* worldview of the Muslims can be traced back to the Mughal concept of *siyasa*, lit. 'politics' in Arabic, Persian, and Urdu, but this literal translation is misleading. For '*siyasa* is more a type of procedural justice, an ethos, rather than a system of politics—more specifically a method of negotiation, of finding resolution to a problem through manipulating or mobilising relationships between people or groups'.[18] This is politics without the messy business of competing interests and popular approval—in a word, anti-politics.

With the coming of Anglo-Muhammadan law in the late-eighteenth century, such impulses acquired greater momentum. Under its terms, the private realm was effectively ceded to the *qazis*, enabling the East India Company to focus on more consequential matters such as regulation and taxation.[19] Two centuries on, little had changed. The Muslim clergy had consolidated power in the circumscribed sphere of influence bequeathed to it. Deoband, for instance, had become a veritable *fatwa* factory, issuing nearly 150,000 of them in the four decades to 1951. Hindu and Muslim alike came to accept the arrangement. This was simply the way things were. Personal law was hallowed ground. The work of lay Muslim politicians and clerics in equal measure, the passage of the Shariat Act in 1937 giving precedence to the *sharia* over local custom amply confirmed the reach of this consensus. In the quarter-century after Partition, no Indian ruler dared to meddle with Muslim personal law in any meaningful way. Indeed, Muslims never felt the need to establish an All-India Muslim Personal Law Board to protect their personal code before 1972.

Small wonder, then, that postcolonial India's Muslim political class, composed in the main of lawyers and clerics, shared in what could be called a jurisprudential habit of mind. The corollary was an odium attached to politics proper. So it was that from 1950 on, Muslim politics became synonymous with the defence of not one but two holy books: the Quran and the Constitution. The decision to plump for cultural over political safeguards in the assembly was of a piece with this worldview. Early intimations of it lay in what has been described in these pages as the three assumptions of the nationalist Muslims: their uncritical loyalty to party and nation, complaisance, and investment in the *Kulturkampf*. Azad's stab at crowning himself *amir-e-hind* and counselling minorities to 'totally give up politics' very clearly illustrated this.

This wasn't a singularly nationalist Muslim standpoint. An important faction of the League, Mohamed Raza Khan's, espoused similar ideas: 'Let us not stand for election'. So did the Fourth Party, with its anodyne name and unconditional support for Bombay's rulers, and the Uttar Pradesh Majlis, framing its entire political programme in relation to clauses of the Constitution, variously Articles 345, 347, 350(A). The Mushāwarat, for its part, railed against 'agitational politics', and Mirza Ismail 'the nation's new-fangled enthusiasm for the common man'. Faridi's final word on the matter said it all: 'we want only those rights which are promised by the Constitution to the minorities'.

Depoliticisation freed up Muslim politicians to focus attention elsewhere. Many of them became unduly fixated on the *umma*, to the detriment of their poorer *confrères* whose loyalties they were purportedly cultivating. Azad and Bari, for example, sent off some 30,000 on a doomed *hijrat*, holy migration, to Afghanistan, a crusade that killed more than a few and tested the faith of many. The Caliphate, likewise, was a far-flung cause. Figures like the nationalist Muslim Hafizka let on that they cared more about al-Aqsa than Ahmedabad, that is, the Jerusalem mosque that was set on fire by a Christian arsonist than the riot closer home that killed four hundred Muslims the same month. The four 'Mushāwarat' Muslim MPs of the Swatantra Party, meanwhile, blithely lost their jobs over their stance on the Six-Day War in which there was no Indian participation.

Evidently, then, seeing the world through *ashraf shariatic* lenses had its limitations. The world of laws set an exceptionally low bar for political engagement. Only constitutional violations, by definition flagrant denials of justice, were deemed worthy of political attention. The word of God, analogously, did not amount to much. Distinguishing between the permissible and the forbidden did not, in itself, constitute a political programme, addressed to the most important question of who gets what, when, and how. Similarly, the Muslim world was little more than a distraction from more pressing tasks.

The contrast with Dalit and 'backward class' politics is striking. Working from positions of more or less equal disadvantage, both fared better. The Dalits, for one, secured reservations at independence, forming unions and organising into relatively cohesive electoral blocs after, even if their millenarian dreams of seceding from India and annihilating caste were never realised.[20] In the late fifties and sixties in Bombay and Uttar Pradesh, they found a voice in the Republican Party of India, whose success in no small part turned on its ability to map class onto caste politics, a heterodoxy that many an old Ambedkarite took to be a betrayal of the Mahar leader's insistence on the specificities of the Dalit experience. Indeed, there was more to the RPI than reservations. It was equally preoccupied with land reform and redistribution, minimum wages and price controls, nationalisation and collectivisation.[21] Its successor organisations— the Backward and Minority Communities Employees Federation (BAMCEF, formed in 1973) that did not contest elections, and the Dalit Shoshit Samaj Sangharsh Samiti (DS4, 1981) and Bahujan Samaj Party (1984), which did—showed a commensurate ecumenicism, if not radicalism.

What of the 'backward classes', another bureaucratic term of art willed into existence by sufficient mobilisation? Like the Scheduled Castes and Muslims, they, too, were divided on questions of strategy: plausible, if incremental, reform from within the Congress or meaningful, if unlikely, change from without? The All-India Backward Classes Federation's first generation opted for the former option, its second the latter. As with the Dalits, an identitarian dimension was topped up with a wider, populist current, most notably in the form of peasant politics. Their transhumance served the cultivating castes well, as is testified by the runaway successes of Charan Singh's successive formations in the late sixties and seventies, one of which propelled him, albeit briefly, to the premiership.[22] The following twenty years, too, were kind to the backward classes, whose mobilisation resulted in the extension of quotas and greater representation in Parliament, while also improving the lot of OBCs more generally.[23]

The Shape of Things to Come

The politics of minorities, to state a truism, are necessarily anti-majoritarian affairs. And there, in the age of mass democracy and dictatorship, lies the rub. Muslim minorities everywhere seem to be locked in struggle with the wider societies they find themselves in. From re-education in Xinjiang to *laïcisation* in France, it has been for the better part a losing battle. Relatively greater levels of toleration in Anglo-America have nevertheless been offset in some measure by discrimination, securitisation, and vilification by the tabloid press since 9/11. The predicament of the Turkish *gastarbeiter* and their heirs in Germany and the mostly Moroccan and Albanian illegals in *jus sanguinis* Italy is no better: in the words of one of the former, they are 'wanted but not welcome'.[24]

Anchoring Islam in such settings is a formidable challenge. The *madrasa*, mosque, veil, dextrosinistral script, and juridical *imperium in imperio*, all as it were essences of Muslim identity, come across as veritable threats to dominant value systems, by turns racial (Han, white), confessional (Hinduism, Christianity), ideological (republicanism, liberalism). Eschewing these and appropriating the universal language of class, on the other hand, offers the prospect of reassuring majority communities but also begs the question of what is 'Muslim' about Muslim politics. It is a paradox. Chagla would have plumped for the latter option, Faridi and Nadwi the former, Azad and Mahmud a *via media*. The weight of Muslim opinion, it appears, would come down in favour of a kind of juridified anti-politics resembling the unavailing worldview of the nationalist Muslims.

Here, then, is pessimism of the intellect. What of optimism of the will? Recent developments seem to indicate that there is enough to warrant some of it. Muslims seem to be overcoming their aversion to politics proper, if not their conservative and juridical character. Put differently, Muslims appear to be rediscovering their agency.

The conversion, literally overnight and *en masse*, of a thousand Dalits to Islam in the village of Meenakshipuram in 1981 powerfully illustrated the re-enchantment of Muslim politics. Here was an angsty response to state neglect, designed to *épater* the Hindus. Predictably enough, it generated outrage, making headlines and drawing Delhi's attention. This was, as it were, the shock of Islam. At the outset, the former Untouchables had contemplated converting to Buddhism before deciding against it, Islam being the epitome of subalternity.

All the more so in the eighties. Already a fig leaf in Nehru's India, Congress secularism all but vanished in Indira's. During her tenure, *tantrics* were consulted before ministerial reshuffles, the prime minister's residence purified by *pandits*, clairvoyants and quacks given an audience with her. Her 1980 campaign culminated in a temple run through a dozen Hindu shrines, a harbinger of Advani's *rath yatra* a decade later. During her final term, the findings of the Riot Enquiry Commission were discarded, Minorities Commission denied statutory status, and National Integration Council dissolved. Some 3,000 Muslims perished in the Nellie massacre on her watch.

The statistics spoke for themselves. By the mid-eighties, Muslims were virtually absent among India's big capitalists (not one in the top fifty), small industrialists (14,000 out of 600,000), and public employees (6.6 per cent). They were, by contrast, overrepresented among the self-employed (53 per cent to the Hindus' 36 per cent). The Muslim literacy rate hovered a good 10 percentage points below the national average of 52 per cent.[25]

Happily, the Sangh Parivar campaigned for Mrs Gandhi's son in 1984. Rajiv's tenure coincided with a period of Muslim assertiveness. If the trend in the age of Azad was for complete depoliticisation, of Faridi for some agency, Syed Shahabuddin's generation displayed a lot more of it. The upshot was, paradoxically, a shot in the arm for Hindu nationalists. I have it on good authority that a portrait of Shahabuddin's is prominently hung at the RSS headquarters. But even if the detail is apocryphal, it is nevertheless illuminating.

A former foreign service mandarin, Shahabuddin traded on his twin platform in Parliament and as editor of *Muslim India* to birth the Babri Masjid Action Committee. Now, Ayodhya's Hindus had been clamouring to bring down Babur's early modern mosque since the forties. Underneath it lay, absurdly, evidence of the premodern birthplace of an incarnation of Vishnu's. Few cared for such millenarian fantasies at the time. It took a postmodern campaign in the eighties—hate speech disseminated on cassettes, the televising of the *Ramayana*—to convince Hindus outside the town of the urgency of flattening Babri Masjid. Importantly, in the Committee, Hindus found a nemesis that cared for their *cause célèbre* just as much as they did.

What followed was a dialectical spiral. Ayodhya was, as it were, brought to Delhi's door by Sanghis and Shahabuddin. The *soi-disant* Muslim Indian could have built a constituency for subaltern politics, underscoring the common predicament of Dalits and Muslims.

Unfortunately for the *qaum*, and fortunately for Hindus, he was cut from the same *ashraf* cloth as his forebears. He had a knack for winning followers and influencing Muslims, but the way he did so, perforce, lost him friends and alienated Hindus. Symptomatic was the national strike he organised in 1987, protesting the district magistrate's decision to open the mosque to Hindu worship. The call to boycott Republic Day celebrations was of a piece with his style. By all accounts, he was a remarkable organiser. He could assemble crowds of 300,000, packing the Rajpath, Delhi's literal corridor of power. In 1989, nearly 4,000 Muslims courted arrest with him in Faizabad after the *shilanyas*, the foundation ceremony of the temple to be built on the ruins of the mosque. Like Sanghis, Shahabuddin was drawn to monuments. Equally, he dismissed national heritage, preferring to think in terms of sacred spaces. And what's more, he had a theatrical flair. This he demonstrated on *shab-e-barat*, a kind of All Souls' Day, commandeering monuments managed by the Archaeological Survey of India to drive home the point that they were, in fact, Muslim places of worship.[26]

Ashraf to the bone, Shahabuddin was obsessed with the *sharia* as well. Here, of course, he had allies in the nationalist Muslims, who were equally concerned with protecting it from the predatory secularists of the state. It is no accident, then, that the clearest manifestation of elite Muslim solidarity since the Mushāwarat surrounded the Shah Bano affair. The facts are these. Ahmad Khan's first wife, the eponymous sexagenarian divorcée, had been left high and dry by her husband of forty years. As it was, the unilateral divorce, a male prerogative, had been secured in Islamic fashion simply by pronouncing the word thrice—*talaq, talaq, talaq!* Penniless, and with five charges to look after, Bano took him to court. The magistracy took a dim view of the *sharia*'s final word on the *iddat*, period of responsibility, of three months, after which men were under no obligation to pay alimony. To the fury of conservative Muslims, nationalist or otherwise, the Supreme Court concurred. Bano was entitled to a monthly maintenance allowance of Rs 400 to support Khan's children.[27]

Enter Rajiv Gandhi, smarting from a series of by-election defeats. Convinced that Muslims were abandoning the Congress on account of its progressivism, he set about putting his party to rights by purging the cabinet of its Muslim secularists. Arif Mohammad Khan was let go for defending the judgement. Thereafter, the government was given over to reactionaries in hock to the Personal Law Board. These were the antitheses of Chagla, the likes of Najma Heptulla (latterly of the BJP), Ziaur Rahman Ansari, and Khurshid Alam Khan, whose Oxford-trained son Salman acted as a go-between for ministers and *mullahs*. To Ansari, obscure clerics were infinitely more competent than seasoned judges on the subject of Muslim law: 'if you have a *tamboli* [*paan* vendor] doing the work of a *teli* [oil seller], things are bound to go wrong'. In other words, personal law only properly belonged to the *mullahs*. Secularists were appalled. To Bano's lawyer Danial Latifi, Rajiv's elevation of the Personal Law Board to the highest circles of decision-making was 'the most flagrant exercise of power-drunk autocracy since Caligula installed Incitatus, his favourite horse, as governor of Rome'.[28]

If the courts couldn't heed conservative Muslim opinion, Rajiv saw to it that Parliament did. The upshot was the passage of the Muslim Women (Protection of Rights on Divorce) Act of 1986, settling the matter for good. The state had no business telling Muslim men to furnish alimony, his government held. Muslim women could well live off the charity of their families, not to mention *waqf* boards.

Three years later, again bending over backwards, Rajiv banned *The Satanic Verses* when the *ulama* took offence. The novel's title insinuated that the Quran was the work of the Devil, clerics cried. Prostitutes were named after Muhammad's wives. The Prophet Abraham was called a bastard. How blasphemous! Interestingly, Delhi's decision came before Tehran's. Khomeini's *fatwa* sentencing Salman Rushdie to death followed a few months later.[29]

If Rajiv was a friend of reactionary Muslims, he was also, intriguingly, a friend of reactionary Hindus. On 9 November 1989, the day the Berlin Wall fell, he did his bit to bring down another monument of old. Appearing before a million Hindus at Ayodhya, he endorsed the VHP's *ram shila pujan*, the ceremonial consecration of bricks to build a temple atop the ruins of the Babri Masjid. His election campaign later that month began in Faizabad, a stone's throw from the mosque, where he promised Ram Rajya, a 'return' to just

334

rule as in the Hindu epics. Here was secular 'equidistance' in practice. 'Tit for tat', was how Rajiv crassly put it. Double-chinned and rather empty-headed, his dithering was too haphazard to be properly manipulative. Machiavellian he wasn't. At all events, if propping up Hindu and Muslim conservatives in order to retain the sensible, centre ground was a calculated strategy, it spectacularly backfired.[30]

For the flattening of the Babri Masjid proved to be the BJP's passport to power. Advani's latter-day *rath yatra*, the chariot cavalcade swapped for a motorised affair, from Somnath to Ayodhya in 1990 impressed upon Hindus the geographical unity of their faith in a manner hitherto unseen. Fast-forward two years and the mosque was reduced to rubble, Rajiv's successor but two, Narasimha Rao, scarcely lifting a finger on the strength of assurances from the Uttar Pradesh chief minister, the BJP's Kalyan Singh. Muslims were slaughtered in a pogrom that ensued in Bombay.

Rao's characteristically Congressite response, a wage hike for *imams*, must have been scant consolation for the *qaum*; just as profitless a wooing gesture as his predecessor V. P. Singh's decree recognising *mawlid*, the Prophet Muhammad's birthday, as a new bank holiday. As it was, Rao could be found in Shirdi the same month giving Hindu idols a lactic shower—in the spirit of secularism, of course.

If the Hindu leadership disregarded the material interests of Muslims, so, too, did the community's *ashraf* leadership. After Ayodhya, more bile was directed at the Ahl-i-Hadith *ulama*, whose 1993 *fatwa* declared triple *talaq* un-Islamic, than at Hindu nationalists. To the delight of the JUH and AIMPLB, the schism was short-lived. Orthodoxy prevailed. *Taqlid* trumped *ijtihad*—purblind conformity trumped creative interpretation.

Language politics, meanwhile, had hit a dead end. Urdu readership had stagnated. In the three decades to 1988, the combined circulation of Urdu dailies grew by 25 per cent to 250,000, whereas the Muslim population grew 115 per cent to 101 million. Maulana Wahiduddin Khan, a card-carrying Jama'ati who renounced Islamism to extol multiculturalism in *Al-Risala*, was only stating the obvious when he observed that English, and to some degree regional tongues, were the *entrées* to technical learning and class mobility. Urdu, by contrast, had become the language of nostalgia, its very parnassian quality synonymous with an unwillingness to come to terms with prosaic modernity.[31]

The diminution of progressive nationalist Muslims continued unabated in the nineties. In a setting where clans sustain political office over generations, surely it was no accident that some of the brightest minds of this persuasion followed not the profession of their forebears but instead migrated to the media? The scion of family friends of the Nehrus who represented Rae Bareilly in the assembly, Saeed Naqvi sought sanctuary in Doordarshan, the state television broadcaster. The story of the Kidwai clan, from Rafi Ahmed Kidwai to Seema Mustafa, is a tale from Parliament to *Pioneer*. Where his parents were on the frontlines of Congress nationalism, Hasan Suroor prefers to periodically pen pamphlets on the quandaries of the *qaum*, lobbing them from London.

Still, it wasn't immediately clear if the *qaum*'s condition had worsened, electorally speaking. Discredited because of Babri, the Congress suffered a string of defeats in the state elections that followed. Muslims abandoned the party *en bloc*. Better to confront an 'open enemy' that confide in a 'treacherous friend' was the popular refrain. This was clear thinking—admirable and percipient. For the early postcolonial hegemony of the 'treacherous friend' was giving way to the late postcolonial one of the 'open enemy'.

In fits and starts, however. At first, Hindu nationalism repelled more than it attracted. After all, riots were bad for business. In the assembly election in UP after Ayodhya, the BJP was easily defeated by a coalition of Muslims (19 per cent of the state's population), Dalits (21 per cent), and Yadavs (17 per cent). As the years wore on, however, the economistic logic lost its resonance. The heteroclite subaltern alliance—never a national phenomenon to begin with—came undone, and an ever-stronger Hindu bloc cemented in opposition to it. Increasingly, the message of Hindu rejuvenation found a sympathetic audience among the lower orders, as the BJP shed its Brahmanical image.

Brigading an aspirant middle class and backward gentry with the left-behinds (just as Mrs Gandhi once did), and promising each the buccaneering rewards of liberalisation (an empty signifier akin to Nehruvian 'socialism'), the BJP came to occupy at the *fin-de-siècle* a position analogous to the Congress' in the mid-century. After its victories in the spring of 1995 in Gujarat and Maharashtra, there was no looking back. Barring an interregnal decade of no particular moment, the Congress' last gasp as it were, the BJP has been in power since 1998, winning five of the last seven elections.

A steady trickle of Muslims back to the party of Azad has taken place, the logic of the Mushāwarat now underscored in reverse, Congressism replacing anti-Congressism. Since 2009, the Congress and its allies have typically taken 45 per cent of the Muslim vote share, the BJP and its partners just under a tenth of it.[32] The League remains influential in Kerala as does the Majlis in Hyderabad. As if habitual wife-swappers in an Updike novel, the Muslims of Uttar Pradesh stagger between the Samajwadi and Bahujan Samaj Party, the vehicle of the Yadavs and Dalits, respectively.

All the same, Muslim representation is at a discount. After achieving highs of 9 per cent in parliaments of the eighties, Muslims are down to 4 per cent in the Modi's India, a return, as it were, to Nehru's India. If the eminent Nehruvians had little standing, the eminent Modians—Najma Heptulla, Mukhtar Abbas Naqvi, M. J. Akbar—have even less. At any rate, none of them lasted very long in government.

Elsewhere, too, Hindu majoritarianism has produced a hostile environment for Muslims. The upshot has been, in the words of Christophe Jaffrelot, nothing less than an 'eviction from institutions'.[33] At 14.25 per cent of the national population, Muslims account for a mere 4 per cent of those who clear the competitive exam for entry into the administrative service.

Similarly, just under 3 per cent of the officers in the police service are Muslim. The result? Some 54 per cent of Muslims fear the police, whereas only 24 per cent of Hindus do. Not without reason. Evidence planted, confessions extracted under torture, and emergency laws invoked, purported Islamists were banged up after the Malegaon bombings of 2006. Only, as it turned out, they were innocent. It was a Hindu group, Abhinav Bharat, that was behind them.

Typically, central institutions more immune to Islamophobia— the Supreme Court, National Investigation Agency, Central Bureau of Investigation—come to the rescue of falsely accused Muslims, but in their own time. To mix metaphors, the sclerotic cogs of justice move slowly. Muslims are often acquitted only after a dozen, sometimes twenty, years in prison, before which they can perish in 'encounter' killings while supposedly staging jailbreaks.

It must be said that the courts themselves are not above prejudice. Under Vajpayee, a commission cleared a Hindu nationalist accused of murdering the missionary Graham Staines. A Haridwar court, meanwhile, issued a warrant for the nonagenarian artist and national treasure M. F. Hussain's arrest after complaints from Hindu organisations protesting his depiction of a naked goddess. Never mind Konark and Khajuraho. More recently, the Bombay High Court exculpated two dozen Hindus who lynched a Muslim computer engineer. The reasoning? His faith, perceptible on account of his beard, quite justifiably 'provoked' them. In another Kafkaesque case, a lynched Muslim's assailants were let go, but his mates detained for cow slaughter when, in fact, they were dairy farmers. In yet another, Hindus sentenced to life imprisonment for killing a Muslim allegedly in the beef trade were released on bail, their legal counsel paid for by a BJP MP who garlanded them on their release.

An index of the shifting Overton window was the Ayodhya ruling, providing ample proof that Modi's India is a Hindu India like none before it since, perhaps, Prithviraj Chauhan. In the immediate aftermath of the demolition, the Supreme Court had sent the chief minister, Kalyan Singh, to prison for a day for allowing Hindus to build a makeshift temple on the site of the mosque. By 2010, secular pretence dropped, the Allahabad High Court ruled that the site was in 'joint possession' by the mosque and Lord Ram, Indian law allowing deities to own property. The land was divided into three tracts, two given to Hindus and one to Muslims, now that the latter—the judgment read—were no longer India's 'rulers' but rather 'junior partners'. Finally, in 2020, after a meandering excursus through pseudo-archaeology and eighteenth-century Jesuit travellers' accounts, the Supreme Court handed the entire land of 67 acres to Hindus, promising Muslims a mere five acres further afield should a suitable site be found for a mosque. Importantly, making quick work of the separation of church and state, the government was tasked with the construction of the temple. Modi himself presided over the *bhoomi pujan*, the cornerstone ceremony, in August 2020. Blurring the spiritual and the temporal, the prime minister was chief guest, master of ceremonies, and grand priest all rolled into one. Here, then, is the making of the world's largest theocracy.[34]

Small wonder Hindus feel emboldened today. In many senses, India at seventy-five evokes year zero: the open hostility to minorities, the absence of a monopoly on violence. Hindu militias set the agenda in the *mofussil* and the media, generating a lexicon so utterly ludicrous were it not also disturbing. There is, to begin with, the Love Jihad of lascivious Muslims, seducing unsuspecting Hindu women only to convert them. The hysteria has made intermarriage quite impossible in large parts of the country, every union now under the watchful eyes of Hindu nationalist wedding registrars, policemen, judges, and neighbours. Then there is the Land Jihad to send real estate prices plummeting. Already, authorities in Ahmedabad have passed laws banning Muslims from buying property in Hindu areas, forcing the community into peripheral ghettoes such as Juhapura. Heeding the dictum 'never let a good crisis go to waste', we now have Corona Jihad. Muslims are the carriers of the new plague, undeserving of hospital beds and unfit for social life.

The fervency has been matched by the government. Property inherited by Muslims from *émigrés* to Pakistan can now be sequestrated under the Enemy Property Act of 2017, a throwback to Evacuee Property. Uttar Pradesh has empowered the magistracy and police to look into conversions driven by marriage, and make arrests if necessary. More risibly, but equally tellingly, its chief minister removed the 'Muslim' Taj Mahal from the state's tourism brochures. For in the Sangh Parivar's artful reconstruction, the history of Islam is a story from Babur to Bin Laden, from medieval tyranny to terrorism. With support from the BJP chief minister, Haryana's Hindus have turfed out Muslims from praying on Gurgaon's streets. The lynching of Muslims for possession of beef across the Republic, too, has brought home the reality that Modi's India is no country for the *qaum*. Video footage of Muslims singing Hindu chants at gunpoint before being killed in cold blood, circulated to intimidate Muslims and entertain Hindus, bear grim testimony to this fact.

The Muslim response to Hindu belligerence has been to retreat from politics proper. The Tocquevillian turn has delivered dignity to the few, but left behind the many. Rightly sceptical of the Islamophobic state, charities such as the Deeni Talimi Council, Hamdard Foundation, and Crescent Schools have endeavoured to fashion a *dar al-Islam* of Muslim-friendly universities, schools, and hospitals. Associationalism has its drawbacks, however. Ghettoisation reinforces prejudice, discouraging even the little interfaith dialogue that there is.

The scholasticism encouraged at the Deeni Talimi schools, moreover, does its millions of students—500,000 in Uttar Pradesh alone—a disservice. Learning is almost entirely confined to religious texts, prayers and the like, leaving pupils woefully unprepared for modern life. Trained for a career in the archaic professions—teaching; sermonising—only so many schools and mosques can absorb them. The toxic alloy of a *de haut en bas* education and *déclassé* existence inevitably gives rise to a crippling sense of resentment.

Meanwhile, elite centres of learning continue to thrive, absorbing the upper crust as once did the great *madrasas* of old: the Shia College and Firangi Mahal in Lucknow, Darul Mussanifin in Azamgarh, Osmania, Aligarh, and Jamia. Calicut's Farook College, the Aligarh of polytechnics as it were, offers the rare promise of social mobility. So, too, does the service industry, at any rate in the few urban enclaves where market capitalism flourishes oblivious, in some measure, to faith so long as obvious religious markers are concealed. Many Muslims are prepared to make this bargain.[35] For Muslims in Malabar, the Gulf labour market remains an attractive proposition. Here, the bargain is reversed. Migrants return home more pious, acquiring a belated suburban respectability after years of backbreaking work in a world without women, leisure, privacy, or even labour rights.[36]

As ever, Muslims scratch a living from such traditional trades as weaving and crafting. Recent decades have seen a leather revival in Kanpur. Varanasi's *sari* interest continues to flourish. Meerut's Muslim weavers have moved into foundries and furniture.

Moradabad remains an important export hub, shipping brassware to the Arab world. In Bhagalpur, the *qaum* has made a start in the silk industry. Muslims are to be found in the coffee plantations in Coorg, and in the surviving textile factories of Ahmedabad and Bombay. The west coast trade still is, to an extent, the preserve of Bohras, Khojas, and Memons.

As with economic, so with legal, activity. Since the nineties, Islamic courts have sprouted across the Republic, a juridical *imperium in imperio* reminiscent of Azad's juristic ghetto, dispensing Quranic justice. They are, in part, a response to—what Muslims perceive to be—the one-sided stringency of the BJP's secularism. Triple *talaq* was criminalised in 2019. Marital abandonment, however, carries no sentence for Hindus. *Sharia* courts, it is true, can be quite progressive. Female judges are not uncommon. Muslim women who otherwise would not have sought justice now do.[37] Still, there's a twofold cost here. The courts further isolate Muslims as well as antagonise Hindus, who cry preferential treatment.

Yet another upshot of the involution of Muslim politics has been the rise of Islamism. That a section of the Muslim youth has taken to insurrectionary millenarianism in a land where the state has only ever tenuously held the monopoly on violence is hardly surprising. From the killing fields of forties Hyderabad to noughties Gujarat, frontier justice has trumped the rule of law. All the same, too much shouldn't be made of the Jama'at's student wing SIMI, Adam Sena, Indian Mujahideen, or ISIS' Indian franchise. As Sara Perlangeli convincingly argues on the strength of her database, the threat posed by the Islamic State has been wildly exaggerated, scarcely a few dozen befuddled and blundering souls attracted to it each year.[38] Not unlike the converts at Meenakshipuram, the Islamists' desire to shock is hardly commensurate with their capacity to act. At all events, their cut-price parody of jihadists abroad—all very *Four Lions*—amounts to little more than a pale imitation of Hindu militants at home.

There are signs, however, that we are today at a new conjuncture. The 2020s, after a fashion, recall the 1920s. The protests that ripped through the Republic's metropolises—some 100,000 gathered at Delhi's Shaheen Bagh; similar crowds were sighted in Allahabad and Ahmedabad, Bangalore and Bombay, Chennai and Calcutta, Pune and Patna—in the early months of 2020 made for vivid images of Muslim agency in action. Khilafatists *de nos jours*, the students of the Jamia Millia Islamia marched on Parliament. Their counterparts at Aligarh combated the paramilitary Central Reserve Police Force.

The immediate provocation, it is true, was not so much a question of material discontent as legal propriety: the passage of the 'unconstitutional' Citizenship Amendment Act, which fast-tracks naturalisation for Afghan, Pakistani, and Bangladeshi migrants so long as they are not Muslim. Once again, Muslims are carping about the Constitution. If the juridical predisposition dies hard, so, too, does the *ashraf* habit. 'Modi, go back to your *chai* shop' read a placard held up by a *burqa*-clad woman. 'I will show my documents if you show me your degree', read another, as though what was most objectionable about Modi's India was the premier's working-class origins.

Even so, popular Muslim disaffection and protest must be taken *faute de mieux* as evidence that hope springs eternal. The emergence of a more progressive brand of Muslim politics cannot be discounted. India's Muslims might prove to be a turbulent, seditious, and factious people after all.

NOTES

INTRODUCTION

1. Hasan, *Legacy of a Divided Nation*, p. 166.
2. Ibid., p. 244.
3. Idem, *Moderate or Militant*, p. 120.
4. Khalidi, 'Muslims in Indian Political Process', p. 43.
5. Akbar, *India: The Siege Within*, p. 312.
6. Naqvi, *Being the Other*, p. 2.
7. *TOI*, 15 July 1951, p. 3.
8. *TOI*, 28 October 1956, p. 10.
9. Shakir, 'Religion and Politics', p. 470.
10. Krishna, 'Electoral Participation and Political Integration', p. 186.
11. Wright, Jr, 'Muslim Legislators in India', p. 255.
12. Gopal, *Jawaharlal Nehru*, vol. 3, pp. 26, 171.
13. Stepan, Linz, and Yadav, *Crafting State-Nations*, p. 41.
14. Lijphart, 'The Puzzle of Indian Democracy', p. 258.
15. Austin, *The Indian Constitution*, p. 13.
16. Idem, *Working a Democratic Constitution*, p. 597.
17. Spear, 'The Position of Muslims', p. 48; Ahmed and Kaviraj, 'Indian Democracy and the World's Largest Muslim Minority', p. 206.
18. Varshney, *Battles Half Won*, p. 26; Mehta, *The Burden of Democracy*, p. 3; Sen, *The Argumentative Indian*, p. 80; Guha, *India After Gandhi*, p. 6.
19. Varshney, *Battles Half Won*, p. 3; Sen, *The Argumentative Indian*, p. 13; Khosla, *India's Founding Moment*.
20. Kothari, *Politics in India*, p. 4.
21. Urdu was a *mélange* of Hindi, Persian, Arabic, and Turkish that developed in Delhi around the time of the Sultanate when the Subcontinent's late mediaeval invaders needed a pidgin to understand locals.
22. Brass, *Language, Religion, and Politics*.

23. Sherman, *Muslim Belonging in Secular India*.
24. Shani, *Communalism, Caste, and Hindu Nationalism*.
25. Jaffrelot and Thomas, 'Facing "Ghettoisation" in "Riot-city"', p. 53.
26. Chatterji, *The Spoils of Partition*.
27. All figures from 1980. See the *Report of the High-Power Panel on Minorities, SC, ST, and Weaker Sections*.
28. Brass, *Language, Religion, and Politics*, p. 185.
29. Wright Jr, 'The Effectiveness of Muslim Representation in India', p. 133.
30. Bhargava, 'On the Persistent Political Under-Representation of Muslims', pp. 83–4.
31. Wilkinson, 'India, Consociational Theory', p. 778.
32. Wright Jr, 'The Effectiveness of Muslim Representation', p. 130.
33. 'Introduction' in Lelyveld, *Aligarh's First Generation*, p. xxxvi.
34. Rehman, *Plight of Indian Muslims*.
35. Harman, *Plight of Muslims in India*.
36. Rahman, *Denial and Deprivation*.
37. See M. R. A. Baig's review of Shakir, *Muslims in Free India* in the *Quest*, November-December 1972, p. 90.
38. Brass, *Language, Religion, and Politics*; Wright Jr, 'Revival of the Majlis', p. 234.
39. *The Spoils of Partition*.
40. *Muslim Belonging in Secular India*.
41. *Mappila Muslims of Kerala*.
42. Ghosh, *The Politics of Personal Law in South Asia*.
43. The Osellas (ed.), *Islamic Reform in South Asia*.
44. *Unequal Citizens*.
45. Khan, *The Great Partition*; Zamindar, *The Long Partition*; Baruah, 'The Partition's long shadow'.
46. See Jürgen Habermas' discussion of Thomas Hobbes in relation to Talcott Parsons: *The Theory of Communicative Action, vol. 2*, p. 210. 'There is no doubt that in his [Parson's] theoretical scheme the object (society) predominates over the subject (the knowledgeable human agent)', Anthony Giddens notes reprovingly in *The Constitution of Society*, p. xx. For a brief critique of Giddens, see Perry Anderson, 'A Culture in Contraflow—Part I', p. 54. Where Giddens writes, 'However subordinate an actor may be in a social relationship, the very fact of involvement in that relationship gives him or her a certain amount of power over the other', Anderson drily suggests that 'Giddens's "type case" is the labour contract in early capitalism— initially strengthening the power of employers over workers, subsequently prompting collective organization against them. It would be more difficult to view the extermination camp in the same light'.
47. 'What is Agency?', p. 968.
48. Näsström, 'Where is the representative turn going?', p. 503.
49. *The Concept of Representation*, p. 107.
50. *Representative Democracy*, p. 132.

51. *Representation.*
52. Pitkin, *The Concept of Representation.*
53. Barnes, *The Sense of an Ending*, p. 17.
54. *Legacy of a Divided Nation.*
55. *Indian Muslims since Independence.*

1.   IDENTITY POLITICS

1.   *Bunch of Thoughts*, p. 154.
2.   *Roses in December*, pp. 151, 380.
3.   *An Autobiography*, p. 138.
4.   Datta, and Cleghorn (eds), *A Nationalist Muslim and Indian Politics.*
5.   Metcalf, 'Nationalist Muslims in British India', p. 25.
6.   Hasan, *A Nationalist Conscience*, p. 181.
7.   Bayly, *Rulers, Townsmen, and Bazaars.*
8.   Robinson, *Separatism among Indian Muslims.*
9.   Eaton, *India in the Persianate Age.*
10. Lelyveld, *Aligarh's First Generation.*
11. Robinson, *Separatism*, pp. 46–77.
12. Ibid., p. 82.
13. While it was founded in Dacca, its leading lights in the main belonged to Aligarh and Lucknow.
14. Cannadine, *Ornamentalism.*
15. Metcalf, *The Aftermath of Revolt*, p. 159.
16. Seal, *The Emergence of Indian Nationalism.*
17. Pandey, *The Construction of Communalism*; Dhulipala, *Creating a New Medina.*
18. McLane, *Indian Nationalism and the Early Congress*, p. 107.
19. Brass, *Language, Religion, and Politics*, p. 133.
20. Robinson, *Separatism*, pp. 82–3.
21. Minault Lelyveld, 'The Campaign for a Muslim University', pp. 145–189.
22. Lelyveld, *Aligarh's First Generation*, p. 76.
23. *My Life*, p. 51.
24. Minault, *The Khilafat Movement*, p. 45.
25. Naziruddin Hasan to Ansari, 26 November 1912 in Hasan (ed.), *Muslims and the Congress*, p. 3.
26. Ansari to A. M. Khwaja, 30 November 1918 and Ansari's circular letter, 1 December 1927, ibid., pp. 11, 24.
27. Hasan, *A Nationalist Conscience*, p. 56.
28. Transcript of the interview with his daughter, Zohra Ansari, Acc. No. 553, NMML Oral History Project.
29. See Ansari's resolution, 30 December 1918 in Zaidi (ed.), *Evolution of Muslim Political Thought*, vol. 2, p. 168.
30. Ali, *My Life*, pp. 32–7.
31. Minault, *Khilafat Movement.*

32. Afzal, *A History of the All-India Muslim League*, pp. 119–31.

33. Owen, 'Negotiating the Lucknow Pact', pp. 561–87.

34. Wolpert, *Jinnah of Pakistan*, pp. 42–60.

35. Qureshi, *Pan-Islam in British India*, p. 100 ff.

36. Devji, *The Impossible Indian*, pp. 9–40.

37. Bari issued 'a *fatwa* declaring that the animal originally slaughtered by Ibrahim was a sheep and not a cow and that cow sacrifice was prohibited in future'. And that was that. See the report on Gandhi's movements of April 1919 in Hasan and Pernau (eds), *Regionalizing Pan-Islamism*, p. 9. Gandhi felt deeply about the matter. 'I would ask the Muslim friends to apply the knife to my neck and kill me rather than the cow': *CWMG*, vol. 16, p. 141.

38. Organised by the reformist Arya Samaj and led by Shraddhanand, the *shuddhi* movement sought, as it saw it, to 'reconvert' lower-caste Muslims in the Punjab and the heartland to Hinduism by ridding it of untouchability. With the help of the JUH, Sufis such as Khwaja Hasan Nizami and clerics like Bari lined up against *shuddhi* activists to form the *tabligh* movement to, as it were, re-reconvert and prevent Arya Samajists from preying on marginalised Muslims. Founded by two other non-cooperation alums, Lala Lajpat Rai and Saifuddin Kitchlew, both Punjabis, the *sangathan* and *tanzim* movements cast an even wider net, their writ running from charity to defence, from converting to rioting.

39. *CWMG*, vol. 25, p. 143.

40. *CWMG*, vol. 16, pp. 33–5.

41. *CWMG*, vol. 18, p. 342.

42. *Imagined Communities*, p. 28.

43. Hardy, *The Muslims of British India*, p. 181.

44. *CWMG*, vol. 16, p. 34.

45. Minault, *Khilafat Movement*, p. 100.

46. Brown, *Gandhi's Rise to Power*, p. 152.

47. Hasan and Pernau (eds), *Documents on the Khilafat Movement*, p. 9.

48. *CWMG*, vol. 17, p. 418.

49. Minault, *Khilafat Movement*, p. 124.

50. Jalal, *Self and Sovereignty*, p. 234.

51. Lewis, *The Middle East*.

52. Keddie, *Sayyid Jamal Ad-Din 'al-Afghani'*.

53. Robinson, *Separatism*, p. 288.

54. Minault, *Khilafat Movement*, p. 77.

55. *India Wins Freedom*, pp. 21, 96, 162, 170.

56. Finkel, *Osman's Dream*, p. 493.

57. Gail Minault, *Khilafat Movement*, p. 229.

58. Ibid., p. 2.

59. Minault, *Khilafat Movement*, p. 87.

60. See the Delhi Province report of 1924 in Hasan and Pernau (eds), *Documents on the Khilafat Movement*, p. 53.

NOTES

61. Robinson, *The 'Ulama of Farangi Mahall*, p. 158.
62. Minault, *Khilafat Movement*, p. 45.
63. Robinson, *The 'Ulama*, p. 160.
64. Azad most certainly was a literary *wunderkind*: Ahmad, 'Azad's Careers', p. 61.
65. Hameed (ed.), *India's Maulana*, p. 14.
66. Minault, *Khilafat Movement*, p. 42.
67. Hardy, *The Muslims of British India*, p. 191.
68. Ibid., p. 194.
69. Metcalf, *Islamic Revival in British India*, p. 158.
70. Minault, *Khilafat Movement*, p. 33.
71. Ibid., p. 320.
72. Dutt, *India Today*, p. 469.
73. Brown, *Gandhi's Rise to Power*, pp. 330–7.
74. Minault, *Khilafat Movement*, p. 184 ff.
75. Hardy, *The Muslims of British India*, pp. 212–5.
76. *A Bunch of Old Letters*, p. 64.
77. Khaliquzzaman, *Pathway to Pakistan*, pp. 94, 89–104.
78. Kamran, 'Majlis-i-Ahrar-i-Islam', pp. 465–82.
79. Hasan, "Congress Muslims' and Indian Nationalism', pp. 103–4.
80. *Language, Religion, and Politics*, p. 44.
81. Robinson, 'Nation Formation', pp. 215–30; Shaikh, 'Muslims and Political Representation', pp. 539–57.
82. Ahmad (ed.), *Some Recent Speeches and Writings of Mr Jinnah*, p. 153.
83. The autumn of 1921 witnessed the Mappila rebellion that pitched notionally 'Khilafatist' Muslim peasants, aided by their recently demobbed *confrères*, against their Hindu landlords in Malabar. What began as a conventional class struggle quickly assumed confessional overtones, Muslims burning temples and converting the Hindu gentry at gunpoint. The next summer, some 30,000 Muslims instigated by Azad and Bari migrated to Afghanistan—a land sold to them as a utopia for Muslims now that the Raj, apparently, had turned against them and 'their' Caliph—only to return disillusioned from this *hijrat*, holy migration, also whittled down by starvation and death.
84. Azad, *India Wins Freedom*, pp. 170–1.
85. Datta, *Humayun Kabir*, p. 38.
86. Gould, *Hindu Nationalism and the Language of Politics*, pp. 223–30; *Pirpur Report*.
87. Dutt, *India Today*, p. 469.
88. Krüger (ed.), *Kunwar Mohammad Ashraf*, pp. 413–4.
89. *Pirpur Report*.
90. *The Partition of India*, p. 35.
91. Azad, *India Wins Freedom*, p. 17.
92. Nehru to Mahmud, 2 December 1939 in Datta and Cleghorn (eds), *Selected Correspondence*, p. 182.

93. Mahmud to Nehru, 9 December 1939 in ibid., p. 184.

94. Nehru to Mahmud, 12 December 1939 in ibid., p. 187.

95. Mahmud to Nehru, 23 March 1940 in ibid., p. 197.

96. Azad, *India Wins Freedom*, p. 99.

97. *TOP*, vol. 5, p. 76.

98. Azad, *India Wins Freedom*, p. 101.

99. Datta and Cleghorn (eds), *Selected Correspondence*, p. 194.

100. *TOP*, vol. 1, p. 362.

101. *TOP*, vol. 5, p. 1279.

102. See his admiring portrait of Wavell in his *India Wins Freedom*, pp. 192–3: 'I found him a rugged, straightforward soldier void of verbiage and direct both in approach and statement. He created in the mind an impression of great sincerity which touched my heart'. Nehru found his fawning embarrassing: ibid., p. 192.

103. *TOP*, vol. 5, p. 1262.

104. *TOP*, vol. 5, pp. 1260–9.

105. *TOP*, vol. 5, p. 1276.

106. *TOP*, vol. 5, pp. 187, 387.

107. *TOP*, vol. 5, p. 250.

108. *TOP*, vol. 5, p. 1185.

109. *TOP*, vol. 4, p. 888.

110. Ahmed, *National Unity and Solidarity*, p. 12.

111. Stephens, *Governing Islam*, p. 167.

112. De, 'Mumtaz Bibi's Broken Heart'.

113. Ahmed, *Jinnah, Pakistan, and Islamic Identity*.

114. Zaman, *Islam in Pakistan*, p. 47.

115. *Language, Religion, and Politics*, p. 164.

116. *TOP*, vol. 6, p. 766.

117. Sho, *Muslims, Nationalism*.

118. *TOP*, vol. 6, p. 852.

119. *TOP*, vol. 7, p. 972.

120. *TOP*, vol. 7, p. 1007.

121. *TOP*, vol. 7, p. 972.

122. *TOP*, vol. 7, p. 967.

123. *TOP*, vol. 8, p. 272.

124. *NYT*, 26 August 1946, p. 1.

125. *TOP*, vol. 8, p. 370.

126. *TOP*, vol. 7, p. 1007.

127. See the *TOIs* of 18 October 1946, p. 1; 7 December 1946, p. 1; 10 December 1946, p. 7.

128. *TOP*, vol. 8, pp. 534, 772.

129. *TOI*, 9 September 1946, p. 1.

130. *TOI*, 11 October 1946, p. 3; *TOI*, 19 October 1946, p. 6.

131. *TOI*, 31 August 1946, p. 8.

132. *TOI*, 31 August 1946, p. 8; *TOI*, 17 September 1946, p. 8.
133. *TOI*, 6 March 1946, p. 10; *TOI*, 5 March 1946, p. 6.
134. *TOI*, 14 October 1946, p. 5.
135. *TOI*, 12 November 1946, p. 5.
136. *TOI*, 26 November 1946, p. 1.
137. *TOP*, vol. 9, pp. 768, 927.
138. *TOP*, vol. 10, pp. 34, 215, 265.
139. *CWMG*, vol. 96, p. 121.
140. *TOP*, vol. 12, p. 601.
141. *India Wins Freedom*, pp. 214–223.
142. *CWMG*, vol. 95, p. 27.
143. Brass, *Language, Religion, and Politics*, p. 181.

2. CULTURE WARS

1. *India Wins Freedom*, p. 11.
2. Zaman, 'Revolutionary History', p. 630.
3. Kabir to Nehru, 28 March 1958, NMML, Kabir Papers, Subject File 1.
4. Nehru to Mahmud, 2 and 7 February 1942 in Datta and Cleghorn (eds), *Selected Correspondence*, pp. 218–26.
5. *India Wins Freedom*, publisher's note and pp. 162, 202, 16–7.
6. Jinnah to Azad, 4 July 1940 in Kumar (ed.), *Selected Works of Azad*, vol. 1, document 71 [no page number].
7. *India Wins Freedom*, pp. 75–6, 96–7, 136–40.
8. *TOP*, vol. 6, p. 155.
9. *TOP*, vol. 6, p. 172. Emphasis added.
10. Kumar (ed.), *Selected Works of Azad*, vol. 11, p. 132.
11. Douglas, *Abul Kalam Azad*, p. 246.
12. Mujeeb, *The Indian Muslims*, p. 442.
13. *TOI*, 23 February 1958, p. 10.
14. *TOI*, 22 March 1955, p. 11. Emphasis mine.
15. Douglas, *Abul Kalam Azad*, p. 252.
16. *TOI*, 22 April 1950, p. 1.
17. Douglas, *Abul Kalam Azad*, p. 245.
18. *TOI*, 22 April 1950, p. 1.
19. *TOI*, 30 September 1952, p. 6.
20. *TOI*, 30 September 1956, p. 1.
21. *TOI*, 10 October 1956, p. 7.
22. Austin, *The Indian Constitution*, and idem, *Working a Democratic Constitution*.
23. Jha, 'Secularism in the Constituent Assembly Debates', pp. 3175–80.
24. See, *inter alia*, ibid.; Retzlaff, 'The Problem of Communal Minorities'.
25. See, *inter alia*, Bajpai, *Debating Difference*; Chiriyankandath, 'Creating a secular state'.
26. *Debating Difference*, pp. 3, 13.

27. Ibid., pp. 52n46, 53–4.
28. Ibid., p. 81.
29. *CAD*, vol. 9, p. 1343.
30. *Religion, Caste, and Politics in India*, pp. 1–21.
31. *The Indian Constitution*, p. 7.
32. Chiriyankandath, 'Creating a secular state', p. 4.
33. *CAD*, vol. 11, p. 733.
34. Appendix II in ibid., p. 334.
35. Rao (ed.), *Select Documents*, vol. 2, p. 394.
36. Ibid., p. 397.
37. Ibid., p. 400.
38. Ibid., p. 409.
39. Galanter, *Competing Equalities*, pp. 133, 150.
40. Rao (ed.), *Select Documents*, vol. 2, pp. 404, 409.
41. Austin, *The Indian Constitution*, p. 150.
42. *Munshi Papers*, vol. 1, p. 207.
43. Ibid.
44. *CAD*, vol. 8, p. 351.
45. Mookerjee to Patel, 17 July 1948 and Patel to Mookerjee, 18 July 1948 in Das (ed.), *Patel's Correspondence*, vol. 6, pp. 322–4.
46. Rao (ed.), *Select Documents*, vol. 2, pp. 416–8.
47. Retzlaff, 'The Problem of Communal Minorities', p. 64.
48. *CAD*, vol. 5, p. 265.
49. *CAD*, vol. 5, pp. 270–1.
50. *CAD*, vol. 5, p. 264.
51. *CAD*, vol. 5, p. 261.
52. *Nehru Report*, p. 36.
53. *Sapru Report*, p. 117.
54. Bajpai, *Debating Difference*, p. 36.
55. *CAD*, vol. 5, p. 272.
56. *The Indian Ideology*, p. 107.
57. *CAD*, vol. 4, p. 580.
58. *CAD*, vol. 4, p. 637.
59. Rao (ed.), *Select Documents*, vol. 2, pp. 400–15.
60. *CAD*, vol. 7, pp. 1168–89.
61. Wilkinson, *Votes and Violence*, p. 108.
62. Austin, *The Indian Constitution*, pp. 131–2.
63. *CAD*, vol. 7, p. 1256.
64. *CAD*, vol. 7, p. 1252.
65. *CAD*, vol. 7, p. 1234.
66. *CAD*, vol. 7, pp. 1234–5.
67. *CAD*, vol. 7, p. 1262.
68. *Munshi Papers*, vol. 1, p. 207.
69. *CAD*, vol. 8, p. 352.

70. *CAD*, vol. 8, p. 336.
71. *CAD*, vol. 8, pp. 332–8.
72. *CAD*, vol. 8, p. 347.
73. *Munshi Papers*, vol. 1, p. 208.
74. *CAD*, vol. 8, p. 311.
75. Bajpai, *Debating Difference*, p. 128.
76. *CAD*, vol. 2, p. 284.
77. *CAD*, vol. 5, p. 213.
78. Khaliquzzaman, *Pathway to Pakistan*, p. 394.
79. Ambedkar, *Annihilation of Caste*, §8.1, §8.4.
80. Idem, *Writings and Speeches*, vol. 5, p. 131.
81. *CAD*, vol. 8, p. 283.
82. *CAD*, vol. 8, p. 305.
83. *CAD*, vol. 8, p. 335.
84. *CAD*, vol. 8, p. 300.
85. *Indian Express*, 14 February 2018.
86. *CAD*, vol. 8, p. 302.
87. *From Purdah to Parliament*, pp. 33, 39.
88. Ibid., p. 121.
89. Ibid., p. 126.
90. Ibid., p. 132.
91. Ibid., p. 134.
92. *Siasat*, 8 October 2020.
93. *TOI*, 21 December 1957, p. 11.
94. Eaton, *India in the Persianate Age*.
95. Stephens, *Governing Islam*.
96. Washbrook, 'Law, State, and Agrarian Society', pp. 649–721.
97. *CAD*, vol. 7, p. 899.
98. Rao (ed.), *Select Documents*, vol. 2, p. 385.
99. *CAD*, vol. 3, p. 503 ff.
100. *CAD*, vol. 7, p. 901.
101. Smith, *India as a Secular State*, p. 348.
102. *CAD*, vol. 7, p. 892.
103. Rao, *The Framing of India's Constitution*, p. 273.
104. *CAD*, vol. 7, p. 902.
105. *CAD*, vol. 7, p. 918.
106. Sumption, *Trials of the State*.
107. Austin, *The Indian Constitution*, pp. 102–13.
108. Ibid., p. 275.
109. Ibid., p. 277.
110. Ibid., p. 275.
111. Ibid., p. 282.
112. *CAD*, vol. 9, p. 1455.
113. *CAD*, vol. 9, p. 1463.

114. Mohani, *Kulliya-i Hasrat Mohani*, p. 228.
115. *CAD*, vol. 9, p. 1456.
116. *Gazette of India: Extraordinary*, 26 November 1949.
117. *Muslim Personal Law*, p. 133.
118. *CAD*, vol. 7, p. 551.
119. Austin, *The Indian Constitution*, p. 80.
120. *CAD*, vol. 7, p. 544.
121. Kugle, 'Framed, Blamed, and Renamed'.
122. Stephens, *Governing Islam*, p. 14.
123. *Peau noire, masques blancs*, p. 8.
124. Som, 'Jawaharlal Nehru and the Hindu Code Bill'.
125. Saxena, 'Commissions, Committees, and Custodians', p. 426.
126. Mullally, 'Feminism and Multicultural Dilemmas in India'.

3.   EMINENT NEHRUVIANS

 1.   Laponce, *The Protection of Minorities*.
 2.   Tendulkar, *Mahatma*, vol. 8, p. 124.
 3.   Brecher, *Nehru*, p. 315.
 4.   Jaffrelot, *The Hindu Nationalist Movement*, p. 160n5.
 5.   Mahmud to S. K. Sinha, *c.* 1948 in Datta and Cleghorn (eds), *Selected Correspondence*, p. 264.
 6.   Mahmud to Desai, 4 December 1964 in ibid., p. 294.
 7.   *Muslim India*, January 1984, p. 5; *Bihar Times*, 15 October 2008.
 8.   Interview with Syed Mahmud, Acc. No. 231, NMML Oral History Project, p. 2.
 9.   Nehru to Mahmud, 16 February 1947 and 30 August 1950, NMML, Syed Mahmud Papers, Correspondence, Subject File 121.
10.   Datta and Cleghorn (eds), *Selected Correspondence*, p. 43.
11.   Emphasis added. Mahmud to Nehru, 13 November 1924 in ibid., p. 51.
12.   *SWJN*, vol. 2, p. 224.
13.   Nehru to Mahmud, 16 November 1953, NMML, Syed Mahmud Papers, Correspondence, Subject File 121.
14.   Nehru to Mahmud, 13 May 1957, ibid.
15.   Nehru to Mahmud, 16 April 1957, ibid.
16.   Indira Gandhi to Mahmud, 17 January 1961 and 20 March 1963, NMML, Syed Mahmud Papers, Correspondence, Subject File 49.
17.   Ansari, Health and Jails Minister to Chagla, 28 October 1965, NMML, Chagla Papers, Subject File 80.
18.   *Link*, 16 January 1966, p. 20.
19.   *Link*, 3 September 1960, p. 17.
20.   Maulana Haque, President of the All-India Muslim Mutaheda Mahaz to Shastri, 2 September 1965, NMML, Chagla Papers, Subject File 80.

21. Abdullah to Mahmud, 31 October 1958, NMML, Syed Mahmud Papers, Correspondence, Subject File 1.

22. *Muslim India*, January 1984, p. 5.

23. Kabir to Patel, 9 September 1950 in ibid., p. 175.

24. Kabir to Roy, 9 April 1956, NMML, Kabir Papers, Correspondence.

25. Kabir to Nehru, 21 August 1962, NMML, Kabir Papers, Subject File 16.

26. Kabir to Nehru, 24 February and 15 March 1958 and 12 December 1959, NMML, Kabir Papers, Subject File 1.

27. Datta, *Humayun Kabir*, p. 23.

28. In the United States, segregation in schools was declared unconstitutional in 1954; busing began in 1971. At the time Kabir made this note, the Soviet Union still had a rather tolerant policy when it came to the education of minorities. Later the same year under Khrushchev's direction, Russification picked up steam.

29. Kabir to Nehru, 1958–63, NMML, Kabir Papers, Subject File 6, *passim*.

30. 'A note on the minorities problem', 30 January 1958, NMML, Kabir Papers, Subject File 4.

31. *TOI*, 22 July 1967, p. 12.

32. *The Proper Study of Mankind*, pp. 191–242.

33. Kabir to Nehru, 29 April 1958, NMML, Kabir Papers, Correspondence.

34. Indira Gandhi to Urs, 28 August 1974, NMML, Miscellaneous Items, Acc. No. 1315.

35. My translation from the Hindi. Indira Gandhi to Anwar Ahmad, 20 January 1981, ibid.

36. Kabir to Nehru, 4 December 1958, NMML, Kabir Papers, Subject File 1.

37. *Link*, 28 September 1959, p. 14.

38. *Link*, 16 July 1961, pp. 17–20.

39. Datta, *Humayun Kabir*, p. 23.

40. Ibid., p. 70; *TOI*, *inter alia*, 19 August 1969, p. 8; 20 August, pp. 8, 10; 21 August, p. 10.

41. Wright Jr, 'The Effectiveness of Muslim Representation', p. 130.

42. *Link*, 1 May 1960, p. 21.

43. Datta, *Humayun Kabir*, pp. 38, 62.

44. *TOI*, 24 November 1967, p. 1.

45. *TOI*, 1 February 1969, p. 13.

46. *TOI*, 3 February 1969, p. 8.

47. Johnson, 'The Relation between Land Settlement and Party Politics', p. 250.

48. Saadulla to Khan, 25 March and 18 May 1945, NMML, Saadulla Papers, Subject File 7.

49. Saadulla to Jinnah, 16 April 1947, NMML, Saadulla Papers, Subject File 13.

50. 'Proceedings of the Assam League', 30 May 1948, ibid.

51. Saadulla to Siddhinath Sarma, Assam PCC President, 30 September 1951, NMML, Saadulla Papers, Subject File 19.

52. Sarma to Saadulla, 6 October 1951, ibid.

53. Medhi, Assam Chief Minister to Saadulla, 10 October 1951, ibid.

54. Saadulla to Nehru, 15 October 1951, ibid.

55. *SWJN*, vol. 16, p. 43.

56. Ibid., p. 50.

57. *Assam Tribune*, 3 November 1951, p. 1.

58. *TOI*, 29 November 1951, p. 5.

59. Abbasi to Govind Ballabh Pant, 16 April 1957, NAI, MHAP, File 2/122/57-S&NG.

60. Ashraf Ali Khan and S. Adityendra, Uttar Pradesh MLA and Rajasthan MP, to the MHA, no date and 27 December 1955, NAI, MHAP, File 2/116/57-S&NG.

61. *TOI*, 13 September 1959 in Siegel, *Hungry Nation*, p. 142.

62. See the *Links* of 7 September 1959, p. 9; 14 September, p. 12; 28 October 1959, p. 28; 23 November 1959, p. 7; 6 August 1960, p. 6.

63. *Link*, 6 August 1960, p. 6.

64. *Link*, 1 December 1963, p. 41.

65. Edgerton, *The Rise and Fall of the British Nation*, p. 459.

66. Sherman, 'Education in early postcolonial India'.

67. *Link*, 26 January 1965, p. 15.

68. *TOI*, 12 February 1937, p. 4.

4.   LOYAL OPPOSITION

1. *Legacy of a Divided Nation*, p. 217.

2. Hasan, 'Introduction' in Lelyveld, *Aligarh's First Generation*, p. xxix.

3. Wright Jr, 'The Muslim League in South India', p. 587.

4. I draw, in part, on Theodore P. Wright Jr's typology. See ibid.

5. Marcuse, *Counterrevolution and Revolt*, p. 55.

6. Interview with Mohamed Raza Khan, Acc. No. 405, NMML Oral History Project, p. 35.

7. Khan, *What Price Freedom?*, p. 425.

8. Wright Jr, 'The Muslim League', p. 592.

9. Raza Khan, *What Price Freedom?*, p. 501.

10. Fortnightly Report for Kerala, 18 February 1957, NAI, MHAP, File 4/1/57-Poll II.

11. *Muslim India*, July 1988, pp. 293–4.

12. *Link*, 25 September 1960, pp. 13–5.

13. *Link*, 13 November 1961, p. 14.

14. Interview with Mohamed Raza Khan, p. 39.

15. Ibid., pp. 47, 62.

16. Fortnightly Report for Kerala, 23 May 1957, NAI, MHAP, File 4/1/57-Poll II.

17. Fortnightly Report for UP, 7 February and 12 August 1957, ibid.

18. Barnett, *The Politics of Cultural Nationalism in South India*, p. 92.

19. Nossiter, *Communism in Kerala*, p. 252.
20. Interview with Mohamed Raza Khan, p. 41.
21. Wright Jr, 'The Muslim League', pp. 590–1.
22. 'Fortnightly Report for Kerala, 10 October 1957, NAI, MHAP, File 4/1/57-Poll II.
23. Namboodiripad to Pant, 18 July 1957, NAI, MHAP, File 26/3/57-Poll II(R); X. Cherian, Convenor of the Christian Education Action Committee to Pant, 18 August 1957, ibid.
24. Kerala Education Bill, ibid.
25. Lieten, 'Education, Ideology and Politics in Kerala'.
26. *Link*, 12 June 1966, p. 14.
27. Wright Jr, 'The Muslim League', p. 593.
28. In 1964, the CPI split. The CPI ('the Communists'), which cleaved to the Centre, was its successor; and the CPI (Marxist), variously 'the Marxists' or the CPM, more on the Left, the breakaway.
29. *Link*, 12 June 1966, p. 14.
30. *Secularist*, vol. 7, no. 1 (July–September 1970), p. 23.
31. *Link*, 13 November 1961, p. 14.
32. For an instance of entryism *sui generis*, see the role of Militant in Labour: Crick, *The March of Militant*.
33. Alexander, *International Trotskyism*, p. 27.
34. Wright Jr, 'The Muslim League', p. 579.
35. Mohamed, 'Muslim Politics in Kerala', p. 147.
36. *TOI*, 4 March 1952, p. 1; *TOI*, 7 December 1952, p. 9.
37. *TOI*, 19 September 1955, p. 3.
38. *TOI*, 3 December 1950, p. 15.
39. Wright Jr, 'The Muslim League', p. 592.
40. *TOI*, 1 April 1967, p. 1.
41. *TOI*, 12 October 1969, p. 3.
42. *TOI*, 9 October 1969, p. 6.
43. *TOI*, 10 July 1967, p. 8.
44. *TOI*, 10 November 1966, p. 10.
45. *India Today*, 23 February 1998.
46. *Times*, 22 July 2008.
47. Interview with Mohamed Raza Khan, pp. 47, 62.
48. *Link*, 6 May 1962, p. 20.
49. Ibid.
50. Interview with Mohamed Raza Khan, p. 39.
51. *SWJN*, vol. 19, p. 551.
52. Wright Jr, 'The Muslim League', p. 583.
53. *Link*, 31 January 1960, p. 12.
54. *Link*, 13 March 1960, p. 17.
55. *Link*, 21 February 1960, p. 10.
56. *Link*, 28 February 1960, p. 20.

57. *Link*, 6 March 1960, p. 15.

58. *Congress Marches Ahead*, vol. 9, p. 101.

59. *TOI*, 30 November, p. 8.

60. Wright Jr, 'The Muslim League', pp. 579–99.

61. Fortnightly Report for Kerala, 23 May 1957, NAI, MHAP, File 4/1/57-Poll II.

62. Wright Jr, 'The Muslim League', pp. 579–99.

63. *Statistical Report on General Elections, 1967*, p. 182.

64. Tocqueville, *Democracy in America*, p. 215.

65. *The First Five-Year Plan*, p. 150; *The Second Five-Year Plan*, p. 73.

66. Wright Jr, 'The Muslim League', p. 599.

67. Fortnightly Report for Kerala, 5 March 1957, NAI, MHAP, File 4/1/57-Poll II.

68. Kochanek, *The Congress Party of India*, p. 343; Nayar, *India*, p. 243.

69. Agwani, 'God's Government', p. 266.

70. Muhsin Ali to the SMU Secretary, 7 September 1962, NAI, Saadulla Papers, Subject File 22.

71. Anderson, 'Voluntary Associations in Hyderabad', p. 177.

72. Faridi to Giri, 29 June 1973 in Khan, 'Role of Muslim Majlis', p. 119.

73. Sampurnanand, *Memories and Reflections*, p. 89 in Hasan, *Quest for Power*, p. 181.

74. *Kripalani Committee Report* in Brass, *Language, Religion, and Politics*, p. 205.

75. Hasan, *Quest for Power*, pp. 176–87.

76. *TOI*, 19 December 1956, p. 11.

77. *TOI*, 24 December 1956, p. 5.

78. *TOI*, 19 December 1956, p. 11.

79. *TOI*, 25 December 1956, p. 9.

80. Mahmud, 23 December 1956 in *Selected Correspondence*, p. 325.

81. *TOI*, 25 December 1956, p. 9.

82. *TOI*, 24 December 1956, p. 5.

83. A. M. Allapichai, MCSI to Ismail, 12 June 1956, NMML, Mirza Ismail Papers, Correspondence.

84. *Searchlight,* 18 March 1958.

85. Ismail to A. Hayles, editor of the Madras *Mail*, 11 March 1954, NMML, Mirza Ismail Papers, Correspondence.

86. *Leader,* 1 October 1954.

87. Gundappa, 'Sir Mirza M. Ismail', p. 27.

88. Ismail to the MCSI Joint Secretary, 14 December 1956, NMML, Mirza Ismail Papers, Correspondence.

89. Ismail, *My Public Life* in Woods to Mirza, 11 November 1955, ibid.

90. Smith, *India as a Secular State*, p. 420.

91. *Link*, 21 May 1961, p. 14.

92. *Link*, 18 June 1961, p. 24.

93. Kothari, 'The Congress System', p. 1163.

94. Anil, 'The Myth of Congress Socialism'.
95. Wright Jr, 'Revival of the Majlis', p. 237.
96. Ibid., p. 238.
97. Ibid.
98. Ibid., p. 242.
99. *TOI*, 26 September 1966, p. 5.
100. *TOI*, 27 April 1964, p. 6.

5. PRESSURE POLITICS

1. Ashraf, *The Muslim Elite*, p. 43.
2. Note prepared by the MHA, NAI, MHAP, File 18/6/63-F.VI.
3. J. D. Khanna, Home Secretary to R. P. Sharma, Under-Secretary, 1 July 1963, ibid.
4. Note prepared by Sharma, 12 June 1956, NAI, MHAP, File 1/19/56-F.IV.
5. Chief Commissioner of Tripura to the Home Minister, 7 April 1956, ibid.
6. Intelligence Bureau summary of the Jabbar Khan Commission, 19 August 1963, NAI, MHAP, File 1/44/63-F.III.
7. Annexures II and III, Rajya Sabha Starred Question 638, 27 August 1962, NAI, MHAP, 17/51/62-F.III.
8. Note prepared by R. P. Sharma, Under-Secretary, 19 June 1958, NAI, MHAP, File 20/30/58-F.III.
9. Letter sent to Assam's Minister of Labour and Planning, 27 June 1963, NAI, MHAP, File 1/4/63-F.III.
10. Biren Dutta, CPI MP to Nehru, 13 June 1962, NAI, MHAP, File 20/73/62-F.III.
11. Mohammad Mian, JUH General Secretary to Nehru, 16 January 1963, NAI, MHAP, File 1/4/63-F.III.
12. Compare the contrasting remarks in Kidwai to Vishwanathan, 26 September 1962, ibid. and *Statesman*, 5 August 1962, p. 1.
13. Bimalaprosad Chaliha, Assam Chief Minister to Nehru, 14 December 1962, ibid.
14. Nehru to the Commonwealth Secretary, 12 September 1962, NAI, MHAP, File 20/78/62-F.III.
15. Note prepared by S. Kochar, Under-Secretary, MEA, 15 May 1963, ibid.
16. *Pakistan Times* (Lahore), 19 May 1963.
17. *Dawn* (Karachi), 30 October 1962.
18. S. Rahman, Nazira-Juktali Congress Secretary to President, 12 June 1962, NAI, MHAP, 1/20/62-F.III.
19. *Assam Tribune*, 5 August 1962.
20. *Organiser,* 27 August 1962.
21. *Nagpur Times,* 21 August 1962.
22. *Hindustan Standard*, 26 June 1962, p. 1.
23. *Radiance,* 27 October 1968, p. 5.

24. *Radiance,* 3 November 1968, p. 11.

25. K. K. Mohiadeen, Islamic Society of India to Home Minister, 22 October 1980, NAI, MHAP, File 68/6/80-HPP.

26. Brass, *Language, Religion, and Politics*, p. 18.

27. Ibid., pp. 190–2.

28. *Radiance,* 8 January 1967 in ibid., p. 188.

29. See his interview with Brass in ibid., p. 198.

30. Note by the Language Department, 23 March 1959, UPSA, Legislature Department, Box 419, File 153/1959.

31. Press communiqué on 'the language question', 20 January 1959, ibid.

32. Brass, *Language, Religion, and Politics*, p. 212.

33. *Vidhan Sabha Debates,* 1 April 1959 in UPSA, Legislature Department, Box 419, File 153/1959.

34. Kabir to Nehru, 8 July 1963, NMML, Kabir Papers, Subject File 16. *Hadith* are anecdotes culled from the life of the Prophet.

35. Brass, *Language, Religion, and Politics*, p. 220.

36. 'Proceedings of the Minority Committee Meeting', 9 September 1957, NMML, Kabir Papers, Subject File 4.

37. Deshmukh to Kabir, 10 February 1958, ibid.

38. Kabir to D. P. Karmarkar, Morarji Desai, G. B. Pant, Swaran Singh. All February 1958, ibid.

39. 'A note on the minorities problem', 4 August 1958, ibid.

40. 'A further note on minorities', 30 January 1958, ibid.

41. Erdman, 'India's Swatantra Party', p. 409.

42. Fortnightly Report for Uttar Pradesh, 13 April 1957, NAI, MHAP, File 4/15/57-Poll II.

43. Brass, *Theft of an Idol*.

44. Berenschot, *Riot Politics*.

45. Tambiah, *Levelling Crowds*.

46. Engineer (ed.), *Communal Riots*.

47. Varshney, *Ethnic Conflict and Civic Life*, p. 46.

48. Brass, *The Production of Hindu-Muslim Violence*, p. 414n44.

49. Varshney, 'Modi the moderate', *Indian Express,* 27 March 2014: 'Modi's campaign has departed, wholly or very substantially, from Hindu nationalist tenets … Governance and development have been the overarching ideas'. Brass takes Varshney to task for his flawed datasets; inappropriate unit of analysis—towns—and hence premise; 'primordialist perspectives'; inability to distinguish between remote and proximate causes; exculpation of Hindu nationalists; and, finally, his 'extraordinary faith in causal explanation … It is truly regrettable that such retrograde work is being brought forth at this stage in our knowledge of Indian politics and society': *The Production of Hindu-MuslimViolence*, p. 414.

50. Wilkinson, *Votes and Violence*, p. 6.

51. Breman, *The Labouring Poor in India*.

52. Jaffrelot, *Religion, Caste, and Politics in India*, p. 368.
53. *Link*, 30 May 1965, p. 11.
54. The Jhas, *Ayodhya*, p. 28.
55. *Link*, 30 May 1965, p. 11.
56. *Link*, 3 May 1959, p. 19.
57. Graff, 'Hindu-Muslim Communal Riots in India'.
58. *Hitavada*, 4 April 1961 in Jaffrelot, *The Hindu Nationalist Movement*, p. 165.
59. *NYT*, 3 April 1964, p. 2.
60. Graff, 'Hindu-Muslim Communal Riots'.
61. Chatterji, *The Spoils of Partition*, pp. 112, 167.
62. Khan, 'The Significance of the Dargah', p. 177.
63. Kanjwal, 'Building a New Kashmir', p. 181.
64. *Times*, 6 January 1964, p. 9.
65. Kanjwal, 'Building a New Kashmir'.
66. Puri, *Kashmir*, p. 46.
67. Zachariah, *Nehru*, p. 256.
68. *Link*, 26 July 1964, p. 18.
69. *Times*, 28 February 1965, p. 10.
70. *Link*, 8 March 1964, p. 12.
71. Kanjwal, 'Building a New Kashmir', p. 231.
72. *Times*, 3 and 4 February 1964, both p. 8.
73. *Link*, 19 April 1964, p. 21.
74. *Link*, 21 June 1964, p. 17.
75. *Times*, 24 October 1965, p. 9.
76. *Times*, 20 January 1964, p. 8.
77. *NYT*, 22 March 1964, p. 1.
78. 'Instructions issued to state governments', 11 January–29 March 1964, NAI, MHAP, File 19/26/64-Poll IA.
79. *TOI*, 26 March 1964, p. 7.
80. *Keesing's Contemporary Archives*, 10 July 1964, pp. 20185–7.
81. *TOI*, 25 April 1964, p. 10; Huda, 'Communal Riots and Jamshedpur', p. 19.
82. *TOI*, 17 April 1964, p. 10.
83. *TOI*, 30 March 1964, p. 7.
84. *TOI*, 20 March 1964, p. 1.
85. Huda, 'Communal Riots and Jamshedpur', p. 19.
86. *TOI*, 18 April 1964, p. 6.
87. *TOI*, 8 May 1964, p. 11.
88. A. B. Shah, Indian Secular Society Director to Deputy Secretary, 28 December 1972, NAI, MHAP, File KWF.6/2/72-R&P.
89. *Ananda Bazar Patrika*, 31 January 1964.
90. Khan, 'Majlis-e-Mushāwarat', p. 49.
91. *Link*, 23 August 1964, p. 9.
92. *Radiance,* 5 April 1964, p. 2.
93. Khan, 'Majlis-e-Mushāwarat', p. 80.

94. *Link*, 23 August 1964, p. 9.

95. Khan, 'Majlis-e-Mushāwarat', p. 63.

96. *Radiance,* 31 July 1966, p. 2.

97. *Secular Democracy*, May 1968, p. 5.

98. Quraishi, 'Electoral Strategy', p. 978.

99. Myrdal, *An International Economy*, p. 211.

100. *Muslim India*, June 1984, p. 245.

101. Khan, *The Stalwarts*, p. 42.

102. Abdullah, 'Abba Jan Maulana Muhammad Muslim'.

103. Khan, *The Stalwarts*, p. 19.

104. Khan, 'Majlis-e-Mushāwarat', p. 99.

105. Ibid., p. 159.

106. Ibid., p. 76.

107. Ibid., p. 134.

108. Wright Jr, 'Muslim Education in India at the Crossroads', p. 61.

109. *Radiance*, 20 September 1964, p. 1.

110. 'Resolution No. 11' in Noorani (ed.), *The Muslims of India*, p. 136.

111. Ibid.

112. *Radiance* of 31 July 1966, pp. 1, 15.

113. Khan, 'Majlis-e-Mushāwarat', p. 103.

114. Shastri to Mahmud, 30 June 1965, NMML, Syed Mahmud Papers, Correspondence, Subject File 143.

115. Mahmud to Shastri, 2 July 1965, ibid.

116. Khan, 'Role of Muslim Majlis', p. 46.

117. Khan, 'Majlis-e-Mushāwarat', pp. 99–188.

118. Quraishi, 'Emergence and Eclipse', p. 1233.

119. Ibid.

120. Faridi, *Presidential Address*, p. 2.

121. *Secular Democracy*, June 1968, p. 4.

122. Khan, 'Role of Muslim Majlis', p. 55.

123. Sayeed, 'Role of Muslim Majlis', pp. 310–29.

124. *Statistical Report on the 1971 General Election.*

125. Faridi to Giri, 29 June 1973 in Khan, 'Role of Muslim Majlis', p. 114.

126. Sayeed, 'Role of Muslim Majlis', p. 328.

127. Khan, 'Role of Muslim Majlis', p. 56.

128. Ibid., p. 84.

129. Khan, 'Majlis-e-Mushāwarat', p. 147.

130. Wright Jr, 'Muslims and the 1977 Indian Elections', p. 1214.

131. Weiner, 'Congress Restored', p. 341.

132. Sayeed, 'Role of Muslim Majlis', p. 316.

6.   ALMOST LIBERAL

1.   *Lok Sabha Debates,* vol. 4, no. 28 (11 September 1953), col. 1872.

2. *Lok Sabha Debates,* vol. 3, no. 39 (6 June 1962), cols 9219–20.

3. *Lok Sabha Debates,* vol. 4, no. 28 (11 September 1953), cols 1872–4; vol. 11, no. 3 (16 March 1972), col. 12; vol. 12, no. 4 (15 February 1968), col. 1177. My translations from the Hindi.

4. Dua, 'The Prime Minister and the Federal System', p. 28.

5. Cordier, 'Challenges of Social Upliftment'.

6. Sikand, 'An Islamist Approach to Inter-Faith Dialogue'.

7. Ahmad, 'Cracks in the 'Mightiest Fortress'.

8. Idem, *Islamism and Democracy in India.*

9. Islam, *Limits of Islamism.*

10. Iqtidar, *Secularising Islamists?*

11. Agwani, 'God's Government', p. 265.

12. Looking for *Radiance*'s sixties' and seventies' numbers, I discovered that the NMML holds an incomplete set on microfilm; these, however, remained unavailable on account of digitisation. In the event, I found the bulk of them uncatalogued at the *Radiance* offices in Okhla. I thank Saumya Saxena for pointing me to it, and the affable staff at the paper for allowing me to rummage through the back issues at leisure.

13. *Legacy of a Divided Nation*, p. 155.

14. Ahmad, *Islamism and Democracy in India*, p. 1.

15. Agwani, *Islamic Fundamentalism in India*, p. 71.

16. Hartung, *A System of Life*, p. 233.

17. Ahmad, *Islamism and Democracy in India*, p. 8.

18. Islam, *Limits of Islamism*, pp. 68, 82.

19. Mitchell, *The Society of the Muslim Brothers.*

20. Curtis, 'Malaysia and Indonesia', p. 20.

21. Nasr, *The Vanguard of the Islamic Revolution.*

22. *Introducing the Jama'at*, pp. 3–8.

23. Nasr, *The Vanguard of the Islamic Revolution*, p. 114.

24. Ibid., pp. 3–46, 103–15; Hartung, *A System of Life*, pp. 122–92.

25. Nasr, *Mawdudi and the Making of Islamic Revivalism*, pp. 34–7.

26. Nasr, *The Vanguard of the Islamic Revolution*, pp. 131–46.

27. Maududi, *Islamic Law and Constitution*, p. 31.

28. Maududi, *Political Theory of Islam*, p. 45.

29. Maududi, *The Process of Islamic Revolution*, p. 21.

30. Maududi, *Nationalism and India*, p. 40.

31. Ibid., p. 15.

32. Ibid., p. 14.

33. Nasr, *Mawdudi and the Making of Islamic Revivalism*, p. 74. Of course, the kind of agrarian capitalism that Maududi defended as Islamic—property rights; ownership; rents; tenure—only appeared in England in about the thirteenth century, more than half a millennium after the coming of Islam, and thousands of miles away from the Islamic heartlands at that: Wood, *The Origin of Capitalism.*

34. Nasr, *Mawdudi and the Making of Islamic Revivalism*, p. 71.

35. Maududi, *Political Theory of Islam*, p. 31.

36. The threat to Islamic order did not stem from capitalistic accumulation but 'working-class dictatorship', the upshot of 'class war': Maududi in Devji, *Muslim Zion*, p. 238. His call for separate electorates and the separation of the sexes, too, stemmed from this allergy to conflict.

37. Curiously, the rabidly anti-communist Maududi's 'theodemocracy'—one of his neologisms—evokes a Leninist parallel: the withering away of the state. The paradox, of course, is that in acting in God's name, Maududi's mandarins become gods by proxy. The risks of such an operation became amply clear when Maududi's men set about killing Ahmadis in His name in fifties Pakistan. There's no escape from conflict. Ibid.

38. Maududi in Nasr, *Mawdudi and the Making of Islamic Revivalism*, p. 71.

39. Maududi in Ahmad, *Islamism and Democracy in India*, p. 79.

40. Maududi in Nasr, *Mawdudi and the Making of Islamic Revivalism*, p. 31.

41. Maududi in Hartung, *A System of Life*, p. 98.

42. 'Statement showing space allotted to communal matters', no date [1972], NAI, MHAP, File KWF.6/2/72-R&P.

43. *Radiance*, 15 September 1963, p. 1.

44. *Radiance*, 6 July 1969, p. 3.

45. *Radiance*, 24 November 1963, p. 4.

46. *Radiance*, 26 April 1970, p. 16.

47. 'Statement showing space allotted to communal matters'.

48. *Radiance*, 5 April 1964, p. 4.

49. *Radiance*, 13 February 1966, p. 12.

50. *Introducing the Jama'at*, p. 10.

51. Ibid., p. 11.

52. Ibid., p. 21.

53. Fortnightly Report for Uttar Pradesh, 18 November 1957, NAI, MHAP, File 4/15/57-Poll II.

54. Fortnightly Report for Bihar, 12 March 1957, NAI, MHAP, File 4/10/57-Poll II.

55. Agwani, 'God's Government', p. 266 ff.

56. *Radiance*, 8 December 1963, p. 1.

57. *Report on Currency and Finance*, p. 108.

58. *Radiance*, 8 December 1963, p. 1.

59. *Radiance*, 15 December 1963, p. 3.

60. Sherman, 'A New Type of Revolution'.

61. *Radiance*, 1 December 1963, p. 1.

62. *Radiance*, 24 November 1963, p. 2.

63. *Radiance*, 11 October 1964, p. 6.

64. *Radiance*, 22 September 1963, p. 8.

65. Hasan, *Legacy of a Divided Nation*, p. 208.

66. *Radiance*, 26 July 1964, p. 5.

67. *Radiance,* 26 April 1964, p. 2.

68. *Radiance,* 5 April 1964, p. 5.

69. Ahmad, *Islamism and Democracy in India*, p. 208.

70. Munir, *From Jinnah to Zia*, p. 65.

71. *Introducing the Jama'at*, p. 17.

72. *Radiance*, 3 May 1964, p. 3.

73. Fortnightly Report for Uttar Pradesh, 1 November 1957, NAI, MHAP, File 4/15/57-Poll II.

74. Fortnightly Report for Bihar, 12 April 1957, NAI, MHAP, File 4/10/57-Poll II.

75. Sikand, 'Emergence and Development', p. 723.

76. *Radiance*, 10 May 1964, p. 13.

77. *Radiance*, 15 December 1963, p. 2.

78. *Radiance*, 10 November 1963, p. 12.

79. *Introducing the Jama'at*, p. 22.

80. Wright Jr, 'Inadvertent Modernization', p. 86.

81. *Radiance*, 6 September 1964, p. 2.

82. *Radiance*, 4 August 1963, p. 6.

83. *Radiance*, 17 August 1969, p. 27.

84. *Radiance*, 22 December 1963, p. 2.

85. Nadwi, *Presidential Address*, p. 26.

86. *Radiance*, 26 July 1964, p. 11.

87. Ahmad, *Islamism and Democracy in India*, pp. 76–89.

88. *Radiance,* 11 August 1963, p. 3.

89. Wright, Jr, 'Muslim Education in India'.

90. *Radiance*, 27 June 1965, p. 3.

91. *Radiance*, 15 September 1963, p. 1.

92. *Radiance*, 17 August 1969, p. 27.

93. *Radiance*, 18 January 1970, p. 3.

94. 'Theodemocracy, in practical terms, is really a theocracy': Jackson, *Mawlana Mawdudi*, p. 142.

95. Fortnightly Report for Uttar Pradesh, 26 December 1957, NAI, MHAP, File 4/15/57-Poll II.

96. *Introducing the Jama'at*, p. 12.

97. Closer to home, Iqbal had penned a poem with the same title in 1936, translated as 'What Should Then Be Done, O People of the East'.

98. Ahmad, *Islamism and Democracy in India*, pp. 196–9, 203.

99. Ibid., p. 204. It is unclear why Nadwi did not exercise his veto.

100. Limaye, *Janata Party Experiment,* vol. 1, p. 133; *Lok Sabha Debates,* vol. 4, no. 28 (13 July 1977), col. 186.

101. *Shah Commission of Inquiry*, pp. 28–30.

102. Dayal and Bose, *For Reasons of State*, p. 45.

103. Ahmad, *Islamism and Democracy in India*, p. 204.

104. Agwani, *Islamic Fundamentalism in India*, p. 67.

105. Fortnightly Report for Uttar Pradesh, 12 August 1957, NAI, MHAP, File 4/15/57-Poll II.

106. *Link*, 17 March 1960, p. 15.

107. *Radiance,* 22 March 1964, p. 5.

108. *Radiance,* 15 September 1963, p. 16.

109. *Radiance*, 25 July 1965, p. 1.

110. *Radiance,* 28 November 1965, p. 5.

111. *Radiance*, 22 November 1964, p. 1.

112. *TOI*, 10 November 1974, p. 4.

113. *TOI*, 16 May 1977, p. 5.

114. *Organiser*, 12 September 1977, p. 6; *Radiance*, 11 September 1977, p. 10.

115. Roy, *The Failure of Political Islam*, p. 21.

116. 'Religion is more trouble than it is worth'; 'the displacement of religion from the centre of human life' will continue unabated: Bruce, *Secularization*, p. 223. True, 'churches are now separate from political structures', vindicating *secularism*, but crucially not *secularisation*, by contrast a self-defeating enterprise with little popular purchase; 'I cannot see the demand for religion just disappearing like that': Taylor, *A Secular Age*, p. 435.

117. His own words were less blunt: Dalwai, *Muslim Politics in India*, p. 102.

118. *Radiance*, 14 September 1969, p. 2.

119. *Radiance*, 21 September 1969, p. 2.

120. *Secularist*, vols 3–4, no. 1 (December 1969), p. 41.

121. *Introducing the Jama'at*, p. iii.

122. Ibid., p. 24.

123. Ibid., p. 25.

124. Nadwi, *Presidential Address at the All-India Conference*, p. 23.

125. *Link*, 13 March 1960, p. 17.

126. Fortnightly Report for Uttar Pradesh, 24 July 1957, NAI, MHAP, File 4/15/57-Poll II.

127. Fortnightly Report for Bihar, 30 May 1957, NAI, MHAP, File 4/10/57-Poll II; Fortnightly Report for Uttar Pradesh, 7 February 1957, NAI, MHAP, File 4/15/57-Poll II.

128. Shaikh, 'Muslims and Political Representation'.

129. Robinson, 'Strategies of Authority'.

130. 'Secularism and its Discontents'.

131. 'What Is Secularism For?'

132. 'The Crisis of Secularism in India', p. 424.

133. 'Secularism in its Place' and 'The Politics of Secularism and the Recovery of Religious Tolerance'.

134. 'Secularism and Tolerance'.

135. *Radiance*, 18 December 1966, p. 1.

136. *Selected Writings*, p. 391.

137. *Il filo e le tracce*, p. 254.

7.   CLASS ACTS

1.   *TOI*, 3 February 1975, p. 1.
2.   'Jama Masjid Riot', p. 343.
3.   *TOI*, 4 and 5 February 1975, both p. 1.
4.   Ahmed, *Muslim Political Discourse in Postcolonial India*, p. 151.
5.   Lewis, *The Political Language of Islam*.
6.   Kozlowski, *Muslim Endowments*, p. 78.
7.   Khan, '*Waqfs* in UP', p. 46.
8.   *Eidgahs*: structures for the commemoration of Eid. *Imambaras*: buildings where the Shia commemorate the killing of Husain, the Prophet's grandson, who in the month of Muharram in 680 CE made a failed stab at deposing Yazid, his nemesis, at Karbala.
9.   Jones, 'The local experiences of reformist Islam'.
10. Beverley, 'Property, Authority, and Personal Law'.
11. Scott, *Seeing Like a State*.
12. *Wakf Administration in India*, p. xii.
13. Ibid., pp. 136, 141, 145, 155–6.
14. *Muslim Wakfs Bill, 1952: Report of the Select Committee*.
15. *Lok Sabha Debates*, vol. 1, no. 6 (12 March 1954), col. 2022.
16. Note by the Deputy Secretary, 10 January 1953, UPSA, Legislature Department, Box 209, File 337/52.
17. Notes on the meeting, 27 August 1951, UPSA, Judicial Department, Box 225, File 2565A.
18. Notes on the meeting, 28 August 1951, ibid.
19. Notes on the meeting, 29 August 1951, ibid.
20. Notes on the meeting, 30 August 1951, ibid.
21. Abbas to Nehru, 19 April 1953, ibid; Abbas' note, 19 December 1952, UPSA, PW Department (A), Box 24, File 19waqfs/1952.
22. Syed Ejaz Husain Jarchavy, UPSC General Secretary to all MLAs, 24 December 1952, ibid.
23. Abbas to Nehru, 19 April 1953, ibid.
24. Note by the Deputy Secretary, 4 November 1952, ibid.
25. Note by the Deputy Secretary, 14 May 1953, ibid.
26. Rashid, *Wakf Administration*, p. 42.
27. Ibid., pp. 78–87.
28. Ibid., pp. 100–110.
29. *In Pursuit of Lakshmi*, p. 62.
30. Kozlowski, *Muslim Endowments*, p. 29.
31. Pandit, 'The Husainabad Trust', p. 1713.
32. Additional Director to the Secretary, 21 March 1955, UPSA, Education Department, Box 267, File 405.
33. Hasan to the District Inspector of Schools, 5 July 1951, ibid.; Nawab of Rampur to the Secretary, 18 April 1953, ibid.; Khan to the Joint Secretary, 12 September 1951, ibid.

34. Singh to M. C. Pant, Under Secretary, 10 June 1955, ibid.

35. Deputy Director of Education to the Manager, Shia College, 9 July 1956, ibid.

36. Nawab of Rampur to Hargovind Singh, Education Minister 18 April 1953, ibid.

37. Syed Abdul Hasan, Honorary Secretary to the Secretary, 16 November 1957, ibid.

38. Note by the Shiksha Sanchalak, 10 June 1960, ibid.

39. Note by the Under Secretary, 13 August 1952, UPSA, Education Department, Box 9, File 622(9).

40. Extracts from the Finance (S) Department, 17 February 1959, ibid.

41. Custodian to the Deputy Custodians, 19 July 1949, UPSA, R and R Department, Box 1, File 501/49(A).

42. Raghunath Prasad Varma, Custodian to District Magistrates, 26 July 1949, ibid.

43. H. D. Pradhan, Under Secretary to Varma, 6 June 1950, ibid.

44. De, 'Evacuee Property', p. 91.

45. Schechtman, 'Evacuee Property'.

46. *TOI*, 11 February 1955, p. 5.

47. *Lok Sabha Debates,* vol. 3, no. 39 (6 June 1962), col. 9129.

48. De, 'Evacuee Property', p. 96.

49. Ibid., p. 100; *TOI*, 6 October 1951, p. 7.

50. Rashid, *Wakf Administration*, p. 144.

51. Nehru to Mir Mushtaq Ahmed, 9 December 1953, NMML, Mir Mushtaq Ahmed Papers, Correspondence.

52. *TOI*, 22 July 1959, p. 8.

53. Rashid, *Wakf Administration*, p. 144.

54. *The Telegraph,* 2 August 2011.

55. *Muslim India*, January 1987, p. 28.

56. 'Transfer of certain *waqf* properties', 14 July 1981, NAI, MHAP, File U-13016/7/81-Delhi Desk I.

57. Note prepared by A. V. Venkatasubban, Deputy Secretary, 6 May 1959, NAI, MHAP, File 47/1/59-Delhi.

58. A. D. Pandit, Chief Commissioner to D. D. Gothi, Under-Secretary, no date, NAI, MHAP, File 16/25/58-Delhi.

59. Note prepared by the Chief Secretary, 28 August 1959, ibid.

60. Note prepared by Gajinder Singh, Under-Secretary, 12 June 1959, NAI, MHAP, File 47/1/59-Delhi.

61. Note prepared by Political I Section, 9 June 1959, ibid.

62. JUH Delhi Secretary to the Delhi Chief Commissioner, 18 April 1959, ibid.

63. *National Herald*, 29 May 1981, p. 6.

64. See his letter in *Muslim India*, February 1988, p. 78.

65. The *pugree* was a lump sum paid to secure a permanent lease. Essentially an instrument designed to enable landlords to get around the Raj's rent

controls—the one-off payment was over and above the monthly rent—it also made the position of tenants less precarious by forestalling eviction.

66. Rashid, *Wakf Administration*, pp. 151, xii.
67. *Muslim India*, February 1989, p. 67.
68. Ibid., pp. 86, viii, 162.
69. 'How to Constitute Better Wakf Boards', 2 December 1980, NAI, MHAP, File 75/1/80-HPP.
70. A. M. Khusro to Khan, 25 September 1980, NAI, MHAP, File 72/1/80-HPP.
71. 'AMU Report of the Working Group II', ibid.
72. *Report of the High-Power Panel on Minorities*, vol. 1, pp. viii, 6, 28.
73. Omar Khalidi, *Muslims in [sic] Indian Economy*, p. 43.
74. *The Social, Economic, and Educational Status of the Muslim Community of India*, pp. 230, 219.
75. *Business Standard*, 28 June 2013.
76. *The Social, Economic, and Educational Status*, p. 231.
77. *Hindu*, 9 September 2014.
78. *Rajya Sabha Debates*, 13 March 2018, p. 480.
79. See the press release (http://nawadco.org.in/page.php?id=37); *Times*, 14 January 1937, p. 6.
80. *Islamic Voice*, August 2015, pp. 1–13.
81. *TOI*, 7 June 2018; *Live Mint*, 10 November 2008; *TOI*, 20 April 1970, p. 1.
82. *Economic Times*, 29 June 2017.
83. See the *TOIs* of 22 May 1998, p. 9 and 7 September 2007, p. 4.
84. Copland, *The Princes of India*, p. 31.
85. Ibid., pp. 55, 11.
86. Ibid., pp. 229–68; Ramusack, *The Indian Princes and Their States*, pp. 245–74.
87. Interview with J. N. Chaudhuri, Acc. No. 426, NMML Oral History Project, p. 30.
88. Note by Vishwanathan, Secretary, no date, NMML, MHAP, File 1/3/64-Poll III; *Link*, 5 December 1965, p. 15.
89. Andhra Pradesh Government to MHA, 29 October 1966, NMML, MHAP, File 1/8/65-Poll III.
90. Note by the Department of Economic Affairs, 30 March 1966, NMML, MHAP, File 1/1/65-Poll III.
91. Note by Vishwanathan, Secretary, no date, NMML, MHAP, File 1/3/64-Poll III.
92. H. C. Heda to Gulzarilal Nanda, Home Minister, 22 April 1964, ibid.
93. *Ahmadunnisa Begum v. Mir Barkat Ali Khan Mukarram*, 29 January 1968, NMML, MHAP, File 1/3/68-Poll III.
94. Note by Vishwanathan, Secretary, no date, NMML, MHAP, File 1/3/64-Poll III.
95. My calculations, based on File 1/9/65-Poll III; *The Times*, 3 October 2019.

96. Note by the Ministry of Finance, HLL Division, 8 January 1960, NMML, MHAP, File 49/1/57-Poll III.

97. Deputy Secretary of the MHA to the Chief Secretary of West Bengal, 8 February 1960, ibid.

98. Note by Vishwanathan, 11 March 1960, NMML, MHAP, 5/1/60-Poll III. Emphasis added.

99. Notes by the MHA, Political III Section, 3 and 24 July 1961, NMML, MHAP, File 11/9/61-Poll III.

100. K. N. V. Nambisan to the chief secretary of the Uttar Pradesh government, 19 August 1961, ibid.

101. Khan to Rao Bahadur, Secretary, States Department, 9 March 1948, NMML, Nawab of Malerkotla Papers, Subject File 1; Khan to V. K. Krishna Menon, 15 March 1948, ibid.

102. Khan to Maharaja Sahib Bahadur of Patiala, 24 March 1948, NMML, Nawab of Malerkotla Papers, Subject File 1; '1941 Census Figures', no date, ibid.

103. Altaf Ali Khan to the general, no date, NMML, Nawab of Malerkotla Papers, Subject File 1.

104. Khan to Bahadur, 20 November 1948, ibid.

105. Khan to Maharaja Sahib Bahadur, 24 October 1948, NMML, ibid.

106. Khan to Nehru, 13 October 1955, NMML, Nawab of Malerkotla Papers, Subject File 3; Khan to Shastri, 17 August 1965, ibid.; Khan to Bahadur, 2 May 1967, NMML, Nawab of Malerkotla Papers, Subject File 5.

107. Khan to Gandhi, 4 May 1967, NMML, Nawab of Malerkotla Papers, Subject File 6.

108. Note by Viswanathan, MHA, 28 August 1957, NMML, MHAP, File 55/5/57-Poll III.

109. Nehru to the Home Minister, 26 September 1957, ibid.

110. Note by the MHA, 30 April 1958, ibid.

111. Note by the MHA, 11 October 1957, ibid.

112. *SWJN*, vol. 33, p. 76.

113. Begum to Nehru, 24 October 1956 and 2 January 1957, NMML, MHAP, File 54/6/57-Poll III.

114. 'Statement showing the present position in respect of pensions of certain political pensioners', 1951, NMML, MHAP, File 54/12/57-Poll III.

115. Note by the MHA, 2 December 1959, NMML, MHAP, File 48/18/59-Poll III.

116. Haque to Nehru, 30 August 1957, NMML, MHAP, File 54/18/57-Poll III; Nehru to Pant, 29 September 1957, ibid.

117. 'Maintenance allowance to the widow of Qazi Abu Ahmad', 24 February 1959, NMML, MHAP, File 54/21/58-Poll III.

118. Frankel, *India's Political Economy*, p. 493.

119. Note by the West Bengal government, 18 December 1957, NMML, MHAP, File 55/8/57-Poll III; Mirza to the Deputy Secretary, Home (Passport Department), 4 December 1957 in ibid.

120. Note by the MHA, 16 February 1964, NMML, MHAP, File 34/1/64-Poll III; Deputy Secretary, UP to the MHA, 24 January 1964 in ibid.
121. Under-Secretary, Ministry of Law to the MHA, 15 May 1957, NMML, MHAP, File 45/4/57-Poll III.
122. Note by M. A. Michael, Under-Secretary, 25 July 1957, NMML, MHAP, 49/2/57-Poll III.
123. UP Government to the MHA, 5 August 1957, NMML, MHAP, ibid.
124. Hardy, *The Muslims of British India*; Robinson, *Separatism among Indian Muslims*.
125. Graff, 'Aligarh's Long Quest'; Wright, Jr, 'Muslim Education in India'.
126. Hasan, 'Aligarh Muslim University', p. 56.
127. Lelyveld, *Aligarh's First Generation*.
128. Ibid., pp. 143, 122, 92.
129. Ibid., pp. 114–25.
130. Jaffrelot, *The Pakistan Paradox*, p. 30.
131. Bayly, *Rulers, Townsmen, and Bazaars*, pp. 346–68.
132. Robinson, *Separatism among Indian Muslims*, p. 110.
133. 'The AMU: An Analysis of the Statutory Provisions', 3 November 1973, MHAP, NMML, File 5/5/73-R&P.
134. Wright, Jr, 'Muslim Education', p. 52.
135. *M. Tajuddin Qurashi v. Union of India*, 15 November 1966, NMML, Gauba Papers, Subject File 2.
136. Zaidi to Kabir, no date, NMML, Kabir Papers, Subject File 4; Hasan, 'Aligarh Muslim University', p. 56.
137. Mahmud to Mrs Gandhi, 11 August 1968, NMML, Prime Minister's Secretariat Papers, File 84(72)/68-69—PMF; Mrs Gandhi to Naim, 26 August 1968, ibid.
138. Interview with B. F. H. B. Tyabji, Acc. No. 312, NMML Oral History Project, pp. 93–8.
139. Reports filed by an anonymous 'Aligarian' in *Blitz*, 17, 24, and 31 July 1965.
140. Gautier, 'Crisis of the Nehruvian Consensus', p. 4.
141. Mahmud to Shastri, 21 May 1965, NMML, Mahmud Papers, Correspondence, Subject File 143.
142. Biyabani to Chagla, 6 August 1965, NMML, Chagla Papers, Subject File 80.
143. *Link*, 5 December 1965, pp. 9–11.
144. *Link*, 24 August 1959, p. 29; *Link*, 28 November 1965, p. 9.
145. Ray, 'Secularism and Political Protest', p. 625.
146. Press release by S. L. Dar, BHU Registrar, 19 November 1965, NMML, Chagla Papers, Subject File 79.
147. Chagla to Brijnarain, 20 February 1965, NMML, Chagla Papers, Subject File 79.
148. Chagla, *Roses in December*, p. 18.
149. Chagla, *Convocation Address*, p. 4.
150. Chagla, 'Urdu in *nagari*', p. 14.

151. Chagla, *Roses in December*, p. 475; *Radiance* in *Illustrated Weekly of India*, 18 November 1973, p. 20; *Organiser,* 24 November 1973, p. 10.
152. Chagla to Nanda, 3 May 1965, NMML, Chagla Papers, Subject File 80.
153. Chagla to Mahmud, 20 May 1965, ibid; Kabir to Chagla, 15 July 1965, ibid.
154. 'Autonomy of the Campus Should Be Preserved', 9 August 1966, NMML, Gauba Papers, Subject File 2.
155. *TOI*, 7 September 1965, p. 8.
156. *Statesman*, 18 July 1965.
157. Wright, Jr, 'Muslim Education', p. 52.
158. Graff, 'Aligarh's Long Quest', p. 1773.
159. Chagla to Madani, 23 May 1965, NMML, Chagla Papers, Subject File 80.
160. 'Round Up of Urdu Press Comments on AMU', 29 June 1965, NMML, Chagla Papers, Subject File 81.
161. Nawab Ali Yavar Jung to Chagla, 14 June 1965, NMML, Chagla Papers, Subject File 80.
162. Wright, Jr, 'Muslim Education', p. 56.
163. 'Round Up of Urdu Press Comments on AMU'.
164. *Statesman*, 25 June 1965.
165. *Patriot*, 9 August 1965.
166. *Patriot*, 11 August 1965.
167. Seerat Vice President to Nanda, 27 August 1966, NMML, Chagla Papers, Subject File 80; Mahaz President to Chagla, 31 August 1965, ibid.; *Link*, 4 July 1965, p. 12.
168. Intelligence Bureau to Chagla, 16 June 1965, NMML, Chagla Papers, Subject File 80.
169. *Hindustan Times*, 24 July 1965.
170. Aligarh Collector's note, 16 June 1966, NMML, Chagla Papers, Subject File 80; *Patriot*, 2 August 1965.
171. Chagla, *Roses in December*, p. 379.
172. Graff, 'Aligarh's Long Quest', p. 1773.
173. *Report of the Committee on Governance of Universities and Colleges*, p. 10; *Link*, 28 November 1965, p. 43.
174. *TOI*, 24 July 1972, p. 5.
175. 'An Analysis of the Statutory Provisions', 3 November 1973, NAI, MHAP, File 5/5/73-R&P.
176. 'CPI's proposals', no date, ibid.
177. Shah, 'Storm over a Non-Issue', p. 57.
178. Aligarh Study Centre pamphlet, 14 June 1972 in Graff, 'Aligarh's Long Quest', p. 1773.
179. *Quest*, May-June 1973, pp. 35–44.
180. Graff, 'Aligarh's Long Quest'.
181. Ibid., pp. 1778–81.
182. *Hindustan Times*, 30 March 1973.
183. Brass, *The Production of Hindu-Muslim Violence*, p. 62.

184. *TOI*, 30 October 1961, p. 1.

185. *TOI*, 15 August 1958, pp. 17, 28.

186. Galonnier, 'Aligarh', p. 139.

187. Hasan, 'Aligarh Muslim University', p. 49.

188. Galonnier, 'Aligarh', p. 148.

189. *TOI*, 22 November 1978, p. 1.

190. Mann, *Boundaries and Identities*, p. 11.

191. Banfield, *The Moral Basis of a Backward Society*, p. 10.

192. Brass, *The Production of Hindu-Muslim Violence*, p. 55.

193. Mann, *Boundaries and Identities*, p. 148.

194. Galonnier, 'Aligarh', p. 140.

195. *TOI*, 21 December 1979, p. 9.

196. Jaffrelot, *India's Silent Revolution*, p. 108.

197. Brass, *The Production of Hindu-Muslim Violence*.

198. Note on Gopal Krishna's CSDS report, 15 March 1978, NMML, MHAP, File 6/4/72-R&P Vol. II.

CONCLUSION

1.   Khilnani, *The Idea of India*, p. 26.

2.   Mann, *The Dark Side of Democracy*.

3.   Subrahmanyam, 'Before the Leviathan'.

4.   Gaborieau, 'From Al-Beruni to Jinnah'.

5.   Bayly, 'The Pre-History of Communalism?'

6.   Hardy, *The Muslims of British India*.

7.   Khan, *The Great Partition*.

8.   Bardhan, *The Political Economy of Development*.

9.   Myrdal, *Asian Drama*.

10. Vanaik, *The Furies of Indian Communalism*.

11. Cooper and Brubaker, 'Identity'.

12. Galonnier, 'Aligarh', p. 154.

13. Lelyveld, *Aligarh's First Generation*, pp. 35–101.

14. Jones, *Shi'a Islam in Colonial India*; Metcalf, *Islamic Revival in British India*.

15. *The Political Language of Islam*, p. 29.

16. This case has been made most persuasively by Wael Hallaq. For a *précis*, see Menski, *Comparative Law in a Global Context*, pp. 339–44.

17. Lewis, *The Political Language of Islam*, pp. 18, 91.

18. Kugle, 'Framed, Blamed, and Renamed', p. 264.

19. Stephens, *Governing Islam*.

20. Jaffrelot, *Dr Ambedkar and Untouchability*.

21. Idem, *India's Silent Revolution*.

22. Brass, *An Indian Political Life*.

23. Hasan, *Politics of Inclusion*.

24. Gatrell, *The Unsettling of Europe*, p. 157.

25. Hasan, *Legacy of a Divided Nation*, pp. 282–9.
26. Madni (ed.), *Syed Shahabuddin*.
27. Mullally, 'Feminism and Multicultural Dilemmas in India'.
28. Hasan, *Legacy of a Divided Nation*, p. 264.
29. Van der Veer, *Religious Nationalism*, pp. 184–90.
30. Noorani, 'Babri Masjid Ramjanmabhoomi Question', p. 115.
31. Hasan, *Legacy of a Divided Nation*, p. 316.
32. Jaffrelot, *Modi's India*, p. 106.
33. Ibid., p. 420.
34. Ibid., p. 438.
35. Williams et al., 'Working at the Margins'.
36. The Osellas, *Social Mobility in Kerala*.
37. Jones, 'Where Only Women May Judge'.
38. Perlangeli and Jaishankar, 'Assessing the Islamic State threat to India'.

BIBLIOGRAPHY

Official Records

National Archives of India, New Delhi
Ministry of Home Affairs Papers
Prime Minister's Secretariat Papers

Uttar Pradesh State Archives, Lucknow
Education Department
Police Department
Legislature Department

Bihar State Archives, Patna
Political Department

Bodleian Library, Oxford
Lok Sabha Debates
Rajya Sabha Debates

Private Papers

Nehru Memorial Museum and Library, New Delhi
Gopal Singh Papers
H. K. Sherwani Papers
Humayun Kabir Papers
K. L. Gauba Papers
M. C. Chagla Papers
Mir Mushtaq Ahmed Papers
Mirza M. Ismail Papers
Syed Mahmud Papers
Syed Mohammad Saadulla Papers

BIBLIOGRAPHY

Oral Histories

Oral History Transcripts, Nehru Memorial Museum and Library, New Delhi
B. F. H. B. Tyabji
J. N. Chaudhuri
Maulana Abdul Latif Farookhi
Mohamed Raza Khan
Syed Mahmud
Zohra Ansari

Newspapers and Journals

Al-Jamiat
Ananda Bazar Patrika
Assam Tribune
Bihar Times
Blitz
Business Standard
Comrade
Dawat
Dawn
Economic Times
Hindu
Hindustan Standard
Hindustan Times
Hitavada
Illustrated Weekly of India
India Today
Indian Express
Islamic Voice
Keesing's Contemporary Archives
Leader
Link
Live Mint
Muslim India
Nagpur Times
National Herald
New Age Weekly
New York Times
Nida-e-Millat
Organiser
Pakistan Times
Patriot
Quest

Radiance
Searchlight
Secular Democracy
Secularist
Siasat
Statesman
Telegraph
Times
Times of India
Zindagi

Official Publications and Other Primary Sources

A Bunch of Old Letters: Written Mostly to Jawaharlal Nehru and Some Written by Him. Bombay: Asia, 1958.

Ahmad, Jamil-ud-Din, ed. *Historic Documents of the Muslim Freedom Movement.* Lahore: Publishers United, 1970.

Ahmad, Jamiluddin, ed. *Some Recent Speeches and Writings of Mr Jinnah.* Lahore: Muhammad Ashraf, 1942.

All-India Congress Committee, *Congress Marches Ahead*, vols 1–12. Delhi: AICC, 1969–74.

Ambedkar, B. R. *Writings and Speeches.* Bombay: Ambedkar Foundation, 2014.

Chagla, M. C. *Convocation Address.* Hyderabad: Osmania University Press, 1965.

Constituent Assembly Debates.

Constitutional Proposals of the Sapru Committee. Bombay: Padma, 1945.

Das, Durga, ed. *Sardar Patel's Correspondence, 1945–1950*, vol. 6. Ahmedabad; Navajivan, 1973.

Datta, V. N. and Cleghorn, B. E., eds. *A Nationalist Muslim and Indian Politics: Being the Selected Correspondence of the Late Dr Syed Mahmud.* Delhi: Macmillan, 1974.

Draft Constitution of the Indian Union Muslim League. Madras: Hindustan Times Press, 1948.

Election Commission of India, *Statistical Reports on General and State Elections.* Delhi: ECI, 1951–2019.

Faridi, A. J. *Presidential Address, at the First Annual Conference of the Muslim Majlis.* Delhi: Muslim Majlis, 28 February 1970.

First Five-Year Plan. Delhi: Planning Commission, 1952.

Gandhi, Mohandas. *Collected Works of Mahatma Gandhi.* Delhi: Publications Division, 1958–84.

Gopal, S., ed. *Selected Works of Jawaharlal Nehru,* 2nd series. Delhi: Jawaharlal Nehru Memorial Fund, 1984–.

Hasan, Mushirul and Pernau, Margrit, eds. *Regionalizing Pan-Islamism: Documents on the Khilafat Movement.* Delhi: Manohar, 2005.

Hasan, Mushirul, ed. *Muslims and the Congress: Select Correspondence of Dr M.A.Ansari, 1912–1935.* Delhi: Manohar, 1979.

Historic Trial of the Ali Brothers & Others: Part II. Proceedings in the Sessions Court. Karachi: New Times Press, 1921.

Introducing the Jama'at-i-Islami Hind. Rampur: JI Publications Bureau, 1960.

Kumar, Ravindra, ed. *Selected Works of Maulana Abul Kalam Azad.* Delhi: Atlantic, 1991.

Lok Sabha Debates.

Mansergh, N. et al., eds. *Constitutional Relations Between Britain and India: The Transfer of Power, 1942–47,* vols 1–12. London: HMSO, 1970–83.

Munshi, Kanaiyalal Maneklal. *Indian Constitutional Documents: Munshi Papers,* vols 1 and 2. Bombay: Bharatiya Vidya Bhavan, 1967.

Muslim Wakfs Bill, 1952: Report of the Select Committee. Delhi: Parliament Secretariat, 1954.

Nadwi, Maulana Abul Lais Islahi. *Presidential Address at the All-India Conference.* Delhi: Markazi Maktaba-i-Islami, 1960.

Nadwi, Sayyid Abul Hasan Ali. *Inaugural Address at the First Conference of the Mushāwarat.* September 1967.

Noorani, A. G., ed. *The Muslims of India: A Documentary Record.* Delhi: OUP, 2003.

Rajya Sabha Debates.

Rao, Shiva B. *The Framing of India's Constitution.* Delhi: Indian Institute of Public Administration, 1967.

Rao, Shiva, ed. *The Framing of India's Constitution: Select Documents.* Delhi: Indian Institute of Public Administration, 1967.

Report of the Committee Appointed by the [All-Parties'] Conference To Determine the Principles of the Constitution for India. Allahabad: AICC, 1928.

Report of the Committee on Governance of Universities and Colleges. Delhi: University Grants Commission, 1971.

Report of the High-Power Panel on Minorities, Scheduled Castes and Tribes, and Weaker Sections, vols 1 and 2. Delhi: Government of India, 1983.

Report of the Inquiry Committee Appointed by the Council of the All-India Muslim League to Inquire into Muslim Grievances in Congress Provinces [sc. *Pirpur Report*]. Delhi: AIML, 1938.

Report of the Review Committee on Education. Delhi: University Grants Commission, 1966.

Reserve Bank of India, *Report on Currency and Finance.* Bombay: RBI, 1962.

Second Five-Year Plan. Delhi: Planning Commission, 1957.

Shah Commission of Inquiry: Third and Final Report. Delhi: Government of India Press, 6 August 1978.

The Indian Constitution. In *Gazette of India: Extraordinary,* 26 November 1949.

Uttar Pradesh Vidhan Sabha Debates.

Zaidi, A. Moin, ed. *Congress and the Minorities: Preserving National Cohesion: A Study of Congress Policy Towards Minorities During the Last 100 Years.* Delhi: Publication Department, Indian Institute of Applied Political Research, 1984.

Zaidi, A. Moin, ed. *Evolution of Muslim Political Thought in India,* vols 1 and 2. Delhi: Michiko & Panjathan, 1959–75.

Published Secondary Sources

Abbas, Khwaja Ahmad. *I Am Not an Island: An Experiment in Autobiography.* Delhi: Vikas, 1977.

Abbott, Freeland K. 'Maulana Maududi on Quranic Interpretation'. *Muslim World*, vol. 48, no. 1, January 1958.

———. 'The Jama'at-i-Islami of Pakistan'. *Middle East Journal*, vol. 11, no. 1, Winter 1957.

Abdullah, Aslam. 'Abba Jan Maulana Muhammad Muslim: Personal Reflections'. *Two Circles*, 23 May 2021.

Abdullah, Sheikh. *Kashmir, India, and Pakistan.* Srinagar: New Kashmir Press, 1965.

Acharya, Ashok. 'Constitutionalizing rights, negotiating difference: The Indian experiment'. In Nanda, Bijayalaxmi and Ray, Nupur. *Discourse on Rights in India: Debates and Dilemmas.* London: Routledge, 2019.

Adams, Charles J. 'The Ideology of Mawlana Mawdudi'. In Smith, Donald E. ed. *South Asian Politics and Religion.* Princeton, NJ: Princeton University Press, 1966.

Adcock, C. S. *The Limits of Tolerance: Indian Secularism and the Politics of Religious Freedom.* Oxford: OUP, 2014.

Afzal, M. Rafique. *A History of the All-India Muslim League, 1906–1947.* Karachi: OUP, 2013.

Agwani, M. S. 'God's Government: Jama'at-i-Islami of India' in Mutalib, Hussin and Hashmi, Taj ul-Islam, eds. *Islam, Muslims, and the Modern State: Case-Studies of Muslims in Thirteen Countries.* London: Macmillan, 1994.

———. *Islamic Fundamentalism in India.* Chandigarh: Twenty-First Century India Society, 1986.

Ahmad, Aijaz. 'Azad's Careers: Roads Taken and Not Taken'. In Ahmad, Aijaz. *Lineages of the Present: Ideology and Politics in Contemporary South Asia.* London: Verso, 2000.

Ahmad, Imtiaz and Reifeld, Helmut, eds. *Lived Islam in South Asia: Adaption, Accommodation, and Conflict.* Delhi: Social Science Press, 2004.

Ahmad, Imtiaz. *Ritual and Religion among Muslims in India.* Delhi: Manohar, 1981.

Ahmad, Irfan. 'Cracks in the 'Mightiest Fortress': Jamaat-e-Islami's Changing Discourse on Women in Pakistan'. *Modern Asian Studies*, vol. 42, nos 2/3, 2008.

———. *Islamism and Democracy in India: The Transformation of Jamaat-e-Islami.* Princeton, N.J.: Princeton University Press, 2009.

———. *Religion as Critique: Islamic Critical Thinking from Mecca to the Marketplace.* Chapel Hill: University of North Carolina Press, 2017.

Ahmad, Mumtaz. 'Islamic Fundamentalism in South Asia: The Jamaat-i-Islami and the Tablighi Jamaat'. In Marty, Martin E. and Appleby, R. Scott, eds. *Fundamentalisms Observed.* Chicago: University of Chicago Press, 1991.

Ahmed, Akbar S. *Jinnah, Pakistan, and Islamic Identity: The Search for Saladin.* London: Routledge, 1997.

Ahmed, Hilal and Kaviraj, Sudipta. 'Indian Democracy and the World's Largest Muslim Minority'. In Stepan, Alfred, ed. *Democratic Transition in the Muslim World*. New York: Columbia University Press, 2018.

Ahmed, Hilal. *Muslim Political Discourse in Postcolonial India: Monuments, Memory, Contestation*. Delhi: Routledge, 2014.

————. *Siyasi Muslims: A Story of Political Islams in India*. Delhi: Penguin, 2019.

Ahmed, Mir Mushtaq. *National Unity and Solidarity*. Delhi: Unity Book House, no date.

Akbar, M. J. *India: The Siege Within*. Delhi: Penguin, 1985.

Alexander, Robert Jackson. *International Trotskyism, 1929–1985: A Documented Analysis of the Movement*. Durham, NC: Duke University Press, 1991.

Ali, Muhammad. *My Life: A Fragment*. Lahore: Muhammad Ashraf, 1942.

Ali, Sayyid Anwar. *Islam, Musalman, aur Hindustan*. Delhi: Markazi Maktaba-i-Islami, 1979.

Ambedkar, B. R. *Annihilation of Caste*. London: Verso, 2014 [1936].

Anderson, Benedict. *Imagined Communities: Reflections on the Origin and Spread of Nationalism*. London: Verso, 2006.

Anderson, Perry. 'A Culture in Contraflow—Part I'. *New Left Review*, no. 180, March-April 1990.

————. *The Indian Ideology*. London: Verso, 2013.

Anderson, Robert T. 'Voluntary Associations in Hyderabad'. *Anthropological Quarterly*, vol. 37, no. 4, 1964.

Anil, Pratinav. 'The Myth of Congress Socialism'. *Himal*, 30 March 2021.

Ashraf, Ali. *The Muslim Elite*. Delhi: Atlantic, 1982.

Austin, Granville. *The Indian Constitution: Cornerstone of a Nation*. Delhi: OUP, 1999 [1966].

————. *Working a Democratic Constitution: The Indian Experience*. Delhi: OUP, 1999.

Azad, Abul Kalam. *India Wins Freedom: The Complete Version*. Delhi: Orient Longman, 1988.

Azizi, Alauddin. *The Saga of a Freedom Fighter*. Delhi: Book Enclave, 2004.

Baig, M. R. A. 'Review of Moin Shakir's *Muslims in Free India*'. In *Quest*, vol. 79, no. 1, November-December 1972.

Bajpai, Rochana. *Debating Difference: Group Rights and Liberal Democracy in India*. Delhi: OUP, 2011.

Balachandran, G. *The Reserve Bank of India, 1951–1967*. Delhi: OUP, 1998.

Banfield, Edward. *The Moral Basis of a Backward Society*. New York: Free Press, 1958.

Bardhan, Pranab. *The Political Economy of Development in India*. New York: Basil Blackwell, 1984.

Barnett, Marguerite Ross. *The Politics of Cultural Nationalism in South India*. Princeton, NJ: Princeton University Press, 1976.

Baruah, Sanjib. 'The Partition's long shadow: the ambiguities of citizenship in Assam'. *Citizenship Studies*, vol. 13, no. 6, 2009.

————. *In the Name of the Nation: India and its Northeast*. Stanford, CA: Stanford University Press, 2020.

Bayly, C. A. 'The Ends of Liberalism and the Political Thought of Nehru's India'. *Modern Intellectual History*, vol. 12, no. 3, 2015.

———. 'The Pre-History of 'Communalism'? Religious Conflict in India, 1700–1860'. *Modern Asian Studies*, vol. 19, no. 2, 1985.

———. *Rulers, Townsmen, and Bazaars: North Indian Society in the Age of British Expansion, 1770–1870*. Cambridge: CUP, 1983.

Benjamin, Walter. *Selected Writings: Volume IV, 1938–1940*. Cambridge, MA: Belknap, 2003.

Berenschot, Ward. *Riot Politics: Hindu-Muslim Violence and the Indian State*. London: Hurst, 2011.

Berlin, Isaiah. 'Two Concepts of Liberty'. In *The Proper Study of Mankind*. London: Chatto & Windus, 1997.

Beverley, Eric Lewis. 'Property, Authority, and Personal Law: Waqf in Colonial South Asia'. *South Asia Research*, vol. 31, no. 2, 2011.

Bhargava, Rajeev. 'On the Persistent Political Under-Representation of Muslims in India'. *Law and Ethics of Human Rights*, vol. 1, no. 1, 2007.

———. 'What is Secularism For?' In Bhargava, Rajeev, ed. *Secularism and its Critics*. Oxford: OUP, 1998.

Bhatia, Udit, ed. *The Indian Constituent Assembly: Deliberations on Democracy*. Abingdon: Routledge, 2018.

Bhatnagar, S. K. *History of the MAO College, Aligarh*. Bombay: Asia Publishing, 1969.

Bilinsky, Yaroslav. 'The Soviet Education Laws of 1958–9 and Soviet Nationality'. *Soviet Studies*, vol. 14, no. 2, October 1962.

Binder, Leonard. *Religion and Politics in Pakistan*. Berkeley, CA: University of California Press, 1963.

Brass, Paul R. *An Indian Political Life*, 3 vols. Delhi: Sage, 2011–14.

———. *Language, Religion, and Politics in North India*. Cambridge: CUP, 1974.

———. *The Politics of India since Independence*. Cambridge: CUP, 1994.

———. *The Production of Hindu-Muslim Violence in Contemporary India*. Seattle, WA: University of Washington Press, 2003.

———. *Theft of an Idol*. Princeton, NJ: Princeton University Press, 1997.

———, ed. *Riots and Pogroms*. London: Palgrave Macmillan, 1996.

———. 'The partition of India and retributive genocide in the Punjab, 1946–47: Means, methods, and purposes'. *Journal of Genocide Research*, vol. 5, no. 1, 2003.

———. *The Production of Hindu-Muslim Violence in Contemporary India*. Seattle, WA: University of Washington Press, 2003.

Brecher, Michael. *Nehru: A Political Biography*. Oxford: OUP, 1959.

Breman, Jan. *The Labouring Poor in India: Patterns of Exploitation, Subordination, and Exclusion*. Oxford: OUP, 2003.

Brown, Judith. *Gandhi's Rise to Power: Indian Politics, 1915–1922*. Cambridge: CUP, 1974.

Bruce, Steve. *Secularization: In Defence of an Unfashionable Theory*. Oxford: OUP, 2011.

Cannadine, David. *Ornamentalism: How the British Saw their Empire*. Oxford: OUP, 2001.

Chagla, M. C. 'Urdu in *nagari*'. In Bhave, Vinoba. *Nagari: The Common Link Script*. Delhi: Gandhi Book House, 1973.

————. *Roses in December*. Bombay: Bharatiya Vidya Bhavan, 1975.

Chatterjee, Partha. 'Secularism and Tolerance'. In Bhargava, Rajeev, ed. *Secularism and its Critics*. Oxford: OUP, 1998.

Chatterji, Joya. *The Spoils of Partition: Bengal and India, 1947–1967*. Cambridge: CUP, 2007.

Chaube, Shibanikinkar. *Constituent Assembly of India: Springboard of Revolution*. Delhi: People's Publishing House, 1973.

Chiriyankandath, James. "Creating a secular state in a religious country': The debate in the Indian constituent assembly'. *Commonwealth & Comparative Politics*, vol. 38, no. 2, 2000.

Chopra, P. N. *Maulana Abul Kalam Azad: Unfulfilled Dreams*. Delhi: Interprint, 1990.

Cooper, Frederick and Brubaker, Rogers. 'Identity'. In Cooper, Frederick. *Colonialism in Question: Theory, Knowledge, History*. Berkeley: University of California Press, 2005.

Copland, Ian. *The Princes of India in the Endgame of Empire, 1917–1947*. Cambridge: CUP, 1997.

Corbridge, Stuart and Harriss, John. *Reinventing India: Liberalisation, Hindu Nationalism, and Popular Democracy*. Cambridge: Polity, 2000.

Crick, Michael. *The March of Militant*. London: Faber and Faber, 1984.

Curtis, Robert. 'Malaysia and Indonesia'. *New Left Review*, no. 28, May-June 1965.

D'Mello, Bernard and Navlakha, Gautam. 'Maoist Insurgency and the State's Counterinsurgency in India: An Anti-Communist Historical Perspective'. In Christian Gerlach and Clemens Six, eds. *The Palgrave Handbook of Anti-Communist Persecutions*. London: Palgrave MacMillan, 2020.

Dalwai, Hamid. *Muslim Politics in India*. Bombay: Nachiketa Publications, 1969.

Datta, Dipankar. *Humayun Kabir: A Political Biography*. London: Asia Publishing House, 1969.

Dayal, John and Bose, Ajoy. *For Reasons of State: Delhi under Emergency*. Delhi: Ess Ess, 1977.

De Cordier, Bruno. 'Challenges of Social Upliftment and Definition of Identity: A Field Analysis of the Social Service Network of Jamaat-e-Islami Hind, Meerut, India'. *Journal of Muslim Minority Affairs*, vol. 30, no. 4, December 2010.

De, Rohit. 'Evacuee Property and the Management of Economic Life in Postcolonial India'. In Prakash, Gyan, Laffan, Michael, and Menon, Nikhil, eds. *The Postcolonial Moment in South and Southeast Asia*. London: Bloomsbury, 2018.

————. 'Mumtaz Bibi's Broken Heart: The Many Lives of the Dissolution of Muslim Marriages Act'. *Indian Economic and Social History Review*, vol. 46, no. 1, 2009.

Devji, Faisal. *Muslim Zion: Pakistan as a Political Idea*. Cambridge, MA: Harvard University Press, 2013.

————. *The Impossible Indian: Gandhi and the Temptation of Violence*. London: Hurst, 2012.

Dhulipala, Venkat. *Creating a New Medina: State Power, Islam, and the Quest for Pakistan in Late Colonial North India*. Cambridge: CUP, 2014.

Douglas, Ian Henderson. *Abul Kalam Azad: An Intellectual and Religious Biography*. Delhi: OUP, 1988.

Dua, B. D. 'The Prime Minister and the Federal System'. In Manor, James, ed. *Nehru to the Nineties: The Changing Office of Prime Minister in India*. London: Hurst, 1994.

Dutt, R. Palme. *India Today*. London: Victor Gollancz, 1940.

Eaton, Richard M. *India in the Persianate Age: 1000–1765*. London: Allen Lane, 2019.

Edgerton, David. *The Rise and Fall of the British Nation: A Twentieth Century History*. London: Allen Lane, 2018.

Edib, Halidé. *Inside India*. London: George Allen & Unwin, 1937.

Emirbayer, Mustafa, and Mische, Ann. 'What Is Agency?' *American Journal of Sociology*, vol. 103, no. 4, January 1998.

Engineer, Asghar Ali, ed. *Communal Riots in Post-independence India*. Delhi: Sangam, 1997.

————. *Islam, Muslims, India*. Bombay: Lok Vangmaya, 1975.

Erdman, Howard L. 'India's Swatantra Party'. *Pacific Affairs*, vol. 36, no. 4, Winter 1963–1964.

————. *The Swatantra Party and Indian Conservatism*. Cambridge: CUP, 1967.

Fanon, Frantz. *Peau noire, masques blancs*. Paris: Éditions du Seuil, 1952.

Faruqi, Shamsur Rahman. 'A Long History of Urdu Literary Culture, Part 1: Naming and Placing a Literary Culture'. In Sheldon Pollock, ed. *Literary Cultures in History: Reconstructions from South Asia*. Berkeley, CA: University of California Press, 2003.

Finkel, Caroline. *Osman's Dream: The History of the Ottoman Empire*. London: John Murray, 2005.

Frankel, Francine. *India's Political Economy: The Gradual Revolution, 1947–2004*. Delhi: OUP, 2005.

Gaborieau, Marc. 'From Al-Beruni to Jinnah: Idiom, Ritual and Ideology of the Hindu-Muslim Confrontation in South Asia'. *Anthropology Today*, vol. 1, no. 3, June 1985.

Galanter, Marc. 'Secularism, East and West'. *Comparative Studies in Society and History*, vol. 7, no. 2, January 1965.

————. *Competing Equalities: Law and the Backward Classes in India*. Delhi: OUP, 1984.

Galonnier, Juliette. 'Aligarh: Sir Syed Nagar and Shah Jamal, Contrasted Tales of a Muslim City'. In Gayer, Laurent and Jaffrelot, Christophe, eds. *Muslims in Indian Cities: Trajectories of Marginalisation*. London: Hurst, 2011.

Gauhar, G. N. *Hazratbal: The Central Stage of Kashmiri Politics.* Delhi: Virgo, 1998.

Gautier, Laurence. 'Crisis of the "Nehruvian Consensus" or Pluralization of Indian Politics? Aligarh Muslim University and the Demand for Minority Status'. *South Asia Multidisciplinary Academic Journal*, 2019.

Ghosh, Partha S. *The Politics of Personal Law in South Asia: Identity, Nationalism and the Uniform Civil Code.* Delhi: Routledge, 2007.

Ghosh, S. K. *Muslim Politics in India.* Delhi: Ashish Publishing, 1987.

Giddens, Anthony. *The Constitution of Society: Outline of the Theory of Structuration.* Cambridge: Polity, 1984.

Gilmartin, David. *Empire and Islam: Punjab and the Making of Pakistan.* London: Tauris, 1988.

Ginzburg, Carlo. *Il filo e le tracce: Vero falso finto.* Milano: Feltrinelli, 2006.

Golwalkar, M. S. *Bunch of Thoughts.* Bangalore: Vikrama Prakashan, 1968 [1966].

Gopal, Sarvepalli. *Jawaharlal Nehru: A Biography,* vol. 2. Cambridge, MA: Harvard University Press, 1979.

—————. *Jawaharlal Nehru: A Biography,* vol. 3. Cambridge, MA: Harvard University Press, 1984.

Gould, William. *Bureaucracy, Community and Influence in India: Society and the State, 1930s–1960s.* Abingdon: Routledge, 2011.

—————. *Hindu Nationalism and the Language of Politics in Late Colonial India.* Cambridge: CUP, 2004.

Graff, Violette. 'Aligarh's Long Quest for 'Minority' Status: AMU (Amendment) Act, 1981'. *EPW*, vol. 25, no. 32, 11 August 1990.

—————. 'Hindu-Muslim Communal Riots in India: Part I, 1947–1986'. *Mass Violence et Résistance*, 15 July 2013.

Guha, Ramachandra. *India After Gandhi: The History of the World's Largest Democracy.* London: Macmillan, 2007.

Gundappa, D. V. 'Sir Mirza M. Ismail'. *Public Affairs*, no date.

Gupta, Jyoti Bhusan Das. *Jammu and Kashmir.* The Hague: Martinus Nijhoff, 1968.

Habermas, Jürgen. *The Theory of Communicative Action, Vol. 2: Lifeworld and System: A Critique of Functionalist Reason.* Boston: Beacon, 1987 [1981].

Hameed, Syeda Saiyidain, ed. *India's Maulana: Abul Kalam Azad.* Delhi: Vikas, 1990.

Hardy, Peter. *The Muslims of British India.* Cambridge: CUP, 1972.

Harman, S. *Plight of Muslims in India.* London: DL Publications, 1977.

Hartung, Jan-Peter. *A System of Life: Mawdudi and the Ideologisation of Islam.* London: Hurst, 2013.

Hasan, Mushirul. "Congress Muslims' and Indian Nationalism, Dilemma and Decline, 1928–1934'. In Jim Masselos, ed. *Struggling and Ruling: The Indian National Congress.* Delhi: Sterling, 1987.

—————. 'Aligarh Muslim University: Recalling Radical Days'. *India International Centre Quarterly*, vol. 29, nos 3–4, Winter 2002-Spring 2003.

—————. 'Introduction'. In Lelyveld, David. *Aligarh's First Generation: Muslim Solidarity in British India.* Princeton, NJ: Princeton University Press, 1978.

—————. 'The Muslim Mass Contact Campaign: An Attempt at Political Mobilisation'. *EPW*, vol. 21, no. 52. 27 December 1986.

—————. *A Nationalist Conscience: M. A. Ansari, the Congress, and the Raj*. Delhi: Manohar, 1987.

—————. *Legacy of a Divided Nation: India's Muslims since Independence*. London: Hurst, 1997.

—————. *Moderate or Militant: Images of India's Muslims*. Delhi: OUP, 2008.

—————. *Mushirul Hasan Omnibus*. Delhi: OUP, 2010.

—————. *Nationalism and Communal Politics in India, 1885–1930*. Delhi: Manohar, 1991.

Hasan, Zoya. *Politics of Inclusion: Castes, Minorities, and Affirmative Action*. Delhi: OUP, 2009.

—————. *Quest for Power: Oppositional Movements and Post-Congress Politics in Uttar Pradesh*. Delhi: OUP, 1998.

Hasan, Zoya and Menon, Ritu. *Unequal Citizens: A Study of Muslim Women in India*. Oxford: OUP, 2004.

Hewitt, Vernon. *Political Mobilisation and Democracy in India: States of Emergency*. Abingdon: Routledge, 2008.

Iqbal. *What Should Then Be Done, O People of the East*. Lahore: Iqbal Academy, 1977.

Iqtidar, Humeira. *Secularising Islamists? Jama'at-e-Islami and Jama'at-ud-Dawa in Urban Pakistan*. Chicago, IL: University of Chicago Press, 2011.

—————. 'Theorizing Popular Sovereignty in the Colony: Abul Ala Maududi's "Theodemocracy"'. *Review of Politics*, vol. 82, no. 1, 2020.

Islam, Maidul. *Limits of Islamism: Jamaat-e-Islami in Contemporary India and Bangladesh*. Cambridge: CUP, 2015.

Ismail, Mirza. *My Public Life: Recollections and Reflections*. London: George Allen & Unwin, 1954.

Jackson, Roy. *Mawlana Mawdudi and Political Islam: Authority and the Islamic State*. Abingdon: Routledge, 2010.

Jaffrelot, Christophe and Anil, Pratinav. *India's First Dictatorship: The Emergency, 1975–1977*. London: Hurst, 2020.

Jaffrelot, Christophe and Thomas, Charlotte. 'Facing "Ghettoisation" in "Riot-city": Old Ahmedabad and Juhapura between Victimisation and Self-Help' in Gayer, Laurent and Jaffrelot, Christophe, eds. *Muslims in Indian Cities: Trajectories of Marginalisation*. London: Hurst, 2012.

Jaffrelot, Christophe, ed. *Hindu Nationalism: A Reader*. Princeton, NJ: Princeton University Press, 2007.

—————. *Dr Ambedkar and Untouchability: Analysing and Fighting Caste*. London: Hurst, 2005.

—————. *India's Silent Revolution: The Rise of the Lower Castes in North India*. London: Hurst, 2003.

—————. *Religion, Caste, and Politics in India*. London: Hurst, 2011.

—————. *The Hindu Nationalist Movement and Indian Politics, 1925 to the 1990s*. London: Hurst, 1996.

————. *The Pakistan Paradox: Instability and Resilience*. London: Hurst, 2015.

————. *Modi's India: Hindu Nationalism and the Rise of Ethnic Democracy*. Princeton, NJ: Princeton University Press, 2021.

Jagadisan, T. N. *V. S. Srinivasa Sastri*. Delhi: Ministry of Information and Broadcasting, 1969.

Jairath, Vinod K., ed. *Frontiers of Embedded Muslim Communities in India*. Abingdon: Routledge, 2011.

Jalal, Ayesha. *Self and Sovereignty: Individual and Community in South Asian Islam since 1850*. London: Routledge, 2000.

Jamal, Amina. 'Feminist 'selves' and feminism's 'others': feminist representations of Jamaat-e-Islami women'. *Feminist Review*, vol. 81, no. 1, 2005.

————. 'Gendered Islam and modernity in the nation-space: women's modernism in the Jamaat-e-Islami of Pakistan'. *Feminist Review*, vol. 91, no. 1, 2009.

Jeffrey, Robin and Sen, Ronojoy, eds. *Being Muslim in South Asia: Diversity and Daily Life*. Oxford: OUP, 2014.

Jensenius, Francesca R. and Verniers, Gilles. 'Studying Indian Politics with Large-scale Data: Indian Election Data 1961-Today', *Studies in Indian Politics*, vol. 5, no. 2, 2017.

Jensenius, Francesca R. *Social Justice through Inclusion: Consequences of Electoral Quotas in India*. Oxford: OUP, 2017.

Jha, Krishna and Dhirendra K., Jha. *Ayodhya: The Dark Night*. Delhi: HarperCollins, 2012.

Jha, Shefali. 'Rights versus Representation: Defending Minority Interests in the Constituent Assembly'. *EPW,* vol. 38, no. 16, 25 April 2003.

————. 'Secularism in the Constituent Assembly Debates, 1946–1950'. *EPW*, vol. 37, no. 30, 27 July–2 August 2002.

Jones, Justin. 'The local experiences of reformist Islam in a "Muslim" town in colonial India: the case of Amroha'. *Modern Asian Studies*, vol. 43, no. 4, 2009.

————. *Shi'a Islam in Colonial India: Religion, Community and Sectarianism*. Cambridge: CUP, 2012.

————. 'Where Only Women May Judge: Developing Gender-Just Islamic Laws in India's All-Female '*Sharī'ah* Courts'. *Islamic Law and Society*, vol. 26, no. 1, 2019.

Kabir, B. M. Monoar. 'The Politics of Religion: The Jamaat-i-Islami in Bangladesh'. In Ahmed, Rafiuddin. *Religion, Nationalism, and Politics in Bangladesh*. Delhi: South Asian Publishers, 1990.

Kamran, Tahir. 'Majlis-i-Ahrar-i-Islam: Religion, Socialism and Agitation in Action'. *South Asian History and Culture*, vol. 4, no. 4, 2013.

Kashif-Ul-Huda. 'Communal Riots and Jamshedpur'. *EPW*, vol. 44, no. 21. 29 May 2009.

Keddie, Nikki R. *Sayyid Jamal ad-Din 'al-Afghani': A Political Biography*. Berkeley, CA: University of California Press, 1972.

Kelly, Saul. '"Crazed in the Extreme": The Silk Letters Conspiracy'. *Middle Eastern Studies*, vol. 49, no. 2, 2013.

Khalidi, Omar. 'Muslims in Indian Political Process: Group Goals and Alternative Strategies', *EPW*, vol. 28, no. 1/2, 2–9 January 1993.

————. *Indian Muslims since Independence*. Delhi: Vikas, 1995.

————. *Muslims in [sic] Indian Economy*. Delhi: Three Essays Collective, 2006.

Khaliquzzaman, Chaudhuri. *Pathway to Pakistan*. Lahore: Longmans, 1961.

Khan, Ajmal. *Malfuzat-e-Azad*. Delhi: Hali, 1959.

Khan, Ateeque. '*Waqfs* in UP: A Socio-Historic [sic] Perspective'. *Islamic Culture*, vol. 64, no. 1, January 1990.

Khan, Mohamed Raza. *What Price Freedom?* Madras: Mohamed Raza Khan, 1969.

Khan, Mohammad Ishaq. 'The Significance of the Dargah of Hazratbal in the Socio-Religious and Political Life of Kashmiri Muslims'. In Troll, Christian W., ed. *Muslim Shrines in India*. Delhi: OUP, 1989.

Khan, Rasheeduddin. 'Muslim Situation and Plight of Urdu', *EPW*, vol. 13, no. 25, 2 September 1978.

Khan, Yasmin. *The Great Partition: The Making of India and Pakistan*. New Haven, CT: Yale University Press, 2007.

Khan, Zafarul-Islam. *The Stalwarts: Builders and Leaders of Mushawarat, 1964–2015*. Delhi: Pharos, 2015.

Khilnani, Sunil. *The Idea of India*. London: Penguin, 1997.

Khosla, Madhav. *India's Founding Moment: The Constitution of a Most Surprising Democracy*. Cambridge, MA: Harvard University Press, 2020.

Kochanek, Stanley A. *The Congress Party of India: The Dynamics of a One-Party Democracy*. Princeton, NJ: Princeton University Press, 1968.

Kothari, Rajni. 'The Congress 'System' in India'. *Asian Survey*, vol. 4, no. 12, December 1964.

————. *Politics in India*. Delhi: Orient Longman, 2005 [1970].

Kozlowski, Gregory C. *Muslim Endowments and Society in British India*. Cambridge: CUP, 1985.

Krishna, Gopal. 'Electoral Participation and Political Integration'. *EPW*, vol. 2, nos 3/5, February 1967.

Krüger, Horst, ed. *Kunwar Mohammad Ashraf: An Indian Scholar and Revolutionary, 1903–1962*. Berlin: Akademie Verlag, 1966.

Kudaisya, Gyanesh. *A Republic in the Making: India in the 1950s*. Delhi: OUP, 2017.

Kugle, Scott Alan. 'Framed, Blamed, and Renamed: The Recasting of Islamic Jurisprudence in Colonial South Asia'. *Modern Asian Studies*, vol. 35, no. 2, 2001.

Kumaraswamy, P. R. and Quamar, Md. Muddassir. *India's Saudi Policy: Bridge to the Future*. Singapore: Palgrave, 2018.

Kuwajima, Sho. *Muslims, Nationalism, and the Partition: 1946 Provincial Elections in India*. Delhi: Manohar, 1998.

Laponce, J. A. *The Protection of Minorities*. Los Angeles: University of California Press, 1960.

Lasswell, Harold. *Political Writings of Harold D. Lasswell*. Glencoe, IL: Free Press, 1951.

Lele, Jayant. *Elite Pluralism and Class Rule: Political Development in Maharashtra, India.* Buffalo: University of Toronto Press, 1981.

Lelyveld, David. 'Three Aligarh Students: Aftab Ahmad Khan, Ziauddin Ahmad and Muhammad Ali'. *Modem Asian Studies,* vol. 9, no. 2, 1975.

———. *Aligarh's First Generation: Muslim Solidarity in British India.* Princeton, NJ: Princeton University Press, 1978.

Lewis, Bernard. *Islam in History: Ideas, People, and Events in the Middle East.* Chicago, IL: Open Court, 2001.

———. *The Middle East: A Brief History of the Last 2,000 Years.* London: Weidenfeld & Nicolson, 1995.

———. *The Political Language of Islam.* Chicago: University of Chicago Press, 1988.

Lieten, Georges Kristoffel. 'Education, Ideology and Politics in Kerala, 1957–59'. *Social Scientist,* vol. 6, no. 62, September 1977.

Lijphart, Arend. 'The Puzzle of Indian Democracy: A Consociational Interpretation', *American Political Science Review,* vol. 90, no. 2, June 1996.

Limaye, Madhu. *Janata Party Experiment,* vol. 1. Delhi: D. K. Publishers, 1985.

Madan, T. N. 'Secularism in its Place'. In Bhargava, Rajeev, ed. *Secularism and its Critics.* Oxford: OUP, 1998.

Madinier, Rémy. *Islam and Politics in Indonesia: The Masyumi Party Between Democracy and Integralism.* Singapore: NUS Press, 2015.

Madni, Mushtaque, ed. *Syed Shahabuddin: Outstanding Voice of Muslim India.* Delhi: Pharos, 2013.

Mahmood, Safdar and Zafar, Javaid. *Founders of Pakistan.* Lahore: Publishers United, 1968.

Mahmood, Tahir. *Muslim Personal Law: Role of the State in the Subcontinent.* Delhi: Vikas, 1977.

Mahmud, Syed. *Hindu-Muslim Cultural Accord.* Bombay: Vora, 1949.

Malik, Jamal. *Islam in South Asia: A Short History.* Leiden: Brill, 2008.

Mann, Elizabeth. *Boundaries and Identities: Muslims, Work, and Status in Aligarh.* Delhi: Sage, 1992.

Mann, Michael. *The Dark Side of Democracy: Explaining Ethnic Cleansing.* Cambridge: CUP, 2004.

Manto, Saadat Hasan. 'Toba Tek Singh'. In *Mottled Dawn,* tr. Khalid Hasan. London: Penguin Modern Classics, 1997.

Marcuse, Herbert. *Counterrevolution and Revolt.* Boston: Beacon, 1972.

Maududi, Syed Abul Ala. *Islamic Law and Constitution.* Karachi: Jamaat-e-Islami Publications, 1955.

———. *Jama'at Islami ki davat.* Rampur: Markazi Maktaba-i-Islami, 1951.

———. *Let us be Muslims.* Leicester: Islamic Foundation, 1985.

———. *Nationalism and India.* Delhi: Markazi Maktaba-i-Islami, 1993 [1947].

———. *Political Theory of Islam.* Lahore: Markazi Maktaba-i-Islami, n.d. [1939].

———. *The Process of Islamic Revolution.* Lahore: Markazi Maktaba-i-Islami, 1955 [1947].

————. *Quran ki char buniyadi istilahein.* Delhi: Markazi Maktaba-i-Islami, 1996.

————. *Tahrik-i Islam ka a'indah la'ihah-i amal.* Lahore: Islamic Publications, 1963.

McLane, John R. *Indian Nationalism and the Early Congress.* Princeton, NJ: Princeton University Press, 1977.

Mehta, Pratap Bhanu. *The Burden of Democracy.* Delhi: Penguin, 2003.

Menski, Werner. *Comparative Law in a Global Context: The Legal Systems of Asia and Africa.* Cambridge: CUP, 2006.

Metcalf, Barbara D. *Islamic Revival in British India: Deoband, 1860–1900.* Princeton: Princeton University Press, 1982.

————. 'Imagining Muslim futures: debates over state and society at the end of the Raj'. *Historical Research*, vol. 80, no. 208, May 2007.

————. 'Living Hadith in the Tablighi Jama'at'. *Journal of Asian Studies*, vol. 52, no. 3, August 1993.

————. 'Nationalist Muslims in British India: The Case of Hakim Ajmal Khan'. *Modern Asian Studies*, vol. 19, no. 1, February 1985.

————. *Husain Ahmad Madani: The Jihad for Islam and India's Freedom.* Oxford: Oneworld Publications, 2012.

Metcalf, Thomas. *The Aftermath of Revolt: India, 1857–1870.* Princeton, N.J.: Princeton University Press, 1965.

Miller, Roland E. *Mappila Muslims of Kerala: A Study in Islamic Trends.* Delhi: Orient Longman, 1992.

Minault, Gail and Lelyveld, David. 'The Campaign for a Muslim University, 1898–1920'. *Modern Asian Studies*, vol. 8, no. 2, 1974.

Minault, Gail. *The Khilafat Movement: Religious Symbolism and Political Mobilization in India.* New York: Columbia University Press, 1982.

Mitchell, Richard P. *The Society of the Muslim Brothers.* Oxford: OUP, 1993 [1969].

Mohani, Hasrat. *Kulliya-i Hasrat Mohani.* Delhi, Nomani, 1977.

Mujeeb, Mohammad. *The Indian Muslims.* London: George Allen & Unwin, 1967.

Mullally, Siobhan. 'Feminism and Multicultural Dilemmas in India: Revisiting the Shah Bano Case'. *Oxford Journal of Legal Studies*, vol. 24, no. 4, 2004.

Munir, Muhammad. *From Jinnah to Zia.* Delhi: New Era Press, 1981.

Munson, Ziad. 'Islamic Mobilisation: Social Movement Theory and the Egyptian Muslim Brotherhood'. *Sociological Quarterly*, vol. 42, no. 4, 2001.

Myrdal, Gunnar. *An International Economy: Problems and Prospects.* New York: Harper, 1956.

————. *Asian Drama: An Inquiry into the Poverty of Nations.* New York: Pantheon, 1968.

Nadwi, Maulana Abul Lais Islahi. *Tashkil-e-Jama'at-i-Islami Hind: Kyon aur Kaise?* Delhi: Markazi Maktaba-i-Islami, 1990.

Nag, Sajal. 'Nehru and the Nagas'. *EPW*, vol. 44, no. 49, 9 December 2009.

Nandy, Ashis. 'The Politics of Secularism and the Recovery of Religious Tolerance'. In Bhargava, Rajeev, ed. *Secularism and its Critics.* Oxford: OUP, 1998.

Naoroji, Dadabhai. *Poverty and Un-British Rule in India.* London: Swan Sonnenschein, 1901.

Naqvi, Saeed. *Being the Other: The Muslim in India*. Delhi: Aleph, 2016.

Nasr, Seyyed Vali Reza. *Mawdudi and The Making of Islamic Revivalism*. Oxford: OUP, 1996.

————. *The Vanguard of the Islamic Revolution: The Jama'at-i-Islami of Pakistan*. Berkeley, CA: University of California Press, 1994.

Näsström, Sofia. 'Where is the representative turn going?' *European Journal of Political Theory*, vol. 10, no. 4, 2011.

Nayar, Kuldip. *India: The Critical Years*. Delhi: Vikas, 1971.

Nehru, Jawaharlal. *An Autobiography*. Delhi: Allied, 1962 [1936].

Newbigin, Eleanor. *The Hindu Family and the Emergence of Modern India: Law, Citizenship, and Community*. Cambridge: CUP, 2013.

Noorani, A. G. 'Babri Masjid Ramjanmabhoomi Question'. In Gopal, Sarvepalli, ed. *Anatomy of a Confrontation: The Babri Masjid Ramjanmabhoomi Question*. Delhi: Viking, 1991.

Nossiter, T. J. *Communism in Kerala: A Study in Political Adaptation*. Berkeley: University of California Press, 1982.

Osella, Filippo and Osella, Caroline, ed. *Islamic Reform in South Asia*. Cambridge: CUP, 2013.

————. *Social Mobility in Kerala: Modernity and Identity in Conflict*. London: Pluto Press, 2000.

Overstreet, Gene D. and Windmiller, Marshall. *Communism in India*. Berkeley, CA: University of California Press, 1959.

Owen, Hugh F. 'Negotiating the Lucknow Pact'. *Journal of Asian Studies*, vol. 31, no. 3, May 1972.

Pandey, Gyanendra. *The Construction of Communalism in Colonial North India*. Delhi: OUP, 1990.

Pandit, Aishwarya. 'The Husainabad Trust: The case of a Shi'a heartland?' *Modern Asian Studies*, vol. 52, no. 5, September 2018.

Perlangeli, Sara and Jaishankar, Dhruva. 'Assessing the Islamic State threat to India', *Times of India*.

Peter Gatrell, *The Unsettling of Europe: The Great Migration, 1945 to the Present*. London: Allen Lane, 2019.

Pitkin, Hanna Fenichel. *The Concept of Representation*. Berkeley, CA: University of California Press, 1967.

Prakash, Gyan. *Emergency Chronicles: Indira Gandhi and Democracy's Turning Point*. Princeton, NJ: Princeton University Press, 2019.

Puri, Balraj. *Kashmir: Towards Insurgency*. Delhi: Orient Longman, 1993.

————. *Muslims of India since Partition*. Delhi: Gyan, 2007.

Qadiri, Khalid Hasan. *Hasrat Mohani*. Delhi: Idarah-i Adabiyat-i Delli, 1985.

Quraishi, Zaheer Masood. 'Electoral Strategy of a Minority Pressure Group: The Muslim Majlis-e-Mushāwarat'. *Asian Survey*, vol. 8, no. 12, December 1968.

————. 'Emergence and Eclipse of Muslim Majlis-e-Mushāwarat'. *EPW*, vol. 6, no. 25, 19 June 1971.

Qureshi, M. Naeem. *Pan-Islam in British India: The Politics of the Khilafat Movement, 1918–1924.* Karachi: OUP, 2009.

Rahman, Abdul. *Denial and Deprivation: Muslims after the Sachar Committee and Rangnath [sic] Mishra Commission Reports.* Abingdon: Routledge, 2019.

Rahman, Hasbullah Haji Abdul. 'The Origin and Development of Ijtihād to Solve Modern Complex Legal Problems'. *Islamic Quarterly,* vol. 43, no. 2, 1999.

Ram, Malik, ed. *Tazkirah.* Delhi: Sahitya Akademi, 1968.

Ramusack, Barbara. *The Indian Princes and Their States.* Cambridge: CUP, 2004.

Rashid, S. Khalid. *Wakf Administration in India.* Delhi: Vikas, 1979.

Rasul, Begum Aizaz. *From Purdah to Parliament.* Delhi: Ajanta, 2001.

Rathore, Aakash Singh. *Ambedkar's Preamble: A Secret History of the Constitution of India.* Delhi: Penguin, 2020.

Ray, Anil Baran. 'Secularism and Political Protest: The Case of the Banaras Hindu University Students' Agitation of 1965'. *Indian Journal of Political Science,* vol. 39, no. 4, October-December 1978.

Redfern, Paul A. 'A New Look at Gentrification'. In Clarke, David B., Doel, Marcus A., Housiaux, Kate M. L., eds. *The Consumption Reader.* London: Routledge, 2003.

Rehman, Habibur. *Plight of Indian Muslims.* Delhi: Atlantic Publishers, 2012.

Retzlaff, Ralph H. 'The Problem of Communal Minorities in the Drafting of India's Constitution'. In R. N. Spann, ed. *Constitutionalism in Asia.* Bombay: Asia, 1963.

Robinson, Francis. 'Nation Formation: The Brass Thesis and Muslim Separatism'. *Journal of Commonwealth and Comparative Politics,* vol. 15, no. 3, November 1977.

————. 'Strategies of Authority in Muslim South Asia in the Nineteenth and Twentieth Centuries'. *Modern Asian Studies,* vol. 47, no. 1, 2013.

————. *Islam, South Asia, and the West.* Oxford: OUP, 2007.

————. *Separatism among Indian Muslims: The Politics of the United Provinces' Muslims, 1860–1923.* Cambridge: CUP, 1974.

————. *The 'Ulama of Farangi Mahall and Islamic Culture in South Asia.* London: Hurst, 2001.

Roy, Asim, ed. *Islam in History and Politics: Perspectives from South Asia.* Oxford: OUP, 2006.

Roy, Olivier. *The Failure of Political Islam.* London: I. B. Tauris, 1994.

Rudolph, Lloyd I. and Rudolph, Susanne Hoeber. *In Pursuit of Lakshmi: The Political Economy of the Indian State.* Chicago: University of Chicago Press, 1987.

Ruthven, Malise. *Islam in the World.* Oxford: OUP, 1984.

Sampurnanand. *Memories and Reflections.* Bombay: Asia Publishing House, 1962.

Sassoon, Donald. *One Hundred Years of Socialism: The West European Left in the Twentieth Century.* London: I. B. Taurus, 2010.

Saxena, Saumya. 'Commissions, Committees, and Custodians of Muslim Personal Law in Postindependence India'. *Comparative Studies of South Asia, Africa and the Middle East,* vol. 38, no. 3, December 2018.

Sayeed, Khalid B. 'The Jamaat-i-Islam Movement in Pakistan'. *Pacific Affairs*, vol. 30, no. 1, March 1957.

Sayeed, S. M. 'Role of Muslim Majlis in UP Politics'. In Kashyap, Subhash C., ed. *Indian Political Parties: Programmes, Promises, and Performance*. Delhi: Research, 1971.

Scarfe, Allan and Scarfe, Wendy. *J.P.: His Biography*. Hyderabad: Orient Longman, 1997.

Schechtman, Joseph B. 'Evacuee Property in India and Pakistan', *Pacific Affairs*, vol. 24, no. 4, December 1951.

Schoenfeld, Benjamin N. 'Emergency Rule in India'. *Pacific Affairs*, vol. 36, no. 3, Autumn 1963.

Scott, James C. *Seeing Like a State: How Certain Schemes to Improve the Human Condition Have Failed*. New Haven: Yale University Press, 1998.

Seal, Anil. *The Emergence of Indian Nationalism: Competition and Collaboration in the Later Nineteenth Century*. Cambridge: CUP, 1968.

Selznick, Philip. 'Foundations of Communitarian Liberalism'. In Etzioni, Amitai, ed. *The Essential Communitarian Reader*. Oxford: Rowman & Littlefield, 1998.

Sen, Amartya. 'Secularism and its Discontents'. In Bhargava, Rajeev, ed. *Secularism and its Critics*. Oxford: OUP, 1998.

———. *The Argumentative Indian: Writings on Indian History, Culture and Identity*. Delhi: Allen Lane, 2005.

Sen, Dwaipayan. *The Decline of the Caste Question: Jogendranath Mandal and the Defeat of Dalit Politics in Bengal*. Cambridge: CUP, 2018.

Shaikh, Farzana. 'Muslims and Political Representation in Colonial India: The Making of Pakistan', *Modern Asian Studies*, vol. 20, no. 3, July 1986.

Shakir, Moin. 'Religion and Politics: Role of Islam in Modern India'. *EPW*, vol. 14, nos 7/8, February 1979.

Shakir, Moin. *Muslims in Free India*. Delhi: Kalamkar, 1972.

Shani, Ornit. 'Conceptions of Citizenship in India and the 'Muslim Question'', *Modern Asian Studies*, vol. 44, no. 1, January 2010.

———. *Communalism, Caste, and Hindu Nationalism: The Violence in Gujarat*. Cambridge: CUP, 2007.

Shapiro, Ian, et al. 'Editor's Introduction' in Shapiro, Ian, et al., eds. *Political Representation*. Cambridge: CUP, 2009.

Sherman, Taylor C. '"A New Type of Revolution": Socialist Thought in India, 1940s–1960s'. *Postcolonial Studies*, vol. 21, no. 4, 2018.

———. 'Education in early postcolonial India: expansion, experimentation and planned self-help'. *History of Education*, vol. 47, no. 4, 2018.

———. *Muslim Belonging in Secular India: Negotiating Citizenship in Postcolonial Hyderabad*. Cambridge: CUP, 2015.

Siddiqi, Mohammad Nejatullah. *Economic Enterprise in Islam*. Delhi: Jamaat-e-Islami Publications, 1968.

Siegel, Benjamin Robert. *Hungry Nation: Food, Famine, and the Making of Modern India*. Cambridge: CUP, 2018.

BIBLIOGRAPHY

Sikand, Yoginder. 'An Islamist Approach to Inter-Faith Dialogue: The Jama'at-i-Islami of India'. In *Muslims in India since 1947: Islamic Perspectives on Inter-Faith Relations*. London: RoutledgeCurzon, 2004.

――――. 'The Emergence and Development of the Jama'at-i-Islami of Jammu and Kashmir (1940s–1990)'. *Modern Asian Studies*, vol. 36, no. 3, July 2002.

――――. *Muslims in India since 1947: Islamic Perspectives on Inter-Faith Relations*. London: Routledge, 2004.

Singh, Gurharpal and Talbot, Ian. *The Partition of India*. Cambridge: CUP, 2009.

Singh, Tripurdaman. *Sixteen Stormy Days: The Story of the First Amendment of the Constitution of India*. Delhi: Penguin, 2020.

Singh, U. B. 'Factors Affecting the Administration of Wakfs and Management of Wakf Properties'. In Singh, S. K., ed. *Wakf Administration: Status and Issues*. Rohtak: Spellbound, 1998.

Skocpol, Theda. *States and Social Revolutions: A Comparative Analysis of France, Russia, and China*. Cambridge: CUP, 1979.

Smith, Donald Eugene. *India as a Secular State*. Princeton, N.J.: Princeton University Press, 1963.

Snedden, Christopher. *Understanding Kashmir and Kashmiris*. London: Hurst, 2015.

Som, Reba. 'Jawaharlal Nehru and the Hindu Code Bill: A Victory of Symbol over Substance?' *Modern Asian Studies*, vol. 28, no. 1, 1994.

Spear, Percival. 'The Position of Muslims, Before and After Partition'. In Philip Mason, ed. *India and Ceylon: Unity and Diversity*. London: OUP, 1967.

Special Correspondent. 'Jama Masjid Riot'. *EPW*, vol. 10, no. 8, 22 February 1975.

Stepan, Alfred, Linz, Juan J. and Yadav, Yogendra. *Crafting State-Nations: India and Other Multinational Democracies*. Baltimore, MD: Johns Hopkins University Press, 2011.

Stephens, Julia. *Governing Islam: Law, Empire, and Secularism in South Asia*. Cambridge: CUP, 2018.

Stokes, Eric. *The Peasant and the Raj: Studies in Agrarian Society and Peasant Rebellion in Colonial India*. Cambridge: CUP, 1978.

Subrahmanyam, Sanjay. 'Before the Leviathan: Sectarian Violence and the State in Pre-Colonial India'. In Basu, Kaushik and Subrahmanyam, Sanjay, eds. *Unravelling the Nation: Sectarian Violence and India's Sectarian Identity*. Delhi: Penguin, 1996.

Sumption, Jonathan. *Trials of the State: Law and the Decline of Politics*. London: Profile, 2019.

Tambiah, Stanley J. 'The Crisis of Secularism in India'. In Bhargava, Rajeev, ed. *Secularism and its Critics*. Oxford: OUP, 1998.

――――. *Levelling Crowds: Ethnonationalist Conflicts and Collective Violence in South Asia*. Berkeley: University of California Press, 1996.

Tang, Zongli. 'Land Distribution in Mao's Investigations: Poverty and Class Struggle'. *Journal of Contemporary China*, vol. 15, no. 48, 2006.

Taylor, Charles. *A Secular Age*. Cambridge, MA: Harvard University Press, 2007.

Tendulkar, D. G. *Mahatma: Life of Mohandas Karamchand Gandhi*, vol. 8. Delhi: Ministry of Information and Broadcasting, 1963.

Thomas, Dana and Thomas, Henry. *Living Biographies of Religious Leaders*. New York: Blue Ribbon Books, 1946.

Tocqueville, Alexis de. *Democracy in America*. New York: Library of America, 2004 [1835].

Tolpadi, Rajaram. 'Context, Discourse, and Vision of Lohia's Socialism'. *EPW*, vol. 45, no. 40, 8 October 2010.

Troll, Christian W. 'Two Conceptions of Dawa in India: Jama'at-i-Islami and Tablighi Jama'at'. *Archives de sciences sociales des religions*, vol. 87, no. 1, 1994.

Urbinati, Nadia. *Representative Democracy: Principles and Genealogy*. Chicago, IL: University of Chicago Press, 2006.

Vanaik, Achin. *The Furies of Indian Communalism: Religion, Modernity and Secularization*. London: Verso, 1997.

Van der Veer, Peter. *Religious Nationalism: Hindus and Muslims in India*. Berkeley: University of California Press, 1994.

Varshney, Ashutosh. *Battles Half Won: India's Improbable Democracy*. Delhi: Penguin, 2013.

———. *Ethnic Conflict and Civic Life: Hindus and Muslims in India*. New Haven, CT: Yale University Press, 2002.

Vieira, Mónica Brito and Runciman, David. *Representation*. Cambridge: Polity, 2008.

Wai, U. Tun. 'Interest Rates in the Organized Money Markets of Underdeveloped Countries'. *IMF Staff Papers*, vol. 5, no. 2, August 1956.

Washbrook, D. A. 'Law, State, and Agrarian Society in Colonial India'. *Modern Asian Studies*, vol. 5, no. 3, 1981.

Weiner, Myron. 'Congress Restored: Continuities and Discontinuities in Indian Politics'. *Asian Survey*, vol. 22, no. 4, 1982.

Wilkinson, Steven Ian. 'India, Consociational Theory, and Ethnic Violence'. *Asian Survey*, vol. 40, no. 5, September-October 2000.

———. *Votes and Violence: Electoral Competition and Ethnic Riots in India*. Cambridge: CUP, 2004.

Williams, Philippa et al. 'Working at the Margins: Muslim middle class professionals in India and the limits of labour agency'. *Environment and Planning*, vol. 49, no. 6.

Wolpert, Stanley. *Jinnah of Pakistan*. Oxford: OUP, 1984.

Wood, Ellen Meiksins. *The Origin of Capitalism: A Longer View*. London: Verso, 2002.

Wright Jr, Theodore P. 'Inadvertent Modernization of Indian Muslims by Revivalists'. *Institute of Muslim Minority Affairs*, vol. 1, no. 1, 1979.

———. 'Muslim Education in India at the Crossroads: The Case of Aligarh'. *Pacific Affairs*, vol. 29, nos 1–2. Spring-Summer 1966.

———. 'Muslims and the 1977 Indian Elections: A Watershed?' *Asian Survey*, vol. 17, no. 12, December 1977.

————. 'The Effectiveness of Muslim Representation in India'. In Smith, Donald E., ed. *South Asian Politics and Religion*. Princeton, N.J.: Princeton University Press, 1966.

————. 'The Muslim League in South India since Independence: A Study in Minority Group Political Strategies'. *American Political Science Review*, vol. 60, no. 3, September 1966.

————. 'Muslim Legislators in India: Profile of a Minority Élite'. *The Journal of Asian Studies,* vol. 23, no. 2, February 1964.

————. 'Revival of the Majlis Ittihad-ul-Muslimin of Hyderabad'. *Muslim World*, vol. 53, no. 3, 1963.

Zachariah, Benjamin. *Nehru.* London: Routledge, 2004.

Zaman, Faridah. 'Revolutionary History and the Post-Colonial Muslim: Re-Writing the 'Silk Letters Conspiracy' of 1916'. *South Asia: Journal of South Asian Studies*, vol. 39, no. 3, 2016.

Zaman, Muhammad Qasim. *Islam in Pakistan: A History.* Princeton, N.J.: Princeton University Press, 1966.

Zamindar, Vazira Fazila-Yacoobali. *The Long Partition and the Making of Modern South Asia: Refugees, Boundaries, Histories.* New York: Columbia University Press, 2007.

Unpublished Secondary Sources

Arshad, Mohammad. 'Hasrat Mohani: A Critical Appraisal of his Political Career and Ideology'. DPhil thesis, Aligarh Muslim University, 2009.

Graham, Ben. '"Congress Misrule and the Swatantra Alternative"? Conservative Politics in India, 1947–64'. MPhil thesis, University of Oxford, 2021.

Johnson, Michael H. 'The Relation between Land Settlement and Party Politics in Uttar Pradesh, India, 1950–69, with Special Reference to the Formation of the BKD'. DPhil thesis, University of Sussex, 1975.

Kanjwal, Hafsa. 'Building a New Kashmir: Bakshi Ghulam Muhammad and the Politics of State-Formation in a Disputed Territory, 1953–1963'. DPhil thesis, University of Michigan, 2017.

Khan, Laiqur Rahman. 'Role of Muslim Majlis in UP Politics from 1967 to 1977'. MPhil thesis, Aligarh Muslim University, 1982.

Khan, Zafar Ali. 'Majlis-e-Mushāwarat'. MPhil thesis, Aligarh Muslim University, 1980.

Mohamed, T. A. 'Muslim Politics in Kerala, 1921–1967'. DPhil thesis, University of Calicut, 2001.

INDEX

Note: Page numbers followed by "*n*" refer to notes.